ROUTLEDGE LIBRARY EDITIONS: THE MEDIEVAL WORLD

Volume 15

THEMES AND IMAGES IN THE MEDIEVAL ENGLISH RELIGIOUS LYRIC

THEMES AND IMAGES IN THE MEDIEVAL ENGLISH RELIGIOUS LYRIC

DOUGLAS GRAY

LONDON AND NEW YORK

First published in 1972 by Routledge & Kegan Paul Ltd
This edition first published in 2020
by Routledge
2 Park Square, Milton Park, Abingdon, Oxon OX14 4RN
and by Routledge
52 Vanderbilt Avenue, New York, NY 10017

Routledge is an imprint of the Taylor & Francis Group, an informa business

© 1972 Douglas Gray

All rights reserved. No part of this book may be reprinted or reproduced or utilised in any form or by any electronic, mechanical, or other means, now known or hereafter invented, including photocopying and recording, or in any information storage or retrieval system, without permission in writing from the publishers.

Trademark notice: Product or corporate names may be trademarks or registered trademarks, and are used only for identification and explanation without intent to infringe.

British Library Cataloguing in Publication Data
A catalogue record for this book is available from the British Library

ISBN: 978-0-367-22090-7 (Set)
ISBN: 978-0-429-27322-3 (Set) (ebk)
ISBN: 978-0-367-18674-6 (Volume 15) (hbk)
ISBN: 978-0-367-18677-7 (Volume 15) (pbk)
ISBN: 978-0-429-19756-7 (Volume 15) (ebk)

Publisher's Note
The publisher has gone to great lengths to ensure the quality of this reprint but points out that some imperfections in the original copies may be apparent.

Disclaimer
The publisher has made every effort to trace copyright holders and would welcome correspondence from those they have been unable to trace.

Themes and Images in the Medieval English Religious Lyric

Douglas Gray
Fellow of Pembroke College, Oxford

Routledge & Kegan Paul
London and Boston

First published 1972
by Routledge & Kegan Paul Ltd
Broadway House, 68–74 Carter Lane,
London EC4V 5EL and
9 Park Street
Boston, Mass. 02108, U.S.A.
Printed in Great Britain by
The Camelot Press Ltd, London and Southampton
© *Douglas Gray 1972*
No part of this book may be reproduced in
any form without permission from the
publisher, except for the quotation of brief
passages in criticism

ISBN 0 7253 8

Contents

	Preface	ix
	Part I The Background	
1	The Inherited Tradition	3
2	Medieval Devotion	18
3	The English Lyrics, I	31
4	The English Lyrics, II	59
	Part II The Scheme of Redemption	
5	Christ and the Virgin Mary	75
6	Annunciation and Nativity	95
7	The Passion	122
8	Resurrection and Assumption	146
	Part III The Life of this World	
9	The Christian Life	153
10	Death and the Last Things	176
	Conclusion	221
	Note on Sources and Abbreviations	227
	Notes	229
	Index	295

Illustrations

		facing page
1	Two illustrated poems (British Museum, MS. Additional 37049, ff. 29v–30r)	22
2	Christ offers Man his Heart (British Museum, MS. Additional 37049, f. 20r)	23
3	A Pattern Poem (Hawes, *The Convercyon of Swerers*, pr. Wynkyn de Worde, 1509; British Museum, C25, k.7)	54
4	Poems from MS. Sloane 2593 (British Museum, MS. Sloane 2593, ff. 10v–11r)	55
5	The Charter of Christ (British Museum MS. Additional 37049, f. 23r)	86
6	Pietà (Devotional Image, late fifteenth-century woodcut; Bodleian Library, MS. Rawlinson D. 403, f. 1v)	87
7	The Man and the Unicorn (British Museum, MS. Additional 37049, f. 19v)	118
8	'Antiochenus' and his Son (British Museum, MS. Additional 37049, f. 87r)	119
9	A painting of 'Earth upon Earth', formerly at Stratford (*Ancient Allegorical, Historical and Legendary Paintings ... at Stratford-upon-Avon*, from drawings by Thomas Fisher, F.S.A. (London, 1838), plate xv)	182
10	Vado Mori (British Museum, MS. Additional 37049, f. 36r)	183

Illustrations

11 Vado Mori (British Museum, MS. Cotton Faustina B. VI part ii, f. 1v)   214

12 A Song of Death (sixteenth-century broadsheet; British Museum, Huth 50)   215

Preface

This book is intended to be an introduction for readers who are interested in making their way into the huge mass of medieval religious lyric poetry. I hope that it will help them to read the poems with increased pleasure, understanding, and discrimination. My discussion of themes and images has much to say about tradition and convention (and sometimes draws its illustrations from verses which are patently of small literary value) since I am convinced that, as Rosemond Tuve used to point out, what is often thought to be 'outside' poems such as these is in fact implicit in them, and that criticism fails if it does not draw attention to it. The treatment of themes even in works which are clumsy or naïve may enhance our understanding of lyrics which are of unquestioned literary quality, since we become aware of the possibilities and the limitations of inherited material and attitudes. However, my emphasis throughout will be on the way in which a tradition may be *used* by a creative intelligence, for it is clear that it cannot do the poet's work for him. I have chosen to treat the lyrics thematically, rather than chronologically, because it seems to me that this is the most useful type of arrangement for those who are just beginning to read the lyrics – the difficulties in discussing 'development' in a genre which is generally conservative and traditional, and of poems whose original date is usually unknown, are greater than is sometimes thought.

In the quotations from Middle English, the symbols þ and ȝ and the use of i/j, u/v, have been modernized, and the punctuation is editorial. Where no stylistic discussion is involved, I have sometimes been content to quote a translation of passages of Latin prose.

I am indebted to many libraries for allowing me to consult

Preface

books and manuscripts – notably to the Bodleian Library, the British Museum, the Cambridge University Library, the Warburg Institute (and especially to its Librarian, Mr J. B. Trapp), but also to the National Library of Scotland, Lambeth Palace Library, University, Magdalen, Merton, and Balliol Colleges, Oxford, Trinity College, Cambridge, the Fitzwilliam Museum, the Pepys Library, and Magdalene College, Cambridge. I should like to thank the Trustees of the British Museum and the Curators of the Bodleian Library for permission to reproduce some of their material as illustrations, and Messrs Faber and Faber Ltd for permission to quote passages from *The Dyer's Hand* by W. H. Auden, and *Early Christian Art* by F. van der Meer. The study of the religious lyric rests upon foundations securely laid by great scholars like Carleton Brown, Rossell Hope Robbins, and R. L. Greene, and no writer on the subject can adequately express his indebtedness to them. Miss Woolf's thorough critical study of the lyrics has been an indispensable companion and guide. Mrs Alison Bond was kind enough to check the Latin passages for me. Finally, I am deeply indebted to my wife for much patient reading and careful criticism.

The Background

The Inherited Tradition

It is hard to overestimate the importance of the Latin background of medieval vernacular literature. For the modern reader, Latin is normally a remote language; for the educated medieval reader (and only the educated were readers) it was immediate. It was the bearer of the Western European literary tradition; its writings dealt with every known area of human experience; its rhetorical handbooks described the craft of oratory and poetry; it was the language of the liturgy, and the language of the Bible. Especially in the field of religious writing, medieval Latin was the mother of the vernacular literatures.

The English religious poets of the Middle Ages inherited an impressive and complex 'imaginary museum', the fruit of twelve centuries of Christian tradition – hymns, religious poetry, commentaries, sermons, and of course, the Scriptures, the Psalter, and the Western liturgy. The tradition was a Western European one, though its roots were in the Eastern Mediterranean and the Middle East, and its spirituality was sometimes fed by the piety of the Eastern Church. From it the poets inherited an elaborate and developed theology, and various sophisticated symbolic or allegorical modes of thought. In it they could find not only ideas and themes, words and phrases, but also a rich array of visual images. In some of its aspects, the inherited tradition had severe limitations: the extremes of austere otherworldliness, the rigid absolutes of some of the homilists, or the frenzied enthusiasms of some popular movements would seem at first sight to suggest a decidedly barren field for poetic inspiration. Yet this was fortunately not the case. It proved to be a tradition of surprising variety, which gave scope for the exploration of human emotions, a tradition which could be (though it was not always) learned, tolerant, and humane.

The Background

Our poets' most obvious inheritance from this tradition was the liturgy of the Western Church. Even the most unlettered and unlearned priest was obliged to say Mass and to repeat the Divine Office. It is easy for us by looking at passages of the liturgy simply as 'sources' for later religious poetry to forget the essential fact that it contains, in its own right, an amazing richness of imaginative material. If we look at the Introits, Offertories and Graduals we find that they are often single verses from the Bible, which, when they are abstracted from their prose contexts to stand alone, become virtually lyrics in miniature. Like this:

> Signum magnum apparuit in caelo:
> Mulier amicta sole
> et luna sub pedibus ejus
> et in capite ejus
> corona stellarum duodecim.*

from the book of Revelation (chapter 12), which was used for the Assumption of the Virgin Mary, a vivid and striking image which particularly appealed to the medieval illustrators of the Apocalypse. Two examples must suffice. On the seven days before the vigil of Christmas were sung the Great Antiphons (they are now seven in number, but in the Middle Ages there were sometimes as many as twelve). This is one:

> O oriens, splendor lucis aeternae, et sol Justitiae:
> veni et illumina sedentes in tenebris, et umbra mortis†

which we find used in English literature already in pre-conquest times, in the Advent section of the poem called 'Christ'.[1] Here again the single (and simple) thought is isolated, giving a lyric power, and making it an obvious base for a meditation or a poem. The exclamatory style, too, is very distinctive (this we find continually in the lyrics, especially those which are in the form of prayers). In prayer, it very frequently takes the form of an address to God, followed by relative clauses which describe his attributes or acts of grace, and ending with a request for favour. In this form it commonly occurs in prayers in medieval secular literature. Thus

---

* And there appeared a great sign in heaven, a woman whose mantle is the sun, and the moon beneath her feet, and on her head a crown of twelve stars.

† O rising star, splendour of eternal light, and sun of justice, come and shine upon those who sit in darkness and in the shadow of death.

The Inherited Tradition

Roland, on the point of death, beseeches God, who has never lied, who has resurrected Lazarus, who has saved Daniel from the lions, to save his soul from all perils:

> Veire Paterne, ki unkes ne mentis,
> Seint Lazaron de mort resurrexis,
> E Daniel des leons guaresis,
> Guaris de mei l'anme de tuz perilz
> Pur les pecchez que en ma vie fis![2]

So, in a humbler English context, the author of *Havelok* is moved to pity for his heroine Goldeboru, as she lies in prison:

> Jesu Crist, that Lazarun
> To live brouhte fro dede-bondes,
> He lese hire with his hondes. . . .[3]

And the prayer with which Chaucer ends *Troilus and Criseyde* uses the same formula, echoing Dante, and mentioning only the attributes of the Trinity:

> Thow oon, and two and thre, eterne on lyve,
> That regnest ay in thre, and two, and oon,
> Uncircumscript, and al maist circumscrive,
> Us from visible and invisible foon
> Defende. . . .

The second example, from the Easter liturgy, is even more interesting. In the Paschal Vigil,[4] the procession bearing the Paschal candle enters the darkened church, and the words *lumen Christi* (the light of Christ) are repeated three times. There follows the *Exultet*, a praise of Easter, and a commemoration of God's works in the Old Testament thus (the passage is long, so I give only an abbreviated translation):

> For this is the Paschal solemnity, in which that true Lamb is slain, by whose blood the doorposts of the faithful are hallowed. This is the night in which Thou didst first cause our forefathers, the children of Israel, when brought out of Egypt, to pass through the Red Sea, with dry feet. This, therefore, is the night which purged away the darkness of sinners by the light of the pillar. This is the night which at this time throughout the world restores to grace and unites in sanctity those that believe in Christ, and are separated

from the vices of the world and the darkness of sinners. This is the night in which, destroying the bonds of death, Christ arose victorious from the grave. For it would have profited us nothing to have been born, unless redemption had also been bestowed upon us. O wonderful condescension of thy mercy towards us! O inestimable affection of charity: that thou mightest redeem a slave, thou didst deliver up thy Son! O truly needful sin of Adam, which was blotted out by the death of Christ! O happy fault, that merited so great a Redeemer! O truly blessed night, which alone deserved to know the time and the hour in which Christ rose again from the grave! This is the night of which it is written, And the night shall be enlightened as the day: and the night is my light in my enjoyments. . . . O truly blessed night, which despoiled the Egyptians and enriched the Hebrews! A night in which heavenly things are united to those of earth and things divine to those which are human. . . .[5]

There are a number of ideas in this passage which occur in the English lyrics: that of the 'happy fault' (*O certe necessarium Adae peccatum . . . O felix culpa*), for instance, is the basis of the poem 'Adam lay iboundyn'. Although by the standards of the Western liturgy this is an unusually extended and poetic section, its rhetoric is quite uncomplicated; it relies largely on simple repetition (*haec nox est*) and exclamation (*o vere beata nox*). The imagery of light and darkness (which we have already seen in the antiphon *O oriens, splendor*) which is fundamental to this passage (and to its dramatic liturgical context of darkened church and Paschal candle) is used in an interesting way. Towards the end, the image of the 'night' becomes first the 'truly blessed night' (*vere beata nox*), then the night to which may be applied the scripture 'the night shall be enlightened as the day' (*nox sicut dies*). Finally, with the loss of the connective *sicut*, and, presumably, with the implication of supernatural reversal of nature, we arrive at the paradox 'the night is my light' (*nox illuminatio mea*).

In this passage the events of the Old Testament are seen as prefigurations or types of the Redemption: 'this is the Paschal solemnity, in which that true Lamb (*verus ille agnus*) is slain, by whose blood the doorposts of the faithful are hallowed . . . this is the night which purged away the darkness of sinners by the light of the pillar', etc. This is much more than taking phrases from the

The Inherited Tradition

Bible and putting them into new liturgical contexts, but depends upon a general principle of interpretation.[6] It is sometimes given rather quaint inconographical expression – in the great south rose-window of the cathedral of Chartres we can see four prophets (Isaiah, Daniel, Jeremiah, Ezekiel) carrying the four Evangelists upon their shoulders. In Malvern, a window (the 'Creed window') shows the twelve apostles next to twelve prophets. The apostles are each given an article of the creed, and the prophets an appropriate sentence from their books. Of all the methods of interpreting the Scriptures, this typological method was that which probably had the most important implications for Christian literature. The more traditional 'types' of the Old Testament were common knowledge; thus Chaucer's Prioress can address the Virgin Mary directly as 'Bussh unbrent, brennynge in Moyses syghte' without any gloss or explanation, since the bush which Moses saw (Ex. 3:2) was commonly taken as a figure or type of Mary's unblemished virginity in the Incarnation. The principle of typology and some of the traditional figures were remembered for a surprisingly long time.[7]

The typological method is found at the beginning of Christianity. Some of the sayings of Christ himself imply that he saw his Passion and death as fulfilments of Old Testament prophecies, and typology is a characteristic mode of thought in the literature and art of the early Church. It has been suggested that it may have afforded a Christian answer to the charge that Christianity was nothing but a new-fangled and short-lived religion – that the whole of history from the creation of man was in fact a series of prefigurations of the coming of the Messiah and Redeemer of mankind.[8] The view of history which it implies is a symbolic one which finds a coherent order and significance in a Divine providential scheme. It is, it may be added, particularly appropriate to Christianity, a religion which combines an insistence on the transcendence of the Creator with an insistence on his immanence and on a particular historical Incarnation. In an interesting book on the art of the early Christians, F. van der Meer says of them:

> They never saw Biblical history merely as a succession of
> single events, connected only by their chronological order.
> Thus history was for them much more a single great whole,
> a whole that was, moreover, made ever-present for them by
> its sacramental re-enactment in the liturgy. And this whole is

The Background

engulfed in the greater radiance of the one unchanging light of the world, the Logos, Christ, the Divine Wisdom that had ordered all things from the beginning to the central moment of the Incarnation and that will bring all things to completion when the Lord returns in glory.[9]

He finds an excellent example among the splendid sixth-century mosaics of San Vitale in Ravenna, where three of the 'shadows' or prefigurations of the redeeming sacrifice of Christ – the sacrifice of Abel (Gen. 4:4), of Melchisidech (Gen. 14:18), and of Abraham (Gen. 22) – are grouped together above the altar at which the sacrifice of the Eucharist would be made; they are, moreover, just those figures which are recalled by the celebrant in the main Eucharistic prayer (*Supra quae*): 'And upon these do thou deign to look with favour and kindliness and to accept them as thou didst deign to accept the gifts of thy just servant Abel, and the sacrifice of thy patriarch Abraham, and that which thy high priest offered to thee, a holy sacrifice, an unblemished victim.'[10]

A number of the implications of this view of history have been discussed at length and brilliantly by Erich Auerbach.[11] A historical or supposedly historical event in the Old Testament (such as the sacrifice of Abraham just mentioned) is regarded as a real event, in time, which at the same time signifies or prefigures the redeeming sacrifice of Christ, another real event, which is its fulfilment (*figuram implere* is a term sometimes used). But the connection between the two events is not one of historical causality; the two are related in the Divine providence, in the mind of God. This means that a present event implies futurity and completion in the divine plan. As Auerbach says, 'The here and now is no longer a mere link in an earthly chain of events, it is simultaneously something which has always been, and which will be fulfilled in the future; and strictly, in the eyes of God, it is something eternal, something omnitemporal, something already consummated in the realm of fragmentary earthly event.'[12] In our passage from the Easter liturgy there is a good example of this 'omnitemporal present' in the use of the present tenses in the sentence 'this *is* the Paschal solemnity, in which that true Lamb *is* slain, by whose blood the doorposts of the faithful *are* hallowed', and it is this which makes possible the symbolic representation of the action – the lighting of the candle, with the words 'now we know the excellence of this pillar, which glowing fire enkindles to the glory of God'. This idea is of fundamental importance both to the liturgy and to devotional and meditative practice, which in a less formal, less symbolic and non-sacramental way seeks an *anamnesis*, a recalling of the significant events of the Redemption. It should also, incidentally, make us wary of ascribing simply to medieval 'anachronism' such things as the presentation of the shepherds in the mystery plays as medieval Englishmen or the way in which Langland (who, like Francis Thompson, was prepared to see 'Jacob's ladder/Pitched between Heaven and Charing Cross'), when he uses the parable of the Good Samaritan, places the 'barn of Unity' to which the wounded man is taken firmly in contemporary England, 'at the Newe Market'. In our passage, by applying the method to objects rather than to events, we can understand the symbolic value of the candle. The words of the prayer 'therefore on this sacred night receive, O Holy Father, the evening sacrifice of this incense, which the Holy Church presents to thee by the hands of thy ministers in the solemn offering of this candle of wax, the work of bees' are precise enough, with only the word *sacrificium* to suggest any symbolic action. With only this warning the text goes on, 'Now we know the excellence of this pillar, which the glowing fire enkindles to the glory of God.' By this word *columna* the concepts of 'candle' and 'pillar of fire' are fused. It is not quite sufficient to say that the candle 'stands for' the pillar of fire. The text clearly indicates that in the figurative sense it *is* the pillar of fire *as well as* being the candle. As the text goes on to say, this is 'a night in which heavenly things are *united* to those of earth, and things divine to those which are human'. And this fusion of the candle and the pillar of fire concentrates in a remarkable way all the previously disparate images of the Exodus and the purging of the darkness by the light.

One of the most important parts of medieval liturgical worship was the singing or reciting of the Psalms. A knowledge of the Psalter was required of candidates for the priesthood; it was copied frequently as a separate work, often sumptuously illustrated, and was turned into vernacular verse and prose.[13] The Psalms were the basis also not only of public offices but of private prayer and devotion. An eloquent passage in St Augustine's *Confessions* describes the effect the reading of them had on one Christian soul:

> In what accents did I speak unto thee, my God, when I read the Psalms of David, those faithful songs and sounds of

The Background

devotion, which allow of no swelling spirit ... how was I by them kindled towards thee, and on fire to rehearse them, if possible, through the whole world, against the pride of mankind.[14]

Alcuin recommends the Psalter for all the Christian's needs; he can find in the Psalms an intimate confession of sins, supplication of the divine mercy, thanksgiving for everything that has befallen him.[15] We are told by Asser, King Alfred's biographer, that the king used to carry with him a little book of devotion, a *libellum* which contained psalms and prayers.[16] And a later Englishman, Sir Thomas More, whose devotion to the Psalms is clear from his works and from the annotated pages of his own prayerbook, quoted the fifty-first Psalm on the scaffold.[17]

There is a book on the medieval religious lyric by Samuel Singer, which has as its subtitle *Das Nachleben der Psalmen*, 'the afterlife of the psalms', and which begins with the sentence, 'The Psalms of the Old Testament are the basis of our whole European Lyric.'[18] This is an impossibly exaggerated claim, but it does have some truth in it. We can certainly find in the Psalms, implicitly or explicitly, a good many of the themes and images of the religious lyrics. The Psalter is itself nothing else than a complete anthology of Hebrew religious lyric poetry. Its emotional range is striking: there are petitions to God, thanksgivings, praises, assertions of violent nationalism, imprecations, expressions of faith, love, hope, fear, celebrations of God's work in nature and in history. By the time all this has filtered through to the English devotional lyrics a great deal has been lost – the sense of the solidarity of Israel, most of the exotic imagery, and the stylistic parallelisms. Isolated images or phrases are most often left. But the lyrics do share with the Psalms a fondness for the poet's 'collective I', where the Psalmist 'speaks in the name of the many', and for elaboration of form – there are alphabetic and acrostic psalms as well as lyrics. One wonders, too, whether the oddness of shape of some of the Psalms, the abrupt emotional changes which can be so disconcerting to the modern reader, might not have been an example for some medieval poets whose own sense of organic form was not strong. But the most obvious connection between the psalms and the later lyrics is in a number of common themes. The sentiments of the penitential psalms, for instance, are familiar enough (though less eloquently expressed) in the medieval lyrics:

The Inherited Tradition

> De profundis clamavi ad te, Domine;
> Domine, exaudi vocem meam.
> Fiant aures tuae intendentes
> in vocem deprecationis meae.
> Si iniquitates observaris, Domine,
> Domine, quis sustinebit?*
>
> (cxxix, Vulg.)

and the medieval poems on death echo the impressive passages on mutability:

> Quoniam mille anni ante oculos tuos
> tanquam dies hesterna quae praeteriit,
> et custodia in nocte;
> quae pro nihilo habentur eorum anni erunt.
> Mane sicut herba transeat;
> mane floreat, et transeat;
> vespere decidat, induret, et arescat . . .
>
> (lxxxix)

> Quoniam ipse cognovit figmentum nostrum;
> et recordatus est quoniam pulvis sumus.
> Homo, sicut foenum dies ejus;
> tanquam flos agri sic efflorebit . . .†
>
> (cii)

Around the liturgy, Western Christianity developed a varied tradition of religious poetry, didactic and reflective devotional poems and, of course, the hymns, which are the sources of many of the vernacular lyrics. It is almost impossible to discover exactly what hymns were sung in the earliest centuries of Christian worship. Christ and the disciples sing a 'hymn', presumably a Jewish hymn, at the Passover before they leave for the Mount of Olives (Mark 4:26); there may be quotations from very early

---

* Out of the depths I have cried unto thee, O Lord. Lord, hear my voice: let thine ears be attentive to the voice of my supplications. If thou, Lord, shouldest mark iniquities, O Lord, who shall stand? (A.V., Ps. 130).

† For a thousand years in thy sight are but as yesterday when it is past, and as a watch in the night . . . they are as a sleep: in the morning they are like grass which groweth up. In the morning it flourisheth, and groweth up: in the evening it is cut down, and withereth. . . . (A.V., Ps. 90).

For he knoweth our frame; he remembereth that we are dust. As for man his days are as grass; as a flower of the field, so he flourisheth. . . . (A.V., Ps. 103).

The Background

Christian hymns in a number of places in the Epistles. In the Eastern Church, some hymns can be traced back to the period before the Council of Nicea (325). The records of Western hymnody begin with St Hilary (d. 367), but the most influential early writer was undoubtedly St Ambrose (d. 397). In the *Confessions*, St Augustine describes the way in which the faithful of Milan, besieged by the Arians, began the singing of hymns,[19] 'after the manner of the Eastern churches', to support their spirits in their trials and anxieties. From these beginnings developed the vast and complex tradition of medieval hymnody (the hymns collected in the *Analecta hymnica* begun by Guido Maria Dreves fill over fifty volumes), to which no brief summary could do justice.[20]

It is time in any case to leave generalities, and to examine one example of a Middle English lyric which is based directly on the liturgy. This is a poem by a fourteenth-century friar, William Herebert.[21] It occurs with some sermons and other rather wooden translations of Latin hymns in a manuscript which is now in the British Museum. We do not really know what purpose these were intended to serve; probably they were to be used in preaching (as other verses were), possibly as private poems for devotion (the hymns of the liturgy itself were of course in Latin). It is certainly not one of the greatest of the English religious lyrics, but it is a striking and vigorous poem. The heroic exaltation of the triumphant Christ (so suddenly varied in lines 16–17 by a glimpse of the solitary, rejected Christ) is quite remarkable.

> 'What ys he, thys lordling that cometh vrom the vyht,
> Wyth blod-rede wede so grysliche ydyht?
> So vayre ycoyntised, so semlich in syht,
> So styflyche yongeth, so douhti a knyht?'
>
> 'Ich hyt am, ich hyt am, that ne speke bote ryht,
> Chaunpyoun to helen monkunde in vyht!'
>
> 'Why thoenne ys thy schroud red wyth blod al ymeind,
> Ase troddares in wrynge with most al byspreynd?'
>
> 'The wrynge ich habbe ytrodded al mysulf on,
> And of al monkunde ne was non other won.
> Ich hoem habbe ytrodded in wrethe and in grome,
> And al my wede ys byspreynd wyth hoere blod ysome,
> And al my robe yvuled to hoere grete shome.

The day of thylke wrech leveth in my thouht,
The yer of medes yeldyng ne voryet ich nouht.
Ich loked al aboute som helpynge mon,
Ich souhte al the route bote help nas ther non.
Hyt was myn oune strengthe that thys bote wrouhte,
Myn owe douhtynesse that help ther me brouhte.
Ich habbe ytrodded the volk in wrethe and in grome,
Adreynt al wyth shennesse, ydrawe doun wyth shome.'

On Godes mylsfolnesse ich wole bythenche me,
And heryen hymn in alle thyng that he yeldeth me.[22]

The poem is a paraphrase of a passage in the book of Isaiah (Isa. 63: 1–7), which was used as one of the *lectiones* for Wednesday in Holy Week, and is an interesting example of the way in which Old Testament material was adapted for the Christian liturgy, and of the way in which this in turn was adapted to the vernacular lyric. The passage in question runs:

> Quis est iste, qui venit de Edom, tinctis vestibus de Bosra? iste formosus in stola sua, gradiens in multitudine fortitudinis suae. Ego qui loquor justitiam, et propugnator sum ad salvandum. Quare ergo rubrum est indumentum tuum, et vestimenta tua sicut calcantium in torculari? Torcular calcavi solus, et de gentibus non est vir mecum; calcavi eos in furore meo, et conculcavi eos in ira mea; et aspersus est sanguis eorum super vestimenta mea, et omnia indumenta mea inquinavi. Dies enim ultionis in corde meo, annus redemptionis meae venit. Circumspexi, et non erat auxiliator; quaesivi, et non fuit qui adjuvaret; et salvavit mihi brachium meum, et indignatio mea ipsa auxiliata est mihi. Et conculcavi populos in furore meo, et inebriavi eos in indignatione mea, et detraxi in terram virtutem eorum. Miserationum Domini recordabor, laudem Domini super omnibus quae reddidit nobis Dominus. . . .*   (Vulg.)

---

* (Thus saith the Lord God: Tell the daughter of Sion: Behold thy Saviour cometh; behold his reward is with him and his work before him.) Who is this that cometh from Edom, with dyed garments from Bosra, this beautiful one in his robe, walking in the greatness of his strength? I that speak justice and am a defender to save. Why then is thy apparel red, and thy garments like theirs that tread in the winepress? I have trodden the winepress alone, and of the gentiles there is not a man with me; I have trampled on them in my indignation and have trodden them down in my

The Background

It is immediately obvious that Friar Herebert has some dramatic sense, and wisely keeps the dialogue form of his original.[23] He also keeps most of the simple rhetorical devices of the Vulgate Latin. The quite effective repetition of *and* in lines 10 ff., for instance, comes directly from an *et . . . et* construction (although in this same line 10 he has sadly lost the emphasis of a Latin repetition: *calcavi eos in furore meo, et conculcavi eos in ira mea*).

But what is more important is the way in which the original passage of Isaiah has been adapted to the liturgy. A celebration of the redemption of Israel, describing how the Messiah returns from Edom (the country which was given to Esau, upon whose head Isaac pronounced the words 'by the sword thou shalt live'), where he has overthrown the enemies of the Hebrews, has been moved from its historical context, and placed in a new Passiontide context. It is a clear result of the typological reading of the Messianic champion as a figure of the Saviour who conquered death. This has two important results. On the one hand it will introduce the possibility of irony; on the other, it may make some of the statements dangerously close to literal inappropriateness. The irony of the passage is concentrated mainly on the figure of Christ as champion (*propugnator*) and on the treading of the winepress (*torcular*). In the 'new' reading and context of the verses, the Messiah is presented as both triumphant and suffering. Consequently, his splendid red garments (*tinctis vestibus, formosus in stola sua, rubrum . . . indumentum*) are at the same time the triumphal robes of the conqueror and the blood-stained garment of the crucified Christ. This gives an ironic ambiguity to words like *formosus* 'beautiful', which it is important to remember when we read crucifixion lyrics in which words like *dulcis* or *swete* are applied to Christ's wounds or to the nails of the cross. The winepress (a common Old Testament image for a crushing slaughter or a disaster)[24] now means as well the 'ignominy of the cross and

---

wrath; and their blood is sprinkled upon my garments, and I have stained all my apparel. For the day of vengeance is in my heart, the year of my redemption is come. I looked about, and there was none to help: I sought, and there was none to give aid; and my own arm hath saved me, and my indignation itself hath helped me. And I have trodden down the people in my wrath and have made them drunk in my indignation, and have brought down all their strength to the earth. I will remember the tender mercies of the Lord, the praise of the Lord for all the things that the Lord our God hath bestowed upon us (tr. G. Lefebvre).

all the torments of the Passion'. St Peter Damian (1007–72) says that Christ 'alone trod the winepress in which he was trodden because by his power he conquered the very Passion that he suffered'.[25] It is sometimes associated with the idea of Christ as the mystic grape, hung on the cross (the reference is to the incident in the book of Numbers (Num. 13), where the bunch of grapes is brought back on a staff from the Promised Land)[26] and is sometimes given a somewhat grotesque visual expression in the 'Mystic Winepress' of late medieval art, which shows the body of Christ being pressed in the *torcular*, and the blood flowing as wine.[27] The fifteenth-century poet Lydgate in his 'Tretys of Crystys Passioun' alludes to this – Christ describes himself thus:

> The vyne of Soreth railed in lengthe and brede,
>   The tendre clustris rent down in ther rage,
>   The ripe grapes ther licour did outshede,
>   With bloody dropis bespreynt was my visage[28]

– as does a later and more famous Herbert, at the end of *The Bunch of Grapes*:

> . . . much more him I must adore,
>   Who of the Law's sour juice sweet wine did make,
>   E'en God himself, being pressed for my sake.[29]

In general, the Old Testament material here is not inappropriate in its new surroundings. But the Middle English poem leaves us with an impression of strangeness, almost of violence, which is accentuated by its rather harsh rhythms. Its stress on the terrible and forbidding aspects of Christ, for instance, is not common in late medieval devotional lyrics (where it is found it is almost always in poems concerned with the resurrection, or the triumphant return of Christ to Heaven, which themselves sometimes echo this same passage of Isaiah). The explanation is that it comes straight from Isaiah's vision of a national Messiah. Christ's indirect response to the question 'who is this?', giving a list of attributes rather than a name seems much nearer to the name-taboo of the Old Testament Jehovah ('I AM hath sent thee') than to the medieval cult of the Holy Name of Jesus. Rather interestingly, Herebert translates *et indignatio mea ipsa auxiliata est mihi* ('my indignation itself hath helped me') as 'myn owe douhtynesse that help ther me brouhte'. Is it that 'douhtynesse' seems to him a

The Background

more knightly quality than *indignatio* (he has transformed *propugnator* into the common image of Christ as Knight), which is a very appropriate quality for a triumphant messianic liberator?

Herebert's treatment of the Latin text amounts in effect to a mild sort of popularization. The unfamiliar names, the typological indicators, Edom and Bosra, have disappeared. Herebert seems more concerned with the vividness and realism of the visual image than with the symbolic overtones. He has a marked tendency to make implicit irony explicit and obvious: *tinctis vestibus* 'dyed garments' becomes *blod-rede wede*, and 'why then is thy apparel red and thy garments like theirs that tread in the winepress' becomes 'why then is thy garment all drenched red with blood?' In one case, this fondness for the direct and the explicit produces a nice paradox – when he turns *propugnator . . . ad salvandum* 'am a defender to save' into *to helen monkunde in vyht*, 'to heal mankind in battle'. This phrase 'to heal . . . in battle' draws out one meaning of the Latin *salvare*, and continues the imagery of warfare, neatly fusing the figures of Christ as warrior and as physician. He sometimes adds explanatory details – *sicut calcantium in torculari* 'like theirs that tread in the winepress' becomes 'treaders in the winepress *all sprinkled with must*', which looks like an attempt to add a vivid and explanatory detail to an image which was perhaps not a particularly familiar one for an English audience. He nearly always prefers the concrete to the abstract – he renders *auxiliator* and *qui adjuvarit* ('a help . . . anyone who might give aid') as *som helpynge mon*, and *circumspexi* ('I looked about') becomes *ich souhte al the route*, which, with its suggestion of the milling, hostile crowds at the Crucifixion, gives a slightly more pathetic picture of the solitary Christ. Difficult or bold images are reduced or blunted – *inebriavi eos in indignatione mea*, 'have made them drunk [i.e. prostrated them] in my indignation', becomes the less exciting 'have drowned them all with humiliation'. And he will occasionally add adjectives or phrases which are much more heavily charged with emotion than the words of the Latin. A typical example is the insertion of the word *grysliche* into the phrase *wyth blod-rede wede so grysliche ydyht*.

The last couplet presents some difficulty. As the poem stands, it seems best to take it as a statement of the poet, an affirmation of faith, concluding the dialogue. The Biblical verse to which it corresponds is in fact the first verse of the next section of the chapter, and seems to be spoken by the prophet Isaiah. So it is

The Inherited Tradition

taken by the medieval commentators: 'The prophet [speaks] in the person of the Jewish people which is penitent, and calls to mind the mercy of the Lord.' In the Bible, there also seems no reason why the two questions at the beginning should not also be attributed to the prophet (some commentators, thinking typologically, take these to be asked at the triumphant entry of Christ into heaven, by the angels, 'not fully knowing the mystery of the Incarnation, Passion, and Resurrection'. In its liturgical context, the last verse still has a collective force – it is spoken *in persona populi Dei*, for the worshipping community, and the plural *nobis* 'upon us' is kept. But this is changed by Herebert into a more directly personal statement 'On Godes mylsfolnesse *ich* wole bythenche *me*'. The idea, presumably, is that the result of this dramatic personal encounter between the poet and the blood-stained champion is that the poet realizes the identity of the 'lordling', and commits himself to God's mercy. The mention of 'Godes mylsfolnesse' immediately after the terrible image of the triumphant, bloodstained lordling is dramatically apt – it is another of those harsh, rather crude switches of emotion like the lordling's own sudden revelation of his solitariness in lines 16–17 – but after the verses which have preceded it this couplet almost inevitably sounds rather flat. The possibilities of the emotional encounter and of the dialogue form have not been completely realized. Two rather impersonal questions are not really a sufficient basis for a sudden, personal spiritual denouement. Perhaps Herebert has stayed too close to his original. Perhaps he should have adapted the passage fundamentally, and not just in details. But the drift of his changes – giving it a greater visual vividness, making it slightly more obviously emotional, and rather less subtle and ironic, is characteristic of many of the Middle English religious lyrics. We have here an attitude to the traditional Christian 'matter' which is clearly the expression of certain tendencies in medieval devotion, and to these we must now turn.

Medieval Devotion

The religious literature of the High and Late Middle Ages in Western Europe is deeply influenced by a fervent and personal type of piety, to which the name of 'affective' devotion is sometimes given. 'Affective' devotion appeals to the emotions and the will rather than to the logical and speculative powers of the intellect; it is not necessarily anti-rational, though it may become so. It likes to dwell with loving enthusiasm on the humanity of Christ, on his name Jesus, on the human and physical details of the Nativity and the Crucifixion. With the same emphasis on human emotion and suffering, it develops Marian devotion; it is fond of the figures of Mary as mother, fondling her baby, or as the Mater Dolorosa, watching the agony of her child upon the cross. In religious literature and art, one of its important results is a heightened sense of tenderness, what Émile Mâle calls 'le sentiment pathétique'. At its best it can, and does, produce impressive works; at its worst it can disintegrate into formlessness, emotionalism, and sentimentality. One late medieval hymn contains the stanza:

> Parvum quando cerno Deum
> Matris inter brachia
> Colliquescit pectus meum
> Inter mille gaudia.*[1]

Colliquescit pectus meum – this is the true spirit of affective devotion, and a sentiment which is echoed throughout the Middle English lyrics.

This style of devotion begins to become dominant from the end

---

* When I see God as a small child in his mother's arms, my heart melts amidst countless joys.

of the eleventh century, and becomes the standard norm of later medieval piety. Dr Pantin's name for it, 'the devotional movement'[2] is perhaps the most convenient title, provided that we do not think of it as a single, unified, organized 'movement', but rather as a general drift underlying a series of separate, though related, movements and expressions of it – the works of St Anselm and St Bernard, Cistercian and Carthusian spirituality, Franciscanism, some aspects of the German mystical writers of the fourteenth century and of Rolle and the English mystics, the various spiritual stirrings in the Low Countries which culminate in the *devotio moderna*. Nor did its profound influence on the way in which Christians looked at the central matter of their devotion end with the Reformation.

The prayers and meditations of St Anselm, Archbishop of Canterbury (1033–1109), are one of the most impressive examples of affective piety, and, because of their literary and intellectual power and because of the *auctoritas* of Anselm, one of the most influential. His modern biographer, Mr R. W. Southern, points out that there were probably more manuscript copies of the prayers in existence in Anselm's lifetime, and for a hundred years after his death, than of any of his other works.[3] The original collection was much enlarged and expanded by other writers. Some of the prayers were sent by Anselm to monastic friends, some to ladies of high birth – Matilda Countess of Tuscany, and Adelaide, probably a daughter of William the Conqueror – a prophecy of things to come for, as Southern says, 'it was the conjunction of monastic piety and the religious impulses of great ladies which chiefly fashioned the private devotions of the Middle Ages'. Interestingly, the meditations were illustrated, possibly at Anselm's own instigation, a testimony to the vividness of their visual imagination, and again, a prophetic example of the close relationship word and visual image were to have in later medieval religious literature.[4] The following brief passage on the Passion and the compassion of the Virgin gives some idea of how Anselm's imaginative power recreates the scene and insistently presses it upon the mind:

> Why, O my soul, has a sword of sharpest sorrow not pierced thee? How canst thou bear to see a lance pierce the side of thy saviour? – since thou wert not able to look upon the hands and feet of thy maker profaned by nails, since thou wert

horrified to see thy Saviour's blood poured out? Why art thou not drunk with bitter tears, since he was given bitter gall to drink? Why dost thou not share the suffering of the most chaste Virgin, his most noble mother, and thy most gentle lady?

O my most merciful lady, how can I tell the fountains of tears that poured from thy pure eyes when thou stood and watched thine only son, innocent, bound before thee, scourged, put to death? What floods of tears must have covered thy holy face, when thou didst see this thy son, thy God, and thy lord stretched out on the cross, though he was guiltless, and this flesh that was taken from thy flesh cruelly torn by the wicked? With what sobs was thy pure breast shaken when thou didst hear him say, 'Woman, behold thy son', and the disciple 'Behold, thy mother'? Thou didst receive the disciple for son in place of the master, the servant in place of the lord.[5]

Anselm goes on to wish (and we are again reminded of later lyrics) that he might have shared the privilege of taking down Christ from the cross, and wrapping the grave-clothes around him, and laments that he was not there to kiss the wounds of the risen Christ, 'the places where the nails went through, and bathe in happy tears the scars that testified that it was thou indeed, in thine own body'.

The 'devotional movement' received further impetus in the twelfth century from the spiritual writings of St Bernard of Clairvaux (1090–1153). Here again we find this urgent personal meditation on the humanity of Christ (which becomes the basis of a Christocentric mysticism), and especially on the details of the Nativity and the Passion. Bernard describes the Nativity with great tenderness, dwelling on the 'sweet kisses' which the Virgin Mary gave her son, and on the smallness of the Christ child ('o parvule, parvulis desiderate'). So too with the *memoria*, the vivid recollection of the grimness of the Passion: 'we saw him and his aspect was no longer that of a man. He who had been the fairest of the sons of men became the accursed of the world, and like a leper, the lowest of mortals, truly a man of sorrows'.[6] His meditations on Christ's humanity inspire a number of imitations (which were later sometimes attributed to the saint himself) and in some of these are to be found the sources of some English lyrics.

Medieval Devotion

Bernard's Marian devotion was equally influential, so much so that his name became proverbial – he was called the *citharista Mariae*, and when in the *Divine Comedy* (*Paradiso* xxxi) he appears to guide Dante to the Virgin Mary and the Trinity, he is introduced as 'her faithful Bernard' (*il suo fedel Bernardo*).

This style of devotion continues through the works of the twelfth-century Victorines, into such thirteenth-century works as the *Merure de Seinte Eglise*[7] by another Archbishop of Canterbury, St Edmund of Abingdon (*c.* 1180–1240) who has given his name to Oxford's only surviving medieval Hall. To this work, which exists in many manuscripts in French, Latin and English, we shall need to refer again, for it contains one of the best of the English Passion lyrics. But the man who for most modern readers embodies the characteristic piety of the Middle Ages, and who certainly seems to many its most attractive product, is St Francis of Assisi (1182–1226). The two incidents in his life which were most popular with the medieval artists – the preaching to the birds and the receiving of the stigmata – illustrate neatly two of the most important aspects of his character and devotion – on the one hand a delight in the created natural world, which is given remarkable poetic expression in his *Canticle of the Sun*, and on the other an affective piety which, not content with the *memoria* of Christ's person and life, is impelled towards the imitation of Christ. In the Middle Ages he was generally regarded as the man who had most successfully imitated Christ, and the story of his reception of the stigmata was taken as final proof of this. After his death, one of his followers, Pier Pettinagno, had a vision in which he saw a procession of apostles, saints and martyrs led by the Virgin Mary 'all walking carefully, and scrutinizing the ground with much earnestness, that they might tread as nearly as possible in the very footsteps of Christ'. At the end of the procession, however, came St Francis, barefoot and in his brown robe; he alone walked easily and steadily in the actual footsteps of Christ.[8] The idea is expressed more literally, and with less charm, in some lines by the fourteenth-century English writer, John Audelay:

> His passion was in the so fervent,
> That He aperd to thi present;
> Upon thi body He set His prynt –
> His v. wondis, hit is no nay.[9]

The Background

Another English testimony to Francis's closeness to Christ was found in some wall-paintings formerly in the church of St John the Baptist, Winchester. In one the figures of St Francis and a layman occupy the traditional places of Mary and John at the Crucifixion, while another shows St Francis at the last Judgment leading the blessed to Paradise.[10]

The saint's affective piety was as much directed to the Nativity, which he represented less as a theological mystery than as an object of loving devotion, with the creator of all as the 'little brother of mankind'. A significant and touching if somewhat grotesque story describes the occasion when

> the saint of God stood before the manger, full of sighs, overcome with tenderness and filled with wondrous joy ... then he preached to the people who stood around, and uttered mellifluous words concerning the birth of the poor king and the little town of Bethlehem. And often when he would name Christ Jesus, aglow with exceeding love he would call him the child of Bethlehem, and uttering the word 'Bethlehem' in the manner of a sheep bleating he filled his mouth with the sound, but even more his whole self with the sweet affection.[11]

Francis and his followers had an enormous influence on medieval devotional art and literature. Scenes from the life of the saint became popular subjects with artists; the *Meditations on the Life of Christ*, one of the works directly inspired by Franciscan piety (it was once attributed to St Bonaventura (1221–74), the theologian and Minister General of the order), which enjoyed an extraordinary prestige and influence, was profusely illustrated, and the cycles of its illustrations were themselves most influential.[12] It has been conjectured that in England (where the Franciscans arrived in 1224) the growth of private devotion among the nobly born resulted in a demand for illuminated psalters, and that the wish of the owners for a deeper and more emotional participation in the sacred events depicted on the pages may reflect the influence of confessors from the new mendicant orders.[13] In the later Middle Ages in England, when the popular image of the friars (at least in the pages of satirical books) was low, the Franciscan interest in and patronage of the fine arts did not go uncriticized. An interesting passage in the late fourteenth-century *Pierce the Ploughman's Crede* sneeringly contrasts the Franciscan profession

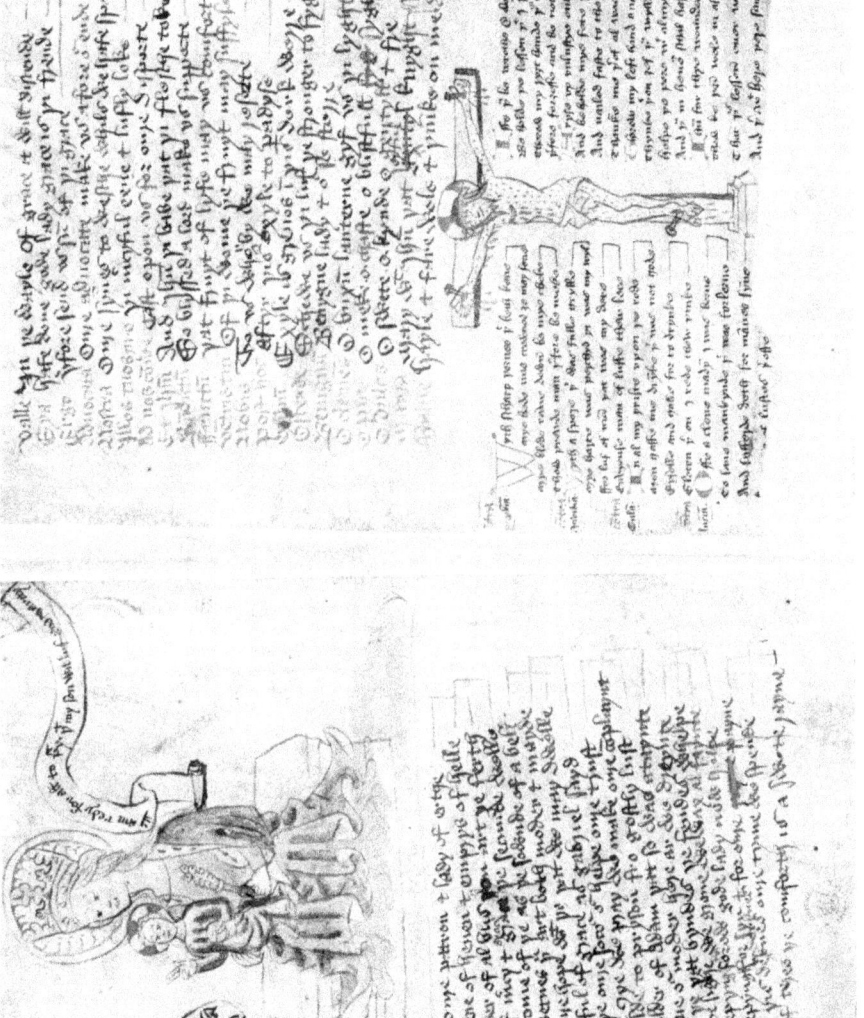

1 Two illustrated poems from a fifteenth-century MS. (cf. pp. 51–2). *Left*: a poem to the Virgin Mary as Queen of Heaven; *right*: the figure of Christ crucified makes an appeal to Man (cf. p. 140).

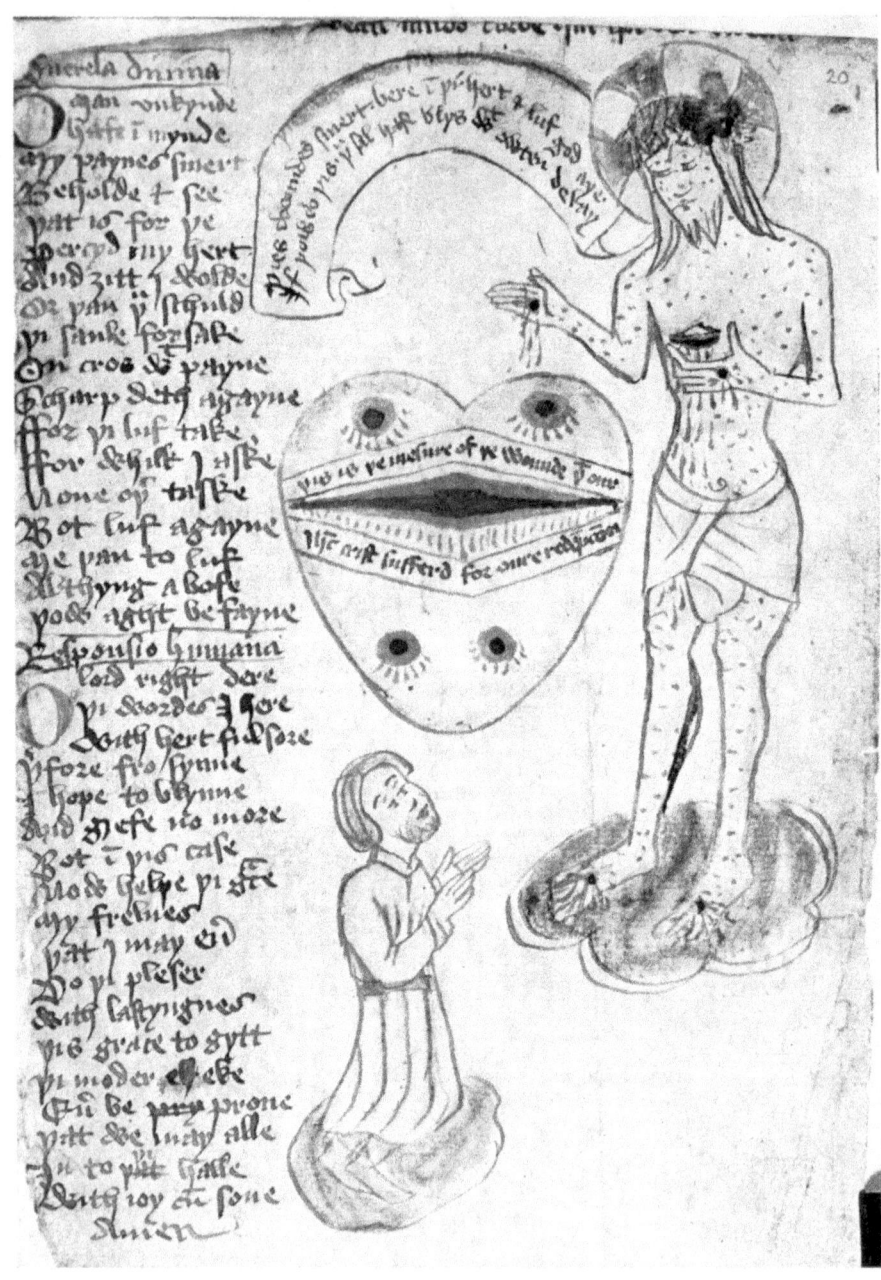

2 Christ offers Man his Heart – an illustrated poem (cf. pp. 52–4).
On the left are the words of Christ's complaint and Man's reply. The Heart, a favourite object of devotion in the late Middle Ages, is marked with the other wounds of Christ and an indication of the 'measure' of the gash made in it by the spear (cf. p. 34).

of poverty with the splendour of their church, with its fine windows in which a patron's figure could be placed – at a price.[14]

Francis himself was a talented poet and musician, and his followers produced a lively tradition of Latin and vernacular verse. A famous story in the *Speculum Perfectionis* tells how he encouraged Brother Pacifico, who had been known as *rex versuum*, and his companions to sing *laude* after their preaching, and that the preacher should say to the people, 'we are the minstrels of the Lord' – for what are the servants of God if not his minstrels who ought to stir and excite the hearts of men to spiritual joy.[15] The most impressive work of the Italian Franciscan poets is to be found in the dramatic *laude* of Jacopone da Todi (*c*. 1230–1306);[16] here, however, some stanzas from a lesser poet of his 'school' which J. A. Symonds quotes in his *Renaissance in Italy* will suffice to give some idea of how Franciscan piety could be transformed into popular verse:

> Veggiamo il suo bambino
> Gammetare nel fieno,
> E le braccia scoperte,
> Porgere ad ella in seno.
>
> Ed essa lo ricopre
> El meglio che puo almeno,
> Mettendoli la poppa
> Entro la sua bocchina . . .
>
> E la sua man manca,
> Cullava lo bambino,
> E con sante carole
> Nenciava il suo amor fino. . . .
>
> Gli angioletti d'intorno
> Se ne gian danzando,
> Facendo dolci versi
> E d'amor favellando.*[17]

* Let us look upon her child, kicking in the hay, and offering to her breast his open arms. And she covers him again as best she can, placing her breast to his little mouth . . . With her left hand she cradled the child, and with holy songs proclaimed her perfect love . . . the little angels all around dancing and making sweet verses and speaking of love.

The Background

The poem creates a beautiful and simple Nativity scene of the type loved by the early Italian painters (it would indeed not be surprising if the writer had such a painting in his mind). Everything from emotion to syntax is reduced; even the angels are diminutive. Its charming simplicity saves it from prettiness and sentimentality, but just how narrow the margin between this and sentimentality is can be seen from the translation of it which Symonds gives:

> Nestling in the hay!
> See his fair arms opened wide,
> On her lap to play!
> And she tucks him by her side,
> Cloaks him as she may!
> Gives her paps unto his mouth,
> Where his lips are laid.
>
> She with left hand cradling
> Rocked and hushed her boy,
> And with holy lullabies
> Quieted her toy. . . .
> Little angels all around
> Danced, and carols flung,
> Making verselets sweet and true
> Still of love they sung.

In England the Franciscans exercised a great influence on the development of the religious lyric.[18] They provided some of the few authors whose names we know – William Herebert, Thomas de Hales, the author of the lyrical meditation called the 'Love Rune', Michael of Kildare, and at the end of the fifteenth century, James Ryman, the author of a large collection of songs and carols. A large number of the earlier lyrics are found in friars' preaching-books; friars were responsible for some of the poetic miscellanies of the thirteenth century, and probably had some share in the development of the religious carol.

Preaching was a distinctive activity both of the Franciscans and of the other new mendicant order of the thirteenth century, the Dominicans, which is significantly named the Order of Preachers. St Francis, like a number of medieval visionary leaders, came from a well-to-do home (his father was a rich cloth-merchant), but his order, in the beginning at least, was connected with the poorest

Medieval Devotion

classes, and the workers of the towns. For this type of audience their preachers adopted a vivid and popular style, full of homely proverbs, striking images and examples to drive home the lessons, and to arouse emotion. A later, and more serene, preacher records his problems with 'country people; which are thick and heavy, and hard to raise to a poynt of Zeal, and fervency, and need a mountaine of fire to kindle them; but stories and sayings they will well remember'.[19] The mendicant preacher, who spoke not only in churches but from open air pulpits to large crowds, often deliberately set out to raise his hearers to a point of zeal; he might affect an emotional and dramatic style,[20] or might resort to some curious or melodramatic devices[21] – the story is told of a preacher, who, to strike terror into his audience, suddenly produced the skull of a dead man from beneath his cloak.[22] But the allusion in Chaucer (the Host's words to the Clerk):

> But precheth nat, as freres doon in Lente,
> To make us for oure olde synnes wepe

sufficiently indicates the reputation the mendicant preachers had. It is not surprising to find some of the most famous of the emotional preachers of the time were among their ranks – one need only mention St Bernardino of Siena, Savonarola, or that Friar Richard whose sermons at the churchyard of the Innocents in Paris (where the Dance of Death was painted) used to last from five in the morning until ten or eleven and caused tears, repentance and the burning of 'vanities'.[23]

Friars and preachers were not the only ones to help in the spread of the 'devotional movement'. The Carthusians, a strict order, were known for their collections of books of mystical and personal devotion.[24] It also finds expression in a remarkable revival of eremitic spirituality.[25] Solitaries and recluses were numerous in England. We have a Latin life of one of the best known, Christina of Markyate, who in the early twelfth century escaped from the persistent attempts of her family to marry her, and after many difficulties found refuge in a cell near St Albans. Her visions and spiritual reputation made her famous.[26] For the populace, the recluses must have been the living representatives of the ascetic ideal; for us now, they are a remarkable testimony to the desire for solitude, introspection, individual and private piety. Their numbers in the later Middle Ages meant that some were idle or vagabonds, and there must have been a number of enthusiastic eccentrics,[27] but many spent much of their time in good works – repairing roads, caring for leper-hospitals, even tending lighthouses – so that even after the Reformation the word 'hermit' still had a certain romantic attraction.[28]

The literature produced for and by recluses is of considerable importance. The spiritual guide for anchoresses, the *Ancrene Riwle*,[29] is perhaps the best known, but there are also accounts of visions, like those of the monk-solitary of Farne,[30] or yet another woman (it is remarkable how important a part women play in the 'devotional movement'),[31] Julian of Norwich.[32] The English recluses do not produce poetry which can equal in quality the earlier 'hermit poetry' of the Celts,[33] but it is interesting that the earliest known author of Middle English religious lyrics, St Godric of Finchale (*c.* 1065–1170), after a life of voyages and pilgrimages, settled as a hermit in the beautiful surroundings of the river Wear near Durham. Three of his poems survive, simple pieces based on Latin hymns addressed to Mary, Mary and Christ, and St Nicholas (the patron of sailors). The chronicler Reginald of Durham says that the Virgin Mary appeared to Godric in his chapel at Finchale and taught him the words and melody of his first piece, and in a later vision sang the second hymn to him.[34] A later literary hermit of some distinction is Richard Rolle, a Yorkshireman, who left Oxford to live as a recluse at Pickering and eventually at Hampole. He is the author of some very influential mystical prose works and of a number of lyrics of mystical 'love-longing' for Christ.[35]

Throughout the works of the 'devotional movement', the 'sweet tears' which are occasioned by the intense and emotional meditation on the humanity of Christ flow unabated. Christina of Markyate shed 'tears of heavenly desire', moved Christ 'with floods of tears', and on one occasion, entering a church 'bathed in tears as was her wont, placed herself in the loving presence of God'. But they never flow so copiously or so extravagantly as in the *Book* of Margery Kempe, a pious woman from Lynn who lived in the early fifteenth century.[36] Margery was so moved by the thought of the Passion of Christ that in church, and during sermons she would burst into tears and roar with anguish (sometimes to the confusion even of the preaching friars). A famous incident gives an extraordinary example of how vivid the recollection of Christ's humanity could be. Margery goes into a church in Norwich and sees a pietà:

Medieval Devotion

sche went to the cherch ther the lady herd hir servyse, wher this creatur sey a fayr ymage of owr Lady clepyd a pyte. And thorw the beholdyng of that pete hir mende was al holy ocupyed in the Passyon of owr Lord Jesu Crist and in the compassyon of owr Lady, Seynt Mary, be whech sche was compellyd to cryyen ful lowde and wepyn ful sor, as thei sche xulde a deyd. Than cam to hir the ladys preste seying, 'Damsel, Jesu is ded long sithyn'. Whan hir crying was cesyd, sche seyd to the prest, 'Sir, hys deth is as fresch to me as he had deyd this same day, and so me thynkyth it awt to be to yow and to alle Cristen pepil. We awt evyr to han mende of hys kendnes and evyr thynkyn of the dolful deth that he deyd for us.'[37]

The transports of a Margery Kempe suggest to us a rather different world from that of the balance of intellect and emotion which is found in the *Meditations* of St Anselm. Since it is from the late Middle Ages that most of our lyrics come, we should perhaps briefly suggest some of the possible connections between the types of affective devotion we have been discussing and other aspects of the culture of that time.

According to the Portuguese artist, Francesco de Holanda, Michelangelo had some scathing things to say about Flemish painting.[38] It pleases the devout more than Italian painting does; unlike Italian painting it makes them shed many tears, but not because of the vigour or goodness of the painting, but because of the goodness of the devout beholders. It pleases women, especially very old ones, or very young ones, and friars and nuns, and some noblemen who cannot understand true harmony. . . . And he goes on to criticize their landscapes, which he says have neither symmetry nor proportion, and aim at rendering minutely many things at the same time. Michelangelo's classical and neo-Platonic imagination can clearly be seen behind this judgment, but it is too sweeping to say, as does Huizinga in his famous book, *The Waning of the Middle Ages*,[39] that what he is judging is the 'medieval spirit' itself – 'the essential traits of the declining Middle Ages: the violent sentimentality, the tendency to see each thing as an independent entity, to get lost in the multiplicity of concepts'. Nonetheless these traits are characteristic of some Northern religious painting, where naturalism of detail and a pietistic imagination can result in grotesque and overstrained expressionism. Michelangelo's remarks on the extreme sensibility of the devout spectators are well exemplified by a person like Margery Kempe; one suspects that her tears would have flowed in the presence of any pietà, no matter what its artistic value was. The vision of the artists, both Northern and Southern (though their technique and concept of form no doubt differed profoundly even before Michelangelo's time) has been deeply influenced by affective piety. The best Flemish painters attempt to see the events of the divine pattern of redemption in human and realistic terms, in contemporary settings, happening in the presence of real men.[40] The traditional idea of the 'omnitemporal present' finds a new expression in Van Eyck's *Virgin of the Chancellor Rolin* (c. 1430), where the divine scene is set against the background of a thickly populated contemporary town. The German painter Cranach in his *Flight into Egypt* shows the Holy Family resting in the midst of a German landscape (which even has a Tannenbaum). Sometimes the passion for 'lifelike' presentation and the human surface of life can mean that the religious content is almost forgotten, so that of a painting like Gherard David's *Virgin with a Bowl of Milk* it can justly be said, 'It is a tender picture, but in no sense a religious image.'[41] But the classicizing criticism of excessive attention to a multiplicity of details is certainly one that can be levelled against many popular religious images of the late Middle Ages, and against some of the elaborate literary meditations on the Passion of Christ, where the rehearsal of grim, naturalistic details of physical suffering can sometimes produce nothing but a sense of unreality.

The subjectivism which marks some aspects of affective piety also perhaps has wider parallels in contemporary trends in theology and philosophy.[42] Some schools of late medieval philosophy are marked by a rigorous empiricism and a stress on the 'thisness' (the famous *haecceitas* of Duns Scotus) of things; the nominalists deny all real existence to universals or abstract concepts ('everything is individual by virtue of itself and by nothing else'). It has been suggested that the great English philosopher Ockham's extreme extension of the concept of the 'absolute power' (*potentia absoluta*) of God (used to denote the omnipotence of God, as against his 'ordained power' (*potentia ordinata*), the divine power devoted to upholding the world, through the laws of creation) to the notion that 'God can if he wills, dispense with all order in awarding man final glory' would destroy all certainty in the discussion of matters of faith, and all ordered categories of grace, and even of good and evil. It lays immense stress on free will and on human autonomy, the autonomy of separate individuals, not of components of a fixed order of things. Certainly in late medieval thought there is a growing tendency to disengage faith from reason (one suspects that outside the schools the two had never been very closely associated). We can detect on the one hand a growth of scepticism (in a limited sense), a doubt, or even a certainty that revealed truths have no *philosophical* validity, and on the other of a simple fideism. Miss Beryl Smalley in her book on an interesting group of English fourteenth-century friars[43] cites a remarkable example from Robert Holcot, who tells the story of a simple Dominican lay brother who converts a heretic (a great clerk), who believes that the human soul is not immortal, by the argument that if it should happen that the Christian view were true, then after death the good Christian will enjoy great bliss and the unbelievers will suffer terrible torments; therefore one should believe the Christian faith because if it is true, one will benefit greatly, and if it is not one will not be a loser, since the soul will not survive at all. It is not far from this to the view that simple faith is the whole essence of religion, without any need of rational support or explanation – 'believe and leave to wonder' as one fifteenth-century English lyric puts it.

If one remembers the great Schism, and the consequent weakening of papal authority, and the growth of disaffected and heretical movements alongside all the fervent enthusiasm of the devout, it is not hard to see how what must have seemed to the orthodox a sort of religious anarchism could easily develop. One Bartholomew, for instance, a fourteenth-century Augustinian friar from Dordrecht,[44] is said to have taught that divinity is dependent on man, that man is perfect God, and has existed from eternity, that every man should lose himself in the nothingness of Godhead, that he is saved through the immanence of the Holy Ghost not through the sacrifice of Christ, that it is a sin to remain under the law of good works, that there is no evil in such imaginary sins as lust, pride, theft, hatred. This fascinating 'underside' of medieval religious life is not directly expressed in the English lyrics at all, but possibly its existence encourages their orthodoxy and their emphasis on unquestioning faith.

My treatment of these suggested wider parallels to the trends in medieval spirituality has of necessity been hasty and highly selective. It is absurd to suggest that there was a single, self-consistent 'late Gothic' culture in Europe, of which every particular aspect is patently related to the whole.[45] Such a simple view can only be produced by careful selection of chosen examples and specimens. Huizinga's picture of the 'declining Middle Ages' which we alluded to earlier is, in fact, grossly oversimplified. After reading *The Waning of the Middle Ages*, we can hardly believe that England could have produced in this period in Chaucer not only one of her greatest poets but one of the sanest and most humane. 'Culture', like the men who make it and who inherit it, is always likely to be complex and inconsistent. Nevertheless, within the limited area of religious literature with which we are concerned, it is not now hard to see that some aspects of the way the inherited tradition had been developed must have made it very difficult for writers to achieve that moderation, that *mesure*, as the English would call it, to which Michelangelo's 'true harmony' is related. In the later Middle Ages, Christian writers sometimes managed to make impressive works from emotional attitudes which were violent, frenzied and even theatrical. It is quite remarkable that so many English lyrics were successful in achieving clarity, simple dignity, and moderation.

The English Lyrics, I

It is time now to consider in more detail the immediate background of the English lyrics: the audience for which they were intended, and the uses to which they were put. We have already seen that laymen and laywomen were coming to play a more important role in the spiritual life of the church. With the spread of literacy and education in the later Middle Ages this increased enormously, so that, as Dr Pantin says, 'It is impossible to exaggerate the importance of the educated layman in late medieval ecclesiastical history.'[1] Private devotional prayers for the laity become increasingly numerous. They are found in both Anglo-Norman and English in Psalters and Books of Hours, copied in blank spaces and on flyleaves. Paraphrases of hymns are made, and prayers in the vernacular for saying during Mass, in private meditation, and before retiring to bed.

It is important here to remember that in medieval England there were three languages available for this mass of devotional literature – Latin, French in its local variety, Anglo-Norman, and English. A well-educated person would be proficient in all three. We have already seen that St Edmund's *Merure de Seinte Eglise* exists in the three languages. There was a lively Anglo-Norman literary tradition, which was especially strong in devotional and religious writing.[2] We have a number of religious lyrics, which are close to their English counterparts. William of Waddington's *Manuel des Péchés*, a guide and aid to confession (a type of work which became common in the later Middle Ages), was turned into English with great gusto by Robert Mannyng of Brunne. Bishop Grosseteste's verse allegory, the *Chasteau d'Amour*, was translated into Middle English. Some of the English religious lyrics have alternate stanzas in French, or are based on French poems. No doubt in many cases Anglo-Norman and English poems would be written by and for the same people. Roughly speaking, in the late Middle Ages, for the clerks there would be devotional works available in Latin, and also in Anglo-Norman and English, for the nobility and the well-educated, in Anglo-Norman, and also in Latin and English, and for the humbler folk in English.

The nobly-born among the laity, who were now such an important part of the audience for devotional literature, were not always simply recipients, but sometimes patrons. Hilton, the fourteenth-century mystic, writes an *Epistle of Mixed Life*, for instance, for a nobleman, to teach laymen 'the which have sovereignty' to live a contemplative life in the midst of their life in the world.[3] Lydgate's *Life of Our Lady* may have been suggested to him by Henry V; his *Virtues of the Mass* was written for Alice Chaucer, the Countess of Suffolk, and other religious poems for the countesses of Warwick and Stafford.[4] They were not only patrons of religious literature but of art as well (although they would not have seen their patronage as a purely aesthetic function). A pious monarch like Henry III (1207-72), given, it seems, to a lavish display of religious emotion which was no doubt the result of contemporary trends in piety, collected relics – the crown of thorns, a phial of the Precious Blood of Christ – those relics of the Passion which play an important part in medieval devotion. At the same time, he was clearly a lover of beautiful things, and took a personal interest in the schemes of decoration which he commissioned.[5] Another devout king, Henry VI (1421-71), was a generous patron of ecclesiastical building. And it would not be hard to continue the list.

Occasionally the nobly-born were themselves the authors of devotional works. A very delightful example is the long Anglo-Norman prose treatise called *Le Livre de Seyntz Medicines*,[6] written in 1352 by Henry, Duke of Lancaster (1310-61), one of the greatest generals of the age, a statesman, and close friend of Edward III, who had fought against the infidels and was renowned for his generosity and his chivalry – a figure indeed who reminds us of the Knight of the *Canterbury Tales*. The *Livre de Seyntz Medicines* discusses the remedies for the disease of sin, in particular the spiritual wounds which are caused by the Seven Deadly Sins. It is a confessional work. Its loose construction possibly suggests that it was composed in the course of the Duke's very active life; certainly his own interests are evident – he tells us in detail how to destroy foxes, and he is obviously very fond of tournaments (possibly a little overfond for the more ascetic conscience of his spiritual director, since he goes to almost comic lengths to justify himself). It is full of intense affective piety (the adjectives *doux, douce* are applied again and again to Christ and the Virgin) and of vivid images from everyday life: the salmon goes upstream to spawn and breed its young, and these in turn have to go to the sea to become salmon – so it is with sin, which breeds its young in the senses of the body, which only become deadly sins after entering the heart. Or, the image of the poor man's house, which, when it is visited by a great lord, has to be cleared of all its furniture. When the lord goes, the furniture is put back into its place, often in worse array than before, and the house is even more cluttered up, and the cat, which had previously fled outside for fear, returns and sits in the place where the lord himself had sat (the poor cat in this adage is the Devil). In other passages we find (as we do elsewhere in devotional literature) intensity and fervour combined with a curious formalism; the Duke elaborates the images of the Virgin's milk, of her tears, of rosewater and the way it is made, in a fanciful and almost euphuistic manner.

It is important to remember the extent and the variety of the audience of late medieval devotional literature – it was in fact virtually the whole of contemporary literate society, from the high nobility to the humblest who could read (and even those who could be read to). There is no need to labour the obvious point that this was a period in which the influence of religion, or at least religious observance, was pervasive. Echoes of devotional cults which are given expression in our lyrics appear in all sorts of odd places. The saintly King Henry VI, who said grace 'like a monk', had a dish with the emblem of the Five Wounds upon which he could look while he ate;[7] the remarkable humanist and patron, John Tiptoft, Earl of Worcester, when he was executed (1470) asked that the executioner should strike three blows in honour of the Trinity and as a sign of his faith.[8] Popular piety was fed not only by the church in its offices, services and sermons, but by festivals and the activities of devout guilds.[9]

The variety of the audience makes comprehensible the extremes of theological awareness shown in devotional literature and practice. It ranges from the sophistication of an important theologian like Anselm to an almost fanatic emotionalism, and to popular beliefs which are often close to magic.[10] It is not surprising to find that devotional images and prayers were sometimes virtually used as charms. Representations of the great wound in Christ's side, as a red lozenge, a straight line, or simply a slit cut in the paper (the *mensura vulneris*,[11] as it is called), are sometimes accompanied by a rubric which claims that an indulgence of seven years may be gained by looking at it, by placing it in one's house, or by wearing or kissing it. The wound in the side, Longinus (the legendary name of the centurion who inflicted it), and the Five Wounds appear together in this charm:

> Longius miles Ebreus percussit latus Domini nostri Jesu Christi; Sanguis exuit etiam latus; ad se traxit + lancea + tetragrammaton + Messyas + Sother Emanuel + Sabaoth + Adonay + Unde sicut verba ista fuerunt verba Christi, sic exeat ferrum istud sive quarellum ab isto Christiano. Amen. And sey thys charme five tymes in the worschip of the fyve woundys of Chryst.[12]

No doubt some aspects of popular devotion and belief would have scandalized theologians. In the seventeenth century a sermon records the story of an old man who was questioned on his death bed by a minister, and 'being demanded what he thought of God, he answers that he was a good old man; and what of Christ, that he was a towardly youth; and of his soule, that it was a great bone in his body; and what should become of his soule after he was dead, that if he had done well he should be put into a pleasant green meadow'. It is not fanciful to suppose that in the Middle Ages there were similar old men with not dissimilar views (the idea incidentally both of the soul as a bone, and of heaven as a green meadow can be found in the traditional ballads).[13] When the Middle English poem *Emare* begins with an emperor obtaining a bull from the Pope to allow him to commit incest with his daughter, we begin to suspect that the theological sophistication of some romancers at any rate was not high.

Popular religion of this sort appears only on the periphery of the corpus of religious lyrics, which are on the whole orthodox and careful, though some of the simple prayers which we shall discuss in a later section sound as though they are almost charms or incantatory verses and formulae. It is of course notoriously difficult at this level to say where religion becomes magic: the genuine Middle English charms (like many of their predecessors in Old English) use much religious imagery – cf. (a formula quoted by the Franciscan, Bromyard) 'Holy Mary enchanted her son from the bite of elves, and the bite of men, and joined mouth to mouth, blood to blood and joint to joint, and so the child recovers'.[14] The most famous, the 'White Paternoster', the *nyghtspel* which is used by the carpenter in *The Miller's Tale*, has a particularly long and interesting history – it still survives as the nursery rhyme,

>Matthew, Mark, Luke, and John,
>Bless the bed that I lie on.[15]

A certain number of verse prayer-charms are preserved in manuscripts. Here, for instance, is one by the Holy Rood:

>Helpe, crosse, fayrest of tymbris three,
> In braunnchys berynge bothe frute and flowr!
>Helpe, banere beste, my fon to doo flee,
> Staf and strencthynge full of socowr!
>On londe, on see, where that I be,
> Fro fyir brennynge be me byforne,
>Now Cristis tree, sygne of pyte,
> Helpe me evir I be nowght lorne.[16]

This (written in an early sixteenth-century hand) rehearses images of the Passion in a strongly incantatory form (it is to be said for the falling sickness and fever):

>What manere of ivell thou be,
>In Goddes name I coungere the.
>I coungere the with the holy crosse
>That Jesus was done on with fors.
>I conure the with nayles thre
>That Jesus was nayled upon the tree.
>I coungere the with the crowne of thorne
>That on Jesus hede was done with skorne.
>I coungere the with the precious blode
>That Jesus shewyd upon the rode.
>I coungere the with woundes fyve
>That Jesus suffred be his lyve.
>I coungere the with that holy spere
>That Longeus to Jesus hert can bere.
>I coungere the never the less
>With all the vertues of the masse,
>And all the holy prayers of seynt Dorathe,
>*In nomine patris et filii et spiritus sancti.* Amen.[17]

These sort of charms survived in folk tradition for centuries. A later poet, Herrick, who was interested in them, produces a nice 'old wives prayer':

> Holy-Rood come forth and shield
> Us i' th' Cities and the Field:
> Safely guard us, now and aye,
> From the blast that burns by day
> And those sounds that us affright
> In the dead of dampish night
> Drive all hurtfull Feinds us fro
> By the Time the Cocks first crow.[18]

Occasionally we find echoes of material from the Apocryphal Gospels, the product of the popular devotion of much earlier times – the idea of Christ's triumphant Harrowing of Hell, or of Joseph's doubts about Mary which are the subject of the traditional *Cherry Tree Carol*. There is however a wider point of greater importance. The reader of our lyrics should not be surprised to find the occasional image which is theologically not very precise. Medieval affective devotion is often not concerned at all with the niceties of dogmatic theology, but with vivid emotion and immediate effect. One example will suffice here. In one lyric Mary is called the 'chambre of the trynyte',[19] a striking image, which combines two lines of thought which are popular in Marian poetry – the idea of the Virgin as the beloved (in one of Ryman's carols she is called 'chast bowre of the Trinitee' – where 'bowre' like 'chambre' probably has some suggestion of secular love poetry) and the idea that in her womb she bore the creator of all things, *immensa deitas*. From the point of view of a theologian however it is not very exact. It requires some sort of equation of Christ with the Trinity which seems to destroy the 'three persons' notion of orthodox doctrine. This image appears in a very literal-minded form in the visual arts. There are in the late Middle Ages statues of the Virgin with small doors in the front which, when opened, reveal inside an image of the Trinity.[20] Gerson, the Chancellor of the University of Paris, discovering one of these in a Carmelite monastery, criticized it not because of its bad taste but because it was heretical. Such images, however, were certainly not meant to be heretical or unorthodox, but are the expression of a fervent popular devotion. The logic which governs this sort of imagery is not so much theological as emotional.

The English Lyrics, I

The devotional lyric was one of the many expressions of medieval religious experience. It was not in its own time a remote 'aesthetic' literary form, but was an integral part of the religious life of contemporary society. This can give an immediacy and an emotional urgency which is not found in some forms of medieval literature, but it also means that it was sometimes fatally easy to write verses which were ephemeral, with devotional or didactic material not transformed into poetry. The lyrics are sometimes put to what we might recognize as 'literary' uses (e.g. in plays), but more often than not the impulse behind them is quite functional and practical. Utility is normally put before beauty, and sometimes, though fortunately not always, excludes it altogether. The lyrics were meant to be, and were, used, sometimes in private devotion and prayer, sometimes for public devotional display, sometimes to emphasize and drive home points in sermons.

French sermons sometimes moralize the popular line from secular songs 'Bele Aelis main se leva' (one of them glosses Bele Aelis as 'the mother of mercy and queen of justice who bore the king and lord of the heavens'),[21] and St Francis himself once adapted a couplet from a secular love song.[22] There is an English parallel to this in a sermon which gives a moral explanation of the lines

> Atte wrastlinge me lemman I ches
> And atte ston-kasting I him forles

– 'wrestling' is a manner of fighting, and truly no one comes to his love or to his bliss unless he is a good champion and manfully fights against his three foes, which are the Devil of hell, his own sinful flesh, and the world (the man who does this may say the first line); by 'stone' is understood the hard heart of man and woman (the hard-hearted can well say the second line of the song).[23]

These are, of course, secular songs which have been adapted by the homilists. But there are a very large number of specifically religious lyrics and verses which were used in sermons. Some of the preaching books which contain notes and exempla for use in sermons have quite extensive collections of lyrics, sometimes couplets or stanzas, sometimes complete poems. A number of the best of our lyrics are, in fact, found in these unlikely sources. In Carleton Brown's anthology of fourteenth-century pieces, for instance, a surprising number come from two of the most famous of the preaching books – that of the friar, John Grimestone, which is now in the National Library of Scotland, and that of Bishop Sheppey, which is now MS. 248 of Merton College, Oxford.[24] Very often these sermon 'tags' as they are called are striking verses (sometimes in not very polished metrical form) which would make a preacher's point memorably and succinctly. Thus (of the Virgin Mary at the cross):

> At his burth thow hurdist angell syng,
> And now seest his frendis wepyng;
> Atte his burth kynggis and schephurdis dede hym
>   humage and worchip,
> And now al maner men doth spit and schenship[25]

or (a statement of a penitent):

> Allas, alas, si haut, si bas!
> So lenger y leved so werchs yc was;
> Alas, alas, ibrocht ic am in perelus pas,
> Alas, alas, the game is ilore for lak of as![26]

or (of Christ's love):

> For my love he ys nou asslawe
> To wynne my love he was wel fawe
> For ys love and for ys sake
> Wol ic now deye, that was my make.[27]

The preachers naturally favoured those which were valuable mnemonic aids. We have for instance a Middle English translation of two verses from an exemplary story told by Robert Holcot of a senator who built a castle with an inscription to the effect that no common person should stay or dine there, but only Achilles, Plato, or Diana – a knight or a philosopher or a beautiful lady. But Christ appeared to him in a dream, and pointed out that since the senator was attempting to exclude him and his people, he might justly exclude the senator from his castle, which is heaven. The senator thereupon decided to devote himself to hospitality, and substituted another inscription:

> At this court this lawe is set:
> Pore man her ne slepeth ne et,
> But sire Achilles the knight of pruesse,
> Platon the wise, ant Dyane the godesse.

The English Lyrics, I

> Change thi lawe if thou wolt wel spede,
> Ant tak into thi hous hem that han nede:
> Martin the naked, and Lazar the seke,
> James the pilgrim, and weri men eke.[28]

A sermon tag is sometimes simply a series of vivid images, which could be used as 'headings' or expanded in the sermon. Here are four images for death:

> Mors
> A lyoun raunpaund wit his powe,
> An ape making a mowe;
> A scriveyn writing on a scrowe;
> An archer drawing in his bowe.[29]

They are fond of repetition. Grimestone has

> Reuthe made God on mayden to lithte,
> Reuthe mad him comen to mannes sithte,
> Reuthe mad his armis on rode sprede,
> And Reuthe mad him wepe and loude grede.[30]

Another (in Balliol College, Oxford, MS. 149) lists seven torments of Christ in seven short monorhyming lines:

> Blod wetyng
> Hard byndyng
> Gret travalyng
> Smert betyng
> Long wakyng
> Croys beryng
> Scherp prikyng.[31]

Sometimes the mnemonic scheme is very obvious. One tag in a manuscript in Cambridge University Library is set out thus:

M .. merowre			of gostly schewyng
O .. orologe	} ys deth {		that wyl wake fro slepyng
R .. robbowre			of al erthely thyng
S .. somenour			to the heye dom comyng[32]

and a quatrain on Christ's Passion in Grimestone's book has directive side-notes, thus:

The Background

Respiciamus
oculis the rede stremes renning
auribus The Jewes orible criying
gustu of Cristes drink the bitternesse
tactu of Cristes wondis the sarpnesse.³³

We have here the homiletic development of an old mnemonic technique, which like much else in medieval civilization can be traced back to classical antiquity. A fascinating account of how the classical 'art of memory' (which was attributed to Simonides) was transmitted to the Middle Ages through rhetorical books like the *Ad Herennium* and Cicero's *De Oratore* and developed and changed has been given by Miss Frances Yates.³⁴ It is hard for us, surrounded by handy reference books, public libraries, and an abundance of documents, not to mention index cards and notepaper, to imagine ourselves back into a time when an elaborate training of the memory was of vital importance. The training of the 'artificial' memory was an important part of rhetorical theory. Two aspects of it are of especial significance for medieval devotional and homiletic literature. Great stress is laid upon *images*. The sense of sight is held to be the strongest of all the senses; Aristotle says that imagination is the intermediary between perception and thought ('the soul never thinks without a mental picture'). Significantly, Miss Yates points out, Simonides, who is the traditional founder of the art of memory, is also said by Plutarch to have called 'painting silent poetry and poetry painting that speaks'. Further, the *Ad Herennium* remarks that as it is in nature the things which are exceptionally base, ridiculous, unusual and so forth which we remember, so images which are devised to aid the memory should be vivid and unusual. In the Middle Ages, when the art was turned to Christian ends, and what it was necessary to remember were the articles of the faith, the virtues, the vices, etc., collections of examples and images and similitudes were made for the use of the preachers (the successors of the ancient orators). And the art of memory itself could be a source of imagery (Miss Yates has interesting things to say on grotesque images in allegory, like Giotto's 'Envy' with the serpent coming out of its mouth, and on the elaborate 'pictures' devised by Ridevall and other fourteenth-century English friars).³⁵ The preachers' liking for violent and extraordinary images is found also in other forms of devotional literature: one meditation compares the swollen head of the suffering Christ to a cake which is baking![36] The traditional techniques of the art of memory no doubt also lie behind some of the schemes of encyclopedic knowledge which are found in medieval books – the allegorical tree-diagrams, for instance, which have inscribed on their leaves the various virtues and vices – and no doubt encourage the use of schemes of sacred numbers (sevens, fives, etc.). There are some interesting examples of mnemonic visual schemes in the 1531 edition of the instructional work *The Pilgrimage of Perfection*.[37] And it relates in a more general way to the various meditative techniques which are used to evoke the *memoria* of Christ incarnate. We have seen already how important this was in affective devotion; significantly the lyrics are full of words like 'remember' 'think on' or 'mynde' (memory):

> The minde of thi passiun, suete Jesu,
> The teres it tollid,
> The eine it bolled,
> The neb it wetth,
> In herte sueteth.[38]

In the light of what has been said of the nature of affective piety and of the art of memory, it is not surprising that images – whether visual images made by artists or craftsmen or mental images made by the words of writers – have such an important function in medieval devotion. Though the Jewish background of Christianity meant that visual and tangible images are slow in appearing at the beginning of the Church's history,[39] the nature of the Christian religion itself, with its stress on the Incarnation in which the Deity takes earthly and visible form, must have been an encouragement to their development.

A late medieval mystic may sometimes austerely recommend that the contemplative should gradually leave behind all visual and mental images of Christ in his humanity and come eventually to have his mind fixed entirely upon the essence of the Godhead, but he will not despise material images at earlier stages of the mystic's 'work'.[40] Indeed a characteristic form which mystical writing takes in the period is significantly the 'vision'.[41] Devotional works will sometimes avoid the vivid and often idiosyncratic images which have been mentioned, and prefer the simple, traditional and homely image – in the main this is true of the religious lyrics. And of course not all lyrics will make extensive

The Background

use of mental images to assist their audience in recollection and meditation. But many do, and very many ask their readers to visualize a scene or an event, often using words like 'look' or 'see', as they call up the traditional and powerful images of the story of redemption – the scenes of the Nativity, the Crucifixion, and so on.

Both writers and artists took their images from the same religious and devotional tradition. The reader of medieval religious literature also needs to remember that the men who wrote it and the people for whom it was written inhabited a world in which the images of the artists were omnipresent. The rich had splendidly illuminated manuscript books and, at the end of the fifteenth century, printed books with woodcuts, as well as tapestries adorned with 'histories', and painted chambers; for all to see were the stained glass and wall-paintings in churches, and innumerable devotional images in stone, carved wood, or alabaster, like the pietà in Norwich which so moved Margery Kempe. The wholesale destruction of images in the sixteenth and seventeenth centuries has made this difficult to imagine. The journal of the notorious seventeenth-century iconoclast, William Dowsing, is full of entries such as

> Ruchmere, Jan. the 27th. We brake down the Pictures of the 7 Deadly Sins, and the Holy Lamb with a Cross about it; and 15 other superstitious pictures. . . . Buers, Feb. the 23rd. We brake down above 600 superstitious pictures, 8 Holy Ghosts, 3 of God the Father, and 3 of the Son. We took up 5 inscriptions of *quorum animabis* (sic) *propitietur Deus*: one *pray for the soul*, and superstitions in the windows and some divers of the Apostles.

The account of the depredations of his deputy, Jessup, at Gorleston has a sombre melancholy:

> In the chancel, as it is called, we took up twenty brazen superstitious inscriptions, *Ora pro nobis*, &c; broke twelve apostles, carved in wood, and cherubims, and a lamb with a cross; and took up four superstitious inscriptions in brass, in the north chancel, *Jesu filii Dei miserere mei*, &c; broke in pieces the rails, and broke down twenty-two popish pictures of angels and saints. We did deface the font and a cross on the font; and took up a brass inscription there, with *Cujus*

The English Lyrics, I

animae propitietur Deus, and 'Pray for ye soul', &c., in English. We took up thirteen superstitious brasses. Ordered Moses with his rod and Aaron with his mitre, to be taken down. Ordered eighteen angels off the roof, and cherubims to be taken down, and nineteen pictures on the windows. The organ I brake; and we brake seven popish pictures in the chancel window – one of Christ, another of St. Andrew, another of St. James, &c. We ordered the steps to be levelled by the parson of the town; and brake the popish inscription, *My flesh is meat indeed, and my blood is drink indeed.* I gave orders to break in pieces the carved work, which I have seen done. There were six superstitious pictures, one crucifix, and the Virgin Mary with the infant Jesus in her arms, and Christ lying in a manger, and the three kings coming to Christ with presents, and three bishops with their mitres and crozier staffs, and eighteen Jesuses written in capital letters, which we gave orders to do out. A picture of St. George, and many others which I remember not, with divers pictures in the windows, which we could not reach, neither would they help us to raise ladders; so we left a warrant with the constable to do it in fourteen days. We brake down a pot of holy water, St. Andrew with his cross, and St. Catherine with her wheel; and we took down the cover of the font, and the four evangelists, and a triangle for the Trinity, a superstitious picture of St. Peter and his keys, an eagle, and a lion with wings. In Bacon's isle was a friar with a shaven crown, praying to God in these words, *Miserere mei Deus*, – which we brake down. We brake a holy water font in the chancel. We rent to pieces a hood and surplices. In the chancel was Peter pictured on the windows, with his heels upwards, and John Baptist, and twenty more superstitious pictures, which we brake; and IHS the Jesuit's badge, in the chancel window. In Bacon's isle, twelve superstitious pictures of angels and crosses, and a holy water font, and brasses with superstitious inscriptions. And in the cross alley we took up brazen figures and inscriptions, *Ora pro nobis*. We brake down a cross on the steeple, and three stone crosses in the chancel, and a stone cross in the porch.[42]

We can see something of what it must have been like in churches where there are still traces of series of wall-paintings (often the legacy of the pious landowners and merchants of the late Middle

The Background

Ages). One random example will serve. In the little church of Combe, near Woodstock, a humble building, and a parish without pretension to ecclesiastical importance, there are the remains of a fifteenth-century scheme of paintings. Over the chancel arch the congregation could see a painting of the Last Judgment with Christ in majesty showing his wounds, the dead rising from their graves on one side, and the damned being driven into hell-mouth on the other. On the north side of the chancel arch was a Crucifixion scene; in the south-east corner of the nave an Annunciation. On the north wall near the door was a picture of St Catherine; on the south wall a picture of St Christopher. If we can refurnish the interior in our imagination with a number of pious images (some of them no doubt brightly painted), we can get some idea of the richness of visual imagery which surrounded the worshippers.[43] Outside the church buildings, the people could see religious processions, and in the towns the events of the divine story were re-enacted for them dramatically and visually in the mystery plays. The medieval church certainly did not fail to realize the strength and power of the sense of sight.

Although the use of religious images of one sort or another had played a traditional part in Christian worship and devotion for centuries, the practice, or some aspects of it, was not without its critics even before the Reformation. The Eastern Church survived a violent controversy in the eighth century (one Patriarch was publicly flogged, blinded, and led in shame through the streets of Byzantium) concerning its most characteristic form of devotional image – the ikon. Later, in the West, there were different manifestations of opposition to devotional images. Wyclif for example attacks those who 'drawen the peple by coryosite of gaye wyndowes, . . . peyntings and babwynerie',[44] and not surprisingly the criticism of the superstitious abuse of images (which was very well-founded) easily turned into an attack on images themselves. The orthodox defence is continually presented, by learned men like Walter Hilton (who makes the point that we have already noticed, that by looking at images laymen can recall to memory the Incarnation of our Lord, and his Passion), Bishop Pecok, and others. The tract *Dives and Pauper* puts the case succinctly:

> They serve for thre thynges. For they be ordeined to stere mannys mynde to thynke on Cristes incarnacion and on his passion and on his lyvynge, and on other seintes lyvynge.

Also they ben ordeined to styre mannys affection and his herte to devocion, for ofte man is more steryt by sight than be herynge or redynge. Also they be ordeyned to be a token and a boke to the leude peple, that they may rede in ymagery and painture that clerkes rede in the boke. . . .[45]

The last argument is a traditional dictum[46] attributed to St Gregory the Great which is often repeated; it was still remembered in post-Reformation times that the Papists' view was that 'images are laiemens books'.[47] Although images were popular at all levels of medieval society, they had an especially important role to play in the instruction of the unlettered. The most remarkable expression of the effect they could have is given in the lines which Villon puts into the mouth of his old mother when she prays to the Virgin:

> Femme je suis povrette et ancienne,
> Qui riens ne sçay; oncques lettre ne lus.
> Au moustier voy dont suis paroissienne
> Paradis paint, ou sont harpes et lus,
> Et ung enfer ou dampnez sont boullus:
> L'ung me fait paour, l'autre joye et liesse.
> La joye avoir me fay, haulte Deesse,
> A qui pecheurs doivent tous recourir,
> Comblez de foy, sans fainte ne paresse:
> En ceste foy je vueil vivre et mourir.*[48]

Since the relationship between devotional art and literature in the Middle Ages is a complementary and close one, it is not surprising to find religious and moral verses sometimes used in inscriptions for public display or as written accompaniments to illustrations – verses which can be conveniently grouped under the heading of *tituli*. Christianity took over the use of *tituli* in verse and prose from classical antiquity (where the inscription and the epigram – which originally simply means 'inscription' – were developed into sophisticated and distinguished literary forms) and adapted the ancient tag *ut pictura poesis*, with its implication of a close relationship between word and visual image, to moral and

---

* I am a poor old woman, who knows nothing, and has never read a letter. In my parish church I see Paradise painted, where there are harps and lutes, and a Hell where the damned are boiled. The one frightens me, the other gladdens and rejoices me. High Goddess, grant me to have the joy, you to whom all sinners must come, filled with faith, without feigning or idleness: in this faith I wish to live and die.

didactic ends. In the Middle Ages, in many places, we find verses carved, inscribed or painted on walls or tombs, or worked in tapestries; verses are engraved on rings or other objects; and in manuscripts, and later in printed books, verses are found in, or accompany illustrations.[49]

Of the 'plain' verse *tituli* (those which are not accompanied by illustrations or images, but which are meant for public display so that the words may seem to speak to the beholders) the largest group are the 'mortality' verses which are used for epitaphs. Since we shall need to consider these as a group later, one example will suffice here, a quatrain which served as an epitaph on the brass of Richard Wenman (d. *c.* 1504) at Witney (it is also found on brasses at Northleach and Luton, and was formerly in the church of Great Tew):

> Man, in what state that ever thou be,
> *Timor mortis* should trouble thee,
> For when thou least wenyst,
> *Veniet te mors superare*.[50]

'Death will take you unexpectedly, whoever you are: therefore repent' is a commonplace of medieval devotional literature. Indeed, one of the carols uses two of these very lines:

> In what estate so ever I be
> *Timor mortis conturbat me.*

The directly penitential and didactic note is characteristic of medieval epitaphs; the verse is designed to be a dramatic admonition to the passer-by, a voice from the tomb. Some are straightforward memorials, but it is usual even in these to find at least the hint of a *memento mori* or a pious prayer. The older tradition of the memorial epigram and epitaph continues as a (not very successful) literary tradition in the Middle Ages, and with the growth of humanist interest in fourteenth- and fifteenth-century Italy comes into its own again, with poets and scholars competing with exquisitely turned Latin verses.

More elaborate and lengthy examples of 'plain' verse *tituli* are rare in England until the end of the Middle Ages. A notable example is the set of thirty-two stanzas of Lydgate that are painted around the Clopton chapel of the Holy Trinity in the church of Long Melford, Suffolk.[51] The selection and the arrangement were planned – thus the stanzas above the altar are an appeal from the crucified Christ to man, or, more specifically, to the worshippers in the chapel:

> Behold O man, lefte up thyn eye and see
> What mortall peyne I suffred for your trespace. . . .

The same sense of arrangement is found on a smaller scale in a verse carved on a splendid early sixteenth-century rood screen in the church of St Mary Magdalene at Campsall near Doncaster. The inscription runs along the middle rail and would be at eye-level for the kneeling worshipper:

> Let fal downe thyn ne and lift up thy hart
> Behald thy maker on yond cros al torn
> Remembir his wondis that for the did smart,
> Gotyn withowut syn and on a virgin bor(n);
> Al his hed percid with a crown of thorne.
> Alas, man, thy hart oght to brast in to!
> Bewar of the Divyl whan he blaws his hor(n),
> And prai thi gode aungel conve(y) the.

The secular lords of the late fifteenth and early sixteenth centuries do not seem to have been repelled by length in *tituli*, nor, it must be said, by tediousness. On the walls of Leconfield and Wressel castles (two Yorkshire seats of the Percy family) were painted ('about the reign of Henry VII') a set of proverbial and moral verses.[52] Whoever used the garret 'over the bayne' at Leconfield could relax by reading a long debate *de contemptu mundi* between 'the parte sensatyve' and 'the parte intellectyve'. Here is a typical remark of the 'parte intellectyve':

> *Vanitas vanitatum* beholde and see,
> In worldly gyftis is mutabilite,
> Gyftis of grace gett the,
> For they be of suerte.
> Erthly thingis be fletynge and vanite,
> And as transitory they passe:
> *Vanitas vanitatum, et omnia vanitas.*

The studious could look up and read 'the proverbes in the roufe of my lordis library' (which begin 'Drede God and fle from syn'), while anyone who slipped into the 'Garet of the Gardynge' for an assignation could divert himself with 'the counsell of Aristotell which he gave to Alexander Kinge of Macedony':

Apply to the best gyftis geven to the,
And vi speciall doctryns thou shalt lern of me. . . .

The use of moral and proverbial verses as *tituli* in secular houses lasted well after the Middle Ages. When, in 1847, it was decided to pull down the old mansion of Hurst House (built 1530) 'in order to re-build it more commodiously, according to modern notions of comfort', a decorated room was discovered under layers of paper, with traces of moral verses.[53] Traces of similar verses are to be found in the decorated panels (probably executed some time between 1564 and 1581) of the beautiful 'Painted Room' at No. 3 Cornmarket, now the property of the Oxford Preservation Trust. The remnants of the set of verses which was once painted around the room strongly suggest a version of some popular moral lines (the so-called precepts in -ly) which are often found in a variety of forms in manuscripts and books of the late fifteenth and the early sixteenth centuries.[54]

Tituli turn up on the most curious objects. It was a fairly obvious step to give visual form to the old rhetorical device of prosopopoeia and to make an inanimate object speak to the onlooker. This was already done in the vernacular in pre-Conquest Northumbria on the Ruthwell Cross, where the cross 'speaks' a portion of *The Dream of the Rood*, or on the Brussels Cross (' + Rod is min nama. Geo ic ricne cynig bœr byfigynde blode bestemed'). The practice is often found in the Middle Ages – indeed, even a gatehouse speaks![55] A mazer (*c.* 1420) adjures its owner:

> Hold yowre tung and sey the best,
> And let yowre neghboure sitte in rest;
> Hoe so lyustth god to plese
> Let hys neybore lyve in ese.[56]

Rather more grimly, a French tankard warns the unfortunate drinker, 'Pense à ta mort, povre sot'.[57] Again, the device continued to be used – at Husborne Crawley in Bedfordshire, there used to be 'an old bier' with

> As I am made to bear many
> Death spares none, nor do I refuse any.[58]

Some tiles (probably of the mid-fifteenth century) give a traditional warning of the wickedness of executors:

Thenke mon thi liffe
Mai not ever endure.
That thow dost thi self
Of that thow art sure;
But that thow kepist
Unto thi sectur cure
And ever hit availe the
His is but aventure.⁵⁹

But strangest of all are the cases where a religious verse accompanies a *sotilte*, an elaborate confection of pastry or sugar. At the coronation banquet of Henry VI there was such a *sotilte* 'of our lady sittyng and hir child in hir lapp and she holding in hir hond a croun and seynt George knelyng on the toon syde and seynt Denyse on the tothir syde presentynge the kyng knelyng to our lady with this reson following' (a stanza of a verse prayer to the Virgin, asking her to guard king Henry).⁶⁰ There was even a jelly, which was (in some way) 'wryten and noted' with a *Te Deum*!⁶¹ So overwhelming is the presence of religious images that it almost seems irrelevant to talk of bad taste.

There are many instances in which verse *tituli* accompany visual images less curious than this. In illustrated manuscripts, *tituli* may be very minor details of the total picture (as in the scrolls which sometimes emerge from the mouths of the figures, rather in the manner of a modern comic strip), or may be of equal importance to the images which they complement. Of the illustrated books of the Middle Ages perhaps the best known is the *Biblia Pauperum*,⁶² the Bible of 'the poor' (which means in fact 'poor clerks'), which is found in illustrated manuscripts and in 'blockbooks' (with the text and pictures printed from an engraved wooden block, not from movable type) of the fifteenth century from Germany and Flanders. It is a very interesting visual adaptation of that traditional typology which we discussed earlier. Each page has a scene from the New Testament, flanked by two Old Testament figures. The images are accompanied by the relevant texts, and by brief explanatory verses in Latin. One page, for example, shows the Crucifixion with two of its types—the sacrifice of Abraham ('signantem Cristum: puerum pater immolat istum' says the verse) and the raising of the Brazen Serpent ('lesi curantur: serpentem dum speculantur'); at the foot, the verse gives a simple devotional message: 'Eruit a tristi: baratro nos passio Cristi'. A fourteenth-century English example of this sort of work is the Holkham Bible Picture Book,[63] a finely illustrated manuscript of the fourteenth century. Here the captions are in octosyllabic couplets (the writer does not always describe what the artist depicts, but what he thinks he sees, and is, as we might expect, concerned to emphasize the emotional quality of the story). They are all in French, with the exception of one scene, where the Shepherds, who are traditionally humble folk, are celebrated in English:

> Songen alle wid one stevene
> Also the angel song that cam fro hevene

Explanatory *tituli* in French also accompanied the images of the 'Painted Chamber' at Westminster, which contains in six bands of painting 'all the warlike pictures of the whole Bible'.[64] In the fifteenth century, English is increasingly used. *Tituli* which accompany pictures of fifteen signs of the coming of the end of the world and of the Last Judgment in a window in the church of All Saints, North Street, York, are couplets taken from the popular English moral poem, *The Pricke of Conscience*.[65] Less fearsome are the proverbial remarks made by a group of birds in a window at Yarnton, Oxfordshire, which together make up a quatrain:

> Make the poure to pray well,
> Be styll or ellis saye well
> And make God thy frende
> At thy last end.[66]

Sometimes the *tituli* are far from being merely explanatory labels: words and images are in a close complementary relationship. For these we might perhaps adapt the German term *Bildgedichte*, and call them 'illustrated poems'. A good example is the late medieval *Dance of Death* or *Danse Macabre*, which appears in books and on the walls of churches.[67] Lydgate translated the famous version which was painted in the churchyard of the Innocents in Paris; his translation was used in the cloister of the old St Paul's cathedral:

> There was also one great Cloyster, on the North side of this church. . . . About this Cloyster was artificially and richly painted, the dance of *Machabray*, or dance of death, commonly called the dance of *Pauls*: the like wherof was painted about S. *Innocents* cloister, at Paris in France: the

meters, or poesie of this daunce were translated out of
French into English, by *John Lidgate*, Monke of Bery, the
picture of Death, leading all estates. . . .[68]

A number of Lydgate's works, in fact, apart from this and the
verses used as *tituli* in Long Melford, seem to have been intended
for 'illustrated' poems. One, called 'A tretys of Crystys Passion'
implies as much in its opening lines:

> Erly on morwe, and toward nyght also,
> First and last, looke on this fygure . . .
> My bloody woundis, set here in picture. . . .[69]

Another poem is meant to accompany a copy of a painting of the
Virgin said by pious legend to have been made by St Luke himself
(because of this sort of tradition, St Luke became the patron of
painters).[70]

A rather curious type of devotional lyric, to which we must
return later, called the *Arma Christi* or 'Arms of the Passion',
consisting of prayers by each of the instruments which caused
Christ's suffering – the crown of thorns, the spear, the sponge,
the nails, etc. – is sometimes found accompanied by illustrations.
Interestingly, some of the manuscripts are rolls, about five inches
wide and usually about six feet long, with coloured drawings of the
'instruments'. It may well be that, as Professor Robbins has suggested, they were intended to be publicly displayed in churches
to stimulate the devotion of the 'lewd' folk (the rubric which is
sometimes found at the end grants an indulgence to those who
behold them). They could, presumably, have been hung on a wall
or over the front of a pulpit or lectern.[71]

One or two fifteenth-century manuscripts are rich in these
'illustrated' poems. MS. Douce 1 in the Bodleian Library is a tiny
book (3 in. × 2⅜ in.), which contains a number of prayers and
illustrated devotional poems and was probably intended for
private use. The simple drawings were meant no doubt to help
the reader in his work of meditation; that this sort of book enjoyed
a continued popularity is suggested by the fact that much of the
material found its way into an early printed book, *A Gloryous
Medytacyon Of Jhesus Crystes Passyon* (printed by Rychard
Fakes, ?1521–3).[72] Additional MS. 37049 in the British Museum
is an elaborate Carthusian compilation which contains a large mass
of didactic and devotional verse, in which the influence of Rolle is

sometimes strongly felt. The range of material it contains is fascinating; it is, to use Saxl's term, a true 'spiritual encyclopedia of the later Middle Ages'.[73] It is profusely illustrated, and though the pictures are not the work of a skilled craftsman, they sometimes have a crude force and vigour, which remind us of some wall-paintings and early woodcuts. We shall have occasion to refer to this important collection several times; our first illustration from it (plate 1) shows two pages with straightforward 'illustrated' poems – on the left a poem based on the *Salve Regina* and on the right an appeal to man from Christ crucified.[74] Again, the purpose of the image seems clearly to be to help the pious reader in his devotion.

Sometimes the relationship between poem and image becomes so close that we have a sort of rudimentary emblem poem. This happens for instance in the passage in the Douce 1 *Arma Christi* verses which deal with the Pelican. The text runs:

> The pellicane his bloode dothe blede
> Therwith his birdis for to fede.
> It figureth that God with his bloode
> Us fede hanging on the rode,
> Whane he us brought oute of hell
> In joy and blis with him to dwel,
> And be oure fader and oure fode,
> And we his childerne meke and good.

Indeed, the Pelican (like the Instruments of the Passion, the Blazon of Christ's Wounds, the Mystic Winepress, and the Fountain of Life) is a medieval religious 'emblem' which goes into the Renaissance books. Here it is in a slightly more sophisticated seventeenth-century form in Wither's *Emblems*:

> Our Pelican, by bleeding, thus,
> Fulfill'd the Law, and cured Us.
>
> Looke here, and marke (her sickly birds to feed)
> How freely this kinde *Pelican* doth bleed,
> See, how (when other *Salves* could not be found)
> To cure their sorrowes, she, her selfe doth wound;
> And, when this holy *Emblem*, thou shalt see,
> Lift up thy soule to him, who dy'd for thee.[75]

Even better examples can be found among the poems in MS. Additional 37049.[76] Our illustration (plate 2) shows the wounded

Christ offering to man his wounded heart (upon which we can see, as one of the Five Wounds, a good example of the *mensura vulneris* mentioned earlier). The text here has an integral relationship with the image. Christ says:

> (*Querela divina*)
> O man unkynde
> hafe in mynde
> my paynes smert.
> Beholde and see
> That is for the
> Percyd my hert.
>
> And yitt I wolde
> Or than thou schuld
> Thi saule forsake
> On cros with payne
> Scharp deth agayne
> For thi luf take.
>
> For whilk I aske
> None other taske
> But luf agayne.
> Me than to luf
> Al thyng abofe
> Thow aght be fayne.

And man (represented in the picture by the praying or meditating figure) is to respond:

> (*Responsio humana*)
> O lord right dere
> Thi wordes I here
> With hert ful sore;
> Therfore fro synne
> I hope to blynne
> And grefe no more.
>
> Bot in this case
> Now helpe thi grace
> My frelnes,
> That I may ever
> Do thi pleser
> With lastyngnes.

The Background

This grace to gytt
Thi moder eeke
Ever be prone
That we may alle
Into thi halle
With joy cum sone.
   Amen.[77]

Such poems as these conform to the more general definitions of 'emblems' which were given in later times, like 'a sweet and morall symbole which consists of picture and words, by which some weighty sentence is declared', but they do not have the witty elaboration and the teasing air of hidden mystery which is characteristic of the later emblem. The Renaissance emblem books, from Alciati's *Emblematum Liber* of 1531, are formed by other intellectual and iconographic traditions,[78] but these illustrated poems of the late Middle Ages are part of the background from which they come.

This type of poem clearly demands a more careful and thoughtful disposition and visual arrangement of the words than had often been the case in medieval manuscripts. It is not surprising therefore to find in the *Convercyon of Swerers* by Stephen Hawes (printed in 1509) an interesting early example of the patterned poem (plate 3)[79] which was to be so elaborated in the seventeenth century. It is an appeal of Christ accompanied by a small figure of the *Imago Pietatis* (swearing will re-open Christ's wounds). The text is arranged more or less as a pair of wings, beginning with lines of one syllable and widening in the middle, though the printer had to carry some lines over to the next page. Artifice and emotion are successfully blended: the image and the words are happily united, so that it becomes a genuine 'speaking picture', the visual pattern of the print is integrated with the intricate metrical and rhythmical patterns of the poem.

It would be misleading to suggest that these experiments in relating images and words often produced remarkable works of art. Generally the problems posed by the differences between the nature of the visual image, with its balance of shade and tone, and its 'frozen' movement,[80] and of the mental images built up by a continuous flow of words, and full of the suggestions and connotations of the words, are hardly faced. It is significant that most of the examples we have mentioned have been very simple poems,

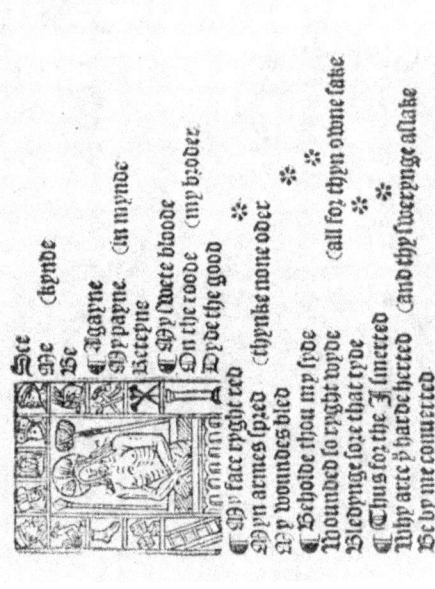

See the kynde
Be Agayne In mynde
My payne Receyue
On the roode My broder
Lyue the good thynke none oder

My face ryght red
My armes spred
My woundes bled   all for thyn owne sake
Beholde thou my syde
Wounded so ryght wyde
Bleyynge sore that tyde

Thus for the I smerted   And thy swerynge a slake
Why arte yu harde herted
Be yu conuerted

Tere me noder no more
My woundes are sore   / and come to my grace
Leue swerynge therfore

I am redy
To graunte mercy   for thy trespace
To the truely
Come nowe nere
My frende dere   / before me
And appere

I
In wo
Dyde go
I

Trye the By

Unto me dere broder my loue and duffette
Turmente me no more with thyn othes grete
Come vnto my loue and agayne reuerte
Frome the Deuyls snare and his subtyll net
Beware of the worlde all aboute the set
Thy fleshe is redy by concupiscence
To burne thy herte with cursed vyolence

Though these thre enmyes do sore the assayle
Vpon euery syde with daungerous iniquite
But yf thou lyst, they may nothynge preuayle
For yet subdue the with all they ertempte
To do good or yll, all is at thy lyberte
I do graunte the grace thyne enmyes to subdue
Where broder accepte it they power to extue

And ye kynges and prynces of hye noblenes
With dukes and lordes of euery dygnyte
Indued with manhode wysdome and rychess
Our the comons hauynge the souerainte
Correcte them whiche so dere me
By cruell othes without repentaunce
Amende by tyme lest I take vengeaunce

3 A Pattern Poem (cf. p. 54) – an appeal of Christ, beseeching Man not to reopen his wounds by swearing.

4 Poems from MS. Sloane 2593, a fifteenth-century collection of religious and secular lyrics.
Left: the unique copy of 'I syng of a mayden that is makeles' (see pp. 101–6); *right:* 'Adam lay ibowndyn' (see p. 76).

and very bold, sometimes crude devotional illustrations. It is rare that the medieval illustrated poem – the *Ship of Fools*, and some versions of the *Dance of Death* are exceptions – can achieve a fruitful and totally successful interaction of image and word.

Finally, it is important to remember that medieval religious literature did not exist in a compartment which was entirely separate from the secular literature of its time. The two ran parallel, and there are many points of contact. The religious poets of Western Europe took over forms and modes of expression from the secular lyric, and sometimes adapted whole poems to their own ends. St Francis, who was familiar with the French courtly tradition, set an example in this: 'a beautiful melody of the spirit sang within him' says Thomas of Celano, one of his biographers, 'and sometimes burst out, and the divine murmur of his soul broke out in transports in a song in French.'[81] There was plenty of ecclesiastical condemnation of 'lascivious' songs—but clerics were quick to make use of them and of the possibilities of the tradition which produced them.

In English, the connections between the secular and the religious lyric can be seen in a number of ways. The religious lyric took over and adapted some of the forms and conventions of the secular, for example, the 'nature-opening'. One thirteenth-century lyric on the redemption begins:

>Somer is comen and winter gon,
>This day biginnith to longe,
>And this foules everichon
>   Joye hem wit songe. . . .

The poet shares their joy, which is for a 'child/that is so milde'.[82] Similarly in penitential and 'mortality' lyrics, the sombre mood of the seasons of autumn or winter affords an appropriate introduction to the poet's reflections:

>Nou skrynketh rose and lylie flour,
>That whilen ber that suete savour,
>   In somer, that suete tyde. . . .[83]

or:

>Wynter wakeneth al my care,
>Nou this leves waxeth bare;
>Ofte y sike, and mourne sare,
>   When hit cometh in my thoht
>Of this worldes joie, hou hit geth al to noht.[84]

The Background

Of the secular forms that are transferred into the religious lyric, one of the most striking is the *chanson d'aventure*. In this the poet introduces himself in a brief narrative preface – which usually opens with the conventional phrase 'as I rode out the other day' – and then pretends to witness or take part in the action that he goes on to describe.

> Under a tre, in sportyng me
> Alone by a wod syd,
> I hard a mayd, that swetly sayd
> 'I am with chyld this tyd'. . . .

but this is not, as a medieval audience might have expected, the introduction to a forsaken maiden's lament. The maid is the Virgin Mary, who sings a song of rejoicing:

> Gracyusly conceyvyd have I
> The son of God so swete.[85]

In the fifteenth century, one or two of the Marian lyrics use the fashionable form of the secular love-epistle – the poem purports to be a letter sent by the poet to his mistress:

> Goe, lytyll byll, and doe me recommende
> Unto my lady with godely countynaunce,
> For, trusty messanger, I the sende.
> Pray her that sche make purvyaunce;
> For my love, thurgh her sufferaunce,
> In her bosome desyreth to reste,
> Ssyth off all women I love here beste. . . .[86]

The religious lyrics (and especially those which are addressed to the Virgin) make extensive use of the language of the *fine amour* of the secular poets. We find rather worldly-sounding descriptions of the Virgin's beauty, and affirmations of the ideal of service, phrased in the traditional feudal terms. More fundamentally, the poets see the Virgin Mary in the way that the secular poets saw their lady. The Virgin, the 'quene of cortaysye' as she is significantly called in *Pearl*, is sometimes a remote mistress who must be approached by her servants humbly, as suppliants, and who like the courtly lady will give her grace of her own free choice, where and when she pleases. In the thirteenth-century poem 'Edi beo thu hevene quene', the poet asks the Virgin to 'have mercy of thy knight', and goes on

The English Lyrics, I

> Levedi milde, softe and swote,
> Ic crie the merci, ic am thi mon,
> Bothe to honde and to fote,
> On alle wise that ic kon.[87]

Here the word 'man' is a feudal term, for 'liegeman' or 'vassal' which was adapted to secular love poetry. So (later) Troilus uses it:

> . . . wheither goddesse or womman, iwis,
> She be, I not. . . .
> But as hire man I wol ay lyve and sterve. . . .
> . . . myn estate roial I here resigne
> Into hire hond, and with ful humble chere
> Bicome hir man. . . .

Sometimes the religious poet will suggest an alternative to the earthly love celebrated by the secular poets; sometimes he will simply adapt, or parody, a secular love song. An example of the first type of poem is the thirteenth-century 'Love Rune' of Friar Thomas of Hales, a learned Oxford Franciscan, who also wrote a graceful Anglo-Norman sermon, and a number of Latin works.[88] Friar Thomas says that he has been asked by a 'maiden of Christ' to write for her a 'love rune'. He does (and, interestingly, chooses English for his nun), but it is a 'love rune' in praise of Christ. He dwells at length on the impermanence of the world in general, and of human love in particular, and rises to an impassioned praise of the precious stone called 'Maydenhod':

> Mayde, al so ich the tolde,
> The ymston of thi bur
> He is betere an hundred folde
> Than alle theos in heore culur:
> He is idon in heovene golde,
> And is ful of fyn amur. . . .

The idea is that gems have each their inherent 'virtue', and that the virtue of this one is 'fyn amur'. Words like 'bur', 'fyn amur', which are full of the suggestions of courtly poetry, are deliberately set in an alien and ascetic context. That this love (that of Christ and of virginity), and not the other, is the true 'fyn amur', is the clear implication.[89]

The more usual method is that of adaptation or 'parody' (though of course there is no sense of burlesque). A number of medieval writers shared with General Booth the view that the Devil should not be allowed to have all the best tunes. According to the chronicler William of Malmesbury, St Aldhelm, the Bishop of Sherborne (d. 709), stood on a bridge singing secular songs until he had won the attention of passers-by – whereupon he began to introduce religious ideas into his songs.[90] In the later Middle Ages Richard de Ledrede, the Bishop of Ossory, a Franciscan, wrote sixty Latin lyrics for his clerics to sing, accompanied in several cases by a scrap of a vernacular love-song ('Have god day my lemon', 'Heu alas par amor/Qy moy myst en taunt dolour', etc.) to indicate the tune.[91] Parodies of various sorts continue into the sixteenth century, where there are moralizations of, for instance, 'The Nutbrown Maid', or 'Come over the Bourn, Bessy' (which is made into an appeal from Christ to sinful man).[92] There is a good deal of variety in the method of these parodies or adaptations. Sometimes there is a simple transference from one tradition to another, which is occasionally so complete that we are hard put to decide whether a poem is 'secular' or 'religious' – one poem which begins

> Trewlove trewe on you I truste,
> Evermore to fynde you perseverawnt,
> Ellys wolde my herte yn sondir brest,
> Bot I cowde love yn expyrant. . . .

might well be called a secular lyric, if it were not for the rubric that accompanies it in the manuscript 'querimonia Christi languentis pro amore'.[93] In other cases we are meant to have a definite sense of shock or surprise.[94] Poems of this sort mostly impress, if they impress at all, by their cleverness or ingenuity. The English devotional lyrics do not attempt that sophisticated exploration of the relationship between divine and earthly love which is characteristic of some of the greatest medieval poets, but there are, as we shall see, a number of lyrics which by their serious use of courtly or erotic imagery, whether taken from secular literature or from the Biblical *Song of Songs*, suggest a different world from that of the 'Love Rune', where earthly love and heavenly love are forever separate and opposed.

The English Lyrics, II

By now something of the nature of the Middle English religious lyrics will be clear. Modern definitions of lyric which emphasize the expression of an individual's emotion will clearly not be applicable to most of them; the student must be content with some such vague description as 'short devotional poems' (though scholars and anthologists differ notoriously about what they regard as 'short') which are usually intended for use by others, whether as song, meditation or prayer. It is important that they are written totally within the inclusive religious tradition of the Middle Ages; Christianity is taken for granted. This results in many inferior, and to our mind, simple and unquestioning poems, but it also means that the poets in this tradition are to a large extent able to by-pass the limitations and problems associated with the writing of religious poetry in later times. They do not, fortunately, feel the need to write self-consciously 'Christian' poetry. Here is a modern poet, W. H. Auden, expressing doubts about personal religious poetry:

> Poems, like many of Donne's and Hopkins', which express a poet's personal feelings of religious devotion or penitence, make me feel uneasy. It is quite in order that a poet should write a sonnet expressing his devotion to Miss Smith because the poet, Miss Smith, and all his readers know perfectly well that, had he chanced to fall in love with Miss Jones instead, his feelings would be exactly the same. But if he writes a sonnet expressing his devotion to Christ, the important point, surely, is that his devotion is felt for Christ and not for, say, Buddha or Mahomet, and this point cannot be made in poetry; the Proper Name proves nothing. A penitential poem is even more questionable. A poet must intend his poem to

be a good one, that is to say, an enduring object for other people to admire. Is there not something a little odd, to say the least, about making an admirable public object out of one's feelings of guilt and penitence before God?[1]

This vividly illustrates the difference between the cultural background and the concept of poetry of a modern poet, who is a Christian, and that of the Christian poets who wrote the English devotional lyrics. They are not primarily concerned with the construction of an enduring object for other people to admire, but rather for other people to *use*. The medieval poet speaks not only for himself, but in the name of the many; if he uses the poetic 'I' it will be in a way which may be shared by his readers. It is a poetic stance which cannot be accurately described either as 'personal' or as 'impersonal'. His devotion may be expressed in fervent and 'personal' terms, but always in a way in which others may share.

The Middle English religious 'lyrics' are a large and somewhat heterogeneous body of verse. One very characteristic and popular type is the reflective or meditative lyric, which directs the reader's mind to the *memoria* of an event in the divine scheme, to the understanding of it, and urges his will to action – to worship or to penitence and reform of life. The aims of medieval meditation are stated in rather general terms – 'these meditacyons or prayers that bene writen in this boke suwyng bene maide to exite and stere the mynde of the reder to the drede of God and to verey knowyng of hymselfe', says one rubric (and the *Pilgrimage of Perfection* defines meditation simply as 'a profounde or studyous cogitacyon about ony certeyn thynge'), so we should not expect the elaborately organized schemes of meditation perfected in the sixteenth century, which were known to and probably influenced later English religious poets.

But meditation is not the only activity of the religious life that finds expression in the lyrics. Prayer, and especially petition, gives impetus and form to many lyrics. Indeed, simple verse prayers are often among the most successful lyrics. Expressions of adoration, thanksgiving, and the celebration of God's goodness and mercy are also found, though more rarely; these are more like the 'singing lyric' familiar to modern readers. Examples may be found among the carols (where the relation of words and music is important in a way in which it is not in the reflective lyrics) or in a few poems like this, from a Tudor manuscript:

The English Lyrics, II

> Pleasure it is
> To hear iwis
>   The birdes sing.
>   The deer in the dale,
>   The sheep in the vale,
>   The corn springing.
>
> Gods purveyance
> For sustenance
>   It is for man;
>   Then we always
>   To him give praise,
>   And thank him than,
>   And thank him than.[2]

There is considerable variety too in the nature of the manuscripts in which the lyrics are found. They vary in size and shape – from the fat heavy volumes of the Vernon and Simeon manuscripts to the tiny Douce 1 and the rolls which we have mentioned. Lyrics are sometimes carefully copied (and sometimes made into collections), sometimes jotted or scribbled on flyleaves or margins. As we have seen, they are found in preaching-books, and as *tituli* on many different surfaces. They are found in poetic miscellanies which contain matter both of 'solace and sentence' like the famous MS. Harley 2253, in which they occur beside some of the best known earlier secular lyrics.[3] Later, in the fifteenth century, they appear in collections which also contain courtly and aureate verse, and, with secular lyrics, in Tudor manuscripts. They occur also in commonplace books, like that made by Richard Hill, grocer of London, in the early sixteenth century.[4] The carols sometimes appear in manuscripts accompanied by polyphonic music; other collections seem likely to be song-books, though they do not contain music, like that in MS. Sloane 2593 which contains 'I syng of a mayden', 'Adam lay ibowndyn' and other well-known pieces. (See plate 4.)[5] A number find their way into early printed books.

This variety is matched by the vastly differing ability of the authors,[6] who range from men of the humblest literary pretension to the best known poets of the time – Chaucer, Hoccleve, Lydgate, Henryson, Dunbar, Skelton – and by the bewildering array of literary forms which the lyrics may take. We find almost everything from the simplest couplets and quatrains to the most elaborate

The Background

rhyme-schemes. They may make use of the traditional forms of secular lyrics. We have already mentioned the characteristic opening of the *chanson d'aventure*, which is used or adapted by the best lyrics with a remarkable boldness and imagination:

> In my bed liying on Cristis day, half slepyng
> Sighhis wondrous hevyng, a voice I hard thus speking,
> 'Wake man, slepe not. . . .'[7]

We can find examples of the courtly *balade*, or the *chanson*, a long, discursive stanzaic form which is capable of almost infinite variation, and which is ideal for reflective and meditative lyrics.

One of the most popular and attractive forms was the *carol*. It was not until the sixteenth century that this became (as it is now) exclusively associated with Christmas; the medieval carols deal with all the themes of the religious lyric, and with secular subjects as well. The carol is meant for singing, and its distinctive formal feature is a burden which recurs after each stanza. The origins of the form are hotly disputed.[8] The word 'carol' is used in Middle English to mean 'ring-dance', and the usually accepted theory is that the literary carols have developed from such dances. In one manuscript among some sermon notes by a Franciscan there is a poem celebrating the Nativity which has as its burden

> Honnd by honnd we schulle ous take,
> And joye and blisse schulle we make,
> For the devel of helle man hath forsake,
> And Godes sone ys maked oure make.

This sounds like a reference to the taking of hands in a dance, although it would be rash to assume that it is evidence that all religious carols were 'danced'.[9]

The dance was an omnipresent feature of medieval life, and naturally became a favourite image in literature and art (besides the grim dance of Death, we have, for instance, the dances of angels, and the cosmic dance of love led by Christ himself).[10] Nor was it such an exclusively secular pastime as it now is. There is a good deal of evidence that sacred dances in churches were still performed.[11] The dance of the *seisos* in Seville at Corpus Christi is one of the few survivals of this practice in modern times, but Aubrey records that in Yorkshire, even as late as the seventeenth century, men danced in country churches at Christmas crying 'yole, yole'.[12] To cite but one medieval example, the canons of

Auxerre used to dance at Easter in the cathedral holding a *pelote* in their left hands, while the dean intoned the prose *Victimae Paschali laudes*.[13] Nor was ecstatic religious dancing unknown.[14] The view that the carol derives from ring-dances has been questioned by Professor Robbins, who suggests that it is patterned on Latin processional hymns. It is, incidentally, hard to distinguish sometimes between solemn religious 'dances' and processions with rhythmic movement. Certainly many of the Middle English carols with their elaborate music, are very far from popular ring-dances, but probably we need not choose between these rival views. The carols are such a varied group of poems that it is not inconceivable that some should be of learned and some of popular origin.

The question of the 'proper' language for devotional literature, which interests the theorists of later times, is never discussed by our poets. They approach what was later regarded as a 'problem' in a typically unselfconscious way. They generally write directly, simply and plainly. In this they follow the usual practice of medieval devotional literature. The author of the *Meditations on the Life of Christ* quotes with approval the dictum that 'plain language reaches the heart, whilst finished speeches merely fill and please the ears': 'It is not beauty of language,' he says, 'but the study of the life of Jesus, to which I ask your attention.' They are not concerned to seek out 'quaint words and trim invention' or 'sweet phrases, lovely metaphors'. Words such as 'simple' or 'homely' have a special resonance in devotional literature. Nicholas Love's fifteenth-century version of the *Meditations* is for 'symple creatures, the whiche as children haven nede to be fedde with mylke of lyghte doctrine and not with sadde mete of grete clergie and of highe contemplacion'.[15] Julian of Norwich and Margery Kempe refer to themselves as 'simple creatures', and one of the most interesting of the mystical works has for its title *The Mirror of Simple Souls*. All of which is an echo of an old and fundamental Christian idea, that, as Herbert puts it

> A peasant may believe as much
> As a great clerk, and reach the highest station.

Devotional writers prefer familiar images, the exactness of particulars which 'ever touch, and awake more than generalls', homely and realistic details. They produce in miniature the verbal equivalents of the homely genre scenes in the splendid Luttrell

Psalter. The English author of *Sawles Warde*, based on Hugh of St Victor's *De Anima* describes Will as the 'wilful housewife'. The lyric poets, too, prefer the homely, proverbial and simple word and phrase – their blossoms simply 'spring'; they avoid the 'painted fields' of the more learned poets.

Erich Auerbach has suggested that what he calls the *sermo humilis*, the 'humble style', is the expression of a basic idea of Christianity – the essential feature of the Incarnation was that Christ did not come as a king but as the humblest of men; his sayings though simple and unadorned were the Word of God.[16] Possibly Auerbach's view that this caused the destruction of the classical notions of the separation of styles is oversimplified, but the concept of *sermo humilis* is a most valuable one for the student of vernacular devotional literature. There are so many references to plainness and simplicity of style that one feels that it was almost a stylistic 'imitation' of Christ. One of the nicest examples (quoted by Auerbach) comes from a late fourteenth-century commentator on Dante, Benevuto da Imola, who remarks on the line in which Beatrice's manner of speaking is described:

e comminciommi a dir soave e piana

'et bene dicit, quia sermo divinus est suavis et planus, non altus et superbus sicut sermo Virgilii et poetarum'. (Well he says this for the divine speech is sweet and plain, not high and proud like the speech of Virgil and the poets.)

Naturally enough there were some devotional poets who felt that the treatment of their divine matter should perhaps be a little more 'altus et superbus'. There is a certain amount of artifice and decoration, and some successful examples of elaborate, more 'literary' styles. Some poets use, as well as rhyme, the technique of alliteration which they had inherited from Old English. In short poems the heavy beat and emphasis can easily become over-insistent for our ear; it is only occasionally that the modern reader will find one of these lyrics – like the poem 'my trewest tresowre sa trayturly was taken' (see p. 132) – pleasing. More extreme forms of artifice are found, examples of what Addison calls 'false wit' and for which he blames monkish ignorance – quite frequent examples of puns, a palindrome (Eva/Ave), as well as acrostics and alphabetical poems.

Two forms of 'decorative' writing are particularly frequent: the use of macaronic verse, and of aureate diction. The interlarding of lines from different languages (the word macaronic is formed from macaroni, 'paste') is not a surprising practice in the light of what has been said about the linguistic situation in England. It is found from thirteenth-century lyrics through to those of the sixteenth. Sometimes it seems to be a verbal equivalent of the 'babwynery' of the artists and sculptors, but it is by no means always simply a frill, as we shall see in a lyric like 'There is no rose of swich vertu'. And some of our poets, notably Dunbar, can make brilliant use of Latin refrains. The golden or 'aureate' diction of the fifteenth century (both the word and the style seem to have been introduced by Lydgate)[17] is almost always abused by critics. It is certainly not hard to find examples which are pedantic to the point of absurdity:

> *Oleum effusum*, to *languentes* medsyne,
> O maria by denominacioun,
> Fulgent as the beame celestyne,
> Called unto hir coronacioun.
> Phebus persplendent made his abdominacioun,
> Devoidyng all in tenebrosite,
> For gret love of hir exaltacioun,
> *Ecce virgo radix Jesse!*[18]

But at its best, as in Dunbar's 'Balet of Our Lady' it can be used with an extraordinary inventiveness and rhythmical virtuosity. There is also usually some sense of decorum in its use. It is most characteristically found in celebrations and gorgeous descriptions of Mary enthroned as Queen of Heaven, where it is the verbal equivalent of the gold and rich colours that are lavished on this scene by the artists.

There are also a few examples of what might be called 'wit-poetry'. We should perhaps linger a little over these and their background since they are usually neglected by critics. There are plenty of examples of this type of writing in medieval Latin, notably in the theological hymns of Adam of St Victor (late twelfth century) and Aquinas, hymns which are full of conceits, puns, paradoxes:

> O Maria, redemptoris
> Creatura, creatoris
>   Genetrix magnifica. . . .*

* O Mary, created by the redeemer, yet the mother of the creator.

The Background

Fr Walter Ong, in a very interesting article which relates these hymns to English seventeenth-century 'metaphysical' poetry[19] (though one suspects that when he uses the word 'metaphysical' it is really Donne of whom he is thinking) compares them very favourably with the Latin poetry inspired by affective devotion, which is for most people exemplified by the *Dies Irae* and the *Stabat Mater Dolorosa*. This 'affective' poetry, he says severely, 'finds the source of its rhetoric in the commonplaces of ordinary life – the love of son for mother, of mother for child . . . encouraging the effort to transfer these or similar emotions to higher and nobler objects'; its most characteristic note is 'anguish and plangent tenderness', there is here 'no need for striking juxtapositions, for the stimulus of insights freshly arrived at, establishing intricate connections between realities apprehended in all sorts of ways and at all levels simultaneously – no need for wit in any form. . . .' No one would deny that bad 'affective' poetry is very bad indeed, and it is certainly possible that these two hymns – especially the *Dies Irae* – do not deserve their reputation. But it is unjust to dismiss all affective poetry. It depends on integrity and precision of feeling rather than on 'wit', but there is surely nothing wrong in principle with this. Nor will all readers be convinced that its lack of concern for 'the dogmatic content of revelation' and its preference for 'the commonplaces of ordinary life' are necessarily bad things. The *Stabat Mater* is in fact a meditative poem. The author first visualizes the scene, then introduces his own (and the reader's) emotional responses, and ends with an extended series of petitions, asking that he may be allowed to share in the Passion. The emotion is controlled; it is certainly emotion of an ecstatic and fervent kind, but it does not become tasteless or extravagant (indeed, in the light of some Middle English treatments of the scene we might criticize the poet for not making the most of its dramatic possibilities):

> Fac me vere tecum flere,
> Crucifixo condolere,
>   Donec ego vixero;
> Iuxta crucem tecum stare,
> Te libenter sociare
>   In planctu desidero.
>
> Virgo virginum praeclara,
> Mihi iam non sis amara;

Fac me tecum plangere,
Fac, ut portem Christi mortem,
Passionis eius sortem
   Et plagas recolere.

Fac me plagis vulnerari
Cruce hac inebriari
   Ob amorem filii;
Inflammatus et accensus
Per te, virgo, sim defensus
   In die iudicii. . . .*[20]

As a greater poet said, even more emotionally and dramatically:

Spit in my face yee Jewes, and pierce my side,
Buffet, and scoffe, scourge and crucifie mee.[21]

A poem by Adam of St Victor, *Splendor Patris et Figura*,[22] is in striking contrast to this. Making use of the traditional 'types', and with some display of paradox, it records the mystery of the Incarnation:

Frondem, florem, nucem sicca
Virga profert, et pudica
   Virgo Dei Filium.
Fert coelestem vellus rorem,
Creatura creatorem
   Creaturae pretium.†

(both the figures of the dry rod and of Gideon's fleece are found in our lyrics; note the pun *virga/virgo*). Adam goes on to explain the significance of the foliage, the flower and the nut. The nut is Christ, the outer bark is the cross, the kernel signifies his deity concealed in flesh and his sweetness, etc. A poem such as this

---

* Make me truly to weep with thee, and share the sufferings of Christ crucified as long as I live; to stand with thee beside the cross, to share gladly in thy lament, is my desire. O virgin, renowned among virgins, do not spurn me now. Grant that I may weep with thee, that I may bear the death of Christ, recall his Passion and his wounds. Grant that I may be wounded with his wounds, that for the love of the Son my cup may be filled by this cross. Inflamed and kindled by love for him, may I be defended by thee, O virgin, on the Day of Judgment. . . .

† The dry rod brings forth branch, flower and nut, and the chaste virgin brings forth the Son of God. The fleece bears the heavenly dew, the creature the creator, the ransom of the creature.

certainly has some of the features associated with later 'metaphysical' poetry. Besides paradox and word-play, it has more than a hint of the 'strong lines', the 'nice speculations of philosophy' and the 'metaphysical ideas and scholastical quiddities'. And yet there is something missing. One difference is that the 'wit' of a theological poem like this is static. The paradoxes are not worked out – they are presented, then left. Though passages may remind us of some of Herbert's poems, there is none of that hammering out of ideas that is characteristic of Donne's. We also miss the personal, colloquial, dramatic tone of Donne's religious poetry. In Adam's poem the 'affective' note is sometimes there, but in a minor and rather unconvincing way in simple exclamations: 'res est ineffabilis/Tam pia, tam humilis/Christi generatio!' or 'O quam dulce sacramentum!' The poem as a whole is markedly impersonal – we invariably have the 'we' of the congregation (*contemplemur adhuc nucem*, 'let us consider the nut further'), and there is all the difference in the world between such an exclamation as *O quam dulce sacramentum!* and Donne's

> Batter my heart, three person'd God; for, you
> As yet but knocke, breathe, shine, and seeke to mend. . . .

It is perhaps significant that when one English metaphysical poet – Crashaw – chose a Latin hymn upon which to write a 'patheticall descant', it was not a poem like *Splendor Patris et Figura*, but the *Stabat Mater* ('Sancta Maria Dolorum or the Mother of Sorrows. A patheticall descant upon the devout Plainsong of Stabat Mater Dolorosa').

Most of our English lyrics clearly belong to the 'affective' tradition (though it would be misleading to separate 'affective' and 'theological' traditions completely).[23] There are many isolated conceits or paradoxes – usually of the kind that are demanded by the mysteries of the Christian Faith: Mary is both maid and mother; as the mother of God she, the creature, bore the creator, etc. But there are some poems that are more consistently and self-consciously witty. A good example is the fifteenth-century lyric which Carleton Brown calls 'The Divine Paradox':

> A God and yet a man?
> A mayde and yet a mother?
> Witt wonders what witt can
> Conceave this or the other.

The English Lyrics, II

> A god, and can he die?
> A dead man, can he live?
> What witt can well replie?
> What reason reason give?
>
> God, truth itselfe doth teach it;
> Mans witt senckis too farr under
> By reasons power to reach it.
> Beleeve, and leave to wonder![24]

It is a successful little poem, which illustrates rather neatly the point made above, in that although it is built up on paradoxes it makes no attempt to work them out or resolve them in any way. It is content with the statement of paradox and a typically late medieval assertion of the need for simple faith. Sometimes in Eucharistic carols and poems we find bolder witty figures:

> In Virgine Mary this brede was bake
> Whenne Criste of her manhoode did take. . . .[25]

or

> *Mirabile misterium*
> In forme of bred ys Godes Son. . . .
>
> Thowgh yt seme whit, yt ys rede;
> Yt ys flesshe, yt semeyth bred.
>
> Yt ys God in his manhed
> As he hong upon a tre. . . .[26]

And occasionally in longer poems we find a figure which reminds us of the extravagances of the seventeenth century – in the *Disputation between Mary and the Cross*, the cross says at one point:

> I was that cheef chargeour;
> I bar flesch for folkes feste,
> Jesu Crist ure saveour,
> He fedeth bothe lest and meste;
> Rosted ayeyn the sonne,
> On me lay the lamb of love;
> I was plater, his bodi above. . . .[27]

In one of the two versions of prose meditations on the Passion attributed to Richard Rolle (the other, in full affective style, makes a direct assault on the reader's emotions) we have a remarkable run of conceits upon the wounds in the scourged body of

Christ (like the witty passages in the *Livre de Seyntz Medicines* mentioned earlier, it coexists happily with an intensely emotional devotion):

> Than was thy body lyk to hevyn. For as hevyn is ful of sterris, so was thy body ful of woundes; bot, lord, thy woundes bene bettyr than sterris, for sterris shynen bot by nyght, and thy woundes bene ful of vertu day and nyght....
> And, yit, Lord, swet Jesu, thy body is lyk to a nette; for as a nette is ful of holys, so is thy body ful of woundes. Here, swet Jesu, I beseche the, cache me into this net of thy scourgynge, that al my hert and love be to the....
> Efte, swet Jesu, thy body is like to a dufhouse. For a dufhouse is ful of holys, so is thy body ful of woundes. And as a dove pursued of an hauk, yf she mow cache an hool of hir hous she is siker ynowe, so, swete Jesu, in temptacion thy woundes ben best refuyt to us....
> Also, swete Jesu, thi body is like to a honycombe. For hit is in euche a way ful of cellis, and euch celle ful of hony, so that hit may nat be touched without yeld of swetnesse. So, swet Jesu, thy body is ful of cellys of devocion, that hit may nat be touched of a clene soule without swetnesse of lykynge....
> More yit, swet Jesu, thy body is lyke a boke written al with rede ynke; so is thy body al written with rede woundes....
> And yit, swet Jesu, thy body is lyk to a medow ful of swete flours and holsome herbes; so is thy body ful of woundes, swet savorynge to a devout soule, and holsome as herbes to euch synful man....[28]

Enough has been said by now to indicate, that although the religious lyrics were written to be used, and although the impulse behind them was devotional rather than narrowly 'aesthetic', it would be wrong to deny to the authors of many of them a developed aesthetic sense. The makers of medieval religious art did not find devotion and a sense of beauty incompatible. The splendour of churches and cathedrals is praised (the word *nitens* 'shining' is a favourite term of approbation)[29] and indeed, in the metrical Latin *Life of St Hugh*,[30] the visual effect of the columns in Lincoln cathedral – 'the little columns which surround the larger column seem to perform a kind of dance' – is caught with an aesthetic precision which almost makes us think of the refined sensibility of a Byzantine poet.³¹ We do not have these direct statements about our lyrics, but we have a certain amount of practical evidence – the sensitive reworking of an earlier lyric in 'I sing of a mayden that is makeles', for instance.³² But the best evidence is the care and craftsmanship which marks the best of the lyrics, and makes them truly into admirable works of art.

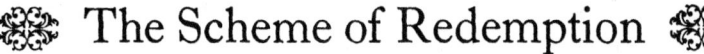
The Scheme of Redemption

Christ and the Virgin Mary

Unlike the vast cycles of the mystery plays, which present the story of the redemption of man as it unrolls from the Fall to the events of Christ's Incarnation, his Passion, his 'harrowing' of hell and triumphant Resurrection, and to the final Day of Judgment, the religious lyrics prefer to find their subjects in the most significant incidents within the story – especially the Nativity and the Passion of Christ – and in the figures whose role in it are most important – those of Christ himself and of the Virgin Mary. Adam's disastrous action is recorded in a little mnemonic tag:

> Adam, alas and waylaway!
> A luther dede dedest thou that day![1]

But usually in devotional lyrics references to the Fall look forward to the redemption ('as in Adam all die, even so in Christ shall all be made alive').[2] Traditionally, Christ was the second Adam, who by his death repaired the fault of the first. So another verse on the same page of the MS. prophesies the joy to come:

> Also Adam wyt lust and likynge
> Broght al his ken into wo and wepynge,
> So shall a child of the kende springe,
> That shal brynge hym and alle hyse
> Into joye and blisse habbynge.

Similarly, Mary, by her humble acceptance of God's command, became the instrument of grace, and a second more fortunate Eve:

> The yates of Parais
> Thoruth Eve weren iloken;
> And thoruth oure swete ladi
> Ayein hui beoth nouthe open.[3]

The Scheme of Redemption

One very well-known known lyric from a fifteenth-century manuscript celebrates with infectious gaiety the fact that the Fall was a *felix culpa*[4] (the phrase is from the *Exultet*) for it brought not only the redemption of man, but the glorious elevation of Mary to be Queen of Heaven:

> Adam lay ibowndyn, bowndyn in a bond,
> Fowre thowsand wynter thowt he not to long.
>
> And al was for an appil, an appil that he tok,
> As clerkes fyndyn wretyn in here book.
>
> Ne hadde the appil take ben, the appil take ben,
> Ne hadde never our lady a ben hevene qwen.
>
> Blyssid be the tyme that appil take was,
> Therfore we mown syngyn *Deo gracias*.[5]

In his *Rationale divinorum officiorum*, Durandus, the bishop of Mende (1230–96), says that there are three ways in which the image of Christ may be depicted in churches: as a child sitting in his mother's lap, as a man hanging on the cross, and as a judge reigning.[6] Of these subjects (which, of course, were not the only ones used by the artists), English devotional lyrics are most fond of the first and the second, those, significantly, of Christ in his humanity. The image of Christ as judge reigning in the sky, so magnificently handled by the artists, receives scanty and unimpressive treatment, although a number of good lyrics celebrate Christ's victory over the fiends and his Resurrection.

One lyric, a not very distinguished piece from the fifteenth century, describes what the appearance of Christ was imagined to be. The poet visualizes the young bearded face with shoulder-length hair parted in the middle which is the standard 'portrait' of Christ in medieval art.[7]

> As walnot barke his hare is yalowe,
> In summer ceson when it is grene. . . .

It is divided in the middle 'as of a custom, I fynde writtyng, Of peppyl of Nazareth. . . .' Christ has a 'playne front' and a 'clere' face. His beard is 'multiplyed wele with hare', and is like down; it is 'noght to bostos (?coarse in texture, shaggy), but longe and smaylle'. His demeanour is sweet, but in his 'correctioun' it is fierce and dreadful:

Christ and the Virgin Mary

And in his tretty ful of plesaunce
And vere blithe when he is plesyd.

In his homely way, the poet is imagining a handsome and dignified figure (the beauty of Christ was traditionally an eternal beauty),[8] with something of the *douceur* of the famous Christ of Chartres, and with more than a touch of its melancholy:

> Both sad and stabyll in his demenaunce,
> And never wald laghe, bot oftyme wepyd.

As Émile Mâle says, 'The Christians of the Middle Ages had their souls filled with Jesus Christ. They sought him everywhere and they saw him everywhere. They read his name on all the pages of the Old Testament.' 'Shadows' or figures of Christ were found not only in the pages of the Old Testament, but in pagan myth and story, and in the pages of the 'book' of nature as it was expounded by commentaries and bestiaries. Such figures are to be found in our lyrics: Lydgate, in his *Testament*, calls Christ

> Our Orpheus that from captivyte
> Fette Erudice to his celestiall tour. . . .[9]

A carol to the Virgin Mary has as its burden:

> A roose hath borne a lilly white,
> The whiche floure is moost pure and bright.[10]

Another poem likens Christ to the fleur-de-lys (with a learned reference to the *Herbarium* of 'Maacer').[11] One carol attempts to work out the image of Christ as an ear of corn which sprang from a maiden, and was reaped on the mount of Calvary; a longer poem which uses the same image (based on John 12: 24–6) produces some conceits worthy of the most exaggerated 'metaphysical' style – Christ, our grain, was ground on the cross, 'Ure cake on crois thei knede', 'Tho was he marked with a launce,/Don(put) in the ovene'; we are instructed to chew on 'ur lof' and be reminded how grim, how hot it is in hell.[12] More successful are the poems which use the nightingale, the traditional messenger of love, as a figure of Christ.[13] In one, possibly by Lydgate, the poet finds the nightingale on her laurel tree and listens to her sing of her impending death:

The Scheme of Redemption

> And aftir this, when Phebus in his spere
>   Over all the world had sprad his bemes bright,
> Causynge the cloudes dym for to be clere,
>   And derke mystes enlumyned with his lyght,
>   Aboute the oure of sixt then she alyght
>   And singynge seet in myddes of the tre:
>   'Ocy, Ocy, O deth, wellcome to me!'[14]

Behind this lies a fine Latin poem *Philomena praevia* by John Pecham (d. 1292) which relates to the legend that the nightingale knows beforehand of the time of her death and when it approaches flies to the top of a tree, and at daybreak begins to sing her songs, her joy and passion increasing until after her cry of 'Oci, oci!', at None she dies.[15] Yet another lyric uses the figure of the nightingale as Christ allusively, 'in a figur of mysty sentence', this time as a remote and mysterious voice, to whose service the poet has devoted himself:

> With notis cleer, and vois entuned clene,
> Lyk the ravisshyng marvelous armony
> Off Jherusalem, I hard the phylomene
> In derk December syng melediously,
> The curious sownyng of whos melody
> With such delyt so in myn eris rong
> That evyr me semyth I her her blisseful song. . . .[16]

But in most of the lyrics the emphasis is on the person of Christ, on his humanity, his 'marvellous courtesy and homeliness' in Julian of Norwich's phrase, which is sometimes expressed in the most intimate terms of human relationship:

> He yaf himself as good felawe,
>   Whan he was boren in wre wede;
> Als good norice he bowh down lowe,
>   Whan wiht himself he wolde us fede.
> Als good schephirde upon [th]e lowe
>   His wed he yaf for wre nede;
> In hevene as king we schulen hin knowe,
>   Qwan he himself schal yiven in mede.[17]

You should remember, says a friar in a sermon,

> That thi brother in heven is maister and kyng,
> Thi suster is maister of all thing;
> He that schal dem the at the dom
> He is thi felaw and thi grom.[18]

Christ and the Virgin Mary

Medieval piety liked to dwell on the beauty and the sweetness of the sacred name of Jesus. The name of the Lord in the Old Testament is remote and awe-inspiring, yet it is in some Old Testament verses – e.g. Ps. 8: 1: 'O Lord our lord, how excellent is thy name in all the earth' and especially Cant. xv, 5 'thy name is oil poured out' (*oleum effusum est nomen tuum*) – that we find the germ of this cult. St Bernard finds the name of Jesus a light, a food, a refreshment, honey for the mouth, melody for the ear, charm for the heart, and a remedy for affliction; by the later Middle Ages devotion to the name of Jesus was flourishing. It became a favourite theme of religious poets. There is a Mass of the Holy Name; popular piety uses the sacred name in prayers and on magical rings. The cult of the Holy Name is now usually associated with the Franciscan St Bernardino of Siena (1380–1444), who in his sermons used tablets with the sacred monogram painted on them, but before this time the devotion was found in England.[19] It is especially marked in the work of Richard Rolle. He says himself that he always held 'the name of Jesu . . . in perfit memoire and gret delite', and in his *Encomium Nominis Jesu* he describes the help it gave him in temptation.[20] The intensely Christocentric devotion which is characteristic of the lyrics associated with his name or with his 'school' often expresses itself through the repeated exclamatory use of the Holy Name:

> Jesu my joy and my lovynge,
> Jesu my comforthe clere,
> Jesu my godde, Jesu my kynge,
> Jesu withowttene pere. . . .

> Jesu my dere and my drewrye,
> Delyte thou arte to synge;
> Jesu my myrthe and my melodye:
> Into thy lufe me bringe.

> Jesu, Jesu, my hony swete,
> Myn herte, my comforthynge:
> Jesu, all my bales thou bete,
> And to thi blysse me brynge.[21]

Poems of this very distinctive type have sometimes been highly praised. However, the ejaculatory style easily becomes monotonous and incoherent; the expression of emotion is often strident and unvaried, a series of ecstatic assertions which, though no doubt effective as devotion, are not embodied in a poetically successful form.

The essential characteristic of Christ, as he is seen in medieval devotional literature, is the love which he shows for mankind. The love which is the nature of God himself (cf. 1 John) finds its supreme expression in Christ's Incarnation and in his sacrifice on the cross. Christ's statement in the gospel of John that God so loved the world that he gave his only son to save it becomes one of the great dominant ideas in devotional literature.[22] It lies behind almost all the lyrics which are concerned with the figure of Christ, and may be developed in a variety of ways. Christ, as the lover of sinful man, may appeal to him from the cross. In one poem he himself is made to express the paradox that it was love which slew him:

> Love me brouthte,
> And love me wrouthte,
> Man, to be thi fere.
> Love me fedde,
> And love me ledde,
> And love me lettet here.
>
> Love me slou,
> And love me drou,
> And love me leyde on bere.
> Love is my pes,
> For love I ches,
> Man to byyen dere.[23]

Man should respond to and return this supreme love; love becomes the basis of the relationship between man and God:

> I hafe set my hert so hye,
> Me likyt no love that lowere ys;
> And alle the paynes that ye may drye,
> Me thynk hyt do me good ywys.
>
> For on that lorde that lovid us alle,
> So hertely have I set my thowght,
> Yt ys my joie on hym to calle,
> For love me hath in balus browght.
> Me think yt do me good iwys.[24]

Christ and the Virgin Mary

There is a very impressive expression of the idea in a song which is recorded long after the Middle Ages. Sandys includes in his *Christmas Carols, Ancient and Modern* (1833) an 'old Cornish poem', 'This have I done for my true love', which begins 'Tomorrow shall be my dancing day'. It is impossible to be sure how old this really is, but some phrases (e.g. 'The Jews . . . with me made great variance') and the nature of the poem suggest that it is not impossible that it should go back to the sixteenth or even to the fifteenth century. Christ tells his 'true love' of his sacrifice

> Then was I born of a Virgin pure,
> Of her I took fleshly substance:
> Then was I knit to man's nature,
> To call my true love to my dance.
>> Sing oh my love, oh my love, my love, my love
>> This have I done for my true love.

and recalls the main events of his life up to his Passion:

> When on the cross hanged I was;
> When a spear to my heart did glance,
> There issued forth both water and blood,
> To call my true love to the dance.
>> Sing oh my love, etc.

and ends with the image of the blessed led by Christ in the cosmic dance of love:[25]

> Then up to Heav'n I did ascend,
> Where now I dwell in sure substance,
> On the right hand of God that man may come
>> into the general dance. . . .

Long before the time that the first of the Middle English religious lyrics were written, the veneration of the Virgin Mary had assumed an important role in Christian devotion.[26] The earliest Christian literature has the Angelic Salutation (Luke 1: 28), which was the germ of so much later poetry and meditation. Mary is spoken of as the second Eve, who by her obedience loosed the knot of Eve's disobedience. Her title of *theotokos*, the bearer of God, was upheld against Nestorian attack at the council of Ephesus in 431. Private prayers to Mary are found in the late fourth century. The apocryphal gospels, which fill out the simple narratives of the canonical books with everyday details of the lives of Mary and her child (it is from these sources that the names of her parents, Joachim and Anna, and such details as that at the Annunciation she was taking a pitcher to fill with water, enter pious legend) indicate considerable popular curiosity, if not necessarily devotion. Already in these early centuries popular cults of the Virgin seem to have gone to extremes. We hear of a fourth-century sect called the Collyridians, 'women in Thrace, Scythia and Arabia', who adored the Virgin Mary as a goddess, and offered sacrificial cakes to her, possibly a survival of the practice of offering cakes to Ceres. They are rebuked by St Epiphanius: 'Let Mary be had in honour, but let the Lord be worshipped.' Thus orthodox Christian theologians have always distinguished between the *latria* (worship) due to her son, and the *hyperdulia* (special veneration) which is due to her, though popular devotion has not always grasped this distinction. By the eighth century, possibly encouraged by the influence of monastic writers, and by a knowledge of Eastern works such as those of Ephraem Syrus (*c*. 306–73), which stressed her perfect sinlessness, Marian devotion was widespread in the West.[27] It became an important and characteristic part of the 'devotional movement'. In Anselm, Mary's vital part in the scheme of redemption is stressed: God is the Father of all created things, and Mary is the mother of all things which are recreated through the Incarnation. Into the mouth of 'her faithful Bernard', in whose works can be found some of Mary's most eloquent praises, Dante puts the great prayer which begins Canto xxxiii of the *Paradiso*:

> Vergine madre, figlia del tuo figlio,
>   umile e alta più che creatura,
> termine fisso d'etterno consiglio,
> tu se' colei che l'umana natura
>   nobilitasti sì, che'l suo fattore
>   non disdegnò di farsi sua fattura. . . .*

The cult of Mary was sometimes taken to some curious extremes. In the *De Laudibus Beatae Mariae Virginis*,[28] an elaborate treatise on the qualities, the virtues, and the figures of the Virgin Mary, her physical qualities are catalogued and expounded with an

---

* Virgin mother, daughter of thy Son, lowly and exalted more than any creature, fixed goal of the eternal counsel, thou art she who didst so ennoble human nature that its maker did not disdain to be made its making. . . . (tr. Sinclair).

Christ and the Virgin Mary

extraordinary dedication. Even her navel reminds the author that she is called 'the navel of the church, since just as the navel is in the centre of the whole body, so she is in the centre of the church'. All of the sensuous imagery of the Song of Songs is applied to Mary – the verse *oleum effusum* which we have just encountered is taken *quasi loquens ad Mariam*, as if speaking to Mary. The author remarks that the name Mary is rightly compared to oil, and proceeds to illustrate the appropriateness of the comparison at considerable length. In another such work, the *Psalterium Beatae Mariae Virginis* (which finds its way into a Middle English version) we have a sort of adaptation or parody of the Psalms, a Marian 'descant' on the opening phrases of each psalm. The fusion of Hebrew imagery with Marian devotion can sometimes produce a splendid exotic effect.[29] There is even a Marian version of the Athanasian creed and of the *Te Deum*: (*Te matrem laudamus; te virginem confitemur....*) 'We praise thee, O mother, we acknowledge thee to be a virgin. The splendour of the eternal father doth illuminate thee, O star of the sea ... to thee Cherubim and Seraphim humbly with us do cry "Virgin, virgin, virgin...".'[30]

The ideas and the images of this extreme Mariolatry are attempts to give expression to the importance of the part Mary had traditionally played in Man's redemption. It is more happily expressed through the ancient opposition of Eve and Mary (*mors per Evam, vita per Mariam*), which is found as late as Milton:

> On whom the angel 'Hail'
> Bestowed, the holy salutation used
> Long after to blest Mary, second Eve.

Medieval devotional writers took some delight in the paradox of the angel's 'holy salutation'. It was a palindrome, with cosmic implications: Gabriel's *Ave* reversed the name of Eva (in Herebert's phrase, he turned 'abakward Eves nome'), and with it the fate of mankind. The author of a famous hymn, *Ave Maris Stella* (which was translated into Middle English) prays to the virgin:

> Sumens illud Ave
> Gabrielis ore,
> Funda nos in pace
> Mutans Evae nomen. . . .*

---

* Taking that 'Ave' from the mouth of Gabriel, establish us in peace, reversing the name of Eva.

The Scheme of Redemption

Some found a punning derivation of 'Ave' from *a ve* (from woe):

> Tibi dicunt omnes 'ave'
> Quia mundum solvens a vae
> Mutasti vocem flentium. . . .*³¹

This is alluded to in a line in the English Coventry plays: 'she is withowte wo and ful of grace'.³² Even more intricate mysteries could be discovered in the salutation by ingenious devotion.³³

Ab initio et ante saecula creata sum – I am created from the beginning and before all time – is a verse applied to Mary in the Office of the Virgin Mary, and the pious imagination could find 'shadows' of the Virgin Mary in scripture and images of her in the created world. Chaucer's Prioress in the prayer to the Virgin at the beginning of her tale, addresses her as 'O bussh unbrent, brennynge in Moyses sighte'. This is an allusion to a traditional and common figure of Mary's perpetual virginity; the bush which the shepherd Moses saw burning with fire, yet not consumed. Like many other Marian figures, it is often found in the visual arts. There is a fine treatment of it by Nicholas Froment in the Cathedral of Aix-en-Provence; here it has been linked with another Marian image, which is also an image of love – the burning bush is a rose-bush.³⁴

Some of the more learned lyrics give what is virtually a catalogue of Marian figures. One fourteenth-century poem, 'Marye, mayde mylde and fre',³⁵ lists her attributes and figures interspersed with brief ejaculatory petitions, and is finally dedicated by the author to her:

> Have, levedy, thys lytel songe
> That out of senfol herte spronge
> Ayens the feend thou make me stronge,
> And yyf me thy wysyssynge. . . .

It is doggedly mediocre, but makes a fine display of Marian learning. It opens with a statement of Mary's attributes – the striking image of Mary as 'chambre of the Trinity' which we have already discussed, and an allusion to her power as shown in one of her miracles. She is called 'Queen of Paradys, Of hevene, of erthe, of al that ys'. Other poets go further, and explicitly include hell as part of her empire. So the *Pearl* poet:

---

* All say Ave to thee, for releasing the world from woe thou hast changed the voice of those who weep.

Christ and the Virgin Mary

> That emperise al hevenz hatz,
> And urthe and helle, in her bayly. . . .[36]

Others press the idea that she is Queen of Heaven. A fifteenth-century carol says

> Thow art emperesse of heven fre;
> Now art thou moder in mageste
> Yknytte in the blessed Trinite. . . .[37]

That the phrase 'yknytte in' probably meant for this poet something like 'in an intimate and special relationship with' is made clear when he goes on to call her 'cosyn to the persones thre', but it is hardly a theologian's phrase. Another poet is so carried away by her excellence that he exclaims:

> Therefore thu maist be called a goddes; yf any be
> Other in heven or erthe, then surely thow art she –
> One spyryte and will with Cryst in his palace![38]

'Marye Mayde mylde and fre' continues with a series of figures from the Old Testament, most of them – like the burning bush – common in Marian tradition. Mary is called 'the yerde of Aaron Me dreiye isegh springande', Aaron's rod, the figure which is punningly alluded to in the *virga/virgo* of Adam of St Victor's *Splendor Patris et Figura*[39] (our poet forgoes the very common Rod of Jesse figure). She is Gideon's fleece, a reference to the story in Judges 6, where as a sign from God the dew falls on the fleece which is put out but not on the ground around it (which Adam also alludes to). Another carol states the figure explicitly:

> This is Gedeonys wulle-felle
> On whom the dewe of heven dyde dwelle;
> The dewe of heven on Mary fel
>   Whan she conceyved Adonay.[40]

Mary is the dove which brought back the olive-branch to Noah (Gen. 8:11), the sling from which David fired the stone (her son) at Goliath (1 Sam. 17:49),[41] the temple built by Solomon (1 Kings 5, et seq.),[42] Ezekiel's gate (Ezek. 44:2), which God said would not be opened 'and no man shall enter in by it; because the Lord, the God of Israel, hath entered in by it',[43] and the hill of which Daniel spoke (Dan. 2:34), from which a stone was cut without hands.[44] The poet lists a number of virtuous women from

The Scheme of Redemption

the Old Testament:[45] Mary is the 'true Sarah' (Abraham's legitimate wife), Judith, 'that fayre wyf' who struck off the head of Holofernes, and Esther, 'that swete thyng' who by her intercession with King Ahasuerus saved the children of Israel from the machinations of Haman. From the pages of the New Testament comes one very unusual figure: 'thou ert Emaus, the ryche castel/Thar resteth alle werye (cf. Luke 24:13, 28),[46] and one very common one – the woman clothed with the sun, with the moon beneath her feet, from the book of Revelation, an image which is often given visual form.[47] Elsewhere, both the sun and the moon are taken as figures of Mary, and such verses as *in sole posuit tabernaculum suum* (Ps. xviii, 6) and *pulchra ut luna, electa ut sol* (Cant. vi, 2) are regularly applied to her. She is often associated with the moon[48] – in one lyric the author, as he 'stood musing on the moon', sees a vision of her as a crowned queen. Elsewhere, she is often the star, especially the star of the sea (cf. the hymn *Ave Maris Stella*), or the star which 'brought forth the sun', or, more generally, the dawn or the daybreak. 'Through Eve,' says the *De Laudibus BMV*, 'night came, for by woman was made the beginning of sin; through Mary the day drew near', an idea which is nicely expressed in an English lyric:

> Al this world was forlore
>   *Eva peccatrice*
> Tyl our lord was ybore
>   *De te genitrice*;
> With *Ave* it went away,
> Thuster nyth, and com the day
>   *Salutis*.[49]

Of the figures of the Virgin which could be found in the natural world, our poet chooses one of the most delightful:

> Ine the ys God bycome a chyld,
> Ine the ys wreche bycome myld;
> That unicorn that was so wyld
>   Aleyd ys of a cheaste:
> Thou hast ytamed and istyld
> Wyth melke of thy breste.[50]

The unicorn, naturally enough a favourite with the artists, will be familiar to many readers from the splendid tapestries of the early sixteenth century in the Musée de Cluny, Paris, and the Cloisters,

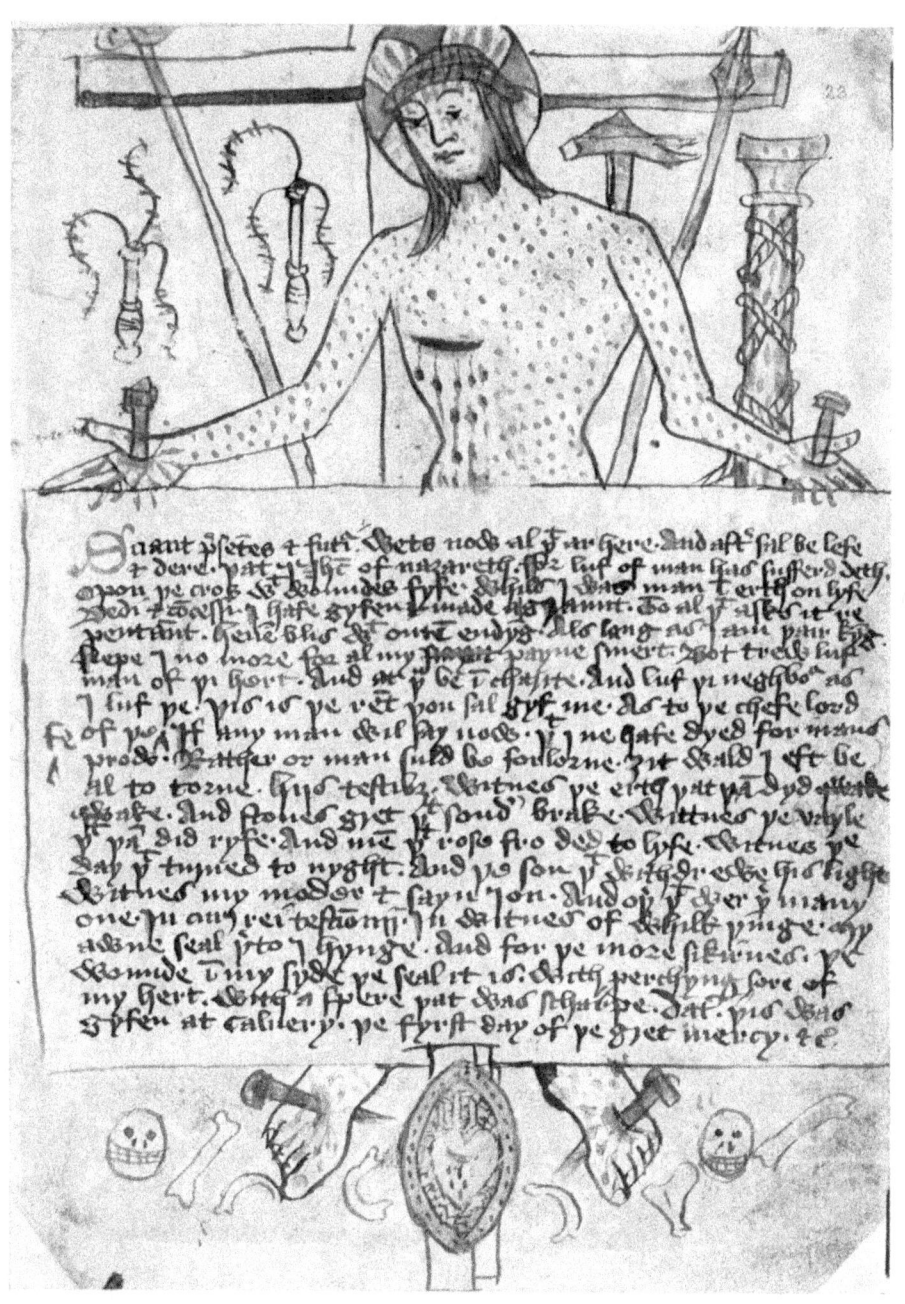

5 The Charter of Christ (cf. p. 130). A crude fifteenth-century illustration shows the wounded Christ, with the cross and the instruments of the Passion behind him, presenting the charter of the grant of Heaven's bliss. The seal at the bottom is Christ's wounded heart.

6 Pietà. A popular devotional image showing Mary holding the dead Christ on her knees (cf. pp. 137–9). In this woodcut it is surrounded by the instruments of the Passion and accompanied by an indulgence which has been partly erased.

Christ and the Virgin Mary

New York. According to the bestiaries he is a small animal, and extremely swift. He is also extremely savage (the *Ancrene Wisse* says that a 'wroth' man is like a wolf, a lion, or a unicorn: the adjective *wyld* in this lyric therefore has strong overtones.[51] But he can be caught by a virgin. As soon as he sees her he comes to her, rests his head in her bosom and lets himself be taken. Honorius 'of Autun' explains the allegorical sense: the unicorn is Christ, the horn is the invincible strength of the Son of God; that he rested on the bosom of a virgin and was taken by the hunters signifies that he took human form in Mary's bosom and consented to give himself to those who look for him. Sometimes in the visual arts the Annunciation is represented in the form of a mystic hunt,[52] with Gabriel, accompanied by three hounds, blowing his *Ave* with his hunting horn to the Virgin, in whose lap the unicorn is resting. Another Middle English poem presents the unicorn-image with some eloquence:

> We blesse the tyme that thou were born,
> For thou hast cauth the unicorn
> That was so fers in the olde lawe;
> Thorw love he is fro heven drawe.
> Thou hast set him upon thy barm
> And homly halsed hym in thin arm. . . .[53]

In medieval devotional literature the images and symbols of the Virgin are innumerable. Mary is compared to a box of perfume, an apothecary's shop, a candelabrum, a censer, various gems (especially the pearl), a library (containing the books of the Old and New Testaments), manna, a rainbow, Jacob's ladder, a ship, snow, the table of shewbread, a wine-cellar, and so on.[54] The reader of a work like the *De Laudibus BMV* may be pardoned for wondering if there is anything in the universe which is not, or cannot be made into an image of the Virgin. Too often these images are simply the product of pious ingenuity, yet in the hands of a great poet they can be startlingly successful – as, when in *Paradiso*, xxxiii (101–2), Mary is called the 'fair sapphire by which the sky is more brightly ensapphired':

> il bel zaffiro
> del quale il ciel più chiaro s'inzaffira.

The English devotional lyrics are in general content with less recondite images. One fifteenth-century carol is built with simplicity and dignity on the traditional image of Mary as the rose:

> Ther is no rose of swych vertu
> As is the rose that bare Jesu.

There is no rose of swych vertu
As is the rose that bar Jesu.
Alleluya.

For in this rose conteynyd was
Heven and erthe in lytyl space,
Res miranda.

Be that rose we may weel see
That he is God in personys thre
Pari forma.

The aungelys sungyn the sheperdes to:
Gloria in excelcis Deo!
Gaudeamus.

Leve we al this wordly merthe,
And folwe we this joyful berthe;
Transeamus.[55]

The style of this little poem is notable for its economy and clarity. Its lines are not crammed with tags or fillers – here a phrase like *gloria in excelcis Deo* is meaningful in its context. The macaronic form is handled in an interesting and skilful way; the rhythmic and semantic patterns of the two languages are varied and related. Very abstract theological concepts are expressed without strain in a simple lyrical form. The great paradox 'heven and erthe in lytyl space' is stated plainly and succinctly, with the precise word *conteynyd* giving an exact emphasis. The structure of the poem seems at first strangely abrupt. The first three stanzas seem evidently a self-contained whole – a simple assertion, 'there is no rose of swich vertu' (*vertu* = inherent power, strength), then a reason for the uniqueness of this rose, then a consequent 'argument' (of an emotional and allusive rather than logical sort), 'Be that rose we may weel see. . . '. The introduction of the angels and the shepherds in the next stanza is sudden, but dramatic. We are brought back to the historical scene of the Incarnation, to the events which happened among men. The nature of the mystery is imparted to the mortal shepherds by the angels' song of praise. We, the audience, then are involved in the scene; the *memoria* of the sacred event comes to be expressed in the 'omnitemporal present' – so that the poem appropriately does not come to a formal conclusion, but leaves us joining the shepherds in adoration and 'following this joyful berthe'. The image of Mary as the rose is full of traditional suggestions.[56] She is the biblical

> purpyl rose
> That whylom grewe in Jericho,
> The Fadres wysdom to enclose.[57]

She is the *rosa inter spinas* or the *rosa sine spina*, pure and sinless in the midst of sin. She is sometimes the wild rose with five petals, which signify the five letters of her name or her five Joys – the Annunciation, the Nativity (sometimes the Epiphany instead of the Ascension), the Resurrection, the Ascension, the Assumption.[58] In one Latin poem the lines

> Virginitatis lilium
> Et rosa per martyrium[59]

oppose the lily of virginity to the red rose of the *martyrium*, the passion she shared with her son at the crucifixion. The image has wider relationships, to a set of Marian images associated with gardens, flowers (especially the lily), spring with its fertility and its promise of renewal of life and beauty. The Virgin is a closed garden, *hortus conclusus* (an image which suggests both the fecundity of nature and the purity and separation of the Virgin from the sinful world), or a fountain – she is often called 'well of grace'. (The artists of the late Middle Ages show her in an idyllic setting, seated in the midst of a walled Paradise Garden, or a garden of roses.)[60] 'The Virgin', says a seventeenth-century poet,

> was a Garden round beset
> With Rose and Lillie, and sweet Violet.
> Where fragrant Sents without distast of Sinne,
> Invited God the Sonne to enter in.[61]

The rose, 'the queen of flowers', was from antiquity an image of love: it gives its name to the great love-vision of the thirteenth-century, *Le Roman de la Rose*. Mary, *umile e alta*, is the mystic rose. In the great north rose-window[62] at Chartres she sits in the centre holding her child, while around her in circles, are four doves, four thrones, the twelve kings of Judah, her ancestors, and twelve prophets. Here she is indeed the 'rose of the world':

The Scheme of Redemption

> Ave virgo gloriosa,
> Caeli jubar, mundi rosa. . . .⁶³

She is the rose in which the Word divine was made flesh: 'Quivi è la rosa in che il verbo divino/Carne si fece . . .' which is exactly the idea behind the unaffected words of our English carol, though with a slight shift of emphasis, for the simple verb *bar* points to Mary rather than her son as the actor – she is, in the words of the Pearl-maiden, 'blessed bygynner of uch a grace'.

The bold image of 'heaven and earth' contained in the 'little space' of the rose is related to other images used of the Virgin's part in the Incarnation. Sometimes it is stated explicitly, less imaginatively, that in her womb she bore the creator of all things:

> Continet hunc genitrix in gremio
> Omnia qui condidit ex nihilo
> Terram, mare, sidera cum infero....*⁶⁴

It is this idea that *tota deitas*, the whole of the Godhead, was enclosed in Mary's womb which leads to the image of her as 'chamber of the Trinity'. The paradox that the creature bore the creator may be elaborated: Mary the Virgin mother is in Dante's phrase 'figlia del tuo figlio', the daughter of God becomes the mother of her Father, and the Father becomes man's brother. So one fourteenth-century English lyric:

> Thou wommon boute vere
> Thyn oun vader bere.
>   Gret wonder thys was
> That on wommon was moder
> To vader and hyre brother –
>   So never nas.
>
> Thou my suster and moder
> And thy sone my brother –
>   Who shulde thoenne drede....
>
> Dame, suster and moder,
> Say thy sone my brother,
>   That ys domesmon,
> That vor the that hym bere
> To me boe debonere –
>   My robe he haveth opon.⁶⁵

---

* The mother holds in her bosom him who created everything from nothing, the land, the sea, the stars, and the infernal regions.

Christ and the Virgin Mary

It is this whole complex of medieval devotional thought that lies behind Donne's fine lines on the Annunciation:

> Yea, thou art now
> Thy Makers maker, and thy Fathers mother,
> Thou hast light in darke, and shuts in little roome,
> Immensity cloisterd in thy deare wombe.

Not surprisingly, Marian devotion found a subject in the Virgin's sacred name. One carol uses it in both its burden:

> Of M.A.R.I.
> Syng I wyll a new song[66]

and its refrain: 'M. and A. R. and I.', and there are more elaborate learned examples.[67] These are the attitudes which in a later age produce a poem like Herbert's *Anagram*:

> How well her name an Army doth present,
> In whom the Lord of Hosts did pitch his tent.

Yet the strongest impulse in affective Marian piety is to infuse into the figure of the Virgin the deepest human emotions and instincts. Both aspects of her character, as mother and as maiden, are expressed in intimate human terms. Not only is she presented as the exemplar of motherhood, but devotion can draw on the emotional power which is made available by the assimilation of the human mother image. Mary is presented as a truly maternal figure – gentle, protective, sheltering, providing food. Poems are written in honour of her breasts, and a number of stories of the miraculous power of her milk are recorded.[68] The figure of Mary the maiden is treated with equal intensity and devotion. There is constant stress on her supreme beauty, both spiritual and physical. Encomia of her beauty nearly always use echoes of the imagery of the Song of Songs, but the poets cannot match the achievements of the artists in the expression of Mary's ideal beauty.[69] Love is a characteristic of the Virgin, as it is of her son. Mary is often seen as a courtly lady, and the poets may express their petitions to her in the erotic language of courtly literature. Most of the English lyrics of this type are not very exciting; more successful are those which use erotic imagery or language allusively or obliquely, as in the final stanzas of the thirteenth-century poem which Carleton Brown calls 'Look on me with thy Sweet Eyes':

> Levedie, ic thonke the
>   Wid herte suithe milde
> That gohid that thu havest idon me
>   Wid thine suete childe. . . .
>
> Maide milde, biddi the
>   Wid thine suete childe,
> That thu erndie me
>   To habbe Godis milce.
>
> Moder, loke on me
>   Wid thine suete eyen:
> Reste and blisse gef thu me
>   Mi levedi then ic deye[70]

where the image of the loving glance, which is found elsewhere in Marian poetry, comes not only from a Biblical tradition (turning the eyes or face towards a person is a sign of favour),[71] but seems also to be echoing the courtly theme of the eyes of the beloved, and of the joy which a loving glance from them can carry.

Another little Marian poem very successfully uses connotations of romance and fairyland. It occurs in an exemplum on confession, which tells how a noble who has fallen into poverty is hindered by shame and by his enemies from coming to court to receive grace:

> At a sprynge-wel under a thorn,
> Ther was bote of bale
> A lytel here aforn.
> Ther bysyde stant a mayde
> Fulle of love ybounde.
> Hoso wol seche trwe love
> Yn hyr hyt schal be founde.[72]

The exemplum explains that the spring under the thorn is the open side of Christ from which flowed blood and water, and that the maiden standing beside it is the blessed Virgin Mary who is always ready to help sinners. The lyric itself however seems much richer in suggestion than this. The great wound in Christ's side is often compared to a fountain or a well (and his other wounds to the four rivers of Paradise) which heals and cleanses those who come to it,[73] and the figure of the maiden who stands sorrowing and compassionate beside the cross (the tree of life, as against Eve's tree of death) is even more deeply charged with traditional

Christ and the Virgin Mary

connotation. But in this lyric these ideas, though present, are surely suggestions, undertones, and not the clearly defined 'meaning' attributed to it by the exegete. In fact the little scene is very reminiscent of medieval romance. There magical and mysterious springs are common (Yvain comes upon a swirling spring shadowed by a fair tree, which is the gateway to the Other World) and the thorn-tree is a thing of magic – it was under a flowering thorn that Viviane enchanted Merlin in the forest of Broceliande, and it is at the thorn of Eldridge Hill that Sir Cawline meets the fairy king.[74] Characteristically, fairy ladies wait for their human lovers at springs[75] – Graelent, following a hart comes upon his lady in a spring of clear, sweet water – and this scene so common in legend and romance is surely suggested in our lyric. And if we think first of a *fée* when we read of this mysterious spring under a thorn, we perhaps share in the confusion of some heroes of ballad and romance, who when they come upon their fairy lady mistake her for the Virgin Mary.[76] Much of the old folk-belief connected with springs and fountains survived in a Christianized or simply superstitious form in the veneration of holy wells.[77] It is not surprising to find thorn-bushes sometimes still regarded as the particular haunt of fairies.[78] And moreover many were especially associated with the Virgin Mary who, in more learned tradition, is regularly called the 'well of grace' the 'fons hortorum', etc.[79]

Our lyric deliberately uses words and phrases which have associations in erotic love poetry. 'Bote of bale' is a phrase which might appear in a lover's complaint.[80] 'Full of love ybounde' is distinctly reminiscent of the many images of the binding power of human love. Achilles, in the *Geste Historiale of the Destruction of Troy*, 'lay in his loge all with love boundon'; some verses in Grimestone's preaching book make a similar devotional adaptation of the image:

> I ne wat quat is love,
> Ne love me never bond;
> But wel I wot wo so lovet
> Reste havet he non.[81]

Sometimes the lover is chained with the chain or yoke of love:

> Forma tua fulgida
> Tunc me catinavit,[82]

The Scheme of Redemption

and the literary image of the *vinculum amoris* has a counterpart in the visual arts, in the chain round the neck of a lover held by a girl on a Limoges casket, or the chain held by Luxuria in illustrations, or those which later in the hands of ladies bind wild men and monsters, *capti cupidinis vinculis*.[83] But the love which this maiden offers is true love; she is not the queen of Elfland but the *virgo fidelis*:

> In all this worlde ye none so tru
> As she that bare our Lorde Jhesu.[84]

Our lyric is taking a traditional phrase from the literature of love, and suggesting, allusively and delicately, the pre-eminent 'trouthe' of Mary's love.

The total result is that in much devotional literature the Virgin appears as a most attractive person, a great lady, indeed the Queen of Heaven, but at the same time homely and simple, ready to help the humblest of her subjects, *umile e alta*. This can be seen nowhere more clearly than in the stories of her miracles (which, judging from their wide diffusion, seem to have appealed to the European imagination[85] – stories such as that of the Tumbler of our Lady who served her with his one talent, his skill in tumbling, of the knight whose place at the tournament was taken by his protectress the Virgin Mary, or the story of the monk Theophilus, the medieval antecedent of Dr Faustus, who made a pact with the devil but was saved by the Queen of Heaven (and Empress of Hell) – the dramatic potential of this story was already realized by some of the many artists who chose to treat it, such as the illuminator of the De Quincy Apocalypse, and by a number of playwrights).[86] It can be seen too in the simple devotion which is revealed in the stories told by some of the visionaries. Christina of Markyate, in the midst of her tribulations, dreams that in a church she meets a lady like an empress, sitting on a dais, who asks her how she is. Christina says that things go ill with her; everyone persecutes and ridicules her, and she cannot stop crying from morning to night. The lady tells her not to be afraid: 'Fear not,' she said. 'Go now, for I will deliver you from their hands and bring you to the brightness of day.'[87]

Annunciation and Nativity

A sense of joy and the imagery of light are characteristic of the poems which celebrate the Incarnation. Light triumphs over darkness; the world is renewed. St Augustine says that Christ chose Christmas Day, the day on which the light begins to increase . . . for the Creator having willed to be born in time, his birthday would necessarily be in harmony with the rest of his creation.[1] Appropriately, the Christian festival of the Sun of Righteousness took over the date of the earlier festival of Sol Invictus. St Bernard says that

> the Sun of Justice had almost set, so that his light or warmth on the earth was scanty; for the light of divine knowledge was very faint, and sin abounding, the heat of charity had grown cold. There was neither angel to visit men, nor prophet to speak to them; both seemed in despair, for the hardness and obstinacy of man had made every effort useless: *then I said* they are the words of our redeemer – then I said, 'Lo! I come'.[2]

Images of light (often verses from the Old Testament) occur frequently in the Advent and Christmas liturgy – we have already met the antiphon *O Oriens splendor* – and are found in profusion in poetry and legend. In one of the Apocryphal gospels, the *Protevangelium*, there is a striking description of the Nativity. It takes place in a cave (which in the East would serve as a stable and a dwelling) overshadowed by a bright cloud. When the cloud goes, a great light appears in the cave. When this goes, a young child appears, and goes to take Mary's breast. In a later vision, of St Bridget of Sweden, the splendour of divine radiance which comes from the body of the child quite outshines the poor light of

The Scheme of Redemption

Joseph's candle. Possibly as a result of this vision, the artists of the later Middle Ages often depict the Christ child surrounded by golden rays while his mother kneels in adoration before him.[3]

The joy of the Incarnation is expressed in the liturgy (notably in the *Laetabundus* sequence)[4] and in many poems. One poet 'parodies' the mournful strains of the *Stabat Mater Dolorosa:*

> Stabat mater speciosa
> Juxta foenum gaudiosa,
>   Dum jacebat parvulus.
> Cujus animam gaudentem
> Laetabundam ac ferventem
>   Pertransivit jubilus.*[5]

This spirit of joy, intensified by Franciscan devotion, is found in many of the English carols. One of the earliest recorded has

> Honnd by honnd we schulle ous take,
> And joye and blisse schulle we make,
> For the devel of helle man hath forsake,
> And Godes sone ys maked oure make;[6]

another has for its burden the lines

> O O O O !
> Exultet mundus gaudio;[7]

another has the stars shining and the angels singing with gay abandon:

> Hit fell upon high mydnyght:
> The sterres shon both fayre and bright;
> The angelles song with all ther myght,
>   '*Verbum caro factum est!*'[8]

One of the best is inspired by an Advent epistle (Rom. 13), 'Brethren, it is time to awake out of sleep; for now is our salvation nearer than we believed. The night is gone, and the day draws near':[9]

> Nowel, nowel, nowel,
> Nowel, nowel, nowel!

---

* The lovely mother stood rejoicing by the hay, while the little child lay there. Her heart, rejoicing and glowing with happiness, was transfixed by joy.

Annunciation and Nativity

Owt of your slepe aryse and wake
For God mankynd nowe hath ytake
Al of a maide without eny make;
   Of al women she bereth the belle.
     Nowel!

And thorwe a maide faire and wys
Now man is made of ful grete pris;
Now angelys knelen to mannys servys,
   And at this tyme al this byfel.
     Nowel!

Now man is brighter than the sonne;
Now man in heven an hye shal wone;
Blessyd be God this game is begonne,
   And his moder emperesse of helle.
     Nowel!

That ever was thralle, now ys he fre;
That ever was smalle, now grete is she;
Now shal God deme both the and me
   Unto hys blysse yf we do wel.
     Nowel!

Now man may to heven wende;
Now heven and erthe to hym they bende;
He that was foo now is oure frende;
   This is no nay that y yowe telle.
     Nowel!

Nowe, blessyd brother, graunte us grace
A domesday to se thy face
And in thy courte to have a place,
   That we mow there synge nowel.
     Nowel!

This is a remarkable poem. From its vivid opening it sustains an extraordinary sense of exaltation. This poet sees the Incarnation almost as much the triumph of man as the triumph of Christ, for it opens up to him infinite possibilities. There is nothing here of that denigration of man which is sometimes supposed to be characteristic of medieval religious poetry: man is here indeed of 'ful grete pris'. The poet's confident optimism is reflected in his tone – the assurance of his address to Christ as 'blessyd brother', and his easy use of a colloquial phrase to express the uniqueness of Mary, 'of al women she bereth the belle'. The *gaudium* of the Incarnation has here become a joy which is momentous but homely, a 'game'.

The 'game' of the season of the Incarnation is reflected in the many stories in pious legend of the miraculous renewal or reversal of nature at that time – the springing of wells, the appearance of a star to the Sybil.[10] That popular tradition did not easily forget this is shown by Marcellus's words at the beginning of *Hamlet*:

> It faded on the crowing of the cock.
> Some say that ever 'gainst that season comes
> Wherein our Saviour's birth is celebrated,
> This bird of dawning singeth all night long;
> And then, they say, no spirit dare stir abroad,
> The nights are wholesome, then no planets strike,
> No fairy takes, nor witch hath power to charm,
> So hallowed and so gracious is that time.[11]

It is reflected too in the jovial late medieval carols in praise of Christmas – 'Wolcum, Yol, thou mery man,/In worchepe of this holy day' – where it is impossible to distinguish between 'religious' and 'secular' joy.[12] Some stanzas from a carol bidding farewell to the bleak season of Advent must suffice to illustrate these:

> Farewele, Advent; Cristemas is cum;
> Farewele fro us both alle and sume. . . .

> While thou haste be within oure howse
> We ete no puddynges ne no sowce,
> But stynkyng fisshe not worthe a lowce;
>   Farewele fro us both alle and sume. . . .

> Thou hast us fedde with plaices thynne,
> Nothing on them but bone and skynne;
> Therefore oure love thou shalt not wynne;
>   Farewele fro us both alle and sume.

> With muskilles gaping afture the mone
> Thou hast us fedde at nyght and none,
> But ones a wyke, and that to sone;
>   Farewele fro us both alle and sume.

> Oure brede was browne, oure ale was thynne,
> Oure brede was musty in the bynne,
> Oure ale soure or we did begynne;
>   Farewele fro us both alle and sume.[13]

Annunciation and Nativity

More learned treatment of the joy of the Incarnation is to be found in the 'Te Deum' carols, and in Dunbar's fine poem on the Nativity, which in the manner of the *Jubilate Omnes*, calls on the created universe to join in the praise:

> Celestiall fowlis in the are
> Sing with your nottis upoun hicht;
> In firthis and in forrestis fair
> Be myrthfull now, at all your mycht,
> For passit is your dully nycht,
> Aurora hes the cluddis perst,
> The son is rissin with glaidsum lycht,
> *Et nobis puer natus est!* . . .
>
> Syng hevin imperiall, most of hicht,
> Regions of air make armony;
> All fishe in flud and foull of flicht
> Be myrthfull and mak melody:
> All *Gloria in Excelsis* cry,
> Hevin, erd, se, man, bird and best,
> He that is crownit abone the sky
> *Pro nobis puer natus est!*[14]

The artists of the Middle Ages in their paintings of the Annunciation not only convey the quiet beauty of the scene but like to exploit the dramatic possibilities of the meeting of two beings from different worlds, of the momentous irruption of the supernatural into the affairs of men. Sometimes they will emphasize the humble purity and timidity of the Virgin in the presence of the awe-inspiring divine messenger; sometimes the angel, a handsome young figure himself, kneels humbly as a courtly suppliant before the handmaid of the Lord for whom so great a destiny is marked out.[15] In the famous painting by Simone Martini in the Uffizi, the Virgin seated with her book in her hand, and the vase of lilies, the traditional symbol of her purity nearby, recoils almost fearfully from the angel who kneels before her with his branch.[16] The drama of the confrontation is expressed through the lines and curves of the figures. The English lyric poets treat the meeting in a more abstract and less dramatic way. They do not encourage us to visualize the scene; they stress Mary's part in it, her humble co-operation and the great effects which her reply has for mankind. A fifteenth-century poem, 'Ecce, ancilla Domini', has an

The Scheme of Redemption

exchange between the two persons; Gabriel 'grett hure graciously', and she replies 'myldely', with the phrase *ecce, ancilla Domini* serving as a refrain, but it is all a little abstract and stiff.[17] Most often the Annunciation is treated as the first of Mary's 'Joys', or the words of the Angelic Salutation are made the basis of prayers to or praises of the Virgin. Thus an incomplete poem in Grimestone's preaching book:

> Heil, Marie and wel thu be
> Of love gunne thu lere
> Wan Gabriel so grette the
> An rounnede in thin eere.
> In blisful time were thu born,
> Oure saveour thu bere;
> Al this werd it were forlorn
> Ne were that thu ne were.
>
> Suete maiden Marie
> Thu rewe nou on me . . .[18]

which is made more interesting than most by the simple dramatic detail that Gabriel 'whispered' in her ear.

At this moment Christ 'takes his abode' in Mary, or is 'biloken' in her. Attempts to find a visual or a literal image for this are sometimes both curious and interesting. Sometimes in pictures of the scene a ray of light (or a chain or a string) stretches from God to Mary down which Christ comes as a small child. Sometimes the idea that the Logos, the Verbum, entered Mary is given a strangely literal expression:

> Glade us maiden, moder milde,
> Thurru thin erre thu were wid childe –
> Gabriel he seide it the.

These lines are in fact a translation of a Latin hymn

> Gaude Virgo, mater Christi
> Que per aurem concepisti
> Gabriele nuntio,[19]

and the idea of conception through the ear is a quite ancient one which occurs in theological as well as devotional works.[20] It has its equivalent in late medieval art, though it is not quite so startlingly literal. In some paintings, as for instance in Simone Martini's

Annunciation and Nativity

Annunciation, Gabriel's greeting extends from his mouth to the Virgin's right ear (a stanza in another English poem specifies the right ear:

> Blessed be, Lady, thy richt ere:
> The Holygost, he liht in there
> Flesch and blod to take).

It has been suggested that the image came into Western art from Byzantium (it is from Byzantine mosaics that Yeats remembers it).[21] Like the related images of conception through wind or breath, it is no doubt an attempt to express a sophisticated doctrine in visual form, but it is hard to think that it has not come from or been contaminated by mythical, legendary and popular patterns of thought.[22]

An image which is poetically rather more successful is found in many poems, both in Latin and the vernacular:

> For so gleam glidis thurt the glas,
> Of thi bodi born he was,
> And thurt the hoale thurch he gload[23]

or, in the poem 'Marye, mayde fre' discussed above:

> Ase the sonne taketh hyre pas
> Wythoute breche thorghout that glas,
> Thy maydenhod onwemmed hyt was
>   For bere of thyne chylde. . . .

Again we find equivalents in the visual arts, in depictions of the Annunciation in which rays of light come in through a window on Mary.[24] Although it is found in the most respectable theologians,[25] it is primarily a poetic rather than a theological image, which is intended only to express the unsullied virginity of the mother of Christ. Its further implications might well suggest that Christ did not take flesh of his mother but simply 'passed through' her (an ancient idea which is not likely in the orthodox contexts in the many poems in which it occurs). Melchior Hofmann, the later Anabaptist, is said by Ronald Knox in his study of seventeenth-century 'enthusiasm' (which does not mention the widespread occurrence of this image in orthodox contexts) to have held that 'the Saviour passed through the virgin as sunshine through a pane of glass'.[26]

We turn from these curious images to what is possibly the finest

The Scheme of Redemption

of all the English religious lyrics, a song in praise of the Virgin Mary in the fifteenth-century MS. Sloane 2593 (plate 4):

> I syng of a m(a)yden that is makeles,
> Kyng of alle kynges to here sone che ches.
>
> He cam also stylle ther his moder was
> As dew in Aprylle, that fallyt on the gras.
>
> He cam also stylle to his moderes bowr
> As dew in Aprille that fallyt on the flour.
>
> He cam also stylle ther his moder lay
> As dew in Aprille, that fallyt on the spray.
>
> Moder and mayden was never non but che –
> Wel may swych a lady Godes moder be.[27]

The excellence of this lyric is due in part to its perfect proportion and balance, but primarily to the skilful way in which it unites a precision of word and meaning with a fullness of suggestion and connotation. It is extremely simple, but far from naïve; its simplicity is the simplicity of art.

The language is remarkable for its precision. Mary (line 2) 'chose' the king of all kings for her son. Doctrinally, what lies behind this is the idea of her active co-operation in the Incarnation; the word *ches* aptly describes her voluntary decision at the Annunciation.[28] As Émile Mâle puts it, 'The angels and God himself waited upon a maiden's answer.' Chaucer's Prioress in her prayer to the Virgin Mary expresses the same dramatic idea in a slightly different way:

> O bussh unbrent, brennynge in Moyses sighte,
> That ravyshedst doun fro the Deitee,
> Thurgh thyn humblesse, the Goost that in th'alighte. . . .

In this lyrical treatment of the Incarnation, Christ the Virgin's son is seen primarily in terms of action: 'he cam . . . ther his moder was'.[29] It is a very Christocentric view of the Incarnation. There is no mention, for instance, of the part played by the Holy Spirit. Here it is the Logos who is 'chosen' and who comes, and our poet concentrates on two persons, the mother and the Son (the event of the Incarnation is presented in isolation,[30] with none of the legendary details of the scene of the Annunciation); after the initial 'I' of the poet, the only pronouns used are 'he' and 'she',

Annunciation and Nativity

referring to the two actors in the event. This is underlined by the precision of the syntax – after the poet's introductory 'I syng', we have the present tenses 'is makeles' (the Virgin is, and remains, 'makeles' *per aeternitatem*) and 'fallyth' (which perhaps suggests both the continuous action of the dew and its brief duration), set against the preterites which indicate historical events in time, 'ches', 'cam' (the fulfilment of the expectation of 'coming' which runs through the Advent liturgy), or historical statements – 'was never non but che'. The final *exclamatio* – 'wel may . . .' – triumphantly concludes the lyrical strain of the first line, and like the culmination of a devotional 'argument' takes up the 'is' of that line and gives an emphatic and confident ending on the verb 'be'. The Incarnation is presented as pure act – it is 'he cam', not 'he came down to earth from heaven'. Further, if we compare it with lines from other poems like 'Hwenne that child bith iboren and on eorthe ifalle',[31] it emphasizes the deliberate voluntary act of the Logos: 'he cam... ther his moder was', *electus ad electam* (similarly in the Coventry plays Christ is eager to become incarnate: 'I have grett hast to be man there').

Simplicity does not forbid paradox and word-play. The traditional contrast of sublimity and humility which is implicit in the Incarnation – a humble maiden becomes the bearer of the Word incarnate (immensity cloister'd in her dear womb) – is here pointed by the contrast between the simplicity of the diction and of the imagery – dew, grass, etc. – and the profundity of the 'doctrine' – king of all kings, Godes moder. The opening phrase 'I syng of' is a most unusual if not unique opening for a religious lyric. Can it be that it is deliberately used to suggest the grandeur, the almost epical grandeur of the subject – almost as if the poet were to say, I sing, but not of arms and the hero who came from Troy, rather of a maiden whose humility raised her to sublimity? Mary is called 'makeles', and the adjective is precisely used. The Virgin is 'matchless', that is, without peer, unequalled; she is also unique (*sola in sexu femina*) – the *Pearl*-poet compares her to the unique and peerless 'Fenyx of Arraby'. There is also probably a further play on the word in that she is 'without a mate' (she conceived *sine virili semine*), and, possibly, like the *Pearl*-poet, the author is thinking of the word *maskeles*, 'without stain'. This verbal play is both artful and exact, but it is worth pointing out that it is not quite 'wit' in the manner of the metaphysical poets – the elements of the paradox are not violently and startlingly yoked together; there is less of harsh surprise than of gentle wonder.³²

There is the same precise control of the suggestions and connotations of the simple words. In the last line the word 'lady' is carefully and suggestively used. It makes a climax, and is appropriate to Mary in one of her most glorious aspects, as bearer of the Incarnate Word (in her passion, as she stands sorrowing by the cross, the embodiment of maternal suffering, she is sometimes called 'woman'). It suggests that Mary is, as she is for the *Pearl*-poet, the 'quene of cortaysye' – there is in fact a nice legend that 'courtesy' came to earth from heaven when Gabriel greeted Mary. Her resting-place is a 'bowr', a word which has submerged and delicate courtly and erotic undertones. We might perhaps compare the famous Latin hymn

>   Angelus ad virginem
>   Subintrans in conclave
>   Virginis formidinem
>   Demulcens inquit 'Ave',*

or a Middle English poem on the Five Joys, which links the 'boure' with a well-known romance simile:

>   Thar thu lay in thi bright boure,
>   Levedi, quite als leli floure,
>   An angel com fra hevene toure,
>   Sant Gabriel,
>   And said, 'Levedi, ful of blis, ai worth the wel'.³³

The figure of Christ as the knight, the lover of man is well-known in medieval literature,³⁴ but it is worth remembering that Mary is also seen as his beloved. 'Thu art Crystes oghene drury' says one poet of her.³⁵ The *De Laudibus BMV* calls her *Dei filio desiderata*; De Guilleville describes how the Son of God sees the young Mary from heaven and how he is charmed by her beauty.³⁶ Possibly here the word *stylle* 'silently' (though it has other and more important associations) may be related to the tradition of 'derne love' and the secret coming of the lover – it would then be closely parallel to *subintrans in conclave* 'creeping silently into the chamber'.

This lyric fully realizes the semantic possibilities of traditional diction.³⁷ The central simile used to describe the coming of Christ (and it is typical of our poet that there is only one) – 'also stylle . . .

* The angel, secretly entering her chamber, softly overcoming the virgin's fear, says to her 'Hail!'

Annunciation and Nativity

as dew in Aprylle' – is at once exquisite, appropriate in its suggestion (the clarity, brightness and purity of dew-drops, the moistening, refreshing, fertilizing power of dew, the gentleness, softness and secrecy of its falling) and rich in traditional associations. The falling of dew is a traditional image of the Incarnation (which we have met in one of its manifestations in the figure of Gideon's fleece), found in many hymns and commentaries,[38] and in a famous liturgical introit which must have been universally familiar, since it was repeated throughout the season of Advent:

> Rorate, caeli, desuper, et nubes pluant justum.
> Aperiatur terra et germinat Salvatorem.[39]

It is part of a wider conception in which the Incarnation is linked with the renewal of nature and the rebirth of fertility in the earth – St Bernard says that 'Christ is . . . a flower of the field, not of a garden; for the flowers of the field bloom without man's care. . . . just so the Virgin's womb, a meadow verdant in an endless spring, has brought forth a flower, whose beauty will never droop.'[40] And it is reflected in popular beliefs in the fructifying power of dew.[41] Probably we have here another subdued erotic undertone, but it is restrained and submerged;[42] there is nothing here of the bold fertility-imagery of some commentators: 'He poured out his dew and his living rain over Mary, the thirsting earth. As the corn sinks into the ground so he descended under the ground. But he arose like the sheaf and its new crop.' (Ephraem Syrus.)[43] These suggestions are emphasized by the April setting (the traditional date of the Annunciation is 25 March), for April is a month which with its 'sweet showers'

> bathed every veyne in swich licour
> Of which vertu engendred is the flour;

it is as it were the 'opener', says one commentator,[44] since in its time the trees are opened to flower and the plants to grow.

The 'stillness' of Christ's coming is just as full of traditional associations. Primarily, of course, the adverb *stylle* refers to the soft and silent falling of the dew. It may also, as we mentioned earlier, suggest the hidden and stealthy coming of Christ the lover. A fine Anglo-Norman poem on the theme of Christ the Lover-knight says that a king who loved a lady who had been seduced by a traitor 'took the arms of one of his bachelors, called Adam, and caused himself to be armed with them by a maiden. He entered the

The Scheme of Redemption

chamber of this beautiful damsel so softly that no one knew it, save the maiden herself. She clad him in curious armour – for acketon she gave him white and pure flesh . . . ' etc.[45] The gentleness of Christ's coming is often remarked on: there is a tradition that the Virgin suffered no pain in her child-bearing, and that Christ was born at the silent hour of midnight[46] – indeed, it is one of the greatest achievements of the medieval artists that in their depictions of the Nativity they so often contrived to give the scene this sense of unearthly stillness. Just possibly there is the further suggestion that he who comes is the Verbum Infans, the paradox found in Augustine[47] and Lancelot Andrewes: 'What, *Verbum infans*, the word of an infant? The Word, and not able to speak a word' and taken over into 'Gerontion':

> The word within a word unable to speak a word
> Swaddled with darkness. . . .

Christ the Word, bringing with him some of the silence said to be at the heart of the Godhead.

These are some of the rich and varied associations with which the genius of this poet has invested forty-five simple words, and created a superb example of the 'humble' style.

Christ's Incarnation is a *mysterium*, a 'mystery': this is a central theme in some of the devotional literature which treats the Nativity, and is present in some way in the background of all of it. Christ the Word clothes himself in human flesh, so that by the flesh he may redeem flesh. One carol has for its burden this statement of the miraculous suspension of the laws of nature:

> Ecce quod natura
> Mutat sua iura;
> Virgo parit pura
> Dei Filium*[48]

and another begins:

> Mirabile misterium,
> The Son of God ys man becum
> Mirabile. . . .[49]

* Lo, Nature reverses her own laws: a pure virgin bears the Son of God.

Annunciation and Nativity

Devotional literature is very fond of using the ancient paradox of the fusion of sublimity and humility[50] in the Incarnation, which we have already encountered several times in poems concerned with the Virgin Mary; in writings on the Nativity it may be expressed in a variety of ways. St Bernard dwells eloquently on the paradox of the Lord Almighty clad in the swaddling clothes of a little child.[51] A writer may use the paradox to show his audience that by sharing in Christ's humility they may be elevated to share in his sublimity; so an English carol:

> He that was riche withowt any nede
> Appered in this world in right pore wede
> To make us that were pore indede
>   Riche withowt any nede trewly.
>
> A stabill was his chambre; a crach was his bed;
> He had not a pylow to lay under his hed;
> With maydyns mylk that babe was fedde;
>   In pore clothis was lappid the Lord Almighty.
>
> A noble lesson here is us tawght:
> To set all worldly riches at nawght,
> But pray that we may be theder browght
>   Wher riches ys everlastyngly[52]

He may express it through ironic understatement, as

> Ne werede he nouther fou ne grey
> The loverd that us alle havet iwroust.[53]

or when another poet addresses the Christ child as 'thu litel barun, thu litel king'. Or he may state the paradox, with a tinge of irony and wonder:

> Of one stable was his halle
> His kenestol on occe stalle
> Sente Marie his burnes alle[54]

or:

He that was al hevene with him that al hat wrouth
Als a wreche he hat him lowed and mad himself as nouth
A thrallis robe thei han him taken that lord of mith that hadde no nede
It semet he hadde himself forsake to ben clad in mannis wede.[55]

The Scheme of Redemption

In the visual arts it is often neatly illustrated by the way in which the onlookers kneel in adoration before the small child.

But, characteristically, it was the humanity of the Incarnate Christ, Francis's 'little brother of all mankind' that was emphasized in medieval devotion. The narratives of the Gospels were filled out with homely and vivid details in the apocryphal gospels, and it is upon these that the Franciscan *Meditations on the Life of Christ* dwell with devout intensity. The reader is emotionally involved in every stage of the story:

> Now take here good hede and have inwardly compassioun of that blessed lady and mayden Marye, how sche so yong and of so tendre age, (that is to saye of xv yere) and grete with childe as nyh the birthe, travailleth that longe way of sixty myle and ten or more in so grete poverte, and yit whan sche cam to the citee forseide there sche schulde reste, and with her spouse asked herborgh in dyvers places, schamefastly as amonge unkouthe folk, alle they werned hem and lete hem goo. . . .[56]

The writer's aim is to make his readers as if present at the scene – 'make the in thy soule present to tho thynges that ben here writen, seide, or done of our lord Jesu, and that besily, likyngly, and abidynge, as they thou herdest hem with thy bodily eeres, or seie hem with thyne eiyen done'. He recreates each scene with striking visual details – that Joseph made a pillow for Mary from the saddle of an ass, that the ox and the ass warmed the child with their breath, and so on. An earlier English work, St Ailred's *De Institutione Inclusarum* (1160), uses the same technique of vivid meditation. The sister is told to go into the cell in which Mary awaits the angels' message, and to participate in the scene of the Nativity:

> With complete devotion follow the mother as she goes to Bethlehem. Go with her into the inn; stand by and assist her when she bears the child. And when the baby is placed in the crib, burst out with a song of joy, crying with Isaiah, 'Unto us a child is born, unto us a son is given!' Embrace that sweet crib, and let your passionate love drive out timidity and fear, so that you place your lips on those holy feet and kiss them again and again.[57]

The 'humilitas' of the Nativity is presented in great detail, not only by the authors of extended prose meditations, but by the artists of the late Middle Ages. The poverty of the scene is insisted on – the *Meditations* say that Christ's simple clothing does not bring comfort to those who go in proud clothing, and his stable and crib do not bring comfort to those that love worldly 'worship'. The combination of an intense and sympathetic portrayal of poverty with a bitter social criticism of the rich and the powerful is characteristic of the shepherds' plays in the Towneley cycle. The nakedness of the Christ child in late medieval painting is, as Mâle says, 'the mark of his humanity'. The coldness of the weather adds to the misery: 'The tyme was mydwynter, when it was maste calde; the houre was at mydnyghte the hardeste houre that es.' In the York play of the Journey to Bethlehem, Joseph says.

> A, lorde, what the wedir is colde!
> The fellest freese that evere I felyd.
> I pray God helpe tham that is alde,
> And namely tham that is unwelde. . . .

and in an Adoration of the Shepherds in St Peter Mancroft Church, Norwich,[58] Joseph is crouching over a brazier trying to keep himself warm (the Western artists and writers are undoubtedly thinking of their own winter conditions, although apparently it *is* cold in Bethlehem at Christmas). It is above all the Flemish painters of the late Middle Ages who convey most realistically the misery and bleakness of the setting of the *mysterium*. In the famous centre panel of the Portinari altar-piece (*c.* 1473–5), now in the Uffizi, by Hugo van der Goes, the naked child lies in lonely isolation surrounded by his parents, the angels and the shepherds, kneeling (except for Joseph who stands a little apart) in grave adoration. The scene is illuminated by the radiance of the child, but it is a bleak world. The faces of the shepherds are full of care and uncertainty and the scene is set in a ruined house.[59]

The English lyrics concerned with the Nativity (which come mostly from the later fourteenth and fifteenth centuries)[60] do not attempt anything as elaborate or as complete as this. The 'humility' of the setting is sometimes suggested by a detail – in one lyric the Christ child says

> Fore he that mad both nyght and day, colde and also hette,
> Now layde I ame in a wispe of hay I cane noder go nore crepe.[61]

It is given restrained yet moving expression obliquely, in dramatic form, in a little poem in which the Virgin addresses her child:

> Jesu, swete sone dere!
>   On porful bed list thou here,
> And that me greveth sore;
> For thi cradel is ase a bere,
> Oxe and asses beth thi fere:
>   Weepe ich mai tharfore.
>
> Jesu, swete, beo noth wroth,
> Thou ich nabbe clout ne cloth
>   The on for to folde,
>   The on for to folde ne to wrappe.
> For ich nabbe clout ne lappe;
> Bote ley thou thi fet to my pappe,
> And wite the from the colde.[62]

The best Nativity lyrics very often express dramatically the relation between the mother and her child; which as in the visual arts becomes a sort of devotional image separated from the setting in the stable, existing in a timeless present.[63] The artists present the relationship as an intensely human and intimate one; they exchange smiles (a well-known English example is the Virgin with the laughing child on the gateway of Winchester College). Mâle puts it very well: 'Il est impossible d'exprimer une communion plus intime entre deux êtres, il semble qu'ils ne fassent qu'un, qu'ils ne soient pas encore séparés. Si ce groupe est divin, ce n'est que par la profondeur de la tendresse.' Cf.

> On her lap she him layde,
> And with her pappe he playde,
> And ever sang the mayde,
>   'Come basse thy mother, dere.'
>
> With lyppes collyng.
> His mouth ofte she dyd kysse
> And sayd, 'Sweete hert myne,
>   I pray you make good chere.'[64]

Like an earthly mother, the Virgin gives suck to her child.[65] It was natural therefore that she should sing to it a lullaby:

> Whan it gan wepe, that child so swete,
> Sho stilled him with mylk of tete;
> Sho clipte hym oft and keste also
> Gret was the joye betwene hem to.
> The yonge child whan it gan wepe,

> With song she lulled him aslepe;
> That was so swete a melody
> Hyt passet alle mynstralcy;
> The nyghtyngale sang also,
> Hure wois is hors and noght therto. . . .[66]

A number of the most attractive English lyrics are lullabies[67] (possibly developed from secular lullabies, and certainly deriving great strength from their closeness to deep human emotions) sung by Mary to her child. Sometimes they are introduced by a vision opening sometimes in a *chanson d'aventure*:

> Alone, alone, alone, alone, alone;
> Here I sitt alone, alas! alone.
>
> As I walked me this endurs day
> To the grene wode for to play
> And all hevyness to put away
>   Myself alone.
>
> As I walkyd undir the grene wode bowe
> I sawe a maide fayre inow;
> A child she happid, she song, she lough –
>   That child wepid alone. . . .[68]

In some the Christ child is imagined to reply to his mother. These exchanges between mother and child can easily become too lengthy (sometimes the child gives a long series of prophecies concerning his life on earth), but even here there is some realism – in one Mary wants to see Christ as a king:

> Suete sone, than seyde sche,
> 'No sorwe sulde me dere,
> Miht I yet that day se
> A king that thu were.'[69]

The best have a fine simplicity, like the burden of the famous carol in MS. Sloane 2593:

> Lullay, myn lykyng, my dere sone, myn swetyng,
> Lullay, my dere herte, myn owyn dere derlyng.[70]

The scene is suggested by details –

> This endres nyght about mydnyght
> As I me lay for to sclepe,
> I hard a may syng lullay

The Scheme of Redemption

> For powaret sor sco wepe.
> He sayd Ba-Bay;
> Sco sayd lullay,
> The virgine fresch as ros in may. . . .[71]
>
> As sche hym held in hyr lape
> He toke hyr lovely by the pape
> And therof swetly he toke a nappe,
> And sok his fyll of the lycour. . . .[72]

which help to involve the devout reader in it, to make him feel as if present at the scene. In the 'cradle-rocking' ceremonies of late medieval Germany, this devotional involvement is given a physical and dramatic form. The crib becomes a cradle which can be rocked by the worshippers as they sing a 'rocking song'.[73] There is a meditative, if not a physical parallel to this in a passage in a Middle English book of spiritual instruction for a mother (c. 1400):

> Go to Marie and make covenaunt with hure to kepe hure
> childe, not for hure nede but for thin, and tak to the the
> swete childe and swetliche swath hit in his (c)radil with swete
> love-bondes. Put fro the the cradul of false love and drawe
> to the the cradul of trewe love, for that liketh this child
> to reste him inne, and so in thi soule singe loveliche and sei
>
> > Loveli litel child, feirest of hewe,
> > Have merci on me, swete Jesu
>
> and the while thou thus singest be sori and thenk hou ofte
> thou haste received thi God and leid him in a foul comyn
> stabele to alle the sevene dedli synnes . . . . therefore ofte sike
> and sorewe and schrif the to God as thou rockist the cradil, and
> sing and sei 'Loveli litel child'. . . .[74]

In two of the best lullabies (both from Grimestone's preaching-book) we find exactly this pattern, for the speaker is not the Virgin Mary, but the poet and his reader, the meditator himself. In one, a carol, with the burden 'Lullay, lullay, litel child, qui wepest the so sore?', there is a striking penitential tone – it is because of my sin, says the poet, that God's son suffers thus. The speaker imaginatively 'becomes' Eve, our parent, who fatally took the apple 'with a reuful res' (the phrase suggests a violent, precipitate action):

Ayenis my fadris wille I ches
An appel with a reuful res;
Werfore myn heritage I les,
    And nou thu wepist therfore.

An appel I tok of a tre,
God it hadde forboden me;
Werfore I sulde dampned be,
    Yef thi weping ne wore.

Lullay for wo, thu litel thing,
Thu litel barun, thu litel king;
Mankindde is cause of thi murning,
    That thu hast loved so yore. . . .[75]

The other has a remarkable expression of the bleakness and hostility of the world into which the child has come:

Child, it is a weping dale that thu art comen inne,
Thi pore clutes it proven wel, thi bed mad in the binne;
Cold and hunger thu must tholen as thu were geten in senne,
And after deyyen on the tre for love of al mankenne.

Lullay, lullay, litel child, no wonder thou thu care,
Thu art comen amonges hem that thi detth sulen yare.[76]

The devotion of the late Middle Ages invested with its characteristic tenderness and pathos all the traditional details of the Nativity scene. Devout veneration of the crib was encouraged by St Francis.[77] Even the animals, the legendary ox and ass, became the focus of pious sentiment.[78] The picturesque detail of their warming Christ with their breath which we have already encountered in the pseudo-Bonaventura *Meditations* is alluded to in a carol:

> The child they knew
> That was born new;
> On hym thei blew. . . .[79]

In popular tradition they play a more vocal part, joining with other animals in their own song of praise. So in a witty French macaronic *noël*:

> Comme les bestes autrefois
> Parloient mieux latin que françois,
> Le coq, de loin voyant le fait,
> S'écria: *Christus natus est.*

The Scheme of Redemption

>Le boeuf d'un air tout ébaubi
>Demande: *Ubi? Ubi? Ubi?*
>La chèvre, se tordant le groin,
>Répond que s'est a Béthléem.
>Maistre Baudet, *curiosus*
>De l'aller voir, dit; *Eamus*,
>Et droit sur ses pattes, le veau
>Beugle deux fois: *volo, volo*.[80]

This delightful idea is not found in our surviving medieval lyrics, though it may well have been known in England since it appears in a later carol, 'The Nailsbourne Beast Song':

>O the beastes all heard the angel call
>When the Cock sang 'Christ is born',
>And they all kneeled to pray down upon the hay,
>When the Cock sang 'Christ is born',
>And the Ruddick sang, O the little Ruddick sang,
>So sweetly sanged he,
>On Chrissimas morn on the Blessed Thorn. . . .[81]

The shepherds, however, play an attractive part in some of our surviving carols (they are so prominent in the French *noëls* that again one suspects that there were once many more of this type). It is impossible not to like the shepherds, who seem to be the epitome of the humble folk for whom Christ came. Even their first brief appearance in Christian literature (for, unlike the animals they appear with the blessing of a canonical book) in Luke 2:8–15: 'and there were in the same country shepherds abiding in the field, keeping watch over their flock by night . . .' calls out for visual representation and for dramatic elaboration.[82] Christian art was long satisfied with the scene of the Annunciation to the shepherds, which it made into a pastoral idyll. As they sit (usually three in number) with their sheep they are surprised by the angelic song; they look up, sometimes shading their eyes against the unearthly radiance. From their predecessors in the ancient pastoral they have inherited a taste for music; unlike St Luke's shepherds they are musicians, and one or more of them has a bagpipe or a flute.[83] In the Holkham Bible picture book they have difficulty with the Latin of the angels' message;[84] in the mystery plays they make a woefully comic attempt to imitate the song they hear. The comic inadequacy of their humanity is shown in the plays in other things

Annunciation and Nativity

– the Chester shepherds chatter on about the diseases of sheep, the Towneley shepherds indulge in an extraordinary rustic banquet, and find themselves involved in boisterous adventures before they make their way to the stable. It was impossible that such lively and real persons should simply 'find' Mary, Joseph and the child, as St Luke says they do. The playwrights make them present the child with touchingly humble gifts – the spirit of the scene is like that of the one simple talent of the Juggler of Our Lady – and the artists of the late Middle Ages develop a separate scene of the adoration of the shepherds, and show them kneeling with their gifts, as very human figures looking in with wonder and amazement on the divine *mysterium*. Their rough faces and simple clothes mark them as the representatives of the ordinary people. They embody not only the devotion and the wonder of the onlookers, but their fears and anxieties as well. In the Towneley plays they are contemporary Englishmen who complain bitterly about the evil of the world, poverty and the harsh weather. In the lyrics, the pastoral background is never forgotten – one *noël* begins:

> Laissez paitre vos bestes
> Pastoureaux, par monts et par vaux – [85]

and in later times this could be more learnedly developed – in the visual arts, for instance by Rubens, in literature, for instance, in the shepherds' hymn of Crashaw, where Thyrsis and Tityrus reappear.[86] The English songs are simple, and perhaps rather more chastely than their French counterparts do not have the two *bergeronnes*, Alison and Mahault, accompanying the shepherds. One carol uses the music of the shepherds for its burden:

> Tyrle, tyrlo,
> So merylye the shepperdes began to blowe.[87]

By far the best is the gay carol in Richard Hill's collection, 'Jolly Wat'. This presents both 'Annunciation' and 'adoration' in dramatic form, as the adventure of a single shepherd. Almost more than any other Middle English lyric, it is full of precise visual details. The poet clearly visualizes each stage in the action, almost as if he had a painting (or a scene from a play) in his mind. It is full of vivid phrases and realistic details, and of that simple piety which expresses the relationship between man and the Christ child in unaffectedly homely and 'companionable' terms. It certainly deserves to be quoted in full:[88]

The Scheme of Redemption

    Can I not sing but hoy,
    Whan the joly shepherd made so mych joy.

The sheperd upon a hill he satt;
He had on hym his tabard and his hat,
His tarbox, hys pype and hys flagat;
His name was called Joly, Joly Wat,
    For he was a gud herdes boy.
        Vith hoy!
    For in hys pipe he made so mych joy.

The sheperd upon a hill was layd;
His doge to hys gyrdyll was tayd;
He had not slept but a lytill broyd
But *Gloria in excelcis* was to hym sayd.
        Vith hoy!
    For in his pipe he mad so myche joy.

The sheperd on a hill he stode;
Rownd abowt hym his shepe they yode;
He put hys hond under hys hode;
He saw a star as rede as blod.
        Vith hoy!
    For in his pipe he mad so mych joy.

'Now farwell Mall, and also Will;
For my love go ye all styll
Unto I cum agayn you till,
And evermore, Will, ryng well thy bell.'
        Vith hoy!
    For in his pipe he mad so mych joy.

'Now must I go ther Cryst was borne;
Farewell, I cum agayn tomorn;
Dog, kepe well my shep fro the corn,
And warn well, warroke, when I blow my horn.'
        Vith hoy!
    For in hys pype he mad so mych joy.

The sheperd sayd anon ryght,
'I will go se yon farly syght,
Wheras the angell syngith on hight,
And the star that shynyth so bryght.'
        Vith hoy!
    For in his pipe he mad so mych joy.

Annunciation and Nativity

Whan Wat to Bedlem cum was,
He swet; he had gon faster than a pace.
He fownd Jesu in a sympyll place
Between an ox and an asse.
    Vith hoy!
    For in his pipe he mad so mych joy.

'Jesu, I offer to the here my pype,
My skyrte, my tarbox, and my scrype;
Home to my felowes now will I skype,
And also loke unto my shepe.'
    Vith hoy!
    For in his pipe he mad so myche joy.

'Now, farewell, myne own herdesman Wat.'
'Ye, for God, lady, even so I hat.
Lull well Jesu in thy lape,
And farewell, Joseph, wyth thy rownd cape.'
    Vith hoy!
    For in hys pipe he mad so myche joy.

'Now may I well both hope and syng,
For I have been a Crystes beryng.
Home to my felowes now wyll I flyng.
Cryst of hevyn to his blis us bryng!'
    Vith hoy!
    For in his pipe he mad so myche joy.

The Magi are prominent in a number of Epiphany carols and longer poems. The scene of their adoration is, of course, splendidly treated by many artists, who adapted for it a theme from Imperial art, the coming of the barbaric kings from the East bearing tribute (a symbolic recognition of the true King by the kings of the world).[89] The poems do not have many details of the adoration or of their hard coming, apart from the obvious gifts, and the names of the three (tradition had settled on the number three apparently for symbolic reasons – they represent, *inter alia*, the three parts of the world, Europe, Asia and Africa – and was firmly enough fixed by 1492 for it to be impossible for an American magus ever to join the group). One carol which distinguishes them as the 'eldest king', the 'medylmest king' and the 'youngest king'[90] perhaps reflects the tradition in which they represent the Three Ages of Man. Whether as astrologers or as 'three kings out of the

East' (which is how they appear in our poems) they are rather mysterious figures (Yeats sees them as 'the pale unsatisfied ones'),[91] and it is not surprising that they became the object of devotion. The relics of the 'three kings of Cologne', which were brought there in 1164, were a most influential centre of this. Prayers to the Magi are found, for instance, in the *Itineraria* of the fifteenth-century antiquary, William Worcestre.[92] Their exotic names are the basis of a pious Latin charm against the falling sickness (apparently because the Magi fell at the feet of Christ):

> Jasper fert myrrham, thus Melchior, Balthasar aurum,
> Hec tria qui secum portabit nomina regum
> Solvitur a morbo Christi pietate caduco.*[93]

This was once on a brass in the church of St Peter Mancroft, Norwich. The names of the Magi occur in other charms as well. But the lyrics make nothing of the mystery or the power of the three kings; they do not come to life like the simple shepherds, who were closer to the experience of the audience.

Joseph, too, is given in the lyrics a more restrained and reverent treatment than he is accorded in other forms of religious literature. One poet sees him as an aged patriarch:

> Be hire sat a sergant
> That sadli seide his sawe,
> He sempte be is semblant
> A man of the elde lawe. . . .[94]

He is puzzled by her pregnancy, but says that he trusts her goodness ('sche wolde no thing misdo'); in one carol he feels so inferior to her virtue that he is afraid to stay with her. In the mystery plays, however, the ancient legend of his 'trouble' (which comes again from the Apocryphal Gospels) is much more sharply expressed, and he is sometimes made into the fabliau type of the old man with a young wife:

> Ya, ya! alle olde men to me take tent,
> And weddyth no wyff in no kynnys wyse
> That is a yonge wench, be myn assent,
> For doute and drede and swyche servyse. . . .[95]

---

* Jasper brings myrrh, Melchior incense, Balthazar gold; whoever will bear on himself the three names of the kings is freed from the falling sickness by the compassion of Christ.

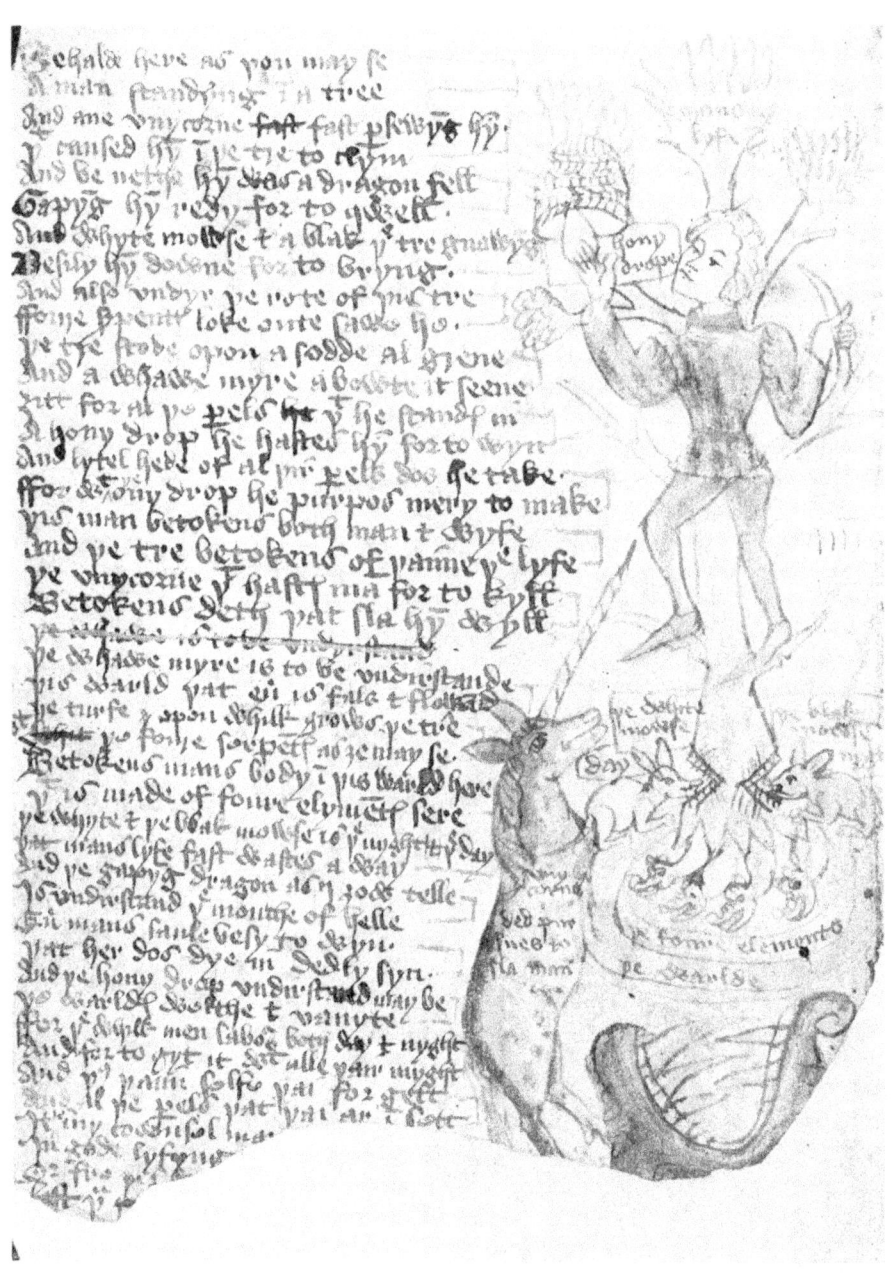

7 The Man and the Unicorn. An illustrated poem based on an incident in the moral legend of Barlaam and Josaphat. Man is pursued by the unicorn, Death (see p. 179).

8 'Antiochenus' and his son. A fifteenth-century illustrated poem. The steward shows the Emperor's son how his father's body lies in its grave and the Emperor delivers a solemn warning (cf. pp. 206–7).

Annunciation and Nativity

It is this tradition which is reflected in the French *noëls* and in the English popular ballad, *The Cherry Tree Carol* ('Joseph was an old man' – recorded first in the eighteenth century but no doubt much older) in which he is convinced by a miracle.[96]

We have already seen that the Nativity, although it is a joyful mystery, is set in a world of misery, cold and doubt. The Christ child already seems rejected by the men he came to save. Joy is deeply mingled with sorrow. In one carol the Christ child already feels menaced by the plots of the wicked:

> Seys thu noghte, thu fayr may, and heris thu noghte also
> How kynge Herod, that keyne knyght, and of his peres mo
> That be abowte nyght and day my body fore to slo?[97]

The cruel slaughter of the Innocents from which the Christ child so narrowly escapes is vividly treated by the artists and the dramatists (their view of Herod as a violent and blustering tyrant is still echoed in Hamlet's phrase 'it out herods herod'). The sorrow and human suffering is most eloquently expressed in the little lullaby which the mothers sing over their children in the Coventry play:

> Lulla, lulla, thow litel tine child,
> By, by, lully, lullay, thow littell tyne child,
> By, by, lully, lullay.

O sisters too,
How may we do
   For to preserve this day
This pore yongling
For whom we do singe,
   'By, by, lully, lullay'?

Herod the king
In his raging,
   Chargid he hath this day
His men of might
In his owne sight
   All yonge children to slay.

That wo is me,
Pore child for thee,
   And ever morne and may
For thi parting
Nether say nor singe,
   'By, by, lully, lullay'.[98]

The emotions which the terrible scene arouses are as powerful today as they were in the Middle Ages; it has indeed been suggested that Picasso's *Guernica* is a twentieth-century expression of the massacre of the Innocents.[99]

The undertone of sorrow in the Nativity scene is intensified because it often is made to look forward prophetically to the scene of the crucifixion. The Portinari altar-piece which we have already referred to not only expresses something of the anxiety and the brooding grief of the onlookers, but also contains symbols of the sorrows of the Virgin.

Sometimes the artists will use proleptic symbolism much more obviously. In an Annunciation in one of the windows of St Peter Mancroft (fifteenth century) rays of light come down towards the Virgin (who wears a coronet, for she has already become, at least in the eye of God, a queen). Down the rays floats a dove, followed by the naked Christ child holding a T-cross, the emblem of his passion.[100] In some French Nativities of the thirteenth century the child lies upon an altar from which there comes the tree of the cross.[101] The poets do not have to resort to such heavy visual symbolism, for they can make Mary speak to her child:

> Ye ben my fadrer eternally
> My sone ye ben so most ye drey
> For Adamys gylt, ye know wel why
> Myn owyn dyre sone lullay.[102]

They often wreck the emotional effect which the prophecy of the coming passion can have in a lullaby by long-windedness and a lack of dramatic sense, but in one poem the connection is cleverly emphasized by rhythmical parallelism, in which the movement of the 'lulling' lines is echoed by the weeping of the child and is taken up and parodied by those which look forward to the buffeting and the beating of the Passion:

> Thys mayden hyghth Mary, she was full mylde,
> She knelyde byfore here oune dere chylde.
>
> She lullyde, she lappyde,
> She rullyde, she wrapped,
>   She wepped wythowtyne nay;
> She rullyde hym, she dressyde hym,
> She lyssyd hym, she blessyd hym,
>   She sange 'dere sone, lullay'.

Annunciation and Nativity

She sayde, 'dere sone, ly styll and slepe.
What cause hast thu so sore to wepe,

   Wyth syghhyng, wyth snobbynge,
Wyth crying and wyth scrycchynge
   All this londe daye;
And thus wakynge wyth sore wepynge
And many salt terys droppynge?
   Ly stylle, dere sone, I the pray.'

'Moder' he sayde, 'for mane I wepe so sore
And for hys love I shall be tore

Wyth scorgyng, wyth thretnyng,
Wyth bobbyng, wyth betyng
– For sothe, moder, I saye –
And one a crosse full hy hanggyng,
And to my herte foll sore styckynge
   A spere on Good Frydaye. . . .'[103]

7

The Passion

The Passion of Christ is the true centre of medieval devotion, and is the subject of a vast number of lyrics.[1] A full discussion of these would extend this book to inordinate length; the following pages, therefore, will simply single out for comment the most common and the most interesting themes and images, and some of the most successful poems. Some stanzas from a fourteenth-century lyric, which echoes the *Jesu Dulcis Memoria*, will serve as an introduction:

> Jesu, swete is the love of thee,
> Noon othir thing so swete may be;
> No thing that men may heere and see
> Hath no swetnesse ayens thee. . . .
>
> Jesu, thi love was us so fre
> That it fro hevene broughte thee;
> For love thou dere boughtist me,
> For love thou hynge on roode tre. . . .
>
> Jesu, for love thou bood so wo
> That blody stremys runne the fro;
> Thi whyte sydes woxen blw and blo –
> Oure synnes it maden, so wolawo!
>
> Jesu, for love thou steigh on roode,
> For love thou yaf thin herte blode;
> Love thee made my soules foode,
> Thi love us bought til al goode. . . .
>
> Jesu my God, Jesu my kyng,
> Thou axist me noon othir thing,
> But trewe love and herte yernyng,
> And love-teeris with swete mornyng. . . .[2]

The Passion

A number of the dominant ideas and attitudes of the Passion lyrics are illustrated here. The relationship of the poet (and of his pious readers) to Christ is one of intense and intimate devotion. It is deeply emotional, but the motion is controlled by its reflective framework. Christ's sufferings should arouse 'love-teeris' and 'swete mornyng'; they are recalled to the mind by brief, but vivid physical and visual details – 'blody stremys', the 'whyte sydes' that became 'blw and blo'. Christ's Passion is the supreme expression of his love (*fortis ut mors dilectio* is a text which is sometimes used in this sort of context),[3] and demands a reciprocal love from the individual soul. The scene of the Passion is the Christian archetype of suffering, but because it is the expression of love and the supreme image of man's redemption it is 'sweet'. So the cross, a cruel instrument of torture, is the instrument of redemption –

> Crux est
> A barge to beren fro depe groundes,
> A targe to weren fro detly woundes,
> A falle to taken in the fend,
> And an halle to glathen in a frend.[4]

Around it gather ancient pious legends,[5] and popular devotion, often associated with particular relics of it such as the 'holy cross of Bromeholm'.[6] One tag, a translation of a stanza from a famous hymn of Fortunatus, puts the devotional paradox nicely:

> Steddefast crosse, inmong alle other
> Thow art a tree mykel of prise,
> In brawnche and flore swylk another
> I ne wot non in wode ne rys.
> Swete be the nalys,
> And swete be the tre,
> And sweter be the birdyn that hangis upon the![7]

When this intense devotion becomes the subject of art or literature it is necessary to maintain a delicate and difficult balance between extreme and conflicting emotions. Failure to do so can easily result in offensive lapses of taste, or over-literal and ridiculous exaggerations, which often suggest a contorted or obsessive interest in suffering for its own sake.

The lyric poets do not pay much attention to the events which immediately precede the Passion proper. One little poem in Grimestone's book uses in a quite dramatic way Christ's words in Gethsemane:

The Scheme of Redemption

> A sory beverech it is, and sore it is abouth
> Nou in this sarpe time this brewing hat me brouth;
> Fader, if it mowe ben don als I have besouth,
> Do awey this beverich, that I ne drink et nouth.
>
> And if it mowe no betre ben, for alle mannis gilth,
> That it ne muste nede that my blod be spilth,
> Suete fader, I am thi sone, thi wil be fulfilt –
> I am her thin owen child, I wil don as thu wilt.[8]

And there is a good thirteenth-century poem (possibly the earliest recorded English ballad) on Judas. In the medieval world, at least as it is presented in literature, there is no more terrible crime than treachery, and the remorse and suicide of this arch-traitor did not seem punishment enough. A grim passage in *Inferno* xxxiv describes him in the very mouth of Satan. At the same time, the popular imagination seems to have recoiled from the idea that a disciple could be capable of such a crime, or at least tried to find some further motivation for it, as in losing the money in gaming or, as in the English poem, in the urging of his sister. *Judas* breaks off abruptly and dramatically with the disciple professing his innocence, and the blustering and vaunting of Peter quietly rebuked by Christ:

> 'Stille thou be, Peter. Wel I the icnowe –
> Thou wolt fursake me thrien ar the coc him crowe.'[9]

It is on the torments of the Passion and the crucifixion scene itself (and on the devotional images connected with, it) that the lyrics concentrate – on Christ 'as a man hanging on the cross'. Ailred tells his sister to have on her altar a crucifix, which will show her the Passion of Christ, 'with arms spread wide apart, inviting you to his embrace'; from his naked breast he will give her the milk of his comfort. If she wishes to praise the excellence of virginity she should have the image of Mary on one side and of John the Baptist on the other.[10] This is the sort of image used as a focus for meditation that is implied by many of the lyrics. So

> Quanne ic se on rode
> Jesu mi lemman,
> An besiden him stonden
> Marie an Johan,
> And his rig isuongen,
> And his side istungen,
>   For the luve of man....[11]

The Passion

Sometimes the poet's imagination will isolate the image of the cross with Christ hanging on it alone as his devotional image; sometimes he will describe the events of the Passion with all their public scorn and clamour.[12] The figure of the hanging Christ is that which had become standard in the visual arts by the late Middle Ages[13] – the head bowed in death 'as if to kiss', the crown of thorns, the arms outstretched 'as if to embrace', the great wound in the right side, the body 'nailed with three nails, naked on the rood'; sometimes, in later manuscripts, the poem is accompanied by an image. Both artists and writers often emphasize the physical torment which Christ suffered – an emphasis which finds it most extreme expression in such works as Grünewald's Isenheim altar-piece, where the contorted body on the cross seems not only dead, but diseased and putrefying, or the scenes in the mystery plays where the body of Christ is stretched by the tormentors with jeers and taunts on the cross as it lies on the ground. The 'terrible precision' which Mâle rightly finds characteristic of this sort of piety is seen clearly in this description from Julian of Norwich of Christ's bleeding head:

> I saw the bodyly sight lesting of the plentious bledeing of
> the hede. The grete dropis of blode fel downe from under the
> garland like pellots, semand as it had cum out of the veynis;
> and in the comeing out it were browne rede, for the blode
> was full thick; and in the spredeing abrode it were bright
> rede; and when it comes to the browes than it vanyshid. . . .[14]

The lyrics, which prefer to imply the scene through selected details, are on the whole more restrained and dignified.

The sorrow of the Passion is succinctly stated in mnemonic sermon-tags, such as these from Grimestone's book:[15]

> Allas, Jesu thi love is lorn
> Allas, Jesu, thi det is suorn
> Allas, Jesu thi bane is born

> Crist criyede. wan he preyyede. foryefnes of oure senne
> Crist criyede. wan he thristede. the helthe of mankenne
> Crist criyede. wan he tholede. harde peynes an wo
> Crist criyede. wan his soule fro the bodi sulde go

(Beside these verses in the margin is a little 'complaint' of Christ:

> Al mi blod for thi is sched
> Reu on me that am forbled.)

It is easy to imagine these being used to emphasize a preacher's point, or being expounded in the course of a sermon. Most of the Passion lyrics, however, are in a real sense poetry of meditation.[16] One of the most popular[17] (preserved in eleven MSS.) is described by the rubric in one copy as a 'holy meditaciun behofliche to be thouht or seyd with devociun'; in other copies instructions are given for its personal devotional use: 'in seiyinge of this orisoun stynteth and bydeth at every cros and thynketh whate ye have seide. For a more devout prayere fond I never of the passioun whoso wolde devoutly say hitte.' Later schemes of meditation were elaborate constructions built upon the traditional division of the mind into three parts (the image of God) – Memory, Understanding and Will. Medieval meditations and especially meditative lyrics were much less formalized. It is immediately obvious that what was later called the 'analysis', the exercise of understanding, is usually very simple. Instead of the elaborate teasing-out of subtle theological points there is usually a simple statement of the *mysterium* or paradox. Sometimes there is some straightforward exegesis of the details of the scene – that Christ's feet are fastened means that he will not flee, etc.[18] Occasionally the 'understanding' is expressed in a more pointed and almost witty way:

> Thi mylde boones love hath todrawe,
> The naylis thi feet han al tognawe;
> The lord of love love hath now slawe –
> Whane love is strong it hath no lawe. . . .[19]

But most of our poets, one feels, would have been satisfied with Julian of Norwich's simple conclusion at the end of her *Revelations* that 'love was our Lord's meaning'. The 'colloquy', the movement of will, is also very simple – it is sometimes a prayer:

> Jesu make me glad to be
> Sympil and pouer for love of the,
> And let me never for more ne lasse
> Love good to myche that sone shal passe.[20]

But the *memoria* of the Passion, the later 'composition of place' is often done with striking detail and personal feeling, applying the insistent injunctions of the Pseudo-Bonaventura *Meditations* (and other such works) to make oneself as if present at the scene, in the midst of every circumstance concerning the Passion, 'with earnestness, zeal, love, and fixed intentness'. The author of the *Medita-*

The Passion

tions is always exclaiming 'observe', 'see', 'behold', and insists that we should carefully regard each particular, 'for it becomes us not to be weary in thinking upon those pains, one by one, which Our Lord wearied not in enduring one by one'. The lyrics too are fond of using 'see' 'behold' – the poet and his readers are transported to the very scene:

> Wan ic myself stond
> And myd herte ysee. . . .[21]

The effect of making the reader 'really there' is achieved by the selection of visual and evocative details, sometimes strikingly vivid – in one poem the scene is precisely located in place and time, 'hey upon a dune', 'a mile wythute the tune', 'abute the midday'; in another, Christ's 'rude' becomes 'grene', and the Jews are said to bristle 'as a mad boar'[22] – but often very traditional: 'defoiled was his face with dispitoue spyttynge', etc.

The poem which is praised in the rubric we have just quoted, 'Jesu that hast me dere ibought' is a very successful example of an extended meditative Passion poem. It is, in fact, a shortened and compressed version of a longer poem, the *Meditations on the Life and Passion of Christ*, which is in its turn a version of a fine Latin poem, *Philomena*, by John of Howden. Though it is technically a compilation – lines selected from the *Meditations* and put together to make a shorter poem – it is the work of an intelligent writer.[23] From his original he takes the striking image which was to be used later by Herbert in *Good Friday*:

> Since blood is fittest, Lord, to write
> Thy sorrows in, and bloody sight;
> My heart hath store; write there, where in
> One box doth lie both ink and sin. . . .

and uses it simply and directly to introduce each section of his meditation:

> Jesu that hast me dere ibought,
> Write thou gostly in my thoght,
> That I mow with devocioun
> Thynke on thy dere passioun:
> For thogh my hert be hard as stone,
> Yit maist thou gostly write theron
> With naill and with spere kene,
> And so shullen the lettres be sene. . . .

The Scheme of Redemption

By substituting 'Jesu' for the more abstract 'Love' of his original, and the second person singular pronoun 'thou' for 'he', he is clearly aiming at constructing a much more intimate and personal sort of meditation, 'a devoute prayere' which may easily be used as a private devotion. His narrative of the crucifixion is no bald recital; the reader's 'memory' of the Passion is made precise by carefully chosen and dramatic details – when the cross is brought forth, Christ begins to 'chever and quake', the nail is said to 'stynt at the bone', the cross is called the 'hard knotty rode tre', and the presence of a hostile crowd is suggested by a brief snatch of direct speech:

> ... cried ay withouten reste:
> 'Honge hym on the rode tre,
> For he wil kynge of Jewes be.'

The poem culminates in a simple affective movement of devotion:

> Jesu, whan I thynke on the,
> How thou were bound for love of me,
> Wel owe I to wepe that stounde
> That thou for me so sore were bounde ...

and a series of prayers.

Sometimes the simplest lyrical statement of the scene as it was, a verbal devotional image, stripped of all preaching and reflection, makes the best poem:

> Wyth was hys nakede brest and red of blod hys syde,
> Bleyc was his fair andled, his wnde dop ant wide,
> And hys armes ystreith hey upon the rode,
> On fif studes on his body the stremes ran o blode.[24]

These lines depend almost entirely for their effect on the sharpness of visual impact and of the allusive and impressionistic use of detail. There is no need to make the emotional appeal explicit: the feeling can be expressed through words which are traditionally 'charged' – 'nakede', 'bleyc', 'ystreith', etc. The poem is one of a number of versions (some of which are much less successful) of some Latin lines in a meditation of John of Fécamp:[25]

> Candet nudatum pectus. rubet cruentum latus. tensa arent viscera. decora languent lumina. regia pallent ora. procera rigent brachia. crura dependent marmorea. et rigat terebratos pedes beati sanguinis unda. ...

The Passion

The dramatic abruptness of the Latin has been transformed into a static image (the verbs 'candet', 'rubet', have become adjectives), which focuses the emotions connected with it into a single moment. The details have been pared down – there is no mention of the eyes, no equivalent for the adjectives 'regia', 'marmorea' (another version in a longer poem uses these details more expansively:

> Mine lonke armes, stive and sterke,
> Min eyin arrin dim and derke,
> Min theyis honket so marbre-ston in werke . . .[26]

and makes the limbs 'hang' with the coldness of a sculpture). The 'beati sanguinis unda' is changed into a fine example of the 'terrible precision' of Passion devotion: 'on fif studes on his body the stremes ran o blode'.

Other meditative poems present the scene obliquely, through more unusual images. One begins strikingly, 'I herd an harping on a hille as I lay undir lynde . . .'[27] and uses a mysterious 'writing on a wall' of the letters X, M, I, C:

> X. for Christ, Goddis son was sett, that duleful ded die gon;
> M. for Mary the chekes wett when he hingked sa hie;
> I. for Jon the teres lett for dole that Crist gon die;
> C. for cros ther thai mett – thir foure fandit to flie. . . .

It is very unusual to find in lyrics the bizarre images which are sometimes used in sermons or in prose meditations (as the likening of the many wounds of Christ to stars, the holes of a net, of a dovehouse, etc. in the passage quoted on p. 70). One little tag gives three images which may be elaborated in a sermon:

> Dolor iste sive passio potest assimilare bene
> to { a man of ple and motyng
> a boke of scripture and wrytyng
> a harpe of melodye mak(y)ng.[28]

These can be found in longer poems. In Scrope's version of Christine de Pisan's *Epistre d'Othéa* Christ is 'streyned as an harpe' upon the cross.[29] The image of Christ's body as a book is used in a couple of rather diffuse 'ABC' poems on the Passion (the reference is to children's hornbooks[30] – originally a leaf with the alphabet, and sometimes numbers, the Lord's Prayer, etc., mounted on a tablet of wood and protected by a layer of translucent horn):

> In everi place men mai see,
> Whanne children to scole sette schulen be,
> A book to hem is brought:
> Nailid to a bord of tre
> That is clepid an a.b.c.
> Parfijtliche wrought. . . .³¹

It is alluded to also in the Digby play of the *Burial of Christ*:

> 'Cum hithere, Joseph, beholde and looke,
> How many bludy lettres ben wreten in this buke,
> Small margente her is'

to which Joseph replies 'Ye, this parchement is trichit owt of syse.'³² A very curious image, which combines it with a legal metaphor, is alluded to in one lyric by Herebert:

> Soeththe he my robe tok
> Also ich finde in bok
>   He ys to me ybounde
> And helpe he wole, ich wot,
> Vor love the chartre wrot –
>   The enke orn of hys wounde. . . .³³

The 'Charter of Christ' is the name given to a number of Passion-complaints which record a grant of heaven's bliss to man, provided that he gives in return his love to God and his neighbour. Plate 5 shows a rather grotesque visual form, with the wounded Christ 'presenting' it before the cross; notice that the seal is his wounded heart. Its structure is based on that of legal charters, and it uses legal formulae – one MS. version ends:

> To my heere under-honged seale
> For the more stable sureness
> This wound in my hearte the seale is
> *Datum*
> Yeoven at Calvary
> The first day of the great mercie . . .

and gives the names of the 'witnesses':

| sealid and deelivered in yᵉ presence of | { Mary mother of God, Mary Cleophe, Mary Iacobi, John yᵉ disciple } | ita fidem facimus | { Matthew, Marke, Luke, John } | Notarii publici |

The Passion

Far more successful as poetic images than any of these, however, are those of the nightingale, which we have already discussed, and of Christ as the knight who because of his love for mankind gives up his life.[34] This story, which directly appeals to the chivalric sentiments of the time, is found in extended form in the *Ancrene Wisse*, and in the *conte* 'of the king who had a beloved' of Nicholas Bozon, which we have already alluded to. It is behind the 'Jousting at Jerusalem' in *Piers Plowman*, and is often used in the lyrics. It is very boldly used in a complaint of Christ from the cross 'Men rent me on rode':

> Biheld mi side,
> Mi wndes sprede so wide,
> Restles I ride.
> Lok up on me – put fro the pride.
>
> Mi palefrey is of tre,
> Wiht nayles naylede thwrh me.
> Ne is more sorwe to se –
> Certes noon more may be.
>
> Under mi gore
> Ben wndes selcowthe sore.
> Ler, man, mi lore;
> For mi love sinne no more.[35]

The allusive use of the image here means that the poet can on the one hand combine it visually with the image of Christ hanging on the cross (possibly his use of the word 'gore' (robe) suggests that he is thinking of the figure clothed in a knightly robe or surcoat, rather than the loincloth which would be most familiar in contemporary depictions of the crucifixion), and that on the other he can underline the irony of the scene with words like 'ride' and 'palefrey' (a cruel adaptation of the sublimity-humility paradox, which is developed with typical grimness by the executioners in the Towneley play of the Crucifixion – as they raise the cross with Christ fastened to it, they jest

> Sir, commys heder and have done,
> And wyn apon youre palfray sone,
> For he is redy bowne . . .).

The image is used very successfully, and again allusively at the climax of a good alliterative poem on the Passion, 'My trewest

The Scheme of Redemption

tresowre sa trayturly was taken'. In this the events of the Passion are rehearsed, with vivid and precise detail – 'thai schot in thi syght bath slaver and slyme', 'ful hydusly hyngand thay heved the on hyght', etc. – and intense personal devotion:

> My dere-worthly derlyng, sa dolefully dyght,
> Sa straytly upryght streyned on the rode;
> For thi mykel mekenes, thi mercy, thi myght,
> Thow bete al my bales with bote of thi blode.

The following stanza sees the deposition from the cross as a scene in which the dead but victorious knight is disarmed:

> My fender of my fose, sa fonden in the felde,
> Sa lufly lyghtand at the evensang tyde;
> Thi moder and hir menyhe unlaced thi scheld –
> All weped that thar were, thi woundes was sa wyde.[36]

Another lyric, from Grimestone's book, suggests the chivalric and romantic aspects of the image:

> Mi love is falle upon a may,
> For love of hire I defende this day,
> Love aunterus no man forsaket,
> It woundet sore wan it him taket;
> Love anterus may haven no reste,
> Quare thouth is newe ther love is f(e)ste;
> Love anterus with wo is bouth,
> Ther love is trewe it flittetth nouth.[37]

So intense is the devotion to Christ's Passion in the late Middle Ages, that almost every detail becomes a focus for meditation or the centre of a 'cult'. 'Chaque heure qui sonne,' says Mâle, 'rappelle au chrétien une souffrance de Jésus-Christ.' Devotional works associate the sufferings with the days of the week or with the canonical hours of the day. A number of English lyrics (not usually of much literary value) use the 'Hours' as a meditative framework.[38] The instruments which inflicted the torments upon the body of Christ before and during the crucifixion also became objects of pious devotion (cf. plates 3, 5, and especially 6, where they have proved too much for a later Protestant, who has erased the indulgence which accompanied them).[39] We have already mentioned the *Arma Christi* poems in Middle English, which are nearly always illustrated with devotional images of the nails, spear, crown

The Passion

of thorns, etc. and with events associated with the road to Calvary – the Jews spitting, the Veronicle (the image of Christ's face left upon St Veronica's cloth),[40] etc. Those poems are the simplest kind of devotional verse. Arranged in heraldic style the instruments form a sort of ironic blazon of the Christ-knight. One little poem makes it into a defence (a shield, if not a *lorica*) for the faithful:

> A scheld of red, a crosse of grene,
> A crowne ywrithe with thornes kene,
> A sper, a sponge, with nayles thre,
> A body ybounde to a tre;
> Whoso this schild in herte wul take,
> Amonge his enimes thar he noght quake.[41]

There were also devotional cults of the Precious Blood of Christ,[42] and of the Wounds which were inflicted on him. Relics of the Precious Blood were brought to England in the thirteenth century (there is a drawing by Matthew Paris of Henry III carrying a phial of the blood to Westminster),[43] at Ashridge and at Hayles (the 'blood of Crist that is in Hayles' which is mentioned in *The Pardoner's Tale*). It is behind such iconographical themes as the 'mystic winepress' and the 'fountain of life' (which, in its simplest form, shows Christ crucified, with blood flowing from his wounds into a fountain around which the faithful pray, or in which they bathe themselves, an idea which like a number of others in medieval affective devotion appears again in Protestant tradition – cf. Cowper's hymn 'There is a fountain filled with blood').[44] Devotion to the Precious Blood sometimes takes a grotesquely statistical turn – there are some little Middle English verses which calculate the number of drops which Christ was supposed to have shed.[45]

Closely related to this is the devotion to the Wounds of Christ.[46] There is a continual stress on the number and the pain of the wounds which were inflicted (crudely expressed by the artists by covering the body of Christ from top to toe with tiny red stains, cf. plates 2 and 5), but it is on the Five Wounds of the feet, hands and heart that devotion concentrates. The cult of the Five Wounds seems to have appealed to all classes of society, from kings to the humblest persons, who used simple prayers and charms based on them. It has some fascinating ramifications in devotional practice and in the visual arts, but its expression in literature is on the whole disappointing. There are some devotional verses which accompany illustrations of the wounds (which are called 'wells'); sometimes

The Scheme of Redemption

the Five Wounds (or the seven sheddings of Christ's blood) are invoked as remedies against sins.[47] One lyric expresses the fundamental idea of the cult very neatly:

> Jesus woundes so wide
> Ben welles of life to the goode,
> Namely the stronde of his syde
> That ran ful breme on the rode.
>
> Yif thee list to drinke
> To fle fro the fendes of helle,
> Bowe thu doun to the brinke
> And mekely taste of the welle.[48]

The great wound in Christ's side was singled out for special devotion (we have already encountered the popular devotional image of the *mensura vulneris*), which developed into the devotion to the Sacred Heart.[49] The fairly common idea that this is a refuge in which the faithful soul can shelter is boldly turned in a poem in Grimestone's book:

> I wolde ben clad in Cristes skyn,
> That ran so longe on blode,
> And gon t'is herte and taken myn in –
> Ther is a fulsum fode. . . .[50]

In a longer illustrated poem by William Billyng the Sacred Heart is addressed (as a 'trusty treulove') with an intricate splendour that reminds us of Crashaw's 'the purple wardrobe of thy side':

> O truest tabernacle of alle the towrys,
> Comlyest closet encensed alle with spyces,
> Most plesaunte pa(ra)dyse, most ryalle in honoure,
> Rychest recyte of joy and dulce deliciis!
> O swettyst honycome aftur our devices,
> Emborde in the syde of the gentylman
> I the salute as humbly as I canne![51]

This type of medieval devotion is often exaggerated, sometimes distasteful or absurd.[52] Yet it is only the extreme manifestation of an intense and fervent devotion to the body and the humanity of Christ which had important consequences in the arts. Few of us would wish to remove the chorale 'O sacred Head sore wounded' from its central position in the *St Matthew Passion*. Here is one of its medieval antecedents, from a poem on the Wounds of Christ:

The Passion

>   Ave, caput inclinatum,
>   Despective coronatum
>   Spinis infidelium,
>   Plagis multis perforatum
>   Circumquaque cruentatum,
>   Exemplar humilium. . . .*[53]

The sorrow of the scene at Calvary is deepened by the presence of Mary. The brief mention of her in the gospels – 'now there stood by the cross of Jesus his mother. . . .' (John 19:25–7) – is the germ of some of the finest art and literature of the Middle Ages. One of the favourite ideas of late medieval devotion is that the Virgin suffers a passion which is parallel to that of her son.[54] She says to St Bridget in her *Revelations*, 'the sorrows of Jesus were my sorrows, because his heart was my heart'. The commentators had, from early times, pointed out that at the foot of the cross the prophecy of Simeon ('yea, a sword shall pierce through thy own soul also') was fulfilled,[55] and this is alluded to often in the lyrics – so the *Stabat Mater Dolorosa*:

>   Cuius animam gementem
>   Contristatam et dolentem
>   Pertransivit gladius.

Though she was spared the pains of childbirth, she suffers deeply now, as she sees her son die. Sometimes the scene is presented visually, with an austere economy of emotion:

>   Jesu Cristes milde moder
>   Stud, biheld hire sone o rode
>   That he was ipined on;
>   The sone heng, the moder stud
>   And biheld hire childes blud,
>   Wu it of hise wundes ran. . . .

That she stands at this moment of anguish is an eloquent testimony to her dignity and self-control – 'stantem illam lego, flentem non lego' (I read that she stood, but not that she wept) says St Ambrose in a consolation.[56] But it was natural that affective devotion (possibly, again, influenced by Eastern models) would prefer to see her subject to the emotions and anguish of a human mother. Not only does she come to weep 'bloody tears', but she swoons, or has

---

* Hail, O head bowed low, shamefully crowned with thorns by the infidels, pierced by many wounds, everywhere covered in blood, the pattern of humility. . . .

to be supported by the other onlookers and this becomes a characteristic gesture of her overwhelming sorrow in late medieval depictions of the scene[57] (though in the visual arts she still retains some dignity; her grief is more restrained than that of Mary Magdalene.[58] The lyrics which express the grief of the Virgin are influenced by two popular Latin meditations, the *Dialogus Beatae Mariae et Anselmi de Passione Domini* and the *Liber de Passione Christi*, in which she tells the story of the Passion as she herself saw it.[59] When this framework is used in the lyrics we usually find some very striking stanzas:

> Than sodenly whan the sonne was downe
> Offe people thou hurdest an hydeouse crye
> Rennyng in the citee with a ferfulle sowne.
> Thou were ful sore affrayed utterli,
> And whan thou knewe not the cause why,
> Than sayde thowe thus, with a pale hewe,
> 'I wolde I were with my swete sone Jesu'[60]

rather than a sustained and successful poem. The best of these lyrics are dramatic realizations of isolated moments in the story. Sometimes the Virgin will engage in a dialogue with her son as he hangs on the cross – a good example is the thirteenth-century sequence 'Stond wel, moder, under rode', in which the extreme emotion of the scene is conveyed sharply and tightly through their exchanges:

> 'Stond wel, moder, under rode,
> Bihold thi child wyth glade mode,
> Blythe moder mittu ben.'
> 'Sune, quu may I blithe stonden?
> I se thin feet, I se thin honden,
> Nayled to the harde tre.'
>
> 'Moder, do wey thi wepinge;
> I thole this ded for mannes thinge –
> For owen gilte tholi non.'
> 'Sune, I fele the dede-stunde,
> The swerd is at min herte grunde,
> That me byhytte Symeon.'[61]

Sometimes, against the background of this scene, the Virgin will give a dramatic *exclamatio*. A terse and eloquent example is found in Grimestone's book; she addresses the Jews:

The Passion

> Wy have ye no reuthe on my child?
> Have reuthe on me ful of murning,
> Taket doun on rode my derworthi child,
> Or prek me on rode with my derling.
>
> More pine ne may me ben don
> Than laten me liven in sorwe and schame;
> Als love me bindet to my sone,
> So lat vus deyyen bothen isame.[62]

In the fifteenth-century lyrics, the most successful laments of the Virgin are those which imply the late medieval devotional image of the pietà, where the Virgin holds the body of the dead Christ in her lap (cf. plate 6) and utters a lament.[63] Hard words are sometimes said about these poems,[64] and it cannot be denied that in many of the *planctus* there is an extreme emotionalism which easily becomes monotonous. It has been pointed out that these poems lack 'a substantial theological frame of reference' unlike the rest of the passion lyrics;[65] this however does not seem to be directly responsible for their excesses and failures – it is rather that the attempt to create a dramatic representation of the extreme grief of a human mother makes emotional and rhetorical demands beyond the scope of many of the poets. Potentially, the treatment of the mother's grief would seem to be a more promising literary topic than an intense meditation on the physical suffering of the crucified Christ, but some poets, bereft of their 'theological frame', seem unable to cope with the human situation. However, some of the Marian laments do show a certain poetic power. One begins with an abrupt and eerie vision:

> Sodenly afraide,
> Half waking,
> Half slepyng
> And gretly dismayde,
> A wooman sate wepyng.[66]

In this poem the narrator is present, and Mary's complaint is directly addressed to his 'hard heart':

> On me she caste hire ey, said 'See, mane, thy brothir!'
> She kissid hym and said, 'swete, am I not thy modir?'
> In sownyng she fill there, it wolde be non othir;
> I not which more deedly, the toone or the tothir. . . .

In another, the Virgin addresses her lament to other mothers.[67]

> ... abyde and se
> How my sone liggus me beforne
> Upon my kne, takyn fro tre.
> Your childur ye dawnse upon your kne
> With laghyng, kyssyng and mery chere;
> Beholde my childe, beholde now me,
> For now liggus ded my dere son, dere. ...

This poem is built upon the contrast between the terrible appearance of her son as he lies in her lap and the happy play of other mothers with their children:

> O woman, thu takis thi childe be the hand
> And seis, 'my son gif me a stroke!'
> My sonnys handis ar sore bledand. ...

Though the final stanzas become less sharp and more diffuse, the eloquence of the complaint is sustained by these pathetic details. There is also some intellectual structure – the Virgin calls attention to the wounds of Christ in order – to his head, breast, hands and feet, and ends (less happily) by making her reproachful complaint to the ordinary mother more explicitly a call to devotion. In yet another *planctus* the poet finds the Virgin not in her usual position beneath the cross, but at a 'citeys ende', sobbing, sighing and tearing her hair.[68] Her complaint is something of a rhetorical *tour de force*, dramatic and heightened, but not theatrical. She utters imprecations against the earth which received her son's blood, the stone of the mortice, the cross, and the scourge, and the Jews. It is a good example of the 'high' exclamatory style which fifteenth-century poets often favoured:

> Thou scourge, with cordis thou brak the skyne
> With hard knottis, I crye upon the!
> Ye bete my sonne that never did synne;
> Why bete thou hym and spare me?
> Made he nott the? thou woldest not blyne –
> Thou teryst hys skynne and wold nott lett;
> Thou myghte nott sett the poynt of a pyne
> Upon hole skynne, so thou hym bett. ...

This is extreme emotion, but it is expressed eloquently and tellingly. We are in the presence of a poet who is certainly more than competent:

The Passion

Gabriel, thu dedeste calle me full of grace –
Nowe full of sorowe thu me seyste:
The terys tryllyd downe be my face,
Filius regis mortuus est.

Yet, as one so often finds in the English religious lyric it is the short, simple, but evocative poem which most impressively expresses a complex of emotion. In the *Merure de Seinte Eglise*, St Edmund of Canterbury quotes an 'Englishman' 'en manere de pite':

Nou goth sonne under wod,
Me reweth, Marie, thi faire rode.
Nou goth sonne under tre,
Me reweth, Marie, thi sonne and the.[69]

The sorrowful moment and the scene with its two figures are austerely and movingly isolated. The darkness which covers the earth is the symbolic parallel to the setting of the true Sun:

Quando sol eclipsabatur
Hora mortis Domini,
Verus sol obscurabatur,
Lucem ferens homini.*[70]

A less well-known little poem of a similar type, which expresses the sorrow of the death (at a later point in the traditional narrative) is the English lament which the author of the Cornish play of the Resurrection makes the three Maries sing like a recurring burden at the tomb of Christ:

Ellas, mornyngh y syngh, mornyng y cal;
Our Lord ys deyd that bogthe ous alle.[71]

It is not surprising to find in a number of lyrics a further development of the Passion scene, in making the wounded or crucified figure of Christ himself address an appeal or a complaint to man – 'Christus potest dicere', as Grimestone's book says:

Christus potest dicere:
Harde gates I have go
That is isene on everi to
To maken my frend of my fo
Love me, man, for al mi wo.[72]

---

* When the sun was eclipsed at the hour of the Lord's death, the true Sun, which bears light to man, was darkened.

The Scheme of Redemption

In fifteenth-century MSS. these poems are sometimes accompanied by devotional illustrations, so that it is as if the image itself speaks directly to the reader[73] (cf. plate 1). The 'complaint of Christ' is potentially a vivid and dramatic lyric form. It is clearly more striking and emotive, if instead of instructing his reader to 'look at' Christ, as

> Loke, man, to Jesu Crist
> Ineiled an tho rode. . . .[74]

the poet makes the figure speak

> Man and wymman, loket to me,
> U michel pine ich tholede for the;
> Loke upone mi rig, u sore ich was ib(e)ten
> Loke to mi side, wat blode ich have ileten. . . .[75]

but the form does make literary demands which not all the writers can meet. Some cannot resist a clumsily didactic introduction:

> Abyde, gud men, and hald yhour pays
> And here what god himselven says,
>   Hyngand on the rode:
> 'Man and woman that bi me gase. . . .'[76]

sometimes Christ's complaint becomes tediously long, or simply querulous:

> I suffre Jewes on me to spete,
> And al nith with hem I wake,
> To loken wan thu woldest lete
> Thi senne for love of thi make. . . .[77]

or heavy with exempla:

> Allso ensaumple may thou luke
> Of saint Peter that me forsoke
>   And sythen rewed it sare. . . .[78]

The best are as usual often the brief taut simple verses, such as this from Grimestone:[79]

> Behold, man, wat is my wo,
> Ther I hange upon the tre;
> Mi blod rennet to an fro
> Be everi side, thu mith wel se.

The Passion

> The spere hat smiten myn herte ato –
> For love of the my blod is spilt.
> Yif thu wilt fro thi senne go,
> My merci is redi quan thu wilt.

Some of the most successful are simply adaptations of a verse in *Lamentations* (1:12): 'O vos omnes qui transitis per viam, attendite, et videte si est dolor sicut dolor meus'; the passer-by is suddenly arrested by the image of the suffering Christ:[80]

> Ye that pasen be the weyye,
> Abidet a litel stounde!
> Beholdet, al mi felawes,
> Yef ani me lik is founde.
> To the tre with nailes thre
> Wol fast I hange bounde;
> With a spere al thoru mi side
> To min herte is mad a wounde.

Christ speaks in 'an eternal present'; the wounds which he calls his 'felawes' to observe are precisely stated, and the restraint of his speech intensifies the emotion.

Other complaints are based on the 'Reproaches' or *Improperia* of the Good Friday liturgy, which are so brilliantly used later in Herbert's 'The Sacrifice', a series of contrasting statements of God's grace shown to man in the Old Testament, and of man's cruel responses in the Passion. One of the Middle English translations is a rather stiff version by William Herebert:[81]

> Ich delede the see vor the,
> And Pharaon dreynte vor the;
> And thou to princes sullest me.
> > My volk, what habbe y do the
> > Other in what thyng toened the?
> > Gyn nouthe and onswere thou me.
>
> In bem of cloude ich ladde the;
> And to Pylate thou ledest me.
> > My volk, etc.
>
> Wyth aungeles mete ich vedde the;
> And thu bufetest and scourgest me.
> > My volk, etc. . . .

The Scheme of Redemption

A number of poems extend the idea of a reproachful complaint (sometimes into a more general type of moral and social satire). One of the best is a lyric which Carleton Brown calls 'Jesus pleads with the Worldling'[82] which is built on a series of contrasts between the sorrows of Christ and the fine dress and habits of a gay gallant. The images are sharply defined and ironic:

> Thyn hondes streite gloved,
> White and clene kept;
> Myne with nailes thorled,
> On rode and eke my feet.
>
> Acros thou berest thyn armes,
> Whan thou dauncest narewe. . . .
> Myne for the on rode,
> With the Jewes wode,
> With grete ropis todraw. . . .

Probably the best of all the appeals to sinful man from the cross is the fifteenth-century poem 'Wofully araide', once attributed (wrongly it seems) to Skelton. In the earliest MS. it is accompanied by a small drawing of the crucified Christ, and in the Tudor 'Fayrfax' MS. by musical settings by William Cornish and Browne.[83] The emotion is expressed in a taut, dramatic style, full of forceful alliteration, vivid phrases and expressive rhythms:

> Thus nakid am I nailid, O man, for thi sake.
> I love the, thenne love me. Why slepist thu? Awake!
> Remember my tender hert-rote for the brake,
> With paynes my vaines constrayned to crake.
> This was I defasid,
> Thus was my flesh rasid,
> And I to deth chasid.
> Like a lambe led unto sacrefise,
> Slayne I was in most cruell wise. . . .

Not all of the complaints of Christ are delivered from the cross. Some imply the devotional image of Christ, as 'Man of Sorrows', the *imago pietatis*, which shows Christ standing, his body covered with wounds (sometimes he himself indicates the wound in his side).[84] It is essentially a devotional image, for it has no part in the traditional chronological pattern of the Passion; the evidence indicates that it was extremely popular in fifteenth-century

The Passion

England (cf. plates 2 and 3). A representation of it accompanies the poem 'O man unkynde' previously mentioned. It is this image which we are meant to visualize at the beginning of this fifteenth-century poem:

> Brother, abyde, I the desire and pray;
> Abyde, abyde and here thy brother speke.
> Beholde my body in this blody aray,
> Broysed and betyne wyth whippis that wold not breke....[85]

Christ then rehearses the events of his earthly life up to his death on the cross; he speaks as the timeless Man of Sorrows whose wounds are a perpetual reproach to mankind. The most successful of the extended laments of Christ is a poem with the refrain *quia amore langueo* which begins 'In the vaile of restles mynd'.[86] Here the poet, seeking for a 'true love', finds true love in the form of a man sitting beneath a tree. The opening is one of the most imaginative in the whole corpus of the lyrics:

> In the vaile of restles mynd
>   I sowght in mownteyn and in mede,
> Trustyng a treulofe for to fynd.
>   Upon an hyll than toke I hede,
>   A voise I herd (and nere I yede)
> In gret dolour complaynyng tho,
>   'See, dere soule, my sydes blede,
> *Quia amore langueo.*'
>
> Upon thys mownt I fand a tree,
>   Undir thys tree a man sittyng,
> From hede to fote wowndyd was he,
> Hys hert blode I saw bledyng –
>   A semely man to be a kyng,
>   A graciose face to loke unto.
> I askyd hym how he had paynyng.
> He said, '*Quia amore langueo.*'

The wounded Christ, sitting wounded and sorrowful (as in the visual arts he is represented as 'Christus im Elend'),[87] tells the story of his treatment by his unkind beloved; his lament uses many of the traditional themes and images which we have encountered, but in every case powerfully and creatively. The 'Reproaches' and the theme of the lover-knight are powerfully combined:

The Scheme of Redemption

>   I clothed hyr in grace and hevenly lyght,
>   This blody surcote she hath on me sett. . . .

and the potential ironies are fully developed:

>   Loke unto myn handys, man!
>   Thes gloves were geven me whan I hyr sowght;
>   They be nat white, but rede and wan,
>   Embrodred with blode (my spouse them bowght!)
>   They wyll not of – I lefe them nowght!
>   I wowe hyr with them where ever she goo.
>   These handes full frendly for hyr fowght,
>   *Quia amore langueo.*

His feet have been 'buckled' with sharp nails. The poet's bold imagination does not shrink from extreme images – Christ's wounded body is the 'bait' for his beloved's heart,[88] the wound of his side is a 'nest' for her, a 'chamber' where she may rest. He uses the traditional language of love-poetry: 'jantilnesse', 'dawngerouse', 'maistrye'. Like the courtly secular poets of his time he handles allegorical images boldly and confidently – 'Loke owt at the wyndows of kyndnesse', like the best religious poets he can give a simple line a visionary splendour – 'I sitt on an hille for to se farre/I loke to the vayle, my spouse I see'. He is not afraid to pile up ecstatic images – Christ is man's lover, husband, brother and even mother.[89] He seems to have assimilated not only the images of the Song of Songs but also something of its poetic technique.

>   My swete spouse, will we goo play?
>   Apples ben rype in my gardine;
>   I shall clothe the in new array,
>   Thy mete shall be mylk, honye, and wyne.
>   Now, dere soule, latt us go dyne;
>   Thy sustenaunce is in my skrypp – loo!
>   Tary not now, fayre spouse myne,
>   *Quia amore langueo.* . . .

>   My spouse is in hir chambre, hald yowr pease,
>   Make no noyse, but lat hyr slepe.
>   My babe shall sofre noo disease,
>   I may not here my dere childe wepe,
>   For with my pappe I shall hyr kepe.

The Passion

> No wondyr though I tend hyr to,
> Thys hoole in my syde had never ben so depe
> But *quia amore langueo*. . . .

It is rare to find a Middle English lyric which is so adventurous in its use of imagery, and even rarer to find one which is so successful. It is a remarkable example of how traditional matter can be moulded into something quite new by a genuine creative imagination.

8

Resurrection and Assumption

A small group of lyrics celebrate Christ's victory over death and his Resurrection. The dominant note of these is one of triumph.[1] They use a technique which is vigorous and emphatic rather than subtle – the simpler, most obviously expressive rhetorical figures, such as anaphora or exclamatio, bold images, a diction which is often full of liturgical echoes. One, from the fourteenth-century MS. Merton 248, is an energetic version of the first two stanzas of the Easter hymn *Aurora lucis rutilat*:

> An ernemorwe the daylight spryngeth,
> The angles in hevene murye syngeth,
> The world is blithe and ek glad,
> The vendus of helle beth sorwvel and mad,
>
> Whanne the kyng, Godus sone
> The strengthe of the deth hadde overcome,
> Helle dore he brak with his fot,
> And out of pyne us wreches he tok.[2]

The Latin lines have perhaps a slightly grander rhythm:

> Aurora lucis rutilat,
> Coelum laudibus intonat,
> Mundus exultans jubilat,
> Gemens infernus ululat
>
> Cum rex ille fortissimus,
> Mortis confractis viribus,
> Pede conculcans tartara
> Solvit catena miseros –

but the English translator has done quite a good job. He has successfully managed the sustained and emphatic syntax, in a way which many of his contemporaries would not have been able to, and by simple and unobtrusive changes he has contrived to make the lines at once more concrete and particular – 'angles in hevene' for *coelum*, the 'vendus of helle' for *infernus*, 'helle dore' for *tartara* – and a little more personal and emotive ('the kyng, Godus sone' or 'us wreches' for the more general *miseros*).

Sometimes the triumphant Christ will himself speak. In the same MS., among a number of striking verses on this theme, we find these lines:

> I come vram the wedlok as a suete spouse, thet habbe my wif with me innome;
> I come vram vight a staleworthe knyght, thet myne vo habbe overcome;
> I come vram the chepyng as a riche chapman, thet mankynde habbe ibought;
> I come vram an uncouthe londe as a sely pylegrym, thet ferr habbe isought.[3]

The idea of Christ's triumphant 'coming' can be forcefully expressed through the 'Quis est iste qui venit de Edom' of Isaiah, which we have already met in the version of William Herebert. The advantage of this passage was that its images powerfully combine the suggestions of the sufferings of the Passion with the consequent triumph of the Resurrection. They are expressed in a more literary and polished style by Lydgate:

> In Bosra steyned of purpil al my weede. . . .
> The vyne of Soreth railed in lengthe and brede,
> The tendre clustris rent down in ther rage,
> The ripe grapis ther licour did out shede. . . .[4]

Another dramatic poem in which Christ (apparently in the tomb) looks forward to his final 'triumph' on the Day of Doom sounds almost like a old Germanic *beot* or vaunt:

> I have laborede sore and suffered deyyth,
> And now I rest and draw my breyth;
> But I schall come and call ryght sone
> Hevene and erth and hell to dome;
> And thane schall know both devyll and mane,
> What I was and what I ame.[5]

The Scheme of Redemption

One Scots poet learnedly suggests the imagery of an antique triumph:

> The mychty, strange, victorius campyoun,
>   With hie imperiall laud hes done returne,
> With palme of glory and with lawre croune,
>   With his allweilding father to sojorne,
> Quhois palice hie schynes abone Saturn,
>   Off quhame etheriall sternes takis licht,
> Quhome hevin and erd dois honour and adurn,
>   Quhois glaid uprissing blithis every wycht.[6]

By far the best of these triumphal poems is Dunbar's 'On the Resurrection of Christ', a work full of poetic vigour and energy:

> Done is a batell on the dragon blak,
> Our campioun Chryst confountet hes force;
> The yettis of hell ar brokin with a crak,
> The signe triumphall rasit is of the croce,
> The divillis trymmillis with hiddous voce,
> The saulis ar borrowit and to the blis can go,
> Chryst with his blud our ransonis dois indoce:
> *Surrexit Dominus de sepulchro.*[7]

The poem is simply but clearly constructed, using simple paradoxes (the sacrificial lamb is 'lyk a lyone rissin up agane', etc) and blending learned reference with vivid imagery and sharp diction. The syntax and the breathless rhythm of the lines convey the excitement of the triumph:

> The fo is chasit, the battell is done ceis,
> The presone brokin, the jevellouris fleit and flemit;
> The weir is gon, confermit is the peis,
> The fetteris lowsit and the dungeoun temit,
> The ransoun maid, the presoneris redemit;
> The feild is win, ourcumin is the fo,
> Dispulit of the tresur that he yemit:
> *Surrexit Dominus de sepulchro.*

The triumph of the Virgin Mary in her Assumption and Coronation as Queen of Heaven is also celebrated by the poets.[8] The longer poems endeavour by rich verbal description to convey something of the splendour of the sight of the Virgin enthroned as Queen surrounded by throngs of adoring angels. So the thirteenth-century *On God Ureisun of Ure Lefdi:*

> Heih is thi kinestol onuppe cherubine,
> Bivoren thine leove sune withinnen seraphine.
> Murie dreameth engles bivoren thin onsene,
> Pleieth and sweieth and singeth bitweonen;
> Swuthe wel ham likieth bivoren the to beonne,
> Vor heo never ne beoth sead thi veir to iselnne. . . .[9]

Fifteenth-century poets often use splendid aureate diction, and images from the Song of Songs (used in the Office of the Assumption), but they can rarely match the achievements of the artists; too often the result is coldly learned or enthusiastically chaotic. Rather better than most is a lyric in which the poet sees a 'crowned queen' in a 'tabernacle of a tower', and hears her complaint:

> In a tabernacle of a toure,
>   As I stode musyng on the mone,
>   A crouned quene, most of honoure,
>   Apered in gostly syght ful sone.
>   She made compleynt thus by hyr one . . .[10]

and another in which Christ calls to his mother to come to be crowned (the refrain is taken from the Song of Songs):

> '*Surge mea sponsa*, so swete in syghte
>   And se thy sone in sete full shene!
> Thow shalte abyde with thy babe so bryghte
>   And in my glorye be, and be called a qwene. . . .
>
> Full swetely shalte thu sytte by me,
>   And were a crowne wyth me in towre;
>   . . . *Veni coronaberis.*'[11]

Like many of these poems it is marred by flat lines and heavy diction, but it makes a passable attempt at the imaginative fusion of the erotic imagery of the Song of Songs with recollections of the maternal tenderness of the relationship between the Virgin and her baby:

> *Vox tua* to me was full swete
>   Whene thu me badde, 'babe be stylle'. . . .
>
> *Favus distillans* that wente wyth wylle
>   Oute of thy lyppes whene we dede kysse. . . .

The Scheme of Redemption

Other poems are based on Latin hymns or antiphons in praise of the Queen of Heaven such as the *Gaude flore virginali*[12] or *Regina Caeli Laetare*.[13] Many poems are simply long lists of exclamatory statements of wonder and praise. To make these successful requires the sustained rhetorical skill and virtuosity of Dunbar, who in his 'Ane Ballat of our Lady'[14] displays the splendours of aureate diction (counterpointed in his usual manner with tough, plain Scots words) and dazzling rhythmical experimentation with theatrical panache:

> Hale sterne superne! Hale, in eterne,
>   In Godis sicht to schyne!
> Lucerne in derne for to discerne
>   Be glory and grace devyne;
> Hodiern, modern, sempitern,
>   Angelicall regyne!
> Our tern inferne for to dispern
>   Helpe rialest rosyne.
>   *Ave Maria, gracia plena!*
>   Haile, fresche floure femynyne!
> Yerne us, guberne, virgin martern,
>   Of reuth baith rute and ryne!

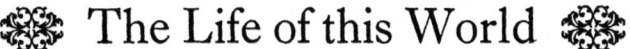

The Life of this World

The Christian Life

A fifteenth-century lyric gaily and optimistically directs the devout Christian to the good life:

> Now is wele and all thing aright
> And Crist is come as a trew knight,
> For our broder is king of might,
>   The fend to fleme and all his.
> Thus the feend is put to flight,
> And all his boost abated is.
>
> Sithen it is wele, wele we do,
> For there is none but one of two,
> Heven to gete or heven forgo;
>   Oder mene none there is.
> I counsaill you, sin it is so,
>   That ye wele do to win you bliss.
>
> Now is wele and all is wele,
>   And right wele, so have I bliss;
> And sithen all thing is so wele,
>   I rede we do no more amiss.[1]

A number of lyrics are expressly designed to assist in one way or another in the task of doing well, of living the Christian life. Many of these extremely practical verses are likely to be prized more by the student of medieval spirituality than by the reader interested in literature, but the latter may find even in the most unpromising places some pleasing (if possibly accidental) felicities. A large number are designed to move the reader to penitence, often by meditation on the prospect of death and the Last Things, but the general tone is by no means always grimly penitential. A poem which is similar in spirit to that which we have just quoted is this version (perhaps a little wordy) of the Latin hymn *Ales diei nuncius*:

> The gladsom byrd, the deys mesanger,
> Synggyng with musical armonye,
> Sayth in hys song the dey gynnyth to clere,
> And byddyth us adressone us and hye
> Toward the lyff, the lyf that schall not dye;
> Thys is the voyce ryght of the byrd of blys
> Syngynge tyll us that the dey cummyng is.
>
> Thys byddyth this heyvynly pursyvant,
> That we schuld all from slomoryng aryse,
> And that we schuld bene holly attendaunt
> To plesen Godd devotly with service;
> Ryghtwos and chast and eke in sobre wyse.
> The lyght of grace is drawyng tyll us nere
> Of our derknes the clowdes for to clere.[2]

There are a number of attractive short prayers in verse.[3] We have already encountered longer lyrics which were either cast in the form of a prayer or ended with a prayer, but these are characteristically very brief ejaculatory prayers which are probably meant for private devotional use. They are cast in the simplest verse forms.[4] Very often they are easily memorable devotional 'tags' or pious ejaculations,[5] just a little more sophisticated than those which the miller's wife in the *Reeve's Tale* uses in a famous comic crisis:

> 'Help, holy cros of Bromholme!' sche sayde,
> '*In manus tuas*, Lord, to the I calle'.

The 'in manus tuas' formula (taken from the words of Christ on the cross) are in fact the basis for verse prayers:

> Into thi handes, lorde, I take my soule,
>   Whom thou boughtist with thi bittur passion.
> Assoyle me, for Seynt Petur and Poule,
> And al thi seyntis supplicacioun;
>   And by the vertu of this confession,
>   Save me fro payne and fro the fende,
>   And bring me to blis that hath none ende.[6]

The Christian Life

As is traditional in Christian supplication these prayers usually recall to the Deity one or more of his acts of grace in the redemption of man; they frequently make reference to one of the objects of the popular devotional cults of the time – the Precious Blood, or the Five Wounds, or the Holy Cross. One rather unusual one is a prayer against 'dispeyre or mysbeleve', based on the verse *illumina oculos meos*:

> Jesu, lythe my sowle with thi grace,
> That y not dispeyre in ony cace.[7]

Often they are addressed to the Virgin Mary. The prayer of Godric (based on a Latin antiphon, and incorporating a nice devotional play on his own name):

> Sainte Marie virgine
> Moder Jesu Cristes Nazarene,
> Onfo, scild, help thin Godric,
> Onfang, bring eghtlech with the in Godes riche.[8]

is, centuries later, still being recommended to a hermit in times of weariness (in Richard Methley's *Epistle of Solitary Life*). Such prayers are sometimes used as *tituli*. In Broughton church, near Banbury, in a series of wall-paintings of the life of the Virgin, a kneeling figure addresses to her a simple prayer by the Five Joys:[9]

> levedy for thi joyyes fyve
> led me the wey of clene (? live) (The last word is now faded.)

A fragment of another, addressed to Christ, was carved on a bench end at Warkworth, not many miles away.[10] A nice variant is the prayer inscribed on a mazer:

> God and Seynt Martyn
> Blysse owre ale and blysse owre wyn.[11]

The verse prayers, whether short or long, are often designed for quite particular practical use.[12] We have, for instance, a prayer at the election of an abbot,[13] and a series of graces to be said before and after meals, which although they have no literary pretensions at all, are sometimes quite touching monuments to simple piety:[14]

> Crist that breed brak
> At the soper there he sat
> With his apostlis twelve,
> Blesse oure breed and oure ale,

> And that we have and heve schale,
> And fede us with him silf,
> And graunte us grace of gostili fode,
> Of breed of lijf that is so goode
> To fede with oure soulis. Amen.

Evening prayers and prayers to guardian angels are often expressions of this same simple, humble devotion. There is a story in the life of Christina of Markyate which describes how when she was a child she had heard that Christ was present everywhere, and therefore used to speak to him in her bed in a loud voice just as if she were speaking to someone she could see.[15] A verse prayer to the Virgin has something of this spirit (and like a number of these simple prayers it seems almost to be a pious charm):

> Upon my ryght syde y me leye,
> Blesid lady, to the y pray,
> For the teres that ye lete
> Upon your swete sonnys feete,
> Sende me grace for to slepe
> And good dremys for to mete,
> Slepyng, wakyng, til morwe daye bee.
> Owre lorde is the frwte, oure lady is the tree;
> Blessid be the blossome that sprange, lady of the!
> *In nomine patris et filii et spiritus sancti*
> Amen.[16]

The verse prayers addressed to various saints are hardly ever of much literary value, though some are not without interest. Ryman's verses to St Francis have some eloquence,[17] Godric's prayer to St Nicholas is agreeably simple.[18] One has some historical interest because of its connection with one of the great English generals of the late Middle Ages, Sir John Talbot (?1388–1453).[19] On a blank page of the splendid 'Talbot Hours', now in the Fitzwilliam Museum, a scribe has written these lines, presumably a prayer for his master's success in war and safe return to England:

> Jesu, whom ye serve dayly,
> Uppon your enemys gyff you victory;
> Off the holy crosse the vertu
> Your gode fortune alwey renew;

The Christian Life

> Oure Lady and Saynt Gabryell
> Geve you long lyffe and gode hele;
> And Saynt George, the gode kynght,
> Over your fomen geve you myght;
> And holy Saynt Kateryne
> To youre begynnyng send gode fyne;
> Saynt Christofre, botefull on see and lond,
> Joyfully make you see Englond!

Not all of the prayer was answered, for Talbot died in France on active service (his body was brought back and interred at Whitchurch, Shropshire). The saints which are invoked are all popular in medieval devotion. In Middle English there is a dull hymn to St Catherine,[20] and St George is also the subject of a carol and of the versified 'Hours' of St George.[21] More interestingly he appears in a charm against the night mare (the night goblin) who settles upon people or animals by night and 'rides' them. It must have proved efficacious, for it appears again in Scot's *The Discoverie of Witchecraft* (1584):

> For the nyghthe mare
> Take a flynt stone that hath an hole thorow of hys owen growyng, and hange it over the stabill dore, or ell over horse, and ell writhe this charme:
> In nomine patris etc.
>
>> Seynt Jorge, our lady knyghth,
>> He walked day, he walked nyghth,
>> Till that he fownde that fowle wyghth;
>> And whan that he here fownde,
>> He here bete and he here bownde,
>> Till trewly ther here trowthe sche plyghth
>> That sche sholde not come be nyghthe,
>> Withinne vii rode of londe space
>> Ther as Seynt Jorge inamyd was.
>
>> St. Ieorge. St. Ieorge. St. (Ieorge)
> In nomine patris &c.
> And wryte this in a bylle and hange it in the hors mane.[22]

St George was very much a national saint; Talbot's men charged with the cry 'Talbot, Talbot, St George!' and the saint was said to have appeared above the battlefield of Agincourt. No verse prayer in English to St Christopher appears to survive, though he too played an important role in popular devotion (Chaucer's Yeoman, it will be remembered wears 'a crystofre . . . of silver shene'). He is an extremely popular subject in wall-painting, no doubt encouraged by the belief that whoever looked upon his image would not that day die a 'bad death'. In one example in the charming village church of Horley, near Banbury, the huge figure of the saint carries the small Christ child across the river (filled with gay fish) and the traditional exchange between them (a naïve example of the 'humility-sublimity' paradox) is recorded in English *tituli*:

> What art thou that art so yynge?
> Bar I never so hevy a thinge.
>
> They I be hevy no wunder nys,
> For I am the kynge of blys.[23]

But we must leave the saints and their legends, for the quality of the verse prayers addressed to them is not at all commensurate with the interest of the subjects.

Since the liturgy was in Latin, it is not surprising that vernacular prayers and meditations (in prose and verse) were made for the private expression of the devotion of the unlearned during the service. The *Layfolks Mass-Book* is the best known collection of this sort of material.[24] For the humble audience the most sacred moment came with the Elevation of the consecrated Host, and a number of pious legends enforce the belief that at this moment Christ is 'really present'. One (which is frequently illustrated) is that St Gregory, while celebrating Mass, saw Christ as Man of Sorrows; another tells of a Jew who, waiting for a Christian outside a church, became tired and curious and went in at the moment of the Elevation – what he saw was not a Host but a 'feir child, iwoundet sore in fot, in hond'.[25] There seems to have been a belief that the act of looking on the Host had an almost sacramental value. So a poem on the 'Merits of the Mass' explains

> When thou his bode hast yseyne,
> Yif thou dey that ilke day,
> Thou schalt be found in the fay
> As thou houseld hadust bene.[26]

In Reformation times, there is a vigorous and unflattering description of the scene at this moment by Thomas Becon, Cranmer's chaplain, in his *Displaying of the Popishe Masse*:

The Christian Life

Before it was *Sursum Corda*, Lift up your hearts unto the Lord, but now it is *Sursum Capita*, come in, Lift up your heads and loke upon your maker betwene the priests hands. . . When the Bell once ryngs (if they cannot conveniently see) they forsake their seates and runne from altare to altare, from Sakering to Sakering, peeping here and touting ther, and gasing at that thing which the pildpate Priest holdeth up in hys handes. And if the Priest be weake in the armes, and heave not up hye ynough, the rude people of the countrey in diverse partes of England wyll crye out to the Priest, holde up Sir Johne, holde up. Heave it a littel hyer. Ane one will say another, Stoupe downe thou fellowe afore, that I may see my maker. For I can not be mery, except I see my Lorde God once in a day.[27]

A number of the verse-prayers are designed for use at the moment of the Elevation.[28] They suggest a setting rather more dignified than this tumultuous scene (though there is no doubt some truth in Becon's satire); they are simple private prayers of the type we have been discussing, often beginning with a formula of address 'Welcome' or 'Hail' – to the Host. A couple of versions of the *Layfolks Mass-Book* recommend this prayer:

> Welcome, lord, in fourme of brede,
> For me thu tholedest a pyneful dede;
> As thu suffredest the coroune of thorne,
> Graunt me grace, Lorde, I be nought lorne.[29]

Another example has a nice simple eloquence:

> O Jesu, lorde, wellcum thu be,
> In forme of brede as y the se;
> O Jesu, for thy Holy Name,
> Schelde me thys day fro sorro and schame,
> And lete me lyfe in trewth and ryght,
> Before my dethe hafe hosyll and schryfte;
> O Jesu, as thu were of a maiden borne,
> Let me never be forlorne;
> And let me never for no syne,
> Lese the blysse that thu art in.[30]

Among the private prayers are some which are ejaculatory expressions of that mystical love-longing which is characteristic of the 'school' of Rolle and which we have already encountered in the longer Christocentric devotional lyrics. Scattered among the prose works written by or attributed to Rolle are little verses like these:[31]

> I slepe and my hert wakes
> Wha sall tyll my lemman say:
> For hys lufe me langes ay?

> Jesu be thou my joy, al melody and swetnes
>   And lere me for to synge
>   The sange of thi lovynge.

> Loued be thou, keyng,
> And thanked be thou, keyng,
> And blyssed be thou, keyng!
> Jesu, all my joyng,
> Of all thi giftes gude,
> That for me spylt thi blude
> And died on the rode;
> Thou gyf me grace to syng
> The sang of thi lovyng!

The same spirit is found in a little tag in MS. Balliol 149:

> For love of Jesu, my swete herte,
>
> y morne and seke wyth teres smert.[32]

Sometimes the simple verse prayer can be expanded and elaborated considerably. One of the most popular of all the religious lyrics, if we may judge from what has survived in MSS., was a prayer by Richard de Caistre, the vicar of St Stephen's, Norwich. Of it and the earlier poem on which it is based twenty-four MS. copies are known.[33] It is a series of stanzas consisting of petitions of the sort we have been discussing, strung together (the order could be and was changed without causing disruption) into a simple devotional poem:

> Jesu, lorde, that madest me,
>   And with thi blessed blod me boght,
>   Foryeve that I have greved the
>   With word, will, werk or thought. . . .

A more ambitious verse prayer of the same general type is found in a MS. containing the Processional of the nuns of Chester. Its enthusiasm often becomes chaotic, for, instead of the simple petitions of Richard de Caistre, it follows the tradition of the *Jesu*

Dulcis Memoria, and strives for more ecstatic effects than the author's style can manage:

> O moste meeke Jesu and mercyfull kynge,
> Gyve me grace, Jesu, yf it be thy lykynge,
> Gladly to covett for thy love to dye,
> And to be gladd for thy love to suffre all envy.
> O mercifull Jesu to thy lovers all,
> O swete derlynge to the sowle that on the dothe call,
> O verey Godd, O verey man, that all thynge hathe wroght,
> Have mercy on me a synnar, thoue hathe me deere boght.
>   Amen.[34]

A small group of lyrics attempt to give expression to the paradoxes and mysteries of the faith. The best of these, 'A God and yet a man', has already been discussed. Similar to this in its insistence on faith rather than reason is a quatrain, which is sometimes attributed to Bishop Reginald Pecok when he was forced to recant in 1457 (for preferring his 'jugement and naturalle resoun before the Newe and the Olde Testament, and the auctoryte and determinacioun of oure moder hooly churche'):

> Witte hath wondir that resoun ne telle kan,
> How maidene is modir, and God is man.
> Leve thy resoun and bileve in the wondir,
> For feith is aboven and reson is under.[35]

The carols on the Eucharist like to use this paradoxical and riddling style:

> Mirabile misterium
> In forme of bred ys Godes son. . . .
>
> Thowgh yt seme whit, yt ys rede;
> Yt ys flesshe, yt semeth bred;
> Yt ys God in his manhed
>   As he hong upon a tre. . . .[36]

The ballad, *The Devil and the Maid* or *Riddles Wisely Expounded* (which first appears in a fifteenth-century MS.),[37] contains a set of similar riddling questions, some of which concern the faith:

> What ys hyer than ys (the) tre?
> What ys dypper than ys the see?. . . .
> What ys swifter than ys the wynd?
> What ys recher than ys the kynge?, etc.

to which the maid wisely gives the answers heaven, hell, thought, Jesus. Another extended paradoxical poem, with the fideistic refrain *Hoc factum est a Domino* even uses contemporary events:[38]

> How gat oure kyng the victory
> At Agyncourt with a smal puissance?
> Who made Prynce Phelyp to flee
> From Calice, with anger and myschaunce?
> Who wrought this worthy purviaunce
> The Scottis from Rokisburgh to go?. . . .

This poem has so many questions crammed into it that it often gives an impression of bewilderment:

> Whi are nat al sterris mevand like,
> For som ben fixed and sette in hevene?
> Som man wise and som man frantike,
> Som blynd born, som halt, som even?
> In erthely thynges planetis seven
> Hath influence; sith it is so,
> Man, of these dowtis the nedis nat mevyn,
> *Hoc factum est a Domino.*

> Why wil Fortune that som man is riche,
> And som man right pore? and whi is pestilence?
> Whi hath nat every man iliche?
> Whi is corne brent by grete violence?
> Whi were these two citees thurgh the peples offence,
> Sodom and Gomor, distroyed both two?
> Man, in this matier to yive a general sentence,
> *Hoc factum est a Domino.*

The poet finds so many questions in Holy Writ and in the world about him that it is hard to believe that he should have been satisfied with his reassuring *Hoc factum est a Domino.*

Occasionally there is an attempt to express one of the mysteries in a more imaginative and oblique way. In one *chanson d'aventure* (sometimes chaotic and obscure)[39] the poet sees a bird 'bryghte of ble' with wings 'of colowrs ryche' which seems like an angel. The bird tells him that she was 'wonte . . . to be in cage' and to play with her fellows. The poet promises to make her a new cage, and we are given a long description of the sort of cage it is to be:

> The flore schold be of argentum,
> Clene sylver alle and sume,
>   That trewe love myghte behold. . . .
> The towres shal be of every,
> Clene corvene by and by,
>   The dore of whallus bone. . . .

The heavenly nature of the 'cage' soon becomes apparent:

> Fyve whelys therein schal be,
> In the medylle schal be the Trinite,
>   That pere has none,
> And the forwte thereabowte,
> To Jesu Criste for to lowte,
>   Marke, Mathew, Luke and Johne.

The 'popejay, your lady fre' will be there, with the 'throstelcoke Gabrielle'

> The wyche gret owre lady welle,
>   With ane *Gracia plene*.

And the poem concludes:

> Thys cage is made withowtyne weme
> For the love of one woman,
>   Mary that is so fre;
> The mane that better cage make canne,
> Take thys byrd to his lemane,
>   That is the Trinite. . . .

In one of the carols, 'And by a chapell as y came' the poet comes upon the striking scene of a Eucharist, with Christ as the celebrant.[40] It probably is, as Professor Greene says, 'true folksong' and quite unlearned; it vividly combines homeliness and mystery:

> And by a chapell as y came,
> Mett y wyhte Jesu to chyrcheward gone,
> Petur and Pawle, Thomas and John,
>   And hys desyplys everychone.
>
> Sente Thomas the bellys gane ryng,
> And Sent Collas the mas gane syng;
> Sent John toke that swete offeryng,
>   And by a chapell as y came.

The Life of this World

> Owre Lorde offeryd whate he wollde,
> A challes off ryche rede gollde,
> Owre Lady the crowne off hyr mowllde—
>   The son owte off hyr bosom schone. . . .

Something like this scene is briefly evoked in the 'Friday spell', from a sixteenth-century MS.:[41]

> This daye is Fridaye
> Faste while we maye
> While wee heare knyll
> Our Lords owne bell
> Our Lorde in his Chappell stoode,
> With his xii appostells soe good
> There came a saynte
> Throughe ryghte robe
> What is yt that shynes soe bryght?
> Our Lorde God alymyghte.
> He was naled sore, farre and in goore
> Throughe lyver, throughe longe,
> Throughe harte, throughe tonge,
> Throughe the holy brayne panne –
> Well is that man tha Fryday spell can.
> He for to saye and his fellowes forto learne
> So manye tymes as youe saye this on Frydaye before noone
> So manye tymes shall your synnes be forgeven youe att
>   Domesdaye. Amen.

Here, too we should perhaps consider what is perhaps the most mysterious and haunting of our lyrics:

> Lully, lulley; lully, lulley;
> The fawcon hath born my mak away.
>
> He bare hym up, he bare hym down;
> He bare hym into an orchard brown.
>
> In that orchard ther was an hall,
> That was hangid with purpill and pall.
>
> And in that hall ther was a bede;
> Hit was hangid with gold so rede.
>
> And yn that bed ther lythe a kynght,
> His wowndes bledyng day and nyght.

By that beddes side ther kneleth a may,
And she wepeth both nyght and day.

And by that beddes side ther stondith a ston,
Corpus Christi wretyn theron.

This is the oldest recorded version of the 'Corpus Christi Carol', in Richard Hill's commonplace book. Three other traditional versions (sometimes called 'The Wells of Paradise' have been found in later printed sources (though their real age is, of course, uncertain).[42] These do not have the 'lullay' opening and differ in a number of details (one has a hound licking the blood, two have a reference to the thorn of Glastonbury, one has a 'flood' under the bed, one half water, one half blood, etc.). All versions have been the subject of intense argument and discussion.[43] In general, the interpretations usually accepted have seen in the poem symbolism suggesting Christ as the wounded knight, the Eucharist, or the legends of the Holy Grail (these are of course by no means mutually exclusive). Recently however, Professor R. L. Greene has proposed a radically different interpretation[44] that the 'Hill' version 'is a song, quite possibly adapted from a song already current in oral tradition (whether or not Eucharistic and related to the Grail legend) which refers specifically to the displacement of Queen Catherine of Aragon by Anne Boleyn in the affections of King Henry VIII'. Crudely summarized, his argument is that Richard Hill's sympathies with the old religion are evident, that the falcon was the well-known heraldic badge of Anne, so that 'to an English reader of 1533 "The fawcon hath born my mak away" would immediately suggest the winning away of the King by Anne Boleyn', and that the image of the weeping and kneeling 'may' recalls Harpsfield's account of the grief of Catherine, who retired to a chamber with a prospect into the chapel, and knelt and wept upon the stones (the 'hall' could be Buckden Palace), or one of her other abodes). I hesitate to disagree with a scholar of Professor Greene's authority, but I must say that I do not find this explanation convincing. The details are not so precise that coincidence cannot be ruled out. An interpretation of this sort needs to be applicable to more than two or three images in the poem. As it stands, the link which is present in the Hill version between the burden and the first stanza is awkward – why should the king carried off by Anne be brought into the orchard of Buckden, etc. to see the weeping queen? The Hill version surely reads more easily if we do not equate the speaker of the poem with the 'may' of stanza 5. Again, the dominant central image of the wounded knight does not seem to have much to do with the royal separation. Professor Greene has to adapt one of the traditional views that he 'stands for' Christ, by suggesting that his wounds are opened afresh by Henry's blasphemy in attacking the Church, but one suspects that had this been the intention it might well have been made a little more explicit. Furthermore, two of the traditional versions are quite unequivocally religious poems.

The poem's power comes, it seems to me, very largely from the enigmatic and suggestive nature of the central scene. It seems to belong rather to the tradition of folk-poetry than to the learned tradition. It may be that some of its mystery comes from the juxtaposition of details which once had a more explicit significance, but to expect a simple 'explanation' which neatly accounts for all the detail seems misguided and likely to impoverish the poem. As it stands in the Hill version it is a lullaby. The speaker (whether a bird, an animal or a human) laments the loss of her 'mak', who has been carried off by the falcon (as some visitors to the Otherworld are carried by birds)[45] to the orchard brown. The mysterious scene in the hall certainly suggests romance. In Marie de France's *Gugemar*,[46] for instance, we have a wounded knight in a rich bed in a rich pavilion on a ship, who is visited by a lady, who takes him to her chamber to tend his wound. It may be that the wounded knight of our poem suggests the wounded keeper of the Grail, though the plural 'woundes' suggests to me rather the many wounds of the Christ-Knight than the wounded groin of the Grail King. The splendour of the hall and the richness of the bed (and the presence of the maiden) are certainly reminiscent of some Grail legends (and so is the thorn of two traditional versions). But it seems that the image most strongly suggested is that of Christ the Lover-Knight, whose armour has been 'unlaced', and whose wounds are a sign of his eternal sacrifice. Some Eucharistic symbolism seems very likely. It has been suggested that the hangings of purple and pall may suggest the hangings of the church and the draped altar.[47] The strange stone with its inscription (which seems to have been 'rationalized' in the traditional versions) is less likely to have been a sort of 'signpost' with explanatory *titulus*, than an altar-stone, or super-altar, on which was consecrated the Lord's body, an *anamnesis* of his perpetual sacrifice. It would then be a more sophisticated, more elusive symbolic expression of the idea put in simple form in 'By a chapell as y came', where Christ offers a chalice. Such altar-stones are in fact recorded,[48] sometimes of jasper or porphyry (the colour of blood), and sometimes inscribed (with a figure of the nimbed lamb and chalice, etc., or with words, e.g. 'Alme Trinitati, agie sopie, sanctae Mariae'). If so, it is a powerful symbol, for it suggests the traditional image of Christ himself as the 'cornerstone'.[49] One English medieval altar-stone, the famous 'sapphire of Glastonbury' (supposed to be the altar slab which St David (in legend, the uncle of King Arthur) had received on a pilgrimage to the Holy Land), suggests a link with the symbolism of the Grail, and it has been very convincingly argued by Dr A. A. Barb that the origin of the Grail is to be found in these stones and in the long tradition of the *mensa sacra* behind them. In Wolfram von Eschenbach's great romance *Parzifal* the Grail itself is a stone. Is it possible that, for all the distance in space and time, we have the same tradition here in Tudor England?[50] Finally, therefore, I would argue that we should read the 'Corpus Christi Carol' along the 'traditional' lines, that its central 'scene' is one which, in a way, can be compared to the Eucharistic visions already mentioned, like the Mass of St Gregory, and in another to such depictions of the eternal sacrifice as the Van Eyck altarpiece of the Mystic Lamb, but that its vision is quite unique and distinctive in its powerful fusion of images of splendour, suffering and eternal sorrow.

Much more humdrum, and much more numerous are the lyrics which concern themselves with the rules and the problems of everyday Christian living. There is a large mass of quite practical instructional verse – paraphrases of the creed, the Ten Commandments, the Beatitudes, etc. – of no literary pretension or quality. Rather more interesting are the general 'moral' poems, although here too it is not hard to find examples of the heaviest and clumsiest didactic verse. Sometimes the sermon-tags have a proverbial force – cf. (from the *Fasciculus Morum*):

> The fende oure foo may not us dere
> Bot we boghen to hym for fere:
> He ys a lyon but thou withstonde
> Not worth a flye yf thou ne wonde.[51]

or, from Grimestone:

> Yungthe ne can nouth but leden me wil,
> Ne elde ne wil nouth techen me skil,
> But sumtime yingthe beginnet a play
> That elde ne can nouth putten away;

The Life of this World

> Therfore as sone as men ben of age
> Wil is a meister and skil but a page.⁵²

General moral reflections of this type are often the basis of more extended poems. Since very few of these achieve anything like genuine literary success, and since, moreover, they are as a group on the periphery of what can reasonably be called the 'religious' lyric, there is no need to attempt a full survey here. Some of the more interesting examples are to be found in a series of refrain poems in the enormous Vernon MS. in the Bodleian Library⁵³ and its sister, the 'Simeon' MS., in the British Museum. These often contain vivid phrases ('sclaundre stynketh in Godes syght', 'our bagge hongeth on a sliper pyn', etc.) or images, and manage their recurring refrains ('each man ought himself to know', 'ever fond (try) to say the best' etc.) with some force, but too often they are prosy and weakly discursive. The moral weight of the poems is hardly equal to the weight of the MSS. which contain them (which must have strained the hearts of many readers since 1400). Of the others, some are treatments of that favourite theme of medieval poets – Fortune. One verse tag succinctly admonishes us:

> The levedi fortune is bothe frend and fo,
> Of pore che makit riche, of riche pore also,
> Che turnez wo al into wele, and wele al onto wo,
> Ne triste no man to this wele, the whel it turnet so.⁵⁴

One or two verses like this may well have been intended to accompany illustrations of the Lady Fortune and her wheel. One poem in fact 'Alle wandreths, welthis in lykingis', consisting of just over one hundred (undistinguished) lines on Fortune's wheel, has in its MS. a space left blank obviously for the picture to be added.⁵⁵ Some other lines in MS. Harley 7322 could well serve as *tituli* for the figures who in some illustrations of the wheel are shown rising, sitting in splendour, and falling:

> 'Kinge I sitte, and loke aboute,
> To morwen y mai beon withoute.'
> 'Wo is me, a kinge ich was;
> This world, ich lovede bote that, ilas!
> Nouth longe gon I was ful riche,
> Now is riche and poure iliche.'
> 'Ich shal beo kinge, that men shulle seo,
> When thou, wreche, ded shalt beo.'⁵⁶

The Christian Life

Occasionally, the poems on this theme are rather homely, proverbial counterparts of the reflective, philosophical short poems, of which the courtly poets from the time of Chaucer are fond. Such is the balade (sometimes ascribed (without much evidence) to 'Squire Halsham') on lack of steadfastness. Both stanzas of it seem to have an independent existence and appear in various combinations. They are smooth, rather uninspired verses, which come alive with the final image from falconry (a 'lune' is a leash for the hawk):

> The worlde so wide, th'aire so remuable,
> The sely man so litel of stature,
> The grove and grounde and clothinge so mutable,
> The fire so hoote and subtil of nature,
> The water never in oon – what creature
> That made is of these foure, thus flyttyng,
> May stedfast be as here in his lyving?
>
> The more I goo the ferther I am behinde,
> The ferther behinde the ner my wayes ende,
> The more I seche the worse kan I fynde,
> The lighter leve the lother for to wende,
> The bet y serve the more al out of mynde.
> Is thys fortune, not I, or infortune?
> Though I go lowse, tyed am I with a lune.[57]

This sort of poem did not lose its popularity after the Middle Ages. One of the fifteenth-century moral poems, 'Sen trew vertew encressis dignytee' appears in the Protestant *Gude and Godly Ballatis* of 1578.[58] Another fifteenth-century poem complaining of the uncertainties and disadvantages of 'court's estate'[59] is part of the background against which we should see Wyatt's fine 'Stond whoso list upon the sliper top' (which is directly adapted from Seneca). Another interesting link may possibly be seen in these lines on *tuta paupertas* (in a fifteenth-century MS.):

> Hiegh towers by strong wyndes full lowe be cast
> When the lowe cotages stand sure and fast;
> Therfor with surenes yt is better in povertie t'abide
> Then hastily to be riche and sodaynly to slyde.[60]

The third and fourth lines are popular proverbial lines which appear separately, and in various longer poems. The first couplet, however, is interestingly reminiscent of a sententious chorus in

The Life of this World

Seneca's *Hippolytus* (ll. 1123 ff.), which develops the idea that the humble are less exposed to the wrath of the gods than the great:

> Minor in parvis Fortuna furit,
> Leviusque ferit leviora deus.
> Servat placidos obscura quies,
> Praebetque senes casa securos. . . .
> . . . non capit unquam
> Magnos motus humilis tecti
> Plebeia domus:
> Circa regna tonat . . .

which is adapted by Wyatt (in a poem written in the 'blodye dayes' of 1536, when Anne Boleyn was executed and he was imprisoned):

> Who lyst his welthe and eas retayne,
> Hym selffe let hym unknowne contayne;
>   Presse not to fast in at that gatte
> Wher the retorne standes by desdayne:
>   For sure, *circa regna tonat*.
>
> The hye montaynis ar blastyd oft,
> When the lowe vaylye ys myld and soft;
>   Fortune with helthe stondis at debate;
> The fall ys grevous frome aloffte:
>   And sure, *circa regna tonat*. . . .[61]

and alluded to by Herrick in a poem to Thomas Falconbridge:

> Lastly, be mindfull (when thou art grown great)
> That Towrs high rear'd most the lightnings threat:
> When as the humble Cottages not feare
> The cleaving Bolt of Jove the Thunderer.

General moral and reflective poems of this kind often shade easily into laments for the wickedness of the world. One poet overhears a semi-pastoral lament over the absence of true friends:

> As I me lend to a lend
> I herd a schepperde makyn a schowte
> He gronyd and seyde with sory syghyng,
> 'A, lord, how gos this word abowte. . . .'[62]

There is always a temptation simply to list the evils which beset the world, often in a very long-winded way; it is only rarely that a succinct force is achieved:

The Christian Life

> Love is out of lond iwent;
> Defaute of love this lond hath shent;
> Reuththe and treuththe and charite
> Beth out of lond alle threo:
> Prude, envye and lecherie,
> Covetise and tricherie,
> Habbeth this lond one here baillye.[63]

This type of poem inevitably becomes more interesting when it becomes a satirical attack on some particular abuse – fashions, or the wickedness of friars,[64] etc. One entertaining little poem describes how the devil Tutivillus[65] records the names of those who chatter in church. In wall-paintings and misericords he is writing down the names of the chatterers or of those who mumble their devotions, and in the Towneley Doom play he appears as a very lively character.[66]

The ancient Christian tradition of penitential literature received a fresh impetus in the later Middle Ages when the Lateran Council of 1215 required of the faithful private confession at least once a year. The need for confessional literature in the vernacular (which, as has been pointed out, probably produced the typical handbooks or manuals for confessors of this period)[67] may be partly responsible for the large numbers of penitential lyrics. These vary enormously, not only in quality, but also in form. Very often, as usual, it is the least elaborate and least pretentious verses which are most successful. A tag in Grimestone's book is in the form of a simple prayer:

> Lord Jesu, thin ore!
> I sorwe and sike sore,
>   That bringet me to grunde.
> I have senned sore,
> With sennes lesse and more;
>   Allas! Allas! the stounde.[68]

Another, from a New College MS., more successful than most because it leaves so much unsaid, is based on a piece of St Augustine's *Confessions*:

> Louerd, thu clepedest me,
> An ich nagt ne ansuarede the
> Bute wordes scloe and sclepie:

The Life of this World

'Thole yet! Thole a litel!'
Bute 'yiet' and 'yiet' was endelis,
And 'thole a litel' a long wey is.⁶⁹

Another adapts the prayer of the prodigal son.⁷⁰ Others imply a dramatic situation – laments of doomed sinners, or an exchange between the Heart and the Eye (accused by the Heart of having destroyed 'us thoru thi fol loking'). In the *Speculum Christiani* the Seven Deadly Sins are each given a little quatrain. Others, both short and long, make use of exemplary figures – the penitent usurer, or the wicked cleric Odo (or Udo) who would not repent and was carried off by demons.⁷¹ One of the Vernon poems uses the earthquake of 1382 as a penitential warning:

> Chaumbres, chimeneys al tobarst,
>   Chirches and castels foule gon fare,
> Pinacles, steples to grounde hit cast;
>   And al was warnyng to be ware.⁷²

The more elaborate penitential lyrics rarely maintain a high standard throughout, though sometimes the *chanson d'aventure* opening is used to give the poem an interesting framework. In one, the poet, walking 'by a forest syde', comes upon a bird with its feathers pulled; it laments the loss of its four feathers (youth, beauty, strength, riches) and its refrain is *Parce mihi domine* (echoing the lament of Job 7:16, *Parce mihi, nihil enim sunt dies mei*).⁷³ In another, the poet is pursuing a pheasant with his hawk and hounds when he catches his leg on a briar, on each leaf of which is written the word *revertere*, turn again.⁷⁴ But the sententious core of such poems is usually crudely didactic (the best version of the *revertere* poem, from a literary point of view, is the shortest, that of four stanzas in Richard Hill's collection). The reader usually has to be content with isolated lines or images, or brilliant openings:

> Nou skrynketh rose and lylie flour
> That whilen ber that suete savour
>   In somer that suete tyde;
> Ne is no quene so stark ne stour,
> Ne no levedy so bryht in bour
>   That ded ne shal byglyde. . . .⁷⁵

of which the effect is slowly dissipated through the lines that follow. The thirteenth-century poem which is called by Carleton Brown 'A Prisoner's Prayer', a macaronic piece in English and

The Christian Life

French, accompanied by musical notes, combines simplicity of expression with formal artifice, but it is again uneven.[76] The best writing in this manner in Middle English (there is a very fine pentitential poem 'Quant fu en ma juvente' in Anglo-Norman)[77] is probably to be found in confessional passages in longer poems by Hoccleve and Lydgate.

A theme which is found in a number of penitential lyrics is the passing of the ages of man's life and the coming of old age. Old age is generally a grim and penitential *Memento Mori*. One poem (in MS. Digby 86 turns the first elegy of Maximianus (a friend of Boethius) into a penitential lament by an old man.[78] The verse is undistinguished, but occasionally something of the force of the original comes through – in 'Maximian's' desire for death:

> Ich wolde ich were on rest,
> Wel lowe leiid in a chest;
> My blisse is al forlore.
> Mi murthe wes monne mest,
> That ilke wile that hit ilest,
> And nou me is wo therfore.
> Ne gladiet me no geest,
> Ne joie of more feest.
> Wat solde ich ibore?
> This world me thinketh west,
> Deth ich wilni mest,
> Wi nis he me icore?

and in the defiant, and hardly penitential ending, addressed to a wife who is weary of him and abuses him:

> Iich may seien alas
> That ich iboren was;
> Ilived ich have to longe.
> Were ich mon so ich was,
> Min eien so grei so glas,
> Min her so feir bihonge,
> And ich hire hevede bi the trasce
> In a derne place,
> To meken and to monge:
> Ne sholde hoe nevere atwiten
> Min elde, ne me bifliten,
> Wel heye I shulde hire honge.

The Life of this World

The old men who make laments and complaints in this type of poetry are never as powerfully presented as the figure in the *Pardoner's Tale*, but what they say usually has some dramatic force. One old man, overheard by the poet 'undure an hold uppone an hylle', compares the stages of his life to the passing hours of the day. His complaint is full of vivid lines and images of his life:[79]

> Witt gronttyng and weppyng was I bore. . . .
>
> At myde-morroo-daye I lernnyd to goo,
> And play as chyldorne done in strete;
> As chyldwood me thoght and taught I dyde thoo,
> Witt my fellous to fyght and beyt. . . .
>
> At under-day to scole I was isete,
> To lerne good as chyldern dothe,
> But when my master woold me bete,
> I wold hym cowrs and wax folle rowthe. . . .
>
> Now age is croppyn on me ful styll,
> He makyt me hore, blake and bowe;
> I goo all dounward witt the hylle. . . .
>
> Now ys this day commyn to the nyght;
> I hawe lost my lewyng;
> A dredfull payne ys for me dyght,
> In cold claye therein to clynge. . . .

His sombre refrain is 'this word (world) ys but a wannyte'. An illustrated poem in MS. Additional 37049 presents a panoramic view of the Ages of Man, an interesting example of the popular devotional tradition which is behind the well-known speech of Shakespeare's Jaques.[80] At the top left-hand corner we see the soul, and beneath it the child in which it dwells, with the good angel on his right and the wicked on his left. Each 'age' of his life speaks. The verses, like the drawings, are crude but not without vigour:

> the crepil: Now must y beddes byd thof my bones ake
> I drede that ded persewes me fast.
> Angel: Goode prayers sal thi paynes slake
> And safe thi saule so at the last.

Finally we see the soul carried from the dying man by the good angel while the fiend laments his failure:

> Here the saule is gone fro me, allas!
> Al my labour is turned in vayne. . . .

10

Death and the Last Things

Lyrics on death are numerous, and sometimes very powerful. Medieval devotional poetry often presents the image of death dramatically, sometimes crudely and stridently. But though death is an important theme in devotional poetry it is not its only subject, nor is it quite as dominant in late medieval culture as has sometimes been claimed. It is easy to oversimplify medieval attitudes towards death: the men of the Middle Ages did not spend all their waking moments thinking upon their end; nor were they always surrounded by shrouds and grinning skeletons.

A number of the images and ideas in devotional poetry are found in ancient literature. This is hardly surprising, since it is obvious that death is a subject which is not without interest for the non-Christian poet as well as for the Christian. Indeed it is remarkable that some medieval 'religious' poems on death seem only nominally connected with Christianity. Commonplaces such as 'death is the end', 'life is but a journey towards death' can be found in classical authors.[1] Horace has a memorable expression of the idea that death comes to all irrespective of degree:

> Pallida mors aequo pulsat pede pauperum tabernas
> Regumque turres.

Even the skeleton with its *memento mori* 'Such as I am such shall we all be' can be found.[2]

But the main tradition which lies behind the lyrics on death is a Christian ascetic and moral one, presented with the characteristic fervour of late medieval spirituality. Most of its themes can be traced back to Biblical, and especially Old Testament sources. Phrases and images from passages on the transience of life such as those in the Psalms, which were mentioned in the Introduction, are echoed again and again in devotional poetry. The great commonplaces of mutability and of the contempt of the world – *media vita in morte sumus* 'in the midst of life we are in death' – are expressed in vivid and memorable images. As the world passes and declines, so do men:

> velut in somniis regnant,
> una hora laetantur,
> sed aeterna tormenta
> adhuc illis parantur. . . .
> pulchritudo hominum
> senescens delabitur
> omnis decor pristinus
> cum dolore raditur.*³

A popular hymn from the thirteenth century, the *Cur Mundus Militat*⁴ (translated into English several times from the Middle Ages to the seventeenth century) warns us of the fragility and untrustworthiness of the world:

> Plus fides litteris scriptis in glacie
> Quam mundi fragilis vanae fallaciae. . . .
>
> Quam breve festum est haec mundi gloria!
> Ut umbra hominis sic eius gaudia. . . .

and addresses that most fragile creature man in grimly ascetic words:

> O esca vermium! O massa pulveris!
> O ros, O vanitas, cur sic extolleris!†

—words which can be found in many homilies and poems.⁵ Vivid, though traditional, images, and proverbial phrases are favoured by the poets and homilists when they treat this theme. Death is a thief, who comes secretly and suddenly.⁶ In one poem death fights with man, pricks and pokes until he unbars all the

---

* They reign as if in dreams; they make merry for one hour but eternal torments are even now being prepared for them.
Men's beauty falls away with age; all their former elegance is stripped off with misery.

† Trust rather to letters written on ice than to the vain deceits of this frail world. . . . How brief a banquet is the glory of this world; its joys are as a man's shadow. . . . O food of worms, O heap of dust, O dew, O emptiness, why wilt thou be glorified thus?

The Life of this World

locks beneath which life lies, leaps out of a leash at him, and beats upon his door.[7] 'Death is hid, man,' says another poet, 'in thy glove.'[8] Man's life passes like a fire of heath or like a 'glentand glem'.[9] There are ironic images of the narrowness of man's last house, the grave – 'the roof will lie upon your nose', or, in another poem:

> quhen thow art ded and laid in layme,
>   and thi ribbis ar thi ruf tre
> Thow art than brocht to thi lang hayme
>   Adew al warldis dignite![10]

It is rare, though not unknown, to find an image which like Herbert's

> Death is still working like a mole,
> And digs my grave at each remove,[11]

is quite startling in its effect. At Gamlingay someone has written a Latin graffito: *Mors comparatur umbre que semper sequitur corpus*, 'Death is like a shadow which always follows the body'.[12] A similar image is finely used by Dunbar:

> My deathe chasis my lyfe so besalie
> That wery is my goist to fle so fast.[13]

One of the Vernon poems, with the refrain 'Think on yesterday'[14] adapts the traditional images very boldly. The author happily uses the homely, semi-proverbial style which is common in this group (the biggest fool is wiser while he lives than he who had a thousand pounds and was buried yesterday), and gives the traditional matter an individual expression – look at the lame, the bedridden and the blind, he says; they are a mirror to your mind to see the shape of yesterday. He finds a remarkably powerful homely image for the transience of life:

> I have wist, sin I cuthe meen,
>   That children hath bi candel liht
> Heor schadewe on the wal isen,
>   And ronne therafter al the niht;
> Bisy aboute thei han ben
>   To cacchen hit with al heore miht. . . .

and in his final stanza he boldly reverses the traditional image of death as a thief:

Death and the Last Things

Sum men seith that deth is a thef,
And al unwarned wol on him stele,
And I sey nay, and make a pref,
That deth is studefast, trewe and lele,
And warneth uche man of his greef,
That he wol o day with him dele. . . .

Plate 7 shows another curious image of the uncertainty of the life of man in an illustrated, emblematic poem in MS. Additional 37049 (the quality of the verses, alas, is banal). It comes from the legend of Barlaam and Josaphat, apparently originally a Buddhist set of apologues *de contemptu mundi*, which were taken over into Christian literature and were widely diffused in Western Europe.[15] Man, pursued by the unicorn, Death, stands in a tree. He can see four serpents (the Four Elements) emerging from beneath the roots, and the base of the tree is being gnawed at by a white mouse (Day) and a black mouse (Night). Beneath is a gaping dragon (the mouth of Hell). Yet in spite of all these perils he has set his eyes upon 'hony drope' (the world's wealth and vanity) on one of the branches.

The grim insistence on the fact of mortality and the rottenness of man, the 'food of worms', which can be found in earlier ascetic writing (there are some lurid examples, for instance, in Old English homilies) is intensified in the later Middle Ages. A visual expression of it which immediately springs to mind are the tombs of the fifteenth century with two tiers, the upper bearing the effigy of the deceased, the lower a decomposed cadaver in its shroud (cf. the drawing in plate 8).[16] Famous examples of such tombs in England are those of Bishop Flemyng (d. 1431) in Lincoln, Archbishop Chichele (d. 1443) in Canterbury, Bishop Bekynton (d. 1451) in Wells, and of Alice, Duchess of Suffolk, at Ewelme. In Burford parish church there is an interesting late example of this type in the tomb of Sir Lawrence Tanfield, who died in 1625.

The deep sense of mortality which pervades this type of literature and art can certainly become an extreme preoccupation with decay and death. But it is questionable whether we should go as far as the great historian Huizinga, who says of his 'waning Middle Ages' that 'no other epoch has laid so much stress . . . on the thought of death'.[17] The letters, journals and much of the literature of the fourteenth and fifteenth centuries hardly give such a clear impression. It is important to remember that religious literature was not the only literature produced in this period, that within religious literature, the ascetic tradition was not the only one, and, indeed, that although the extremes and exaggerations of the ascetic writers are real enough (amounting sometimes to an almost dualistic opposition of spirit and flesh), even these can be exaggerated further by selection and quotation out of context. To revert for a moment to the 'transi' tombs, which we have just suggested as an example of the intensified image of death in the late Middle Ages, it ought to be pointed out that the decomposing corpse is only half of the total visual ensemble and that the effigies of the dead persons are often portrayed with a fineness and sad beauty which seem to defy the ravages of death. What we have in the extreme ascetic insistence on the fact of decay, the 'macabre' imagination, is in fact an exaggeration of one aspect of the Christian tradition. It was not always easy to maintain a balance between two claims – on the one hand, an emphasis on the transience and contingency of human life, which could be expressed in an otherworldly and admonitory way, and which stressed that death was a grim reminder to us all, could lead to an obsession with death (so that the Emperor Julian the Apostate could criticize the Christians for having filled everything with graves and corpses),[18] and, on the other, an insistence that the possibility of immortal life had removed the sting from death, which became a gentle and peaceful door to a better life.[19] It perhaps should also be pointed out that the 'macabre' imagination did not cease with the fifteenth century. Worms, graves, bones, and winding-sheets are by no means unknown in the poetry of the sixteenth and seventeenth centuries. Death's heads in rings will also be familiar to readers of Elizabethan drama – Falstaff, who can use this sort of imagery lightly, bids the prince 'Do not speak like a death's head; do not bid me remember mine end', and he wittily uses the image at the expense of Bardolph's face (alluding incidentally to another medieval exemplum): 'I make as good use of it as many a man doth of a death's head or a memento mori. I never see thy face but I think upon hell-fire, and Dives that lived in purple; for there he is in his robes, burning, burning. . . .' And skeletons and other grim funerary images can be found without difficulty in the sixteenth and seventeenth centuries (and even later, in more popular tradition).[20]

However, with all these limitations, it is possible to speak of an intensification of the way in which the image of death was presented. Not only do skeletons and images of mortality become more frequent in the visual arts, but some new forms of 'mortality' literature – notably the Dance of Death – seem to be developed in this period. One wonders if there was something like the 'saturation of the religious atmosphere' which Huizinga discusses and if homilists and moralists were, or felt, forced to find novel, even melodramatic, ways of arousing penitence and emotion. Possibly this reflected to some extent changing social conditions: violence and war (no new things in themselves) and schism were sometimes seen in an apocalyptic way as signs of the imminence of the end of the world.

It is easy for us to forget that death and decay were public affairs in the Middle Ages, and not tucked discreetly away behind the doors of hospitals. It therefore seems likely that the plagues of the later Middle Ages may well have had some effect on this ascetic and penitential tradition (though over-large and ambitious claims have been in the past made for the social effects of the Black Death).[21] The Black Death, a type of bubonic fever, came from the East. In 1347 it made its appearance in Cyprus, Sicily, Marseilles and some Italian seaports. It spread rapidly; by January 1348 it was in Avignon, by August in England. Outbreaks recurred throughout the fourteenth century. The chroniclers present it as an unparalleled catastrophe: 'the dreadful pestilence penetrated the seacoast by Southampton and came to Bristol, and there almost the whole population of the town perished, as if it had been seized by sudden death; for few kept their beds more than two or three days, or even half a day. Then this cruel death spread everywhere around following the course of the sun.'[22] No doubt the estimates of the mortality given by chroniclers are often exaggerated (as are the estimates of the social and historical effects which were made by earlier modern writers on the subject). But the emotional effect, at least as it is presented by writers, must have been considerable. The most powerful piece of writing on it, the introduction to the *Decameron*, which describes the ravages of the plague in Florence in 1348, may not be a completely historical account, but it gives the sense of an extraordinary imminence of death, and of the emotional consequences of the plague, which ring true.

Some forms of social and religious unrest, which were already in existence, may well have been intensified by the plagues. Apocalyptic and messianic preachers saw in them a sign of the end. The greatest of the flagellant movements swept through Germany in 1348–9, bringing with it an eerie premonition of later history, large

The Life of this World

pogroms of Jews. Other enthusiastic religious aberrations are recorded at the same time.

Whether the plague had indirect effects on the tradition of mortality literature or not, it did produce a small clearly defined group of works of art and literature which are directly connected with it. In art the figure of the Virgin Mary sheltering the faithful under her mantle is adapted to show her defending them against the plague (sometimes shown as javelins hurled down by an angry God).[23] There were popular devotional images,[24] popular 'plague saints' – notably St Anthony, St Sebastian, St Roch – whose help could be invoked, and masses against the plague.[25] There are also verse tracts of practical instruction, and some verse prayers addressed to the Virgin Mary, the healer of the sick, or to God (the best of which is Henryson's *Prayer for the Pest*).[26]

It might well seem from what has been so far said that the theme of death as it is presented in the literature and art of the late Middle Ages is not one which would offer much in the way of imaginative possibilities. Its expression is certainly often violent and simplified. Huizinga's strictures on the 'macabre vision', that it has assimilated only one of the 'great complex of ideas relating to death' – the sense of the perishable nature of things, that it stresses the cruder and more horrific aspects of death, that it does not represent the 'emotions of tenderness or consolation', that it is essentially self-seeking and earthly, playing only on man's fear of his own death, etc., are, if we limit ourselves to the ascetic and penitential tradition, to a large extent justified. Outside this, they are much more dubious. The ancient tradition of consolation literature continued and produced some impressive poems (*Pearl* for one). Tenderness, pathos, elegiac sentiments can certainly be found in the treatment of death in English non-ascetic literature. Chaucer's treatment of death (notably in the *Book of the Duchess*) is remarkably humane and compassionate. And sophisticated and complex treatments of death can be found in European works as well.[27] The limitations of the theme as it is presented in penitential and devotional works are obvious. The thought of death is an excellent penitential weapon – to adapt Dr Johnson's remark, it 'concentrates the mind wonderfully'; there is therefore no room in most of these poems for complexity of emotion or for compassionate understanding – they are interested in absolutes, and attempt to achieve a general and universal message. It is possible (though it requires a literary skill greater than most practitioners possess) to make from the

9 A painting of 'Earth upon Earth', formerly at Stratford. This early nineteenth-century copy shows the stanzas of the poem arranged around the figure of an angel. At the bottom, above the body in the shroud, is a scroll with another devotional lyric (cf. pp. 196–8).

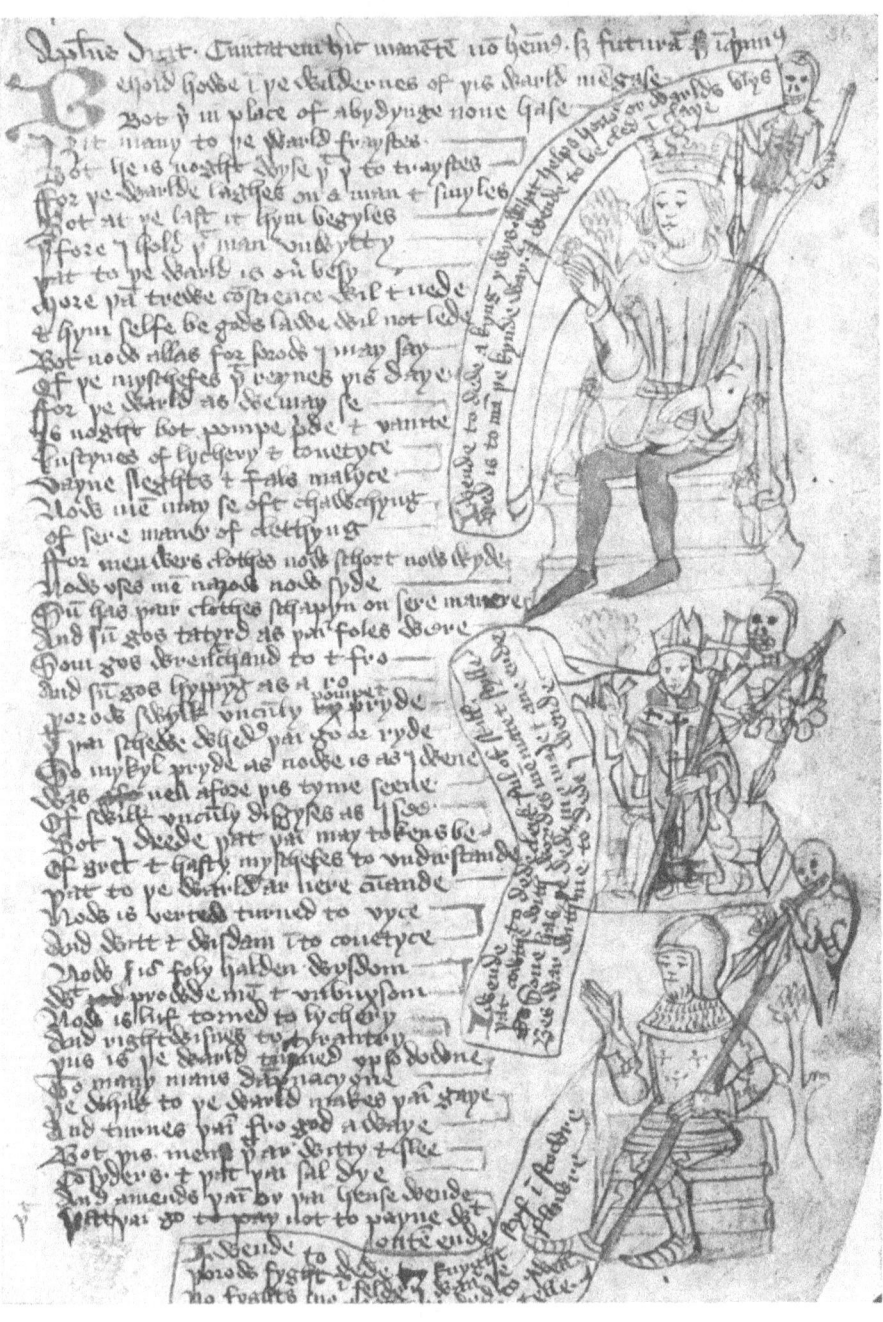

10 Vado Mori. A fifteenth-century illustrated poem in which a king, a 'clerk' and a knight are carried off by Death (see pp. 209–11).

macabre tradition powerful and imaginative works of art, impressive in their relentless and total austerity of vision, which never allow us to slide away from the vision of the undignified, and often grotesque fate from which no one can escape:

> La mort le fait fremir, pallir,
> Le nez courber, les vaines tendre,
> Le col enfler, la chair mollir,
> Joinctes et nerfs croistre et estendre. . . .

It is true, as Huizinga says, that this sort of view is earthly rather than spiritual. Often a fundamental materialism seems to assert itself through layers of penitential comment. Sometimes the penitential or religious codas are emotionally quite separate from the body of the poem. Indeed, in some macabre forms like the Dance of Death, specifically 'religious' comment is sometimes not present at all.

It is also, fortunately, rather difficult to exclude complexity of emotion or an elegiac tone altogether. Any rehearsal of the vanished or transient joys of life, any enumeration of men who have died may, whether 'intentionally' or not, develop a nostalgic or melancholy tone. Poets of stature have minds comprehensive enough to allow a variety of tone and conflicting emotions to exist. Some writers, adopting a more rigidly homiletic attitude, attempt to exclude this altogether. Sometimes then in a curious way the poem seems to develop within itself a contrary voice which surreptitiously seems to try to gainsay the voice of the preacher, and encourages us to linger with just a little nostalgia over the life which we are told is transitory, vain, and false. This is nowhere more obvious than in the most famous of all medieval mortality themes, the *ubi sunt* formula.

The two finest literary treatments of this in the Middle Ages are widely different in date, traditional background, and tone, but they illustrate what good poets can do with this. The first is the group of lines which occurs towards the end of the Old English poem *The Wanderer*:

> Hwær cwom mearg, hwær cwom mago? hwær cwom maþþumgyfa?
> Hwær com symbla gesetu? Hwær sindon seledreamas?
> Eala beorht bune, eala byrnwiga,
> Eala þeodnes þrym! Hu seo þrag gewat
> genap under nihthelm, swa heo no wære![28]

The Life of this World

The dignity and gravity of these lines is remarkable. The poet carefully chooses images and concepts which symbolize the nature of the heroic life whose transience he laments. His attitude to the passing of human life and honour is both Christian and gravely classical; one suspects that if Boethius could have read this passage he would have approved and admired it. Significantly this poet answers his own rhetorical questions not with an ascetic *moralitas* in the manner of the homilists, but with a further lament: 'Eala beorht bune. . . .'[29]

In the later Middle Ages the poet who handles all the commonplaces and formulae of mortality literature with the greatest originality and imagination is undoubtedly François Villon. The first of his *ubi sunt* ballades, the *Ballade des Dames du Temps Jadis*, with its haunting refrain 'mais ou sont les neiges d'antan', is well known, but it is rarely considered in its context in the *Testament* which is responsible for much of its complexity.[30] Villon has been discussing poverty. His heart tells him not to complain, for it is far better to live in poverty than to have been a lord and lie rotting in a rich tomb. Death is the leveller who will take off all men, and whoever dies, dies in pain. This is expanded in grim lines on the manner of death which we have already quoted, and prompts the question whether the soft and tender female body will also suffer these horrors. It will indeed, he says, 'unless she goes alive into heaven'. Then comes the ballade:

> Dictes moy ou, n'en quel pays,
> Est Flora la belle Rommaine,
> Archipiades, ne Thaïs,
> Qui fut sa cousine germaine,
> Echo parlant quant bruyt on maine
> Dessus riviere ou sus estan,
> Qui beaulté ot trop plus qu'humaine.
> Mais ou sont les neiges d'antan?
>
> Ou est la tres sage Helloïs,
> Pour qui chastré fut et puis moyne
> Pierre Esbaillart a Saint Denis?
> Pour son amour ot ceste essoyne.
> Semblablement, ou est la royne
> Qui commanda que Buridan
> Fust geté en ung sac en Saine?
> Mais ou sont les neiges d'antan?

Death and the Last Things

La royne Blanche comme lis
Qui chantoit a voix de seraine,
Berte au grant pié, Bietris, Alis,
Haremburgis qui tint le Maine,
Et Jehanne la bonne Lorraine
Qu'Englois brulerent a Rouan;
Ou sont ilz, ou, Vierge souvraine?
Mais ou sont les neiges d'antan?

Prince, n'enquerez de sepmaine
Ou elles sont, ne de cest an,
Qu'a ce reffrain ne vous remaine:
Mais ou sont les neiges d'antan?

Here we are at once struck by the way that the tension between a gentle lyricism of tone and the grim fact of death is sensitively exploited; it is epitomized by the magnificent image of the 'neiges d'antan', which both refines the old mortality images of the fragility of life, and suggests the fragility of female beauty ('poly', 'suef', 'si precieux'). The presence of a lively and original mind is felt in every line. The poet startles us with the incongruity of Buridan in a sack in the Seine (in the following *ubi sunt* ballade on the 'seigneurs du temps jadis', he refers to the Scottish king, 'half of whose face was as red as an amethyst', and the good king of Spain 'whose name I do not know'). Nothing could be further from the detached attitude of the poet of *The Wanderer* (at least in his *ubi sunt* lines) than the questioning, ironic, self-centred attitude of the part of the *Testament* in which this ballade occurs. Villon concludes that since all the great ones are 'buried dead and cold', poor Villon must die too, but this announcement is given a typical twist – 'as long as I have had my fun (mais que j'aye fait mes estrenes) I don't fear an honest death'.

Needless to say, the devotional poems which use the theme do not treat it with the confidence and originality of these poets – indeed more than once one has the impression that it is the theme which is using them – but their efforts are by no means despicable. The *ubi sunt* seems to come into devotional literature from Biblical sources,[31] and when it appears in homiletic contexts it usually has a very clear and didactic framework. This is evident in an influential sermon by Caesarius of Arles.[32] He tells his audience to look at the tombs of the rich, 'I ask you, brethren, look at the tombs of the rich.' This introduces the traditional rhetorical questions – when you pass by consider and diligently regard where are their adornments, where are their rings, etc. – and concludes with an emphatic homiletic answer – certainly they have all passed as a shadow. The reader of the *Testament* will notice how neatly and cleverly Villon has adapted this framework.

The rhetorical questions usually list either a series of objects or general classes – riches, robes, hunting-dogs, etc., the symbols of the rich or heroic society – or of the names of historical or legendary characters, used as exemplary figures – from the Bible, David 'most worthy king', Solomon (called 'wise' or 'prudentissimus'), 'beautiful' Absolom, 'sweet' Jonathan, etc. – or figures from romance, or, especially in poems with the classical interests of the twelfth century, figures from ancient history – Caesar, 'Tullius', Aristotle 'summus ingenio', etc. Occasionally, for greater emphasis, the name of some well-known figure who has recently died is inserted. One fine twelfth-century poem has an impressive list of philosophers, in addition to David and Solomon, 'Tullius' and Virgil, and a pair of lovers, Helen and Paris. Its ending is abrupt and stark:

> Transierunt rerum materies,
> Ut a sole liquescit glacies.
> Ubi Plato, ubi Porphyrius,
> Ubi Tullius aut Virgilius;
> Ubi Thales, ubi Empedocles,
> Aut egregius Aristoteles?
> Alexander ubi rex maximus,
> Ubi Hector Trojae fortissimus;
> Ubi David rex doctissimus;
> Ubi Helena Parisque roseus?
> Ceciderunt in profundum ut lapides,
> Quis scit an detur eis requies?*[33]

Of the numerous examples in Middle English, it will be sufficient to note one or two of the most interesting. The first part of the 'Love Rune' of Thomas of Hales which we mentioned in

* The substance of things has passed away, just as ice is melted by the sun. Where is Plato, where Porphyry, Cicero or Virgil? Where is Thales, Empedocles, or the supreme Aristotle? Where is Alexander, the greatest of kings, Hector, the most mighty hero of Troy, David, the wisest ruler, or Helen and rosy Paris? They have all fallen into the abyss like stones; who knows if any peace be granted them?

the introductory chapter, is concerned with the traditional themes of transience. The noblemen that once were so bold have passed away:

> Theos theines that her weren bolde
> Beoth aglyden so wyndes bles;
> Under molde hi liggeth colde
> And faleweth so doth medewe gres.

A series of further traditional topics is followed by the *ubi sunt* passage:

> Hwer is Paris and Heleyne
> That weren so bryht and feyre on bleo,
> Amadas and Dideyne,
> Tristram, Yseude, and alle theo,
> Ector, with his scharpe meyne,
> And Cesar, riche of wordes feo. . . .
>
> Thus is thes world of false fere
> Fol is he the on hire is bold.
>
> Theyh he were so riche mon
> As Henry ure kyng,
> And al so veyr as Absalon
> That nevede on eorthe non evenyng,
> Al were sone his prute agon,
> Hit nere on ende wrth on heryng. . . .

The first three pairs of names here are appropriately enough those of famous lovers.[34] Hector and Caesar, from the traditional 'Nine Worthies', are a less happy choice. There is a sort of continuity between these exemplary figures and earlier remarks on wealth, and on the instability of the world in general, but it is hard to avoid a sense of imprecision here, a sense that the poet is following a set theme rather mechanically. Friar Thomas uses his *ubi sunt* passage intellectually as part of his argument that earthly love is frail and transient. His lines have a clarity and a certain eloquence, but he is careful to exclude as completely as he can any suggestion of an elegiac lament for the great ones of the past. Man's 'pride' is brutally rejected with the words 'nere . . . wrth on heryng', a dismissive phrase which one cannot imagine the poet of *The Wanderer* using.

Quite different in tone are some lines from a thirteenth-century poem:

The Life of this World

Uuere beth they biforen us weren,
Houndes ladden and hauekes beren
And hadden feld and wode?
The riche levedies in hoere bour,
That wereden gold in hoere tressour
With hoere brightte rode;

Eten and drounken and maden hem glad;
Hoere lif was al with gamen ilad,
Men kneleden hem biforen,
They beren hem wel swithe heye –
And in a twincling of on eye
Hoere soules weren forloren.

Were is that lawing and that song,
That trayling and that proude yong,
Tho hauekes and tho houndes?
Al that joye is went away,
That wele is comen to weylaway,
To manie harde stoundes. . . .[35]

These lines occur towards the end of a rather dull homiletic poem usually called the 'Sayings of St Bernard', which is based on a prose meditative work, the *Meditationes piisimae de conditione humanae*. The equivalent Latin passage runs:

> Tell me where are the lovers of the world, who lived but a short while before us? Nothing of them has remained save ashes and worms. Attend carefully to what they are, and to what they were. They were men just as you are: they ate, they drank, they laughed, they passed their days in delights, and in a moment they went down to hell. . . . Of what benefit was to them that vain glory, that brief happiness, power in the world, desire of the flesh, false riches, great family, and wicked concupiscence? Where is the laughter, the jesting, where the vain glory, where the pride? From so much happiness how much sorrow; after so little pleasure what heavy misery! . . .[36]

At this point the English poem suddenly comes to life, and the homily is transformed into literature. The transitory life of the lovers of the world is dramatically presented in a series of small scenes or images (derived from the simple verbs of the Latin, 'ate', 'drank', 'laughed', etc.), in particular details – the bright gold on the frets of the ladies, the servants kneeling – rather than in abstract concepts. For a while at least the poem manages to sustain a balance between the sympathetic recreation of the earthly life and the moralist's view that it is all gone, and that their souls are lost in the 'twinkling of an eye'. After this passage it quickly relapses into weak moral exhortation; that it retains any interest at all for the modern reader is entirely due to the possibilities of the traditional *ubi sunt* theme.

Different again is the fluent and polished *ubi sunt* passage in Lydgate's reflective poem 'Al stant on change like a mydsomer rose'. Here there is no attempt to jerk the hearer into an awareness of the penitential significance of the questions. We have rather a gentle meditation on transience, without the individuality or the tensions of Villon's ballade, but relaxed and lyrical, with a sort of melancholy beauty:

> Where is Tullius with his sugryd tonge,
>   Or Crisistomus with his goldene mouthe?
> The aureat dytees, that be red and songe
>   Of Omerus in Grece, both north and south?
> The tragedyes divers and unkouth
>   Of morall Senek, the mysteryes to uncloose,
> By many example this mateer is ful kouth
>   Al stant on chaung like a mydsomer roose.
>
> Wher been of Fraunce all the dozepeers,
>   Which in Gawle had the governaunce;
> Vowes of the Pecok, with al ther proude chers?
>   The worthy nyne, with al ther hih bobbaunce?
> Trojan knyhtes, grettest of alliaunce;
>   The flees of golde conqueryd in Colchoos?
> Rome and Cartage, moost sovereyn of puissance?
>   Al stant on chaung like a mydsomyr roos. . . .[37]

The *ubi sunt* formula was not forgotten with the passing of the Middle Ages. Here, for instance, is a stanza from an eloquent Elizabethan translation of the hymn *Cur Mundus Militat* (which condemns, says the rubric in the *Paradyse of Daynty Devises*, 'the unstable felicitee of this wayfaring world'):

> Where is that Caesar nowe, whose hygh renowned fame,
> Of sundry conquests wonne throughout the world did sound?

Or Dives riche in store, and riche in richely name,
Whose chest with gold and dishe with daynties did abound?
Where is the passing grace of Tullies pleding skill?
Or Aristotles vayne, whose penne had witte and wyll?[38]

In Shakespeare, too, we often find echoes of the medieval literature of death, though transformed and refashioned. It is interesting to look at Hamlet's reflections on the skulls in the light of the tradition which we have just discussed. He does not quite 'go to the tombs of the rich' and his wryly individual moralities would probably not have satisfied the homilists, though they might have pleased Villon, but he does say of one skull: 'There's another: why may not that be the skull of a lawyer? Where be his quiddities now, his quillets, his cases, his tenures, and his tricks? . . .', and and again, of Yorick, 'Where be your gibes now? your gambols? your songs? your flashes of merriment, that were wont to set the table on a roar?' He even introduces the good old exemplary figure of Alexander: 'Dost thou think Alexander looked o' this fashion i' the earth?'[39] But let us take leave of the *ubi sunt* formula with its delightful adaptation in Byron's *Don Juan*, canto xi: the world is a globe of glass – 'Statesmen, chiefs, orators, queens, patriots, kings/And dandies, all are gone on the wind's wings:

Where is Napoleon the Grand? God knows:
  Where little Castlereagh? the devil can tell:
Where Grattan, Curran, Sheridan, all those
  Who bound the bar or senate in their spell?
Where is the unhappy Queen, with all her woes?
  And where the Daughter, whom the Isles loved well?
Where are those martyr'd saints the Five per Cents?
  And where – oh, where the devil are the rents?

Where's Brumel? Dish'd. Where's Long Pole Wellesley? Diddled.
  Where's Whitbread? Romilly? Where's George the Third?
Where is his will? (That's not so soon unriddled). . . .

Where are the Lady Carolines and Franceses?
  Divorced or doing thereanent. . . .

There were two ways in which the *memoria* of death could be made vivid, so that the reader might be shocked into penitence.

Death and the Last Things

The poet could stress the physical facts of the decay of the body, and he could present man's encounter with death in a dramatic way. The two are, naturally enough, sometimes combined. There are poems in which the dead man 'speaks' to us, and tells us the gruesome details of decomposition, and we sometimes find depictions of worm-covered skeletons accompanied by warning *tituli*, as if they were speaking to the beholder.[40]

It is a difficult task to transform the commonplaces of physical corruption into poetry; poems which lean heavily on these very often become simply disgusting or ludicrous. Images of physical decay are found, of course, in ancient religious literature (in the Old Testament, Job's sayings, e.g. 'I have said to corruption "thou art my father"; to the worm "thou art my mother and my sister"', often seem curious premonitions of the 'macabre' imagination); in the penitential tradition of the later Middle Ages they are intensified. 'Rot', 'pourrir', 'putrescere' become favourite words. In one Latin poem *De Morte*, a dialogue between a living man and a corpse, the dead man rehearses the commonplaces of mortality, but elaborates the idea of the decay of the body with gruesome relish: 'scorpions and serpents gnaw us with their teeth' –

> Putret caro, patent ossa. . . .
> Intestina computrescunt
> Ibi vermes requiescunt
>   Corrodentes omnia. . . .*

The operations of the 'worms' (the natural history is somewhat vague) are rounded off with a truly remarkable exclamation:

> Esca vermis sum effectus,
> Cibus eis et electus,
>   O quam rodunt dulciter!†[41]

The fifteenth-century MS. Additional 37049 contains a curious English example of this sort of thing. The medieval passion for the debate as a literary form produced some odd results, but few can be odder than the 'Disputacioun betwyx the body and wormes'.[42] It is accompanied by a picture of the tomb of a lady, complete with corpse and worms. A few introductory lines moralize on this

---

* The flesh rots, the bones lie bare . . . internal organs decay; there the worms take their rest, gnawing everything.
† I am made into food for the worms and chosen for their meal. O how sweetly they gnaw!

figure; then comes the disputation itself. The poet goes off on pilgrimage, during the plague ('in the ceson of huge mortalite'); he goes into a church, sees a tomb, and reads the epitaph 'in manner of a dialogue'. It is in fact a *titulus* poem within a *titulus* poem. One of the exchanges will be sufficient to give an idea of its tone and quality:

> 'Wormes, wormes,' this body sayd,
> 'Why do ye thus? What causes yow me thus to ete?
> By yow my flesche is horribilly arayed,
> Whilk was a fygure whylom fresche and feete,
> Right amyabyll and odorous and swete. . . .
>
> Moste unkynde neghbours that ever war wroght!
> Dynner mete and sowper al to lyte,
> Now fretyng and etyng ye hafe me thorow soght
> With ane insaciabyll and gredy appetyte.
> No rest – bot alway ye synk, sowke and byte. . . .
>
> When ye fyrst began to drawe me to,
> It semes me ye wer fed in a faynt pasture;
> Now fatte waxen and ugly rownde and gret also.
> Of curtasy and gentilnes lefe me of your cure,
> And with sum other dwelle and endure,
> Whilk may yow rewarde with better wardone,
> For ner am I wasted, consumed and gone.'
>
> Wormes spekes to the body:
>
> 'Nay, nay, we will not yit departe the fro
> While that one of thi bones with other wil hange;
> To we hafe scowred and pollysched to
> And made als clene as we can thaim amange.
> For our labour we aske no maner of thing to fange,
> Gold, sylver, ryches, ne no other mede,
> Bot onely us wormes on the to fede. . . .'

Charnel-imagery of this sort is not unknown in later times. So Donne, on man: 'between that excremental jelly that thy body is made of at first, and that jelly which thy body dissolves to at last there is not so noisome, so putrid a thing in nature'.[43] Even the the worms do not die with the 'waning of the Middle Ages'. Hamlet in a memorable punning phrase refers to 'a certain convocation of politic worms', the supper at which Polonius does not eat, but is eaten, and the old homiletic tag *esca vermium* is also jestingly used by Mercutio: 'They have made worms' meat of me.'[44] Some of this macabre material was taken up in Romantic literature.[45] In the original version of *The Ancient Mariner* some 'Gothick' verses (fortunately removed in revision) describe the figures on the spectre-bark:

> His bones were black with many a crack,
>   All black and bare I ween;
> Jet-black and bare, save where with rust
>   Of mouldy damps and charnel crust
>   They're patch'd with purple and green. . . .
>
> A gust of wind sterte up behind
>   And whistled thro' his bones;
> Thro' the holes of his eyes and the hole of his mouth
>   Half-whistles and half-groans.

The worms crawling around the skeleton appear in an extraordinary incident in that masterpiece of Gothic fiction, M. G. Lewis's *The Monk* (1796). Here Antonia goes into a little library, where the eerie atmosphere inspires her 'with a melancholy awe'. Trimming the taper 'which now drew towards its end', she reads the Spanish ballad of 'Alonzo the Brave and the Fair Imogene'.[46] Alonzo and Imogene are promised. Alonzo goes off to fight in the Holy Land, and Imogene vows never to wed another. If she breaks her word, she says, may Alonzo's ghost sit beside her at the wedding, claim her as his bride and bear her off to the grave. Within the year, as might be expected, she is to be married to a baron. At the feast, when the bell strikes one, Imogene finds a stranger by her side:

> His air was terrific: he uttered no sound;
> He spoke not, he moved not, he looked not around,
>   But earnestly gazed on the bride.

He is asked to open his vizor:

> The lady is silent: the stranger complies.
>   His vizor he slowly unclosed:
> Oh! God! what a sight met fair Imogene's eyes!
> What words can express her dismay and surprise,
>   When a skeleton's head was exposed!

The Life of this World

All present then uttered a terrified shout;
  All turned with disgust from the scene.
The worms they crept in, and the worms they crept out,
  And sported his eyes and his temples about,
    While the spectre addressed Imogene.

Like other heroines in this type of ballad, she is carried off to the grave. From this or some similar source, the delightful image of the worms creeping and sporting must have caught the popular imagination, for it is still found in a children's song.[47]

One of the most curious types of the medieval 'macabre' lyric is the *Proprietates Mortis* or 'Signs of Death'. It is simply a catalogue of the symptoms of the ebbing away of life, which came into penitential literature from the medical lore of the ancients.[48] A good example is this thirteenth-century version:

Wanne mine eyhnen misten,
And mine eren sissen,
And mi nose koldet,
And mi tunge foldet,
And mi rude slaket,
And mine lippes blaken,
And mi muth grennet,
And mi spotel rennet,
And min her riset,
And min herte griset,
And mine honden bivien,
And mine fet stivien;
Al to late, al to late,
Wanne the bere ys ate gate.
Thanne ye schel flutte
From bedde te flore,
From flore to here,
From here to putte,
And te putt fordut.
Thanne lyd min hus uppe mon nose,
Off al this world ne gyffe ic a pese.[49]

The monotonous rehearsal of the progression from bed to grave is impressive in its cumulative way. It comes to a climax with the final couplet (the first line of which is traditionally almost proverbial)[50] which seems (at least to the modern reader) to 'drop' the tone to an ironic nihilism.

Death and the Last Things

The *Proprietates* appear, directly or indirectly, in many places (I have already quoted an example from Villon).[51] Some versions include the striking detail 'the nose sharpeth', which is found in one of the Elizabethan echoes in the account of Falstaff's death – 'his nose is sharp as a pen'. There are a number of later examples in homily, or derived from popular medical lore[52] – among modern echoes we could cite Mr Bloom's reflections on the coming of death:

> The death struggle. His sleep is not natural. Press his lower eyelid. Watching is his nose pointed is his jaw sinking are the soles of his feet yellow.[53]

or Raymond Chandler's description of the aged General Sternwood, who, it will be remembered, spends much of his time in a greenhouse:

> The rest of his face was a leaden mask, with the bloodless lips and the sharp nose and the sunken temples and the outward-turning ear-lobes of approaching dissolution.[54]

Few of the lyrics in this tradition are better than curiosities. One good example is this little thirteenth-century verse:

> Wen the turuf is thi tuur,
> And thi put is thi bour,
> Thi wel and thi wite throte
> Ssulen wormes to note.
> Wat helpit the thenne
> Al the worilde wnne?[55]

It is accompanied in the manuscript by its Latin equivalent:

> Cum sit gleba tibi turris
> Tuus puteus conclavis,
> Pellis et guttur album
> Erit cibus vermium.
> Quid habent tunc de proprio
> Hii monarchie lucro?

The usual commonplaces – the earth will be your house, your beautiful body will be eaten by worms, what use will be all the world's joy then? – are here handled concisely and forcefully. The poem consists simply of two neatly balanced statements bound together by 'when . . . then', and followed by a rhetorical question. The opposition of turf and 'tower' is sharpened in the English lines by the alliteration; tower suggests the panoply of knighthood and riches, while 'bour' with its suggestions of ladies and love, finds an effectively grim contrast in 'pit'. The rhetorical question is as usual more successful than a direct appeal to penitence. Here again, the English lines are slightly superior – 'helpit' is more forceful than 'habent', and the retention of the 'thou' form of address is preferable to the more impersonal 'they'. 'Al the worilde wnne', though a conventional phrase, gives a sonorous and full ending. On the whole the English is neater and more pointed throughout.

Another interesting poem is a riddling expansion, a witty elaboration of the old tag *memento homo quod cinis es et in cinerem reverteris*:

> Erthe toc of erthe erthe wyth woh,
> Erthe other erthe to the erthe droh,
> Erthe leyde erthe in erthene throh –
> Tho hevede erthe of erthe erthe ynoh.[56]

It remarkably suggests the movement from the earth to the earth, the lowest and heaviest of elements. The final line has something of the irony which we saw in the *Proprietates Mortis*. There are a number of longer expansions, which on the whole lose the grim concision of the quatrain; they contain varying amounts of interpolated material – one in Balliol 354 has a reference to the Nine Worthies and William the Conqueror and Henry I 'that was of knyghthode floure' as well as to the Dance of Death painted at St Paul's. But the longer versions are not entirely despicable. These verses, for instance, from one of the 'B' versions, though uneven, contain some good lines:

> Erthe appone erthe wolde be a kynge,
> Bot howe that erthe to erthe sall thynkis he no thynge.
> When erthe b(e)dis erthe his rentis home brynge,
> Thane schalle erthe of erthe hafe full harde partynge. . . .
>
> Erthe gose appone erthe as (m)olde uppon (m)olde,
> He that gose appone erthe gleterande as golde,
> Lyke als erthe never more goo to erthe scholde,
> And yett schall erthe unto erthe (r)athere than he wolde. . . .

Death and the Last Things

These longer versions were certainly popular. They were sometimes used, like so many of these poems, as *tituli*. One MS. (that of William Billyng, which survives only in a nineteenth-century copy) was in the form of a roll, and the 'Earth upon Earth' poem was preceded by a figure of a naked body with a mattock and spade, and was followed by the prone figure of a skeleton. This may well have been used for public display. Another copy was formerly painted on the wall of the Trinity chapel in Stratford-on-Avon:[57]

> Against the West wall of the nave, upon the South side of the arch was painted the martyrdom of St. Thomas à Becket, whilst kneeling at the altar of St. Benedict in Canterbury Cathedral; below this was represented the figure of an angel (probably St. Michael) supporting a long scroll, upon which were written the following rude verses: *Erthe out of erthe* &c. Beneath were two men, holding another scroll over a body wrapt in a winding sheet, and covered with some emblems of mortality with these lines:
> *Whoso hym be thowghte* &c.

(The *Whoso hym be thowghte* verses are another common mortality lyric, called by Carleton Brown '*Memorare Novissima tua*'.) A drawing by Thomas Fisher in the early nineteenth century gives a good idea of the arrangement (plate 9). Echoes and snatches of 'Earth upon Earth' are found as epitaphs and tomb inscriptions for centuries. The seventeenth-century antiquarian John Weever, in his great collection of epitaphs, records one stanza at Edmonton, in a manner which emphasizes the melancholy nature of human mutability:[58]

> Here lyeth one whose name is worne out of his Monument, his Tombe covered with a faire marble stone, his bodie figured in brasse armed, with a gorget of Maile; under his feet a Lion cowchant. His wife lieth portrayed by him; he is thought by some to have bene one of that ancient and honourable familie of the Mandevills, by others to be one of that noble familie of the Darcies. These verses remaining:
>
>> Erth goyth upon erth as mold upon mold
>> Erth goyth upon erth al glysteryng in gold,
>> As thogh erth to erth ner turne shold,
>> And yet must erth to erth soner then he wold.

The Life of this World

This verse occurs in tomb inscriptions even in the eighteenth century, and as late as 1837 'Earth upon Earth' is found on a headstone.[59] 'Earth must to earth' becomes a proverbial phrase – it is quoted as 'an old said saw' by Peele in *Edward I*.[60] Its most interesting occurrence in more sophisticated contexts is in Shakespeare's Sonnet lxxiv:

> But be contented. When that fell arrest
> Without all bail shall carry me away,
> My life hath in this line some interest,
> Which for memorial still with thee shall stay.
> When thou reviewest this, thou dost review
> The very part was consecrate to thee.
> The earth can have but earth, which is his due;
> My spirit is thine, the better part of me.
> So then thou hast but lost the dregs of life,
> The prey of worms, my body being dead;
> The coward conquest of a wretch's knife,
> Too base of thee to be remembered.
> The worth of that is that which it contains,
> And that is this, and this with thee remains.

The literary echoes in this sonnet (of Ovid and possibly of Ronsard) have been illuminatingly discussed by J. B. Leishman.[61] It would, however, be entirely typical of Shakespeare's comprehensive mind to use as well an allusion to this homely proverbial phrase that comes ultimately from the mortality tradition, with all its associations. One cannot help wondering if he had read the old 'Earth upon Earth' poem in the chapel at Stratford. Two other phrases in this sonnet, interestingly enough, come from this same medieval mortality tradition – 'the prey of worms', and 'that fell arrest', which like the image in *Hamlet* of death as the 'fell sergeant' has its medieval antecedents (in the Lydgatian *Dance of Death*, for instance, the Constable and the Sergeant are 'arrested' by Death; according to Leland, a version of the Dance of Death was also painted in the Trinity Chapel).

Perhaps the most successful of these poems is Skelton's 'Uppon a deedmans hed'.[62] It is a 'gostly medytacyon' on this 'token' of mortality, but it wastes no time in a loving description of the ugly object – all its emphasis is upon the effect its sight produces. The driving insistence of the Skeltonic lines presses the lesson home. The skull imaginatively suggests the grim figure of death himself:

It is generall
To be mortall:
I have well espyde
No man may hym hyde
From deth holow-eyed,
With synnews wyderyd,
With bonys shyderyd,
With hys worme-etyn maw
And hys gastly jaw
Gaspyng asyde,
Nakyd of hyde,
Neyther flesh nor fell. . . .

then becomes the particular image of our own dissolution:

Oure days be datyd
To be chekmatyd,
With drawttys of deth
Stoppyng oure breth;
Oure eyen synkyng,
Oure bodys stynkyng,
Oure gummys grynnyng,
Oure soulys brynnyng!

The dramatic type of poem in which man is directly confronted and addressed by death, an image of death, or a dead man, is generally much more interesting. As we have seen, the homilist was fond of directing his hearers to look at the tomb. 'If you will hear, O man,' says Caesarius of Arles, 'these dry bones can preach to you. . . .' And they do.

> The dead man calls to thee from the tomb: 'Take heed of me, and recognize thyself; consider my bones and so may your lechery or your avarice be hateful to thee. What thou art, I was; what I am, thou shalt be. . . . Look upon my dust, and give up evil desire. . . .'[63]

The idea is turned into many poems, and it is not at all surprising to find it used in the drama. In a striking scene in the Towneley play of Lazarus, Lazarus comes forward in answer to Christ's command and addresses the audience, presumably still clad in his shrouds. His speech is full of the commonplaces of this sort of literature – no man, whatever his estate, can escape death; such

The Life of this World

shall you all be; after your death you will be forgotten; your wife and your children will not have masses sung for you; you cannot trust executors (executors in this tradition have a notoriously bad reputation), and so on – but these are somehow made impressive by the dramatic setting, and by the irony and macabre details:

> Under the erthe ye shall thus carefully then cowche;
> The royfe of your hall yowre nakyd nose shall towche....
>
> Youre rude that was so red, youre lyre the lylly lyke,
> Then shall be wan as led, and stynke as dog in dyke;
> Wormes shall in you brede as bees dos in the byke.

The dramatic presentation of death's grim message to man is very often found in the *tituli* and epitaphs which accompany tombs and monuments. Here we find again and again that ancient warning phrase 'such as I am shall you be' which like 'earth upon earth' long remained a favourite in funerary inscriptions.[64] Archbishop Chichele's tomb (he died in 1443) at Canterbury has a Latin version of it:

> Quisquis eris qui transieris rogo memoreris
> Tu quod eris mihi consimilis qui post morieris,
> Omnibus horribilis, pulvis, vermis, caro, vilis.

At Higham Ferrers in Northamptonshire his brother William and his wife Beatrice voice the same sentiments in the vernacular. They use also the ancient *orate* formula, beseeching the passer-by to pray for their souls:[65]

> Such as ye be such wer we
> Such as we be such shall ye be
> Lerneth to deye that is the lawe
> That this lif now to wol drawe.
> Sorwe or gladnesse nought letten age
> But on he cometh to lord and page.
> Wherfor for us that ben goo
> Preyeth as other shall for you doo
> That God of his benignyte
> On us have mercy and pite
> And nought remember our wykedness
> Sith he us bought of hys goodnesse
>   Amen.

Death and the Last Things

These epitaphs are usually extremely simple and quite unpretentious. Sometimes they rarely go beyond a plain commemoration, a request for prayer, and a warning memento mori:

> John Barton lyeth under here,
> Sometimes of London, citizen and mercere,
> And Jenet his wife, with their progenie,
> Beene turned to earth as ye may see:
> Friends free, what so ye bee,
> Pray for us we you pray,
> As you see us in this degree,
> So shall you be another day.[66]

Occasionally, with a touching pride they mention their benefactions. Henry Notingham and his wife, at Holme-by-the-Sea (c. 1400) say that they 'made' church steeple, choir, two vestments and bells;[67] John Spicer (d. 1431) mentions the rood-loft:

> The wiche rode-soler in this chirche
> Upon my cost y dede do wirche
> With a laumpe brenyng bright
> To worschip God both day and nyght.[68]

The witty and facetious literary epitaph is significantly absent in these surroundings. Very occasionally we find a gentle pun:

> Palmers all our faders were
> I a Palmer livyd here
> And travyld sore till worn with age
> I ended thys worldes pylgramage
> On the blyste Assention daye
> In the cherful moneth of Maye
> On thousande with foure hundrede seven
> And tooke my jorneye hense to heven.[69]

or a single grim jest:

> Qwan the Belle ys solemplye rownge,
> And the messe wyth Devosyon songe,
> And the mete meryly hete,
> Sone shall Sere Thomas Bettys be forgete. . . .[70]

What imagery there is is of the simplest and most traditional kind:

> As flowers in feeld thus passyth lif,
> Nakyd then clothyd, feble in the end;
> It sheweth by Robert Daluss and Alyson his wyf,
> Chryst them save fro the power of the fiend.[71]

The epitaphs of the simple and the great share a liking for the traditional commonplaces. In Brightwell Baldwin church, the fourteenth-century epitaph of 'John the Smith' (apparently the earliest known English inscription in a brass) speaks to the passer-by:

> Man com and se how schal alle dede be:
> Wen thow comes bad and bare
> Noth hab ven ve away fare:
> All ys werines that ve for care:
> Bot that ve do for Godys luf ve have nothyng yare:
> Hundyr this grave lys John the smyth
> God yif his soule heven grit.[72]

while in Canterbury Cathedral, the elegant French epitaph of the Black Prince reminds us that death comes suddenly, 'such as you were I was', and that now his house is very narrow ('moult est estroit ma meson').[73]

Almost all without literary pretensions, these epitaphs have a simplicity and a piety that attracted the early antiquarians like Weever (whose taste for elegant inscriptions did not prevent him from recording many of these homely epitaphs):

> Of all funerall honours (saith Camden) Epitaphs have always beene most respective; for in them love was shewed to the deceased, memorie was continued to posteritie, friends were comforted, and the Reader put in minde of humane frailtie: and indeed the frequent visiting, and advised reviewing of the Tombes and monuments of the dead (but without all touch of superstition) with the often reading, serious perusall, and diligent meditation of wise and religious Epitaphs or inscriptions, found upon the tombes or monuments, of persons of approved vertue, merit, and honour, is a great motive to bring us to repentance.[74]

and a later poet like Wordsworth.[75]

Sometimes we have extended epitaphs or 'laments' for prominent men who have recently died. These may in some cases have been intended for the private circle of mourners, or may have been exhibited on a scroll near the tomb. They would thus be the antecedents of the sixteenth-century epitaphs on 'tables', referred to slightingly by Puttenham ('for they make long and tedious discourses, and write them in large tables to be hanged up in churches and chancells over the tombes of great men and others'),[76] and in a more neutral tone by the Friar in *Much Ado* ('Maintain a mourning ostentation,/And on your family's old monument/Hang mournful epitaphs'). Others seem to be completely 'literary' works, which have close affinities with the admonitory verses spoken by the anonymous dead, or with the laments of fallen princes which are to be found in *The Mirror for Magistrates*. There is, for instance, a fifteenth-century epitaph in Lydgatian style on Humphrey, Duke of Gloucester (d. 1447),[77] and a number of Tudor examples – Skelton's poem on Jasper, Duke of Bedford (d. 1495), More's Lamentation of Queen Elizabeth, a virelay attributed to Earl Rivers on the eve of his execution (1483), an epitaph of Sir Gryffyth Ap Ryse, a 'lamentation' of Edward, Duke of Buckingham (which ends on a most exemplary note: 'Therefore all gentyll bolde, take ensample by me/Of Buckyngham late Duke of ryght noble degree'), etc. These pieces have some interest for the student of late fifteenth and early sixteenth century literature, but they are hardly distinguished poems. One of the most successful (though it is uneven) is the *Lament of the Soul of Edward IV* sometimes attributed to Skelton,[78] which is incorporated later into *The Mirror for Magistrates* (where it is said to be an 'oracion' of Skelton's and is headed 'how king Edward through his surfeting and untemperate life sodainly died in the mids of his prosperity' – it seems quite likely that Edward IV did in fact die of apoplexy or acute indigestion in consequence of what the chronicler Hall calls 'superfluous surfeit'). This dramatic monologue is stately, sometimes slow in its movement. It begins with a Latin phrase 'Miseremini mei, ye that ben my fryndys', and each of its stanzas ends with the solemn refrain *ecce nunc in pulvere dormio*. It is adorned with learned diction (*ymperiall, terrestyall*, etc.), and some high sentence of the usual general kind:

> Evyre forto lyve who may be swre?
> What is hit to trust the mutabilite
> Off this world whan no thyng may endure?

and so forth. Nor is it hard to find the usual commonplaces (earth unto earth . . .) and the favourite images of mortality literature:

the world is 'no sertayne butt a chery fere full of woo' (the image of the 'cherry-fair', the gay fair held in cherry-orchards, is found in a number of these lyrics).[79] But as often in this type of poem the traditional figures have a sombre force – false fortune smiled on him 'with hure sewger lyppus';[80] she took him 'by the hond and led me the dance';[81] 'owtt off this lond sho hath (me) exylyd' – where the word 'exiled' with its semi-political overtones aptly expresses the plight of the dead king, and suggests the enforced, unhappy and unnatural manner of his parting from life.[82] The poet does not shrink from expressions of proverbial generality: 'example to take evyre off had-I-wist'.[83] The king's monologue is not without its personal, almost humorous touches:

> xxiii^{ti} yeres I reyned this ymperiall,
> Som men to plesoure, and som men nott to lykyng . . .

but usually these remarks are submerged in uninspired catalogues – as for example of the king's achievements in building.[84] It is interesting however to find the *ubi sunt* formula in this sort of setting:

> Where is my gret conquest and vyctory?
> Where be my rentis and my ryall aray?
> Where be my coursors and my horsys so hy?
> Where is my grett plesure, solas and play?
> As vanite to noughte all ys gon away.

Coming immediately after this, the pathetic lines which the king addresses to his lady Besse have a haunting melancholy:

> Lidy Besse, for me long may ye call,
> Whe be departyd untyll domusday!
> I lovyd you, lady, my soverayne overall.

But the homiletic impulse soon overpowers the dramatic imagination; the king rather ponderously quotes St Bernard on the end of man, and those well-known exemplary figures Alexander, Samson, Solomon and Absalom are cited. Then in the beginning of the last stanza, the quality of the writing improves yet again, with two images – life as a brief pageant[85] and as a battle – given some dramatic force, and a tone of gentle resignation achieved through the words *In manus tuas* . . . , so full of Christian connotation (the last words of Christ on the cross, they are used in private prayer, and in compline, the final office of the liturgical day):

> I have pleyd my pagent and now am I past,
>   I wyll that ye wytt I was off no grett elde.
> Butt all thing consumeth att the last;
>   Whan deth apperith lost ys the feld.
> Sith this world no lenger upheld
>   Mo, conservyd to me my place.
> *In manus tuas,* domine, my spryte up I yeld;
>   Humbley I besech the off thy grace. . . .

In this poem as in others of the type the attempt to adapt the devices and ideas of the essentially anonymous and general 'dead man's lament' or warning to a particular historical individual is not completely successful. This is evident if we compare it with another fifteenth-century poem, entitled by Carleton Brown 'Farewell, this world is but a cherry fair'.[86] This opens:

> Farewell, this world! I take my leve for evere,
>   I am arested to apere at Goddes face.
> O myghtyfull God, thu knowest that I had levere
>   Than all this world, to have oone houre space
> To make asythe for all my grete trespace.
> My hert, alas, is brokyne for that sorowe;
> Som be this day that shall not be tomorow. . . .

Here again we have commonplaces and traditional phrases – death 'arrests' the man, he is the leveller, 'sotell' and swift and implacable:

> Today I sat full ryall in a cheyere,
> Tyll sotell deth knokyd at my gate,
> And on-avysed he seyd to me 'chekmate!'. . . .

Again, they are deployed with a dramatic sense. But since this dead man's discourse is deliberately general, without the 'personal' catalogues of building achievements which the previous author thought appropriate to Edward IV, we do not have the awkward shifts and juxtapositions which marred that poem. This poet is more successful in suggesting the tone of a speaking voice, sometimes gentle and pathetic in tone:

> Speke softe, ye folk, for I am leyd aslepe!
> I have my dreme, in trust is moche treson . . .

sometimes anguished and despairing:

The Life of this World

Wold to God, I had remembyrd me beforne!

His control of the verse is much tighter and more confident; his poem rises to a stately and impressive climax in a stanza which was popular as a separate epitaph:

> Farewell, my frendis! the tide abidith no man:
> I moste departe hens and so shall ye,
> But in this passage the best song that I can
> Is *Requiem eternam* – I pray God grant it me!
> When I have endid all myn adversite,
> Graunte me in paradise to have a mancyon,
> That shede his blode for my redempcion.

This characteristic simplicity and gravity, this homely diction which does not despise the proverbial and the general commonplace, is brilliantly used by Hawes in the most famous of early English epitaphs, that of Grande Amoure in *The Passetyme of Pleasure*:

> O mortall folke, you may beholde and se
> How I lye here, somtyme a myghty knyght.
> The ende of joye and all prosperyte
> Is dethe at last, through his course and myght.
> After the day there cometh the derke nyght
> For though the day be never so longe,
> At last the belles ryngeth to evensonge.[87]

Sometimes the confrontation between death and man is expressed in the form of a dialogue. In MS. Additional 37049 there is a curious exchange between the emperor 'Antiochenus' and his son.[88] The emperor, notorious for his pride, was buried in a tomb of gold. His son, who succeeds him, proves even more wicked. The steward advises him to take heed how his father lies in the grave. When the son comes to the tomb (see plate 8: the artist has naturally and effectively made it a fashionable 'transi' tomb), 'than he sawe the body stynkyng, and wormes and snakes etyng opon hym'. He speaks to his father:

> 'Fader sum tyme what was thou'
> A voyce awnswerd and sayd,
> 'Swilk as I was artu nowe'
> Than sayd the son to the fader

Death and the Last Things

> 'A fowle stynke I fele of the'
> The voyce awnswerd
> 'Son, wele fowler sone sal cum of the'
> Than sayd the son
> 'Horrybil bestes restys with the'
> The voyce sayd
> 'Thow sal cum and reste with me'
> Than sayd the son
> 'Thy fayr flesche falles and fadys away'
> 'Son, so sal thine do, that is now so gay.'

It will be seen from the illustration how these verses (with some minor variations of spelling) have been abstracted and arranged in quatrain form as *tituli*. The upshot of the story is a striking example of the power of the visual image in late medieval devotion – the son has a painter make for him the likeness of his father as he lay in his grave, 'and when he was styrred to any syn, he beheld the ymage of his fader, knawyng wele that he come fro the erthe and suld turne to the erthe'.

In the Hungerford chapel of Salisbury cathedral there was once a painting which showed a fashionably dressed gallant meeting death enveloped in a shroud. Each of the figures spoke a single rather undistinguished stanza:[89]

[Gallant] Alasse, Dethe, alasse, a blessful thyng y(t) were
Yf thow wolldyst spare us in our lustynesse,
And cum to wretches that bethe of hevy chere
When they ye clepe to slake there dystresse.
But owte, alasse! thyne owne sely selfwyldnesse
Crewelly werieth them that seyghe, wayle and wepe,
To close there yen that after ye doth clepe.

[Death] Grasles galante in all thy luste and pryde,
Remembyr that thow ones schalte dye.
Deth shold fro thy body thy sowle devyde;
Thou mayst him not ascape certaynly.
To the dede bodys cast downe thyne ye
Behold thaym well, consydere and see,
For such as thay ar, such shalt yow be.

This sort of confrontation is naturally not limited to the lyrical or shorter poems of the late Middle Ages. The reader will remember its finest expression in dramatic literature in the early sixteenth-century play *Everyman*.[90] There is also the most celebrated 'illustrated poem' of the fifteenth-century, the *Dance of Death* or *Danse Macabre*, in which Death confronts many social types – pope, emperor, king, etc., and rejecting their pleas leads them off in his terrible dance. The famous version of this at the church of the Innocents in Paris was translated into English by Lydgate. It was painted in St Paul's churchyard, and traces of it remain in a number of places in England. It is perhaps the most extreme example of the grim, macabre spirit, to which it has given its name; Death here is completely victorious, man doomed and totally defeated. There is no room for the melancholy nostalgia, or the defiant voice of life which we have noticed in other poems of death. There are brief touches of pathos – in the exchange with the labourer, whose life has been so terrible that he longs for death, or with the child who can only say A! A! – but they are quickly extinguished. Nor, curiously, is there much room in this grim view of man's end for Christian consolation or hope. Death's meeting with the Abbot is a typical example of the sardonic irony of the work:

> Come forth sir Abbot, with youre brood hatte,
>   Beeth not abaisshed, though ye have right.
> Greet is your hood, your bely large and fatte.
>   Ye mote come daunce, though ye be no thing light. . . .[91]

The *Dance of Death* cannot really be classed as a lyrical work, but one or two related forms have left traces in our lyrics. The Legend of the Three Living and the Three Dead,[92] which can be traced back to French poems (by Baudouin de Condé, Nicholas de Margival, and two anonymous authors) of the thirteenth century, was a great favourite with English painters; traces of it can be found in many wall-paintings throughout the country.[93] The basic situation is simple enough: three living men, usually nobles (they sometimes represent the Three Ages of Man), are suddenly confronted by three dead men, and recoil in horror. The better artists are able to convey something of the dramatic potential of the terrifying moment. In this legend the dead do not, as does Death in the *Dance of Death*, implacably carry off the living, but warn them of their coming end. The scene does not have therefore quite the grim finality of the confrontations of the *Dance of Death*, and allows the expression of the humans' horror and of

Death and the Last Things

their passion for life. In the French versions words and pictures were already associated (some manuscripts have a preface making the connection explicit: 'ceste diverse portraiture/nous presente une aventure'), and there are traces of this in England. The best known MS. depiction of the scene, in the fourteenth-century Arundel Psalter,[94] has some English verses above the figures:

> [Men] 'Ich am afert.' 'Lo whet ich se.'
>   'Me thinketh hit beth develes thre.'
> [Dead] 'Ich wes wel fair.' 'Such scheltou be.'
>   'For Godes love be wer by me.'

One of the fragmentary surviving wall-paintings with the legend, in Wensley church in Yorkshire,[95] also has traces of verses between the figures of the dead:

> [As] we a[re] nove/[Thus] sal the be/[B]ewar wyt [me]

There is a complete literary version in Middle English in an alliterative poem by John Audelay.[96] It is perhaps too long to be classified as a 'lyric', but it deserves a mention here, since it is almost totally neglected by critics. It is very uneven, and is sometimes marred by the uninspired use of conventional diction, but the best sections are powerful. Here the poet sees a boar at bay, and gives a lively description of the hunt. The mist comes down, and the three kings see three spectres gliding towards them. This is very well done:

> Schokyn out of a schawe thre schalkys at ene,
> Schadows unshene were chapid to chow,
> With lymes long and lene and leggys ful lew,
> Hadyn lost the lyp and the lyver sethyn thai were layd loue. . . .
> . . . was no beryn that ther was dorst bec nor bewe,
> Bot braydyn here brydilys agayne, her blongis can blow;
>   Here blonkis can blow and abyde.
>   Seche barns thai can hom byde,
>   Thai se no sokur hom besyde,
>   Bot oche kyng apon Crist cryde
>   With crossyng and karpyng o crede. . . .

There follow the usual exchanges between the living and the dead.

The Latin verses known as the *Vado Mori*,[97] found in MSS. of the thirteenth and fourteenth centuries, in which a number of figures arranged in roughly hierarchical order – king, pope,

The Life of this World

knight, physician etc. – complain that they must go to die (the words *vado mori* begin and end each couplet), is clearly closer in shape to the *Dance of Death*. There is a fifteenth-century English version which includes three of the 'complaints'.[98] If the verses are compared with the relevant Latin lines it will at once be obvious that much of the tautness and point has been lost:

> I wende to dede, knight stithe in stoure,
> Thurghe fyght in felde I wane the flour;
> Na fightes me taght the dede to quell –
> I weend to dede, soth I yow tell.
>
> I weende to dede, a kynge iwisse;
> What helpis honor, or werldis blysse?
> Dede is to mane the kynde wai –
> I wende to be clade in clay.
>
> I wende to dede, clerk full of skill,
> That couth with worde men mare and dill.
> Sone hase me made the dede an ende –
> Beese ware with me, to dede I wende.
>
> (Vado mori, rex sum, quid honor, quid gloria mundi?
> Est via mors hominis regia: vado mori.
>
> Vado mori, miles, belli certamine victor,
> Mortem non didici vincere: vado mori.
>
> Vado mori, logicus, aliis concludere novi;
> Conclusit breviter mors mihi: vado mori. . . .)

The English has lost the sharp irony of words like *regia* and *concludere . . . conclusit*; the rough force of its homely phrase 'clade in clay' does not make up for a series of flat tags and fillers. But though the English *Vado Mori* is no literary masterpiece, it has considerable interest, for it was conceived of as an 'illustrated poem'. All three MS. versions are accompanied by pictures, and the technique varies interestingly. In MS. Additional 37049 (plate 10) the treatment is typically crude and forceful. The skeletons with their spears lurk behind three seated figures, and the whole is crowded in as a side illustration of another *contemptus mundi* poem. In MS. Stowe 39 the treatment is rather more handsome, and more formal. The figures are confronted by a skeleton (in this version Death is also given a stanza). In MS. Cotton Faustina (plate 11) the scene has been drawn by a real artist. The finely drawn and sensitive faces of his figures express real grief, and the whole is filled with an air of melancholy. He has found no room for the crude depiction of the presence of death, but has preferred to let the sorrow of the victims speak for itself.

It would be tedious to prolong this list of lyrics which use the inherently dramatic situation of man's encounter with death. Leaving aside therefore laments of damned souls and complaints of souls to their wicked bodies,[99] we shall go on to consider a small group of lyrics which make remarkably imaginative use of the themes and images of the mortality tradition.

The first[100] takes up the traditional idea of the homilists that man is born to die, and that therefore the child comes weeping into the world (a twelfth-century sermon says that the child suffers bitter distress in his birth, comes into a grim dwelling, and shows this by its weeping; a later sermon records the cry of the weeping babe – 'Welaway! why was I resceyved in anny womans barme')[101] – a sentiment which Lear comes to echo:

> we came crying hither....
> When we are born, we cry that we are come
> To this great stage of fools.

The lyric boldly adopts the form of the lullaby, with all its suggestions of maternal tenderness and intimacy; the speaker is not the Virgin Mary, but a human mother, whose words transform the commonplaces of tradition into what is perhaps the bleakest statement of the human condition in early English literature:

> Lollai, lollai, litil child, whi wepistou so sore?
> Nedis mostou wepe, hit was iyarkid the yore
> Ever to lib in sorow, and sich and mourne ever,
> As thin eldren did er this, whil hi alives were.
>   Lollai, lollai, litil child, child lolai, lullow,
>   Into uncuth world icommen so ertow!

The recurring lament of the refrain emphasizes the grimness of the theme: other creatures may 'do themselves some good' by being born, but for the wretched seed of Adam only one thing is certain in this unstable world:

The Life of this World

> Child, thou ert a pilgrim in wikidnes ibor,
> Thou wandrest in this fals world, thou loke the bifor
> Deth ssal comwith a blast ute of a wel dim horre,
> Adamis kin dun to cast, him silf hath ido before. . . .

There is a confidence in the handling of images in this lyric which is rarely found:

> Child, thou nert a pilgrim bot an uncuthe g(est),
> Thi dawes beth itold, thi jurneis beth i(ke)st. . . .
>   Lollai, lollai, litil child, this wo Adam the wroght,
>   Whan he of the appil ete, and Eve hit him betacht.

One of the poems in the Vernon collection[102] is a reflection on mortality which exhibits in a remarkable and distinctive way the sombre pessimism and scepticism that is sometimes found in late medieval religion. It is based largely on the Old Testament book of Ecclesiastes (which Heine called the 'canticles of scepticism'). This author, 'the Preacher', sees existence as an ever-turning wheel, 'fruitless and purposeless, or, if there be a purpose . . . it is beyond the wit of man and hidden from him by God'. The Middle English poem elaborates with skill and power the idea starkly expressed in another quatrain:

> All hyt is fantome that we withe fare,
> And for othere mennes goode is all oure care;
> Alle come we hyder nakude and bare,
> Whenne we hethene passe, is there no mare.[103]

It opens in a questioning mood:

> I wolde witen of sum wys wiht
>   Witterly what this world were:
> It fareth as a foules fliht,
>   Now is hit henne, now is hit here,
> Ne be we never so muche of miht,
>   Now be we on benche, now be we on bere;
> And be we never so war and wiht,
>   Now be we sek, now beo we fere;
> Now is on proud withouten peere,
>   Now is the selve iset not by;
> And whos wol alle thing hertly here,
>   This world fareth as a fantasy.

Death and the Last Things

Following the Preacher, the poet illustrates change from the natural world:

> The sonnes cours, we may wel kenne,
>   Aryseth est and geth doun west;
> The ryvers into the see thei renne,
>   And hit is never the more almest;
> Wyndes rosscheth her and henne,
>   In snouw and reyn is non arest. . . .

It is against this background that he sees the life of man (neatly using a favourite image) – 'each man glides forth as a gest (guest, stranger)'. Echoing the Preacher's words he presents the mutability of man:

> Kunredes come, and kunredes gon,
>   As joyneth generacions;
> But alle hee passeth everichon,
>   For al heor preparacions;
> Sum ar foryete clene as bon
>   Among alle maner nacions;
> So schul men thenken us nothing on
>   That nou han the ocupacions . . .

sharply and effectively contrasting the sonorous abstract words of Latin origin with the homely expression 'forgotten clean as bone' (which is grotesquely appropriate to its mortality context). The recurring refrain 'This world fareth as a fantasye' emphasizes the inevitability of change.

At this point in the poem there is introduced the idea of the uselessness of discussion and argument. All these 'disputations', the poet says, 'idelyche all us occupye', for Christ 'maketh the creacions', with the implication that we cannot know his 'privete'. He asks the Psalmist's question, 'what is man?' but does not go on 'that God is mindful of him', but with a different question – who knows whether he is 'ought or nought'? His answer is that as a gnat 'grows up' out of earth and air, so does man, and that although man grows 'gret and fat' he will 'melt away' like a moth. He believes with the Preacher that there is little difference between men and beasts:

> Dyeth mon and beestes dye,
>   And al is on ocasion;
> And alle o deth bos bothe drye,
>   And han on incarnacion. . . .

The Life of this World

The only thing that distinguishes man is that he is more 'sleyye' (wise, cunning). Who knows if animals' souls sink down, and man's soul rises up (he uses the word 'soul' without theological distinction; the Vulgate version of Ecclesiastes has *spiritus*). Only God who understands the 'soun' of animals knows their 'intention'.

Man's intellect is of no more avail than his strength. Boldly, the poet introduces the question of differing religious belief. Each 'sect' he says (the word 'sect' could have either its modern sense, or that of 'religion') hopes to be saved, and 'baldeth bi heore bileeve'; they each think that the other 'raves', but they all call upon God and hope in him. The poet passes no judgment, but simply gives a fideistic expression of the need for God's mercy:

> Thus many maters men don meve,
> Sechen heor wittes hou and why;
> But Godes merci us alle biheveth,
> For this world fareth as a fantasy.

The stumbling beliefs of men are like children learning to talk. The anti-intellectual mood of the poem deepens – to what end do we wish to know the 'poyntes of Godes privete'?

> More then him lustes forte schowe
> We schulde not knowe in no degre;
> And idel bost is forte blowe
> A mayster of divinite.
> Thenk we lyve in eorthe her lowe,
> And God an heigh in mageste;
> Of material mortualite
> Medle we and of no more maistrie.
> The more we trace the Trinite
> The more we falle in fantasye.

We should leave our 'disputation' and simply believe in the creator of all. We cannot prove 'bi no resoun' how He was born. His power is infinite; he can turn 'kinds' upside down (this sounds a little like Ockham's 'absolute power' of God –

> Whon al ur bokes ben forth brouht,
> And al ur craft of clergye,
> And al ur wittes ben thorwout sought,
> Yit we fareth as a fantasye.

11 Vado Mori. The same illustrated poem as plate 10, here treated by an artist of genuine talent (see pp. 209-11).

12 A Song of Death. This illustrated poem from an Elizabethan broadsheet is an interesting survival of the *Dance of Death* (see p. 224).

Death and the Last Things

Like the Preacher, the poet launches into a *carpe diem* passage (though it is now in a very pietistic context):

> Of fantasye is al ur fare,
>   Olde and yonge and alle ifere;
> But make we murie and sle care,
>   And worschipe we god whil we ben here;
> Spende ur good and luytel spare,
>   And uche mon cheries othures cheere.
> Thenk hou we comen hider al bare
>   (Ur wey wendyng is in a were)
>   Prey we the prince that hath no pere,
>   Tac us hol to his merci
>   And kepe ur concience clere,
>   For this world is but fantasy

and the poem ends with yet another sombre reminder of mutability:

> Thus waxeth and wanieth mon, hors and hounde,
>   From nought to nought thus henne we hiye;
> And her we stunteth but a stounde,
>   For this world is but fantasye.

The coexistence of the different moods – the sombre pessimism, the questioning spirit, the doubts of man's value and of the capacity of his reason, together with the absolute insistence on faith and the need for God's mercy, and the hopeful advice to man to make virtue of necessity, which is almost optimistic yet has undertones of despair – results in a remarkable emotional power. This is an extraordinary and a unique religious poem, and it would be rash to find it typical of the 'spirit of the age', but it is a very interesting exercise to read it alongside something from a quite different context, Theseus's remarks on man's condition at the end of *The Knight's Tale*. One would like to know more about this author and his reading. It has been suggested that he has been influenced by the thought of Thomas Bradwardine, who takes a strongly Augustinian view of grace.[104] But the indications given by the poem are not clear enough, it seems, for us to fit him into any particular philosophical school. Certainly, however, it is hard to find a more powerful expression of that distrust of reason and philosophical scepticism and the consequent reliance on simple faith which have been seen in much late medieval thought.

We have already seen in other types of religious lyric that some of the most individual and brilliant treatments of traditional matter are the work of the Scottish poet Dunbar. The themes of mortality are no exception. They are prominent in a number of his poems, and are treated with typical vigour and energy. Many of the ideas and images which we have been discussing are found expressed with a new eloquence:

> Haif mynd that eild ay followis yowth;
> Deth followis lyfe with gaipand mowth,
> Devoring fruct and flowring grane:
> All erdly joy returnis in pane. . . .[105]

> Thy lustye bewte and thy youth
> Sall feid as dois the somer flouris;
> Syne sall the swallow with his mouth
> The dragone Death that all devouris.
> No castell sall the keip, nor touris,
> Bot he sall seik the with thy feiris;
> Thairfore, remembir at all houris
> *Quod tu in cinerem reverteris*. . . .[106]

> Walk furth, pilgrame, quhill thow hes dayis lycht,
>   Dres fra desert, draw to thy duelling place;
> Speid home, for quhy anone cummis the nicht,
>   Quhilk dois the follow with ane ythand chaise;
>   Bend up thy saill and win thy port of grace;
> For, and the deith ourtak the in trespas,
>   Than may thow say thir wourdis with 'allace'
> *Vanitas vanitatum, et omnia vanitas*.[107]

Two poems, however, deserve special mention. The first is the well-known 'Lament for the Makaris'[108] with its haunting traditional refrain *Timor mortis conturbat me*. The poet's own sickness ('I that in heill wes and gladnes/Am trublit now with gret seikness. . . .') is the emotional framework for the old themes of mutability and of the levelling power of death:

> On to the ded gois all estatis,
> Princis, prelotis, and potestatis,
> Baith riche and pur of al degre:
> *Timor mortis conturbat me*.

Death and the Last Things

> He takis the knychtis in to feild,
> Anarmit under helme and scheild;
> Victour he is at all mellie;
> *Timor mortis conturbat me.*
>
> That strang unmercifull tyrand
> Takis, on the moderis breist sowkand,
> The bab full of benignite. . . .

Death has taken all of Dunbar's 'brothers', the poets; the list of their names gives them fame and some measure of revenge, but the remorseless death is triumphant at the end of the poem:

> Sen he has all my brether tane,
> He will nocht lat me lif alane,
> On forse I man his nyxt pray be;
> *Timor mortis conturbat me.*
>
> Sen for the deid remeid is none,
> Best is that we for dede dispone,
> Eftir our deid that lif may we;
> *Timor mortis conturbat me.*

In the 'Meditatioun in Wyntir',[109] the theme of mortality is treated in a more personal and more subtle manner. The heaviness of the season embodies the poet's sorrow and 'dule spreit':

> In to thir dirk and drublie dayis,
> Quhone sabill all the hevin arrayis
>   With mistie vapouris, cluddis, and skyis,
>   Nature all curage me denyis
> Off sangis, ballattis, and of playis.
>
> Quhone that the nycht dois lenthin houris,
> With wind, with haill, and havy schouris,
>   My dule spreit dois lurk for schoir,
>   My hairt for languor dois forloir
> For laik of symmer with his flouris. . . .

As he turns in his vexed sleeplessness the poet's thoughts are assailed by suggestions from Despair, Patience, Prudence, Age and Death. The gentle tone of Age's speech:

> My freind, cum neir,
> And be not strange, I the requeir:
> Cum, brodir, by the hand me tak . . .

contrasts sharply with Death's abrupt address:

> Syne Deid castis upe his yettis wyd,
> Saying, 'This oppin sall the abyd;
>   Albeid that thow wer never sa stout,
>   Under this lyntall sall thow lowt:
> Thair is nane uther way besyde.'

The poet's melancholy is not completely removed by the coming of summer; the poem ends on a tentative and hesitant note:

> For feir of this all day I drowp;
> No gold in kist, nor wyne in cowp,
>   No ladeis bewtie, nor luiffis blys,
>   May lat me to remember this,
> How glaid that ever I dyne or sowp.
>
> Yit, quhone the nycht begynnis to schort,
> It dois my spreit sum pairt confort,
>   Off thocht oppressit with the schowris.
>   Cum, lustie symmer! with thi flowris,
> That I may leif in sum disport.

In most of the lyrics on death there is, as we said earlier, little room for tenderness, and little of the humble, even grateful acceptance of death after a good life (cf. St Francis, *Canticle of the Sun*, 'praised be my lord for our sister the death of the body, from whom no man escapeth'). These sentiments are however occasionally found. The idea that death is the end of the 'world's woe' and the beginning of true life is not unknown in moral poetry:

> Thynk and dred noght for to dy,
>   Syn thou sall nedis therto;
> Thynk that ded is opynly
>   Ende off werdes wo;
> Thynk als so, bot if thou dy,
>   To God may thou noght go;
> Thynk and hald the payed therby,
>   Thou may noght fle therfro. . . .[110]

It is given most eloquent expression in a few poems from the end of the Middle Ages. Some lines from one of the lyrics in the *Pilgrimage of the Soul*, the song of welcome sung by the angels to the victorious souls, have something of the spirit of *Pilgrim's Progress*:[111]

> How passed bene youre perilous aventures,
>   And all youre travaile hath an ende take.
> Ryght welcome be ye, blessid creatures!
>   Tyme is that scrippe and burdoun ye forsake,
>   For now ye schul no lenger journey make;
> And after labour time is of quiete,
> And hevynesse and angwysshe to foryete.

And, for an example of a more personal type of lyric, there is this not undistinguished poem by Ryman:[112]

> O dredeful deth, come make an ende!
>   Come unto me and do thy cure!
> Thy payne no tunge can comprehende,
>   That I fele, wooful creature.
>   O lorde, how longe shall it endure?
>   Whenne shall I goo this worlde fro,
>   Out of this bitter payne and woo?
>
> Full harde it is for to departe,
>   And harde it is this payne to abyde.
> O good lorde, that in heven art,
>   Thou be my helpe, comfort and guyde,
>   Bothe nyght and day and every tyde,
>   And take my soule into thy blis,
>   Wherof the joye shall nevir mys.

The best known of these poems is a verse written on the margin of an early sixteenth-century manuscript:[113]

> (N)owe cometh al ye that ben ybrought
>   In bondes, full of bitter besynesse
> Of erthly luste abydynge in your thought.
>   Here ys the reste of all your besynesse,
>   Here ys the porte of peese and resstfulnes
>   To them that stondeth in stormes of dysese,
>   Only refuge to wreches in dystrese,
>   And al comforte of myschefe and mysese.

Although it is sometimes a little diffuse and loose, it has a grave and simple dignity. Carleton Brown, who gave it the title of 'Death, the Port of Peace', said, rather rashly, that in it 'we recognize clearly the spirit of the Renaissance. At the threshold of the sixteenth century we are already looking forward to

The Life of this World

Spenser.' One suspects that he was thinking of the lines in Book One of *The Fairie Queene* in which Despair attempts to persuade the Redcross Knight to commit suicide, which is perhaps not the best place to look for the 'spirit of the Renaissance', but in any case it was later pointed out by Professor Greene that the verse comes from Walton's fifteenth-century translation of Boethius (III, *metrum* x) and that its primary reference is to God, not to death. This is made quite clear in Chaucer's gloss on this metre of Boethius: 'This is to seyn, that ye that ben comryd and disseyvid with worldly affeccions, cometh now to this sovereign good, that is God, that is refut to hem that wolen com to hym.' But, of course, the idea of death is present by implication. The images of 'rest' and 'port' have these overtones, as we can see from the stanzas from the *Pilgrimage of the Soul* just quoted; their most celebrated antecedent occurs in Cicero's work on old age[114] where Cato compares the coming of death to entering harbour after a long voyage. It is hard to think that Boethius did not have this passage in his mind when he wrote

> Haec erit vobis requies laborum,
> Hic portus placida manens quiete,
> Hoc patens unum miseris asylum. . . .

It is not, however, an image which found much favour with the more ascetic and didactic poets. It is wonderfully developed in a passage in Dante's *Convivio*, which will serve both to end this section and to place the 'macabre' lyrics of our tradition in perspective:

> She (the noble soul) in her last age returns to God, as to the port whence she departed when she came to enter upon the sea of this life . . . she blesseth the voyage that she hath made, because it hath been straight and good and without the bitterness of tempest. And here be it known that, as Tully says in that *Of Old Age*, 'natural death is as it were our our port and rest from our long voyage'. And even as the good sailor, when he draws near the port, lowers his sails, and gently with mild impulse enters into it, so ought we to lower the sails of our worldly activities and turn to God with all our purpose and heart; so that we may come to that port with all sweetness and all peace.[115]

Conclusion

It remains to say something about the fate of the religious lyrics after the first few decades of the sixteenth century, and the influence of medieval devotional literature; to do justice to this subject would require another volume. In the preceding pages I have been at pains to point out parallels and echoes of their images and themes in the poetry of the sixteenth and seventeenth centuries. It may therefore come as a surprise to begin this coda by saying that the medieval English lyrics seem to have had little *direct* influence on later religious lyrics (in that there is, for example, no evidence that a later poet like Donne ever read the poems of MS. Sloane 2593), and that it is rare to find examples of medieval lyrics copied or recorded after 1540–50. But this is hardly surprising in view of the considerable changes in religious beliefs and forms which took place at this period. The medieval lyrics, though numerous, had been a rather humble and workaday type of literature, with a practical and devotional bent; there was therefore less need for extreme reformers to use drastic methods of censorship, as seems to have been done with the public religious dramatic performances and festivals. No doubt many devotional books containing lyrics were destroyed by enthusiasts, but in the books which survive it is rare to find evidence of the disapproving marks which have erased the indulgence at the bottom of the devotional image in plate 6.[1] The old religious lyrics seem rather to have faded and declined. That group which touched most closely the courtly secular lyric was bound to suffer, partly because of its liking for Marian subjects, but also because of changing fashions in lyric style. The newer literary religious lyrics developed in their own way, and were more obviously the work and the property of self-conscious poets, who more and more had to face the 'problems' of religious literature. The large mass

Conclusion

of lyrics meant to be used, as prayers, mnemonics, meditations, etc., also suffered from changes in the social and literary milieu. Already in the fifteenth century verse was becoming less of a maid of all work, and the extension of prose for most practical and didactic purposes was no doubt encouraged by the influence of the printing presses.

And yet it is possible to find, especially in popular tradition, survivals and echoes of the themes, forms, and sometimes even the spirit of the medieval poems. We have seen examples of medieval prayer-charms, proverbial phrases from 'mortality' literature, or epitaphs occurring in the sixteenth and seventeenth centuries. The carol, though it loses its distinctive medieval form with the recurring burden, and becomes increasingly limited to Christmas songs, survives the Reformation as a genre of popular poetry.[2] And a few of the old carols do themselves survive in traditional form. The 'Corpus Christi Carol' is the most celebrated example, but there are others – 'When Cryst was born of Mary fre/In Bedlem, in that fayre cyte' was heard in a version sung by a gypsy in the beginning of the twentieth century; the Boar's Head carol of the Queen's College Oxford is a case where a text has been preserved in a small academic community. Occasionally we find a verbal echo – Professor Greene has shown that the Shropshire version of 'The Seven Virgins' ('Under the Leaves of Life' – a remarkable folk-song of which the greater part is a very traditional dialogue between Mary and Christ on the cross) seems to echo a line ('For to se my dere sone dye, and sones have I no mo') of a medieval carol. The same sort of survival is found in ballads and other forms of popular song. The old subjects of Joseph's trouble, Herod and St Stephen, and various infancy stories (cf. *The Bitter Withy*, *The Holy Well*) recur.[3] Aubrey records a famous and impressive example which we have not yet mentioned:[4]

> The beliefe in Yorkshire was amongst the vulgar (perhaps is in part still), that after the persons death the soule went over a Whinny-moore, and till about $\frac{1616}{1624}$ at the Funerall a woman came (like a Praefica) and sang the following song:
>
> > This ean night, this ean night,
> > every night and awle:
> > Fire and Fleet and Candle-light
> > and Christ recieve thy Sawle.

Conclusion

When thou from hence doest pass away
   every night and awle
To Whinny-moor thou comest at last
   and Christ recieve thy silly poor sawle.

If ever thou gave either hosen or shun
   every night and awle
Sitt thee downe and putt them on
   and Christ recieve thy sawle.

But if hosen nor shoon thou never gave nean
   every night, &c:
The Whinnes shall prick thee to the bare beane
   and Christ recieve thy sawle.

From Whinny-moor that thou mayst pass
   every night &c:
To Brig o' Dread thou comest at last
   and Christ &c:

From Brig of Dread that thou mayest pass
   no brader than a thread
   every night &c:
To Purgatory fire thou com'st at last
   and Christ &c.

If ever thou gave either Milke or drinke
   every night &c:
The fire shall never make thee shrink
   and Christ &c.

But if milk nor drink thou never gave nean
   every night &c:
The Fire shall burn thee to the bare bene
   and Christ recive thy Sawle.

Sir Walter Scott, who includes a different version in *The Minstrelsy of the Scottish Border*, describes it as 'a sort of charm sung by the lower ranks of Roman Catholics, in some parts of the north of England, while watching a dead body, previous to interment. The tune is doleful and monotonous, and, joined to the mysterious import of the words, has a solemn effect'.[5] This powerful dirge has parallels in European folk-poetry;[6] the student of medieval

Conclusion

literature will recognize not only survivals of the idea of Purgatory, and the corporal works of mercy, but also that narrow, dangerous bridge, found in the visions of the Other World, which links Purgatory and Paradise.[7]

The broadside ballads of Elizabethan and later times preserve some of the older themes, especially of the mortality tradition.[8] One song of death begins with a typically grim and ironic question–

> Canne yea dance the shakinge of the sheetes,
>   A daunce that everie man must dooe?
> Can yea trime it up with daintie sweetes,
>   And everie thinge that longs there too?
> Make readie then your winding sheete,
> And see how yea canne besturre youre feete,
> For death is the man that all must meete. . . .

Others use the old dramatic device of the unexpected meeting of Death and man – one such, *Death and the Lady*, is still found with a lurid illustration at the end of the eighteenth century.[9] One or two of these illustrated death ballads are very clearly in the tradition of the old *Dance of Death*. In one (plate 12) the dance circles around an open grave and the figure of 'Sycknes Deathes minstrel', while in the four corners Death comes to take off miser, prisoner, judge and lovers (two at least may be faint echoes of Holbein's 'Images' of the Rich Man and the Judge). The accompanying verses are neatly arranged as *tituli*. In the same collection, on another sheet Death drives off a bishop, a king, a harlot, a lawyer and a labourer, and again the whole is arranged as an illustrated poem. The verses in these ballads do not have the grim force of their macabre antecedents, but they are in a direct line of continuity.

In one way, even the learned religious poetry of the later sixteenth and seventeenth centuries maintained an unbroken link with the past in that the Christian Latin tradition (with a surprising number of its medieval developments and accretions) continued with full authority and influence. Apart from the few great disputed points of dogma, the spiritual inheritance of Catholic and Protestant was often surprisingly similar. Though the Dowsings and the Jessups ordered the destruction of 'IHS the Jesuit's badge' and other popish images, the translation by Quarles of the Jesuit Hermann Hugo's *Pia Desideria* (concealing its Jesuit origins, but reproducing its counter-Reformation

Conclusion

plates) was popular reading, especially it seems, among Puritans! The Psalms continued to be used for meditation and for confessional poetry: they played an important part, for instance, in the life and worship of the remarkable community at Little Gidding[10] (the spirit of which has been compared to that of the medieval Brethren of Common Life). The Latin hymns continued to be known and echoed in poetry; passages of the old liturgy such as the *Improperia* were not forgotten. The medieval doctors of the spiritual life continued to be read; the writings, genuine or otherwise, of 'Bernard' lie behind many meditations. And, as we have seen, even the cults and themes of late medieval devotional literature – the Five Wounds, the Precious Blood, the Instruments of the Passion, the Debate of the Soul and Body – appear again.

Even more importantly, in a deeper, more intangible way, much of the spirit of medieval devotion continues, not only in a special community like that of the Ferrars, but in religious literature of very varied sorts. Gregory Dix points out amusingly how much of the intensely Christocentric affective devotion of the Passion prayers said by the medieval laity privately during Low Mass has found its way into the new liturgy, not only into the *Book of Common Prayer* but even into the reformed liturgy offered by Baxter and the Puritans.[11] The stress on 'being there' in meditating on the scenes from the life of Christ continues as strongly as ever – John Davies has a poem with the significant title *The Holy Roode or Christs Crosse: containing Christ crucified, described in speaking pictures*, which has an appeal of Christ from the cross (based on the *Improperia*). In fact, the characteristic emphases of medieval spirituality – a personal relationship with Christ, love, simplicity – had become part of the Western Christian tradition. That typical product of medieval devotion, the significantly named *Imitation of Christ*, was destined to be the favoured reading of Catholic and Protestant alike. Whether they were aware of it or not, the view that the later religious poets had of the traditional 'matter' of Christianity had been influenced and moulded by the work of Anselm, Bernard, Francis, and the rest. With the Reformation (and its Catholic counterpart) there went out much of the superstition and extravagance of late medieval religion, but also something of the simplicity of a totally popular religion – no longer do we find references in church accounts to 'a pair of gloves for him that played Christ on Corpus Christi

Conclusion

day'.[12] Yet the great religious poets of the seventeenth century are in a sense the inheritors of that delicate balance of emotion and intelligence, of learning and simplicity, and of that profound and humble style that is characteristic of the best of the medieval religious lyrics.

Note on Sources and Abbreviations

The most complete modern editions of the lyrics are the volumes of Carleton Brown – *English Lyrics of the Thirteenth Century*, Oxford, 1932 (*CB XIII*), *Religious Lyrics of the Fourteenth Century*, revised by G. V. Smithers, Oxford, 1952 (*CB XIV*), *Religious Lyrics of the Fifteenth Century*, Oxford, 1939 (*CB XV*) – and R. L. Greene's *The Early English Carols*, Oxford, 1935 (*EEC*), and wherever possible I have referred to these. Further information on the MSS. or editions of particular lyrics can be found under the relevant entries in *The Index of Middle English Verse*, by Carleton Brown and Rossell Hope Robbins, New York, 1943, and its *Supplement*, by Rossell Hope Robbins and John L. Cutler, Lexington, 1965 (*Index*). Many lyrics are collected in the anthologies of R. T. Davies, *Medieval English Lyrics*, London, 1963 (Davies), and E. K. Chambers and F. Sidgwick, *Early English Lyrics*, London, 1921 (*EEL*). The Clarendon Medieval and Tudor Series has *A Selection of English Carols*, ed. R. L. Greene, Oxford, 1962 (*SEC*); this will be joined by *A Selection of Religious Lyrics*, ed. Douglas Gray. Apart from references to discussions of themes and poems in the remarkably full and authoritative study by Rosemary Woolf, *The English Religious Lyric in the Middle Ages*, Oxford, 1968 (Woolf), I have not swollen the notes with references to interesting critical comments in such books as George Kane, *Middle English Literature* (London, 1951), Stephen Manning, *Wisdom and Number* (Lincoln, Nebraska, 1962), etc. The following other abbreviations are commonly used in the notes:

Archiv: *Archiv für das Studium Neueren Sprachen.*
Brieger: Peter Brieger, *English Art 1216–1307*, Oxford (Oxford History of English Art), 1957.
Child: F. J. Child, *The English and Scottish Popular Ballads*, Boston, 1857–8.
Dreves: *Analecta Hymnica*, ed. Guido Maria Dreves (continued by C. Blume), Leipzig, 1886– .
EETS: Early English Text Society ((ES): Extra Series).

Note on Sources and Abbreviations

EHR: *English Historical Review.*
ELH: *Journal of English Literary History.*
Eng. St.: *Englische Studien.*
Evans: *English Art 1307–1461* by Joan Evans, Oxford (Oxford History of English Art), 1949.
JEGP: *Journal of English and Germanic Philology.*
JFSS: *Journal of the Folk-Song Society.*
J. Arch. Ass.: *Journal of the British Archaeological Association.*
JWCI: *Journal of the Warburg and Courtauld Institutes.*
LM: *Lexikon der Marienkunde*, ed. K. Algermissen and others, Regensburg, 1957– .
MÆ: *Medium Ævum.*
Mâle, *Fin*: E. Mâle, *L'Art religieux de la Fin du moyen âge en France*, Paris, 1946 ed.
Mâle, *XIII*: idem. *L'Art religieux du XIIIe siècle en France*, Paris, 1958 ed.
MLN: *Modern Language Notes.*
MLR: *Modern Language Review.*
Mone: F. J. Mone, *Lateinische Hymness des Mittelalters*, Freiburg, 1853.
MP: *Modern Philology.*
NM: *Neuphilologische Mitteilungen.*
NQ: *Notes and Queries.*
OBMLV: *Oxford Book of Medieval Latin Verse*, ed. F. J. E. Raby, 1959.
PL: *Patrologia Latina*, ed. Migne.
PMLA: *Publications of the Modern Language Association.*
RDK: *Reallexikon zur deutschen Kunstgeschichte*, ed. O. Schmitt, Stuttgart, 1937– .
Réau: L. Réau, *Iconographie de l'Art chrétien*, vol. II, Paris, 1957.
RES: *Review of English Studies.*
Robbins, *Sec. Lyr.*: Rossell Hope Robbins, *Secular Lyrics of the XIVth and XVth Centuries*, Oxford, 1952.
RS: Rolls Series.
SP: *Studies in Philology.*
STC: *Short-Title Catalogue of English Books, 1475–1640*, ed. A. W. Pollard and G. R. Redgrave, London, 1926.
STS: Scottish Text Society.

Notes

Chapter 1 The Inherited Tradition

1 Ed. A. S. Cook (Boston, 1900), ll. 104 ff. On the literary aspects and potential of the liturgy, see F. di Capua, 'Preghiere liturgiche, poesia ed eloquenza', *Archivio Italiano per la Storia della Pietà* i (1951), 1–24.
2 Ed. F. Whitehead (Oxford, 1947), ll. 2384 ff.
3 Ed. W. W. Skeat and K. Sisam (Oxford, 1915), ll. 331 ff.
4 On the ceremony of the blessing of the Paschal Candle, see T. Klauser, *A Short History of the Western Liturgy* (tr. J. Halliburton, Oxford, 1969), pp. 81, 210–11, B. Capelle, 'La Procession du Lumen Christi au Samedi-Saint', *Revue Bénédictine* xliv (1932), 105–19, A. Baumstark, *Liturgie comparée* (1952), 149, 161 ff. It can be traced back as far as the seventh century. The *Exultet* was sometimes, in Italy, from the eleventh to the thirteenth centuries, written out with the music on MS. rolls, each section accompanied by illustrations placed upside down so that they could be seen by the congregation when they were laid over the back of the *ambo* or lectern; see E. Bertaux, *L'Art dans l'Italie méridionale*, I (1903), 216–40 (with a supplement on iconography), M. Avery, *The Exultet Rolls of Southern Italy*, II (Princeton, 1936).
5 The translation is primarily that of Dom G. Lefebvre, *The Daily Missal* (Bruges/London, 1924).
6 On typological interpretation, see, for example, J. Daniélou, *From Shadows to Reality* (London, 1960), G. W. R. Lampe and K. J. Woolcombe, *Essays on Typology* (London, 1957). The Alexandrian Jewish background of the technique is discussed in G. Kittel, *Theologisches Wörterbuch zum neuen Testament*, I, 260–4. A. C. Charity, *Events and their After Life* (Cambridge, 1966), in a most interesting discussion of typology, applies it to Dante's *Commedia*.
7 To cite but two examples from the seventeenth century: the east window of Lincoln College chapel, Oxford, has a number of traditional types and antitypes (the creation of Adam and Eve with

Christ's Nativity, the crossing of the Red Sea with the Baptism, the Passover and the Last Supper, the Brazen Serpent and the Crucifixion, the ascent of Elijah and the Ascension of Christ), and a series was included in the decorative scheme by Rubens for the Jesuit church in Antwerp. Simple examples (e.g. the tree of death in Eden with the tree of life) still appear on tombstones in the eighteenth and early nineteenth centuries (F. Burgess, *English Churchyard Memorials* (London, 1963), pp. 188–9).

8 F. van der Meer, *Early Christian Art*, tr. P. and F. Brown (London, 1967), pp. 92 ff.
9 Ibid., p. 93.
10 Ibid., p. 95.
11 In 'Figura', *Archivum Romanicum*, xxii (1938), 436–89, and at length in *Mimesis, dargestellte Wirklichkeit in der abendländischen Literatur*, Bern, 1946; tr. W. R. Trask as *Mimesis, the Representation of Reality in Western Literature* (Princeton, 1953. References are to this ed.)
12 *Mimesis*, p. 74.
13 The Psalms were turned into English verse in the Old English period; unfortunately, both this version, and the later Middle English verse translations are poetically undistinguished.
14 *Confessions* ix, tr. E. B. Pusey.
15 *PL* ci, 465–6; see R. W. Southern, *St. Anselm and his Biographer* (Cambridge, 1963), p. 39.
16 Ed. W. H. Stevenson, pp. 21, 73.
17 See *Thomas More's Prayer Book. A Facsimile Reproduction of the Annotated Pages* transcribed and translated by Louis L. Martz and Richard Sylvester (New Haven, 1969), with an interesting discussion of the placement of More's lines in the pages of his Book of Hours and of his marginalia in the Psalter.
18 Samuel Singer, *Die religiöse Lyrik des Mittelalters (Das Nachleben der Psalmen)*, (Bern, 1933).
19 *Confessions*, ix.
20 See J. Szövérffy, *Die Annalen der lateinischer Hymnendichtung* (Berlin, 1964–5); shorter accounts are to be found in F. J. E. Raby, *Christian Latin Poetry* (Oxford, 1953) and Peter Dronke, *The Medieval Lyric* (London, 1968). For the hymns known in pre-conquest England, see Helmut Gneuss, *Hymnar und Hymnen im englischen Mittelalter* (Tübingen, 1968).
21 *CB XIV*, 25. On Herebert and his translations, see Helmut Gneuss, 'William Hereberts Übersetzungen', *Anglia* lxxviii (1960), 169–92; he was obviously a learned man, since he was *lector* in the Franciscan house in Oxford.
22 I have rearranged the order of the last two couplets (restoring the order of the Biblical passage) according to what seems to me to be the sense of a note in the MS.

23 Common in the Old Testament; cf., for example, Ps. xxiii (Vulgate) ('Lift up your heads O ye gates, and be ye lift up ye everlasting doors; and the king of glory shall come in.' 'Who is this king of glory?' etc.), which is put to dramatic effect in an exchange between Christ and the devils in the York Harrowing of Hell play, Isa. xl, Cant. iii, 6–10, vi, 1–3, etc.
24 Cf. Lam. 1: 15, Joel 3:12–13, and in the New Testament, Rev. xiv, 19–20, xix, 15.
25 *PL* cxlv, 1162.
26 St Augustine (*PL* xxxvi, 649) in his comment on Ps. lv makes the connection: Christ is the grape, the *botrus*, who has been put under the press – *primus botrus in torculari pressus est Christus*.
27 On the 'mystic winepress', see L. Lindet, 'Les Représentations allégoriques du Moulin et du Pressoir dans l'art chrétien', *Revue archéologique* (3e sér.) xxxvi (1900), 403 ff., Mâle *Fin*, figs 63 ff. (in Bellegambe's 'Fountain of Life' at Lille (fig. 62) two of the questions from the *Quis est iste* passage are held by angels, and the verse *torcular calcavi solus* is above the cross), M. Vloberg, *L'Eucharistie dans l'art* (Grenoble, 1946) pp. 172 ff., *RDK* s.v. 'Christus in der Kelter'. There is a good post-Reformation example in Van Haeften's *Schola Cordis* (1629; turned into English by Christopher Harvey as *The School of the Heart*, 1647), Emblem xlvii.
28 *Minor Poems*, ed. MacCracken, EETS (ES) cvii, p. 251.
29 For a more modern example, see G. M. Hopkins, 'Barnfloor and Winepress'.

Chapter 2   Medieval Devotion

1 A. Daniel, *Thesaurus hymnologicus* (1841) ii, 342.
2 W. A. Pantin, *The English Church in the Fourteenth Century* (Cambridge, 1955), p. 190. There are many accounts of medieval spirituality; see, for example, P. Pourrat, *La Spiritualité chrétienne*, II (Paris, 1951), Dom A. Wilmart, *Auteurs spirituels et textes dévots du moyen âge latin* (Paris, 1932), J. Leclerq, F. Vandenbroucke and L. Bouyer, *The Spirituality of the Middle Ages* (London, 1968). It is hard to believe that (as is sometimes implied) 'affective' devotion suddenly 'began' in the late eleventh century. It is much more likely that fervent and personal devotion to Christ was an aspect of Christian spirituality which was present from the beginning (cf. the Gospel stories of Mary Magdalene's devotion to Christ), even if it was not given such emphatic (or exaggerated) expression as in the Middle Ages. Fr A. Hamman's collection of *Early Christian Prayers* (tr. W. Mitchell, Chicago, 1961) contains some impressive examples, notably from the Eastern Church (see especially Nos 65

(Origen on the wounds of love), 257 (Gregory of Nazianzus)). St Augustine's expressions of faith and devotion are often both personal and fervent (cf. the discussion of the *Confessions* by Peter Brown in *Augustine of Hippo* (London, 1967). Fr E. Colledge has some interesting remarks on the ejaculatory and intense private prayers from Irish sources which are found in some Old English manuscripts (in *Pre-Reformation English Spirituality*, ed. J. Walsh (London, 1966), pp. 26ff., and in the Introduction to his *The Medieval Mystics of England* (London, 1962)). Cf. also Dom L. Gougaud, *Christianity in Celtic Lands* (London, 1932), pp. 334 ff., and 'Étude sur les loricae', *Bull. d'ancienne litt. et d'archéol. chrétiennes*, i (1911), ii (1912). Probably this strain of personal devotion was taken up and given memorable literary form by powerful intellects like Anselm and Bernard, and with the weight of their authority as leaders and spokesmen of the ascetic and eremitic revival became the accepted and expected form of expression.

3 Southern, op. cit., pp. 37–8. The genuine prayers and meditations are in Vol. III of Anselm's *Opera*, ed. Schmitt (1946).

4 See O. Pächt, 'The Illustrations of St Anselm's Prayers and Meditations', *JWCI* xix (1956), 68–83, who points out, *inter alia*, that the renewal of asceticism was not necessarily hostile to representational art, but that 'its urge towards introspection, its emphasis on affective feeling and pious compassion ... fermented visual imagination and led to new artistic experience which ultimately had a humanizing effect on the imagery of Christian art'.

5 Schmitt, op. cit., III, pp. 7–8.

6 *Inferia IV^a hebd. sanctae, Opera*, ed. J. Leclerq (Rome, 1968), V, p. 58.

7 Ed. H. W. Robbins (Lewisburg, 1925). This devotional work remained popular for a long time – the English version appears in early printed books (see *STC* 965–7).

8 Cf. E. Underhill, *The Mystics of the Church* (London, 1925), p. 93, Cristofori, 'Memorie del B. Pietro Pettinagno da Siena', *Miscellanea Francescana* v (1890), 34–52, F. W. Moorman, *A History of the Franciscan Order* (Oxford, 1968), p. 223. He was a comb-maker and a Franciscan Tertiary; Dante alludes briefly to him (*Purg.* xiii, 127–8).

9 Ed. B. J. Whiting, EETS clxxxiv, 213. Cf. the later Franciscan Ryman (*Archiv* lxxxix, 318): *Salve decus pauperum,/In* whom be vertuys ryve,/*In quo Cristus iterum*/Schewith his woundes five.

10 See E. W. Tristram, *English Medieval Wall Painting* (London, 1944), p. 620, F. J. Baigent, 'On the church of St. John, Winchester, and the paintings newly discovered on the north wall', *J. Arch. Ass.* ix (1854), 1–14.

Notes to pp. 22–5

11 Thomas of Celano, *First Life*, ch. xxx, tr. A. G. Ferrers Howell (London, 1908, Latin text in Rome ed. (1906), p. 87).
12 See Ida Ragusa and Rosalie B. Green, *Meditations on the Life of Christ: An Illustrated MS. of the Fourteenth Century* (Princeton, 1961). On Franciscan influence on the visual arts, see H. Thode, *Franz von Assisi und die Anfänge der Kunst der Renaissance in Italien* (1885), *Franciscan History and Legend in English Medieval Art*, ed. A.G. Little (British Society of Franciscan Studies, 1937).
13 Brieger, p. 171 (cf. pp. 98–9 etc.).
14 Ed. W. W. Skeat, EETS xxx (1867), ll. 118 ff.
15 Ed. P. Sabatier, Br. Soc. of Franciscan Studies, xiii (1928), ch. 100.
16 See E. Underhill, *Jacopone da Todi, Poet and Mystic, 1228–1306* (London, 1919) and the discussion by Peter Dronke, *The Medieval Lyric*, pp. 58–63.
17 J. A. Symonds, *The Renaissance in Italy. Italian Literature*, I (London, 1881), pp. 298, 533–4.
18 See Rossell Hope Robbins, 'The Authors of the ME Religious Lyrics', *JEGP* xxxix (1940) 230–8, 'The Earliest Carols and the Franciscans', *MLN* liii (1938) 239–45, and R. L. Greene, *EEC* Introduction, 'The Franciscans and the Carol'.
19 Herbert, *A Priest to the Temple* (*Works*, ed. F. E. Hutchinson, p. 233).
20 On medieval sermons, see H. G. Pfander, *The Popular Sermon of the Medieval Friar in England* (New York, 1937), G. R. Owst, *Preaching in Medieval England* (Cambridge, 1926), and *Literature and Pulpit in Medieval England* (Cambridge, 1933, 1961) (the limitations of Owst's methods are pointed out in a review by Leonard Boyle, *MÆ* xxxiii, 227–30). Cf. also L. Toulmin Smith, 'English Popular Preaching in the Fourteenth Century', *EHR* vii (1892), 25–36.
21 As Francis's imitation of the sheep bleating. St Bernardino of Siena (a Franciscan) is said to have amused his audience by imitating the croaking of a frog.
22 Owst, *Preaching*, p. 351.
23 See *Journal d'un Bourgeois de Paris 1405–49*, ed. A. Tuetey (Paris 1881), pp. 233 ff. *Pierce the Ploughman's Crede*, which is full of virulent attacks on the friars, complains, curiously enough, that they do not preach penitence as they should, but simply entertain their audience with nice Marian sermons.
24 See D. Knowles, *The Religious Orders in England*, II (Cambridge, 1955), pp. 136–8, 343, E. Margaret Thompson, *The Carthusian Order in England* (London, 1930), G. C. Williamson, 'The Books of the Carthusians', *Bibliographica* III (1897), 213.
25 See R. M. Clay, *The Hermits and Anchorites of England* (London,

1914). There is a general survey of the whole eremitic tradition by P. F. Anson, *The Call of the Desert* (London, 1964).
26 The Life is ed. and tr. by C. H. Talbot (Oxford, 1959). There is some evidence that there was a continuous eremitic tradition in England from pre-conquest times; Talbot (p. 12) points out that the hermits of these early post-conquest period often have Saxon rather than Norman names – Wulfric, Sigar, Godric. Indeed, the Latin life of Christina records that her spiritual director called her by the homely English title 'myn sunendæge dohter'.
27 Anson, p. 167, mentions one English hermit who kept himself chained like a tethered goat, and moved himself each Saturday.
28 The oddest manifestations are the ornamental hermits favoured by gentlemen of the eighteenth and nineteenth centuries (cf. Anson, pp. 193 ff., Edith Sitwell, *English Eccentrics* (London 1958), pp. 48–67); there is even an advertisement (1810) requesting 'employment' from a young man, 'who wishes to retire from the world and live as a hermit, in some convenient spot in England'.
29 Ed. in various volumes of EETS; tr. by Mary Salu (London, 1955). G. Shepherd's edition of Parts VI and VII of the *Ancrene Wisse* (London, 1959) contains much useful information on its spirituality.
30 (He was probably John Whiterig.) Ed. by H. Farmer, *The Monk of Farne* (London, 1961). Cf. W. A. Pantin, 'The Monk-Solitary of Farne: a Fourteenth-Century English Mystic', *EHR* lix (1944), 162–80.
31 See E. Colledge, *Mediaeval Netherlands Religious Literature* (Leyden, London, 1965), Introduction, H. Grundmann, *Religiöse Bewegungen im Mittelalter* (Hildesheim, 1935), esp. pp. 170–354, 452–75, 'Die Frauen und die Literatur im Mittelalter', *Archiv. f. Kulturgeschichte* xxvi (1936), 129–61.
32 Her *Revelations of Divine Love* are accessible in modernized versions by Grace Warrack (London, 1901, 1950), R. Hudleston, J. Walsh, A. M. Reynolds, etc.
33 See Robin Flower, *The Irish Tradition* (Oxford, 1947), ch. ii.
34 See Zupitza, *Englische Studien* xi, 401–32. Cf. the essay by C. H. Talbot in *Pre-Reformation English Spirituality*, ed. J. Walsh.
35 See Hope Emily Allen, *Writings Ascribed to Richard Rolle* (N.Y., 1927), *English Writings of Richard Rolle* (Oxford, 1931).
36 Ed. S. Meech and H. E. Allen, EETS ccxii (1940). There is a modernized version by W. Butler-Bowden (1936, 1954).
37 Meech and Allen, op. cit., p. 148.
38 See *Four Dialogues on Painting*, tr. A. F. G. Bell (London, 1928), pp. 15–16.
39 J. Huizinga, *The Waning of the Middle Ages* (English ed., London, 1924), p. 244. All page references are from the 1948 reprint.

40 The English artists, of course, attempted the same thing. A famous passage in the chronicle of the abbey of Meaux in Yorkshire (*Chronica Monasterii de Melsa*, ed. E. A. Bond, R.S. 43c (1868), III, 35) describes how Abbot Hugh (1339–49) had a new crucifix made, and the sculptor had a naked man standing before him as he worked so that from his beautiful form he might make the crucifix more fairly.
41 Margaret Whinney, *Early Flemish Painting* (London, 1968), p. 115.
42 These trends are interestingly discussed by G. Leff in 'Changing Patterns in Medieval Thought', *Bulletin of the John Rylands Library* xliii (1961), 354–72, and *Medieval Thought. St. Augustine to Ockham* (London, 1958).
43 B. Smalley, *English Friars and Antiquity in the Early Fourteenth Century* (Oxford, 1960).
44 A. Hyma, *The Christian Renaissance. A History of the 'Devotio Moderna'* (Hamden, Conn., 2nd ed., 1965), pp. 30–1. Bartholomew was a follower of the 'Free Spirit'; our knowledge of his doctrine is derived from the letters of Gerald Groote (*Epistolae*, ed. J. G. R. Acquoy, pp. 28 ff.). This aspect of late medieval religion is discussed by N. Cohn, *The Pursuit of the Millennium* (rev. ed., 1970). Cf. also G. C. Coulton, 'The Plain Man's Religion in the Middle Ages', *Hibbert Journal* xiv (1916), 592–603.
45 As, for all its suggestive ideas, is the underlying tendency in Erwin Panofsky's *Gothic Architecture and Scholasticism* (Latrobe, 1951). Cf. E. Gombrich, *In Search of Cultural History* (Oxford, 1969).

Chapter 3   The English Lyrics, I

1 Pantin, op. cit., p. 189 (and *passim*). Cf. also G. R. Owst, 'Some Books and Book-owners of Fifteenth-century St. Albans', *Trans. St. Albans and Herts. Archaeological Society* (1929), 175–94, Robbins, *Sec. Lyr.*, pp. xxviii ff., and *PMLA* lxv, 249–80, H. S. Bennett, *English Books and Readers 1475–1557* (Cambridge, 2nd ed., 1969), ch. ii, J. W. Adamson, 'The Extent of Literacy in England in the Fifteenth and Sixteenth Centuries', *Library* (4th ser.) x (1929–30), 164–5.
2 See M. Dominica Legge, *Anglo-Norman Literature and its Background* (Oxford, 1963), and *Anglo-Norman in the Cloisters* (Edinburgh, 1950).
3 Tr. Dorothy Jones, *Minor Works of Hilton* (London, 1929).
4 See W. F. Schirmer, *John Lydgate* (tr. A. E. Keep, 1961), Derek Pearsall, *John Lydgate* (London, 1970). One of the most interesting of the pious noble ladies of the late Middle Ages was Cicely, Duchess

of York, the mother of Edward IV and Richard III: see C. A. J. Armstrong, 'The Piety of Cicely, Duchess of York: A Study in Late Mediaeval Culture' in *For Hilaire Belloc. Essays in Honour of his Seventy-second Birthday*, ed. D. Woodruff (London, 1942), pp. 73-94. She read 'Bonaventure' (probably Nicholas Love's English paraphrase of the *Meditations*), Hilton's *Mixed Life*, an apocryphal narrative of Christ's infancy (the *De Infantia Salvatoris*), the *Legenda Aurea*, 'St. Maude' (apparently the mystical *Liber Specialis Gratiae* of Mechtild of Hackeborn in an English version), 'St. Katherine of Senys' (possibly the Life of St Catherine of Siena by Raymond de Vincis), and the 'Revelacions of St. Bridgett', the English version of the intense visions of St Bridget of Sweden, which were both popular and influential.

5 See Brieger, pp. 96 ff., T. Borenius, 'The Cycle of Images in the Palaces and Castles of Henry III', *JWCI* vi (1943), 40-50.

6 Ed. E. J. Arnould (Oxford, 1940). See also Arnould, 'Henry of Lancaster and his "Livre des Seintes Medicines"', *Bulletin of the John Rylands Library* xxi (1937), 352-86 (one MS. was owned by a later 'good duke', Humfrey of Gloucester). On Henry's life see K. Fowler, *The King's Lieutenant: Henry of Grosmont, First Duke of Lancaster, 1310-1361* (London, 1969).

7 See Blacman's *Memoir*, ed. M. R. James (Cambridge, 1919), pp. 13, 35.

8 R. J. Mitchell, *John Tiptoft* (London, 1938), p. 143.

9 On guilds see G. Unwin, *The Guilds and Companies of London* (London, 1938). Parish fraternities in particular attended to the spiritual needs of parishioners. Religious observances were an important aspect. The Guild of Salve Regina of St Magnus Church, for example (Unwin, p. 115), sang the anthem 'in honour and reverence of the Five Joys of Our Lady'. There was a *puy* or *confrérie* like the French *puys* of minstrels in London during the fourteenth century (Unwin, pp. 98-100); its functions were religious, convivial and literary, and it is most unlikely that religious lyrics, in Anglo-Norman if not in English, were not sometimes presented.

10 Cf. the interesting material collected by Owst from sermons and sermonbooks in 'Sortilegium in English homiletic literature of the fourteenth century', *Studies presented to Sir Hilary Jenkinson*, ed. J. Conway Davies (London, 1957).

11 See Gougaud, 'La Mesure de la plaie du côté', *Revue d'Histoire ecclésiastique* xx (1924), 223 ff., W. Sparrow Simpson, *J. Arch. Ass.* xxx (1874), 357 ff., Gray, *NQ* ccx (1963), 87-8.

12 J. Brand, *Observations on Popular Antiquities* (with the Additions of Sir Henry Ellis, London, 1877), p. 729.

13 Quoted by G. L. Gomme, *Folklore as a Historical Science* (London, 1908), p. 189, from a sermon (1659) by a Mr Pemble. See L. C.

Wimberly, *Folklore in the English and Scottish Popular Ballads* (Chicago, 1928), pp. 68–72, 149 ff. An important study by Keith Thomas, *Religion and the Decline of Magic* (London, 1971), appeared too late to be used in this book.

14 Owst, 'Sortilegium', pp. 294–5. Cf. the seventeenth-century Norwegian folk-charm quoted by Robbins, *Encyclopedia of Witchcraft and Demonology* (New York, 1960), pp. 363–4: 'Christ walked to the church with a book in his hand. Came the Virgin Mary herself walking. "Why are you so pale, my blessed son?" "I have caught a powerful grippe." "I cure you of powerful grippe – cough grippe, intestinal grippe, back grippe, chest grippe – from flesh and bone, to beach and stone, in the name of the Father, Son and Holy Ghost".'

15 See Iona and Peter Opie, *Oxford Dictionary of Nursery Rhymes* (Oxford, 1957) 303–35 (where examples from other European languages are quoted), A. A. Barb, 'Animula Vagula Blandula', *Folklore* lxi (1949), 15–30.

16 Robbins, *Sec. Lyr.* No. 61. There were a number of prayers by the cross, ranging from the simple ejaculation 'Christ cros me spede' to charms. Cf. also B. Bischoff, 'Ursprung und Geschichte eines Kreuzsegens', *Volk and Volkstum* i (1936), 225–31.

17 Robbins, *Sec. Lyr.*, No. 65. A later version occurs (as a charm against toothache) in a seventeenth-century MS. in the Bodleian Library (e mus. 243, f. 37r).

18 Cf also other poems: *Poetical Works*, ed. Moorman (Oxford, 1915), pp. 217, 258, 284, 322.

19 *CB XIV* No. 32, discussed below, pp. 84ff. Ryman's carol is *EEC* No. 205. Cf. the phrase in Latin hymns (*totius*) *trinitatis triclinium* (e.g. Mone II, Nos 335, 364, 524); the Latin word is taken over as a learned word, *triclyne*, in Ryman's carols (*EEC* Nos 199, 224).

20 There is a fifteenth-century *vierge ouvrante* of this type in the church of St Mathieu, Morlaix. The 'Lady of Boultone' at Durham seems to have been an example: see Fowler, *Rites of Durham* (Surtees Soc. cvii, 1903), p. 30, 'Every principall daie the said immage was opened that every man might se pictured within her, the father, the sonne, and the holy ghost, most curiouslye and fynely gilted.' (God the Father was represented holding 'a fair and large crucifix of Christ all of gold'.) Gerson's remarks (*Opera*, ed. L. Ellies du Pin (Antwerp, 1706), III, p. 947): '. . . quae in ventribus earum unum habent Trinitatem, veluti si tota Trinitas in Virgine Maria carnem assumpsisset humanum. . . . mea namque sententia nulla in eis est pulchritudo, nec devotio, et possunt esse causa erroris et indevotionis' are mentioned by Huizinga, p. 140. Cf. the stage direction in the *Ludus Coventriae* (EETS (ES) cxx, p. 107): 'Here the Holy Ghost discendit with iij bemis to Our Lady; the Sone of the Godhed nest with iij bemys to the Holy Gost; the Fadyr Godly with iij bemys to the

Sone; and so entre all thre to here bosom.' See also *LM*, pp. 1448–9.
21 See *The Exempla of Jacques de Vitry*, ed. T. F. Crane (London, 1890), pp. 252–3.
22 P. Sabatier, *Life of St. Francis of Assisi* (London, 1894), p. 172.
23 *Index* 445. See Förster, *Anglia* xlii, 152, Carleton Brown, 'Texts and the Man', *Modern Humanities Research Association*, ii, 106–7.
24 On Grimestone's book (written 1372), see *CB XIV*, pp. xvi ff.; on Sheppey, *CB XIV*, p. xv, and A. B. Emden, *A Biographical Register of the University of Oxford to 1500*, III, 1683.
25 Balliol College, MS. 149, f. 11r.
26 Cambridge University Library, MS. Ii. 3.8, f. 88r.
27 Ibid., f. 61r.
28 See Gray, *NQ* ccxiii (1968), 125. The story is quoted by B. Smalley, *English Friars*, p. 169.
29 From the same MS. as the Holkot tag; G. Meyer and M. Burckhardt, *Die mittelalterlichen Handschriften der Universitätsbibliothek Basel*, Abt. B., I, p. 853. It is a description of a 'picture' of the sort discussed in Miss Smalley's book: 'Mores . . . antiquitus depingebatur quasi niger miles fortis . . . habens scutum magnum in 4^{or} partes divisum. In prima parte depingebatur leo rapax. In 2^a symia cachinnans. In 3^a scriptor scribens. In 4^a sagittarius sagittans. Anglice sic . . .' Other examples can be found in Pfander, op. cit., pp. 49–50.
30 National Library of Scotland, MS. Adv. 18. 7. 21, f. 119r (Grimestone).
31 Balliol College, MS. 149, f. 33r.
32 Cambridge University Library, MS. Dd 10. 15, f. 23r.
33 MS. Adv. 18. 7. 21 f. 122r.
34 Frances Yates, *The Art of Memory* (London, 1966). Considering the importance given to the training of the memory, it is not surprising to find stories of fantastic feats of memory: St Augustine had a friend who is said to have been able to recite the whole of Virgil backwards; the elder Seneca could repeat 2,000 names in the order in which they had been given, and when a class of two hundred students spoke in turn lines of poetry, he is reputed to have been able to recite all the lines in reverse order (Yates, p. 16). In the Middle Ages remarkable powers of memory were attributed to Eadmer, Anselm's biographer, and Aquinas.
35 The whole of her chapter 'Medieval Memory and the Formation of Images' is immensely suggestive.
36 See *Laudate* xiii (1935), 37 ff.
37 *STC* 3277. Cf. the crucifixion facing f. m. ii. There are similar schemes of nine graces and a tree of Vice; ff. R v^v, R vi^r have mnemonic English verses. The late date need occasion no surprise: the

Notes to pp. 41–4

tradition of the art of memory continued into the seventeenth century. Miss Yates (p. 370) quotes Aubrey on Bacon's painted glass windows at Gorhambury 'and every pane with severall figures of beast, bird and flowers: perhaps his lordship might use them as topiques for locall use' (which might echo the traditional technical terms, *loci, imagines*). Mnemonic verses in Latin and Middle English are common. There are versified paternosters and creeds, and lists of virtues and vices (one poem begins 'kepe well .x. and flee from .vii.'). Among the secular examples in Robbins *Sec. Lyr.* is the ancestor of the modern jingle on the numbers of days in the months (No. 62) and a verse on the number of bones and sinews. No doubt mnemonic practice and necessity encourage formal schemes of prayer, whether numerical or alphabetical (cf. the Hindu alphabetical rosary discussed by Eithne Wilkins, *The Rose-Garden Game* (London, 1969), p. 201). Cf. J.-F. Bonnefoy, 'La Mystique des nombres', *Rev. d'Ascétique et de mystique* xxv (1949), 533–50, F. Dornseiff, *Das Alphabet in Mystik und Magie* (Leipzig/Berlin, 1922).

38 *CB XIII*, No. 56A.
39 The earliest Christian images appear about A.D. 200. Cf. A. Grabar, *Christian Iconography. A Study of its Origins* (London, 1969). There are Jewish experiments with images in the third century also.
40 Cf. *The Cloud of Unknowing*, ed. P. Hodgson, EETS ccxviii, chs 7, 59 ff.
41 Among English visionaries Julian of Norwich is especially interesting for the way in which she discusses her images; cf. the passage on Christ's bleeding head, mentioned on p. 239, where she explains (Warrack, ed., p. 16) that 'these three' came to her mind at the time: pellets for roundness (of the drops), the scale of herring, in the spreading in the forehead, and drops off the eaves after a great shower of rain, for plenteousness.
42 *The Journal of William Dowsing*, ed. C. H. Evelyn White, *Proc. Suffolk Inst. of Archaeology* vi (1888), 236–95.
43 On wall-paintings see E. W. Tristram, *English Medieval Wall Painting* (London, 1944), *English Wall Painting of the Fourteenth Century* (London, 1955), A. Caiger-Smith, *English Medieval Mural Paintings* (Oxford, 1963). The paintings are often inspired by the same popular devotion which produces the lyrics; the same is true of alabaster images (see W. L. Hildburgh, 'English Alabaster Carvings as Records of the Medieval Religious Drama', *Archaeologia* xciii (1949), 51–101). Some idea of the richness of the interior decoration of a pre-Reformation parish church can be gained from the account of Roger Martin (d. 1580) of Long Melford church 'as I remember it' (*Gentleman's Magazine* (1830), p. 206): he remembers the many images, the gilt tabernacles, the rood loft, painted boards, the roof

Notes to pp. 44-8

beautiful with fair gilt stars, and he describes the Corpus Christi day processions about the church green. Even more sumptuous is the description of Durham Cathedral printed in Fowler, *Rites of Durham*. The colourful and dramatic ceremonies of Holy Week are described by H. J. Feasey, *Ancient English Holy Week Ceremonial* (1893).

44 *Leaven of the Pharisees*, EETS lxxiv, p. 8.

45 *Dives et Pauper*, ed. Pynson (1493). Cf. Myrc's *Festial* (EETS (ES) xcvi, p. 171): 'I say boldly that ther ben mony thousand of pepull that couth not ymagen in her hert how Crist was don on the rood, but as thei lerne hit by sight of images and payntours.' On Hilton, see J. Russell-Smith, 'Walter Hilton and a Tract in Defence of the Veneration of Images', *Dominican Studies* vii (1954), 180–214. Cf. Owst, *Literature and Pulpit*, pp. 137 ff., Caiger-Smith, ch. 8.

46 See L. Gougaud, 'Muta praedicatio', *Revue Bénédictine* xlii (1930), 168–71.

47 Yates, op. cit., pp. 277–8, quoting the Elizabethan Puritan, William Perkins.

48 *Grand Testament*, ed. A. Longnon and L. Foulet, (Paris, 1932), ll . 893 ff.

49 Cf. E. Steinmann, *Die tituli und die kirchliche Wandmalerei in Abendlande vom V bis zum XI Jahrhundert* (Leipzig, 1892), H. Rosenfeld, *Das deutsche Bildgedicht* (Leipzig, 1935).

50 Gray, *NQ* ccv (1960), 403–4.

51 See J. B. Trapp, 'Verses by Lydgate at Long Melford', *RES* n.s. vi (1955), 1–11. Interestingly, the work of a well-known poet was used. Later, at the time of the Field of Cloth of Gold, a letter to Wolsey asks for another known poet, Alexander Barclay, to be sent 'to devise histoires and convenient raisons to florisshe the buildings and banket house'. Rossell Hope Robbins's account of the proverbial wall verses at Launceston Priory (*Arch.* cc (1963) 338–43) contains much information on M.E. verse *tituli*. See also J. Evans, *Pattern* (Oxford, 1931), especially I, iv, 'Literature and Decoration'.

52 Printed by Flügel, *Anglia* xiv (1891) 472–97; cf. P. Wilson, *The Musicall Prouerbis in the Garet at the New lodge in the Parke of Lekingfelde* (London, 1924).

53 See A. A. Cameron, *A Few Words about Hurst* (Reading, 1882).

54 For the 'precepts in -ly' see *Index* 317, 324, 799, 2794.8, 3087, 3102 (cf. 596). The painted room verses which remain run:

> ... in the mornynge earlye
> serve God devoutlye ...
> ... feare God above allthynge. ...
> ... And last of thi rest
> be thou gods servante for that hold i best.

55 Evans, p. 122. Among many other 'speaking objects' may be mentioned the Alfred Jewel, or a lectern in the Museum at Vienne, which says: ' + Est sacro sanctorum mihi sarcina grata librorum nam qui verba dei predicat aptor ei.' For rings, cf. *Index* 4203, 798, 3273–5; J. Evans, *English Posies and Posy Rings* (London, 1931). Bells, naturally enough, may 'speak'; some inscribed bells are discussed in, e.g. J. J. Raven, *The Church Bells of Cambridgeshire* (Cambridge, 1882), and G. Holles, *Lincolnshire Church Notes* (Lincoln Record Society I), 246 (cf. e.g. *Sum rosa pulsata mundi Maria vocata*). One of the purposes of ancient inscribed *tituli* was magical ('may Thor hallow these runes'), and sometimes in the Middle Ages magic is not far away: the practice of ringing 'christened' bells during thunderstorms is criticized in the fiercely anti-Catholic *The Popish Kingdome* of 'Naogeorgus' (Thomas Kirchmaier (d. 1577)), translated by B. Googe (ed. R. C. Hope, London, 1880):

I sawe myselfe at Numberg once, a towne in Toring coast,
A bell that with this title bolde, hirselfe did prowdly boast,
By name I Mary called am, with sound I put to flight
The thunder crackes, and hurtfull stormes, and every wicked spright.

56 Evans, p. 90 (cf. *Index* 938, 942, 2796.5, 3751.8, 675.5, 1172.8).
57 Mâle, *Fin*, p. 353.
58 L. Meynell, *Bedfordshire* (London, 1950), p. 271.
59 *Index* 3565.4. One is still at Malvern Priory (it may have been produced there in the kiln nearby which was discovered last century). Encaustic tiles (of which perhaps the most splendid examples are in the Chapter House at Westminster) were sometimes adorned with scenes from romance, or with religious or moral symbols (e.g. the Pelican wounding herself to feed her young, the Instruments of the Passion) or inscriptions. Warnings against executors are extremely common in moral verse; there is even a carol with the burden (*EEC* No. 382):

> Have in mynd, in mynd, in mynd
> Secuters be oft onekynd.

60 E. P. Hammond, *Eng. St.* xliii, 23. *Index* 1929, 3886. Some idea of what these were like can be gained from the terracotta cakemould figure of St Catherine reproduced as pl. xciii of the *London Museum Medieval Catalogue*. The same sort of thing is recorded later, in the feasts given for Queen Christina of Sweden in seventeenth-century Rome – the tables were laid with sculptured *trionfi* (of sugar, etc.), sometimes depicting the sufferings of Christ in the Passion, the Last Supper, the Virgin pierced with seven swords, Jesus as Man of Sorrows, etc. (see Per Bjurström, *Feast and Theatre in Queen*

Christina's Rome (Stockholm, 1966), pp. 53–69, which has reproductions of Sevin's drawings and watercolours of the tables and *trionfi*).
61 Evans, p. 111.
62 See Gerhard Schmidt, *Die Armenbibeln des xiv. Jahrhunderts* (Graz/Cologne, 1959), P. Heitz and W. Schreiber, *Biblia Pauperum* (Strasbourg, 1903), Mâle, *Fin*, pp. 232 ff. Similar typological illustrated books are the *Bible moralisée*, the *Speculum humanae salvationis*, a long verse work, possibly by Ludolph of Saxony, and the *Concordantia caritatis* (see J. B. Trapp, 'The Iconography of the Fall of Man' in *Approaches to Paradise Lost*, ed. C. A. Patrides (London, 1968), pp. 243–7).
63 Facsimile ed. W. O. Hassall (London, 1954).
64 W. R. Lethaby, 'English Primitives. The Painted Chamber and the Early Masters of the Westminster School', *Burlington Magazine* vii (1905), 257–69. The phrase is that of two visiting friars in 1322, Simon, and Hugh the illuminator: 'the celebrated chamber, on the walls of which all the warlike pictures of the whole Bible are painted with ineffable skill, and explained and completed by a regular series of texts beautifully written in French, to the great admiration of the beholder.' The subjects also included figures of the Virtues, and the Coronation of Edward the Confessor. See also ibid., xxxiii (1918), 3–8, 169–72.
65 A reproduction is in E. Liddell Armitage, *Stained Glass* (London, 1959), pl. 17.
66 J. D. Le Couteur, *English Mediaeval Stained Glass* (London, 1926), p. 152, fig. 51, Bouchier, *Notes on the Stained Glass of the Oxford District* (Oxford, 1918), p. 99.
67 There is a vast literature on this. A straightforward account in English is J. M. Clark, *The Dance of Death in the Middle Ages and the Renaissance* (Glasgow, 1950).
68 John Stow, *A Survey of London*, ed. C. L. Kingsford (Oxford, 1908), I, pp. 327–8.
69 *Index* 702; ed. MacCracken EETS (ES) cvii, pp. 250–2. Other Lydgate poems which may have been intended to accompany illustrations include the *Life of St. George*, *A Tretys of Crystys Pasyoun*, *On the Image of Pity*, *Bygorne and Chicheface*.
70 *Index* 490; ed. MacCracken, EETS (ES) cvii, pp. 290–1 (there is no illustration in the MS.). William Wey, in his *Itineraries* (ed. Roxburghe Club, 1857), p. 147, mentions this image in S. Maria del Populo, as well as another such in Rome. A number of Madonnas were claimed to be the work of the Apostle, e.g. the twelfth-century Madonna di S. Luca at Monte della Guardia near Bologna (see *LM*, s.v. 'Bologna'). Cf. Maerten van Heemskerck's 'St Luke Portraying the Virgin' (E. Panofsky, *Renaissance and Renascences in Western*

Notes to pp. 51–2

Art (London, 1970 ed.), p. 190, fig. 144). St Luke was also supposed to have produced authentic likenesses of Christ (see Réau, pp. 70–1). Cf. also Owst, *Literature and Pulpit*, p. 140, Smalley, *English Friars*, p. 225.

71 See Rossell Hope Robbins, 'The Arma Christi Rolls', *MLR* xxxiv (1934), 415–21. Other lyrics are found on rolls – the 'Love Rune' of Thomas de Hales, and William Billyng's prayer to the Five Wounds (which now survives only in a nineteenth-century facsimile book). Charms are sometimes found on rolls – see W. Sparrow-Simpson, 'On a magical Roll preserved in the British Museum', *J. Arch. Ass.* xlviii (1892), 38–54, C. F. Bühler, 'Prayers and Charms in Certain Middle English Scrolls', *Speculum* xxxix (1964), 270–80 (cf. W. Heneage Legge, *The Reliquary* x (1904)). It seems possible that they could have been carried on the person for protection or displayed for devotional purposes on the wall of a house – as may have been done with the *mensura vulneris* (*NQ* ccviii, 88).

72 On this MS. see Gray, *NQ* ccviii, 83, J. C. Hirsh, *NQ* ccxiii, 6–7.

73 The MS. is briefly discussed in *CB XV* p. 315, Allen, *Rolle*, pp. 306 ff.; the illustrations (briefly) by F. Wormald in *Miscellanea pro Arte* (*Festschrift für Hermann Schnitzler*, Düsseldorf, 1965), pp. 279–85. It is important and interesting enough to deserve a facsimile. Nearly all of the themes of late medieval devotion are fully represented: the Passion of Christ (and especially his wounds, his loving appeal to sinful man) is central, but there are groups of Marian poems, mystical songs of love-longing, and a large section concerned with death and the last things. The phrase 'a spiritual encyclopaedia of the later Middle Ages' is the title of a brilliant article by Saxl (*JWCI* v (1942), 82–134), which discusses similar Latin MSS. There are differences – the Carthusian MS. is rather less concerned with the order of society – but much of the material is similar, and Additional 37049 would certainly fit Saxl's description, 'collectanea spiritalia wherein various materials for the progress of spiritual life are contained'.

74 The poems are *Index* 1073 (*CB XV*, No. 26) and 4200 (Cf. *CB XIV*, No. 127, for another MS. version).

75 *NQ* ccviii, 168. The pelican survives even longer on graveyard memorials (see Burgess, op. cit., p. 245). A very full and fascinating discussion of some medieval prototypes of later devotional emblems (with material largely drawn from Additional 37049) is K. J. Höltgen 'Arbor, Scala, und Fons vitae' in *Chaucer und seine Zeit* (Symposion für Walter F. Schirmer), ed. A. Esch (Tübingen, 1868), pp. 355–91.

76 Cf. Thomas W. Ross, 'Five Fifteenth-Century "Emblem Verses" from British Museum, Additional MS. 37049', *Speculum* xxxii (1957), 274–82.

77 *Index* 2504. This poem occurs twice in the MS. (f. 20r and, without the *responsio*, f. 24r); cf. Woolf, pp. 185–6. Christ's complaint is found used as a *titulus* in Almondbury church, Yorkshire, 'round the nave, on the roof plate' (dated 1522), *J. Arch. Ass.* xxx (1874), 230–2. In a copy of the poem in a Bodleian MS., Christ's last word *herte* is replaced by a drawing of a heart, a simple devotional sort of *rebus* (more enigmatic and facetious examples are sometimes found in churches: in a boss at Sherborne, for instance, P + a ram + SAM records Abbot Ramsam; the name of Kidlington, Oxfordshire, is disguised in two in the parish church, while at Lydgate (Suffolk) graffiti with musical notes and the four at dice appear – Well (fa)(re) (mi) (la)dy (Cater)yne (V. Pritchard, *English Medieval Graffiti* (Cambridge, 1967), p. 145)).

78 Cf. Rosemary Freeman, *English Emblem Books* (London, 1948), Mario Praz, *Studies in Seventeenth-Century Imagery* (2nd ed., Rome, 1964).

79 Cf. p. 290, note 70. For all the scorn that is heaped upon it (cf. Addison, *Spectator* lviii, ed. D. F. Bond (Oxford, 1965), I, pp. 244–8, or Butler's 'character of a small poet': 'As for Altars and Pyramids in poetry, he has outdone all men that way; for he has made a gridiron and a frying-pan in verse'), the pattern poem has not ceased to challenge poets – Mallarmé, Apollinaire, and Dylan Thomas are but three who have attempted it (and cf. the Mouse's tail in *Alice*). M. Church, 'The First English Pattern Poems', *PMLA* lxi (1946), 636–50, says something about the ancient antecedents (notably in the Greek anthology); Dieter Schaller, 'Die karolingischen Figurengedichte des Cod. Bern. 212' in *Medium Aevum Vivum* (Festschrift für Walther Bulst), ed. H. R. Jauss and D. Schaller (Heidelberg, 1960), discusses an interesting Carolingian group of 'carmina figurata' (pr. E. Dümmler, *Poetae Latini* I (MGH), 1881, pp. 152–9, 224–7, 482 (Alcuin is one of the authors)) and places them in the tradition of Optatianus Porfyrius (of the time of Constantine). Cf. also Bischoff, *Volk und Volkstum i* (1936), 225–31, J. von Schlosser, *Jahrb. der kunsthistorischen Sammlungen des A. H. Kaiserhauses* xiii (1892), 1–36. For illustrations, cf. O. Homburger, *Die illustrierten Handschriften der Burgerbibliothek Bern* (Bern, 1962), pp. 162–3, pl. lxiii, and two popular accounts, which include modern examples – C. Boultenhouse, 'Poems in the Shapes of Things', *Art News Annual* xxviii (1959), 64–83, 178, Berjouhi Bowler, *The Word as Image* (London, 1970).

80 Cf. Dante's description of the Annunciation sculpture in *Purg.* x, ll. 29 ff. – the image is so truly graven 'that it did not seem silent'; Mary's words, '*Ecce ancilla Dei*' are imprinted in her bearing and motion. Here the visual image 'speaks' in its own language, without recourse to scrolls and *tituli*. See also the lively comments of

E. P. Pickering, *Literature and Art in the Middle Ages* (London, 1970).
81 Cf. *First Life*, ch. 7, *Second Life*, chs 8, 90.
82 *CB XIII* No. 54.
83 *CB XIV* No. 10.
84 *CB XIV* No. 9.
85 *EEC* No. 261. On this form see H. E. Sandison, *The 'Chanson d'aventure' in Middle English* (Bryn Mawr, 1901). Elsewhere in Europe even the *alba*, the form most deeply associated with love poetry is 'converted': cf., e.g., the religious *alba* of Folquet de Marseille (in A. Berry, *Florilège des Troubadours* (Paris, 1930), pp. 336–40) where the dawn rises over Jerusalem and bids the lovers of God rise and adore him.
86 *CB XV* No. 46.
87 *CB XIII* No. 60.
88 See Legge, *Anglo-Norman Literature* pp. 227–8, Betty Hill, *MLR* lix (1964), 321–30. The 'Love Rune' is printed in *CB XIII* (No. 43); there is a very sympathetic discussion of it in Woolf, pp. 57, 60–3.
89 The praise of virginity, the *laus virginitatis*, is of course an important theme in much early and medieval ascetic and devotional literature. There are some interesting parallels in Anselm's letters to Matilda and Gunhilda (see Southern, op. cit., pp. 182 ff. (Schmitt, *Ep.* 177, 168, 169), and in the visual arts in the motif (from apocryphal literature) of St John, the beloved disciple leaving his wife to follow Christ (see Pächt, *JWCI* xix, 78).
90 *PL* clxxix, 1621.
91 See *EEC*, p. cxviii, St J. D. Seymour, *Anglo-Irish Literature 1200–1582* (Cambridge, 1929), pp. 73–5, 96–8.
92 *Index* 3318.4; Cf. *Index* 467, 3820.5, 4094.3, 4098.6. See also the discussion in Woolf, pp. 192 ff.
93 *CB XV* No. 110.
94 As in an Anglo-Norman poem which begins with the poet rising up in the morning and thinking of 'love affairs which are to be prized', which turn out to be addressed to God (Legge, *Anglo-Norman Literature*, p. 351, *Reliquiae Antiquae*, ed. T. Wright and J. O. Halliwell (London, 1841), i, p. 104).

Chapter 4   The English Lyrics, II

1 *The Dyer's Hand* (London, 1962), p. 458.
2 *Index* 2757.5; *EEL*, p. 160.
3 See the facsimile, ed. N. R. Ker, EETS cclv.
4 The poems are printed in EETS (ES) ci (1907), ed. Dyboski.
5 See the description of this MS. in *EEC* p. 330 and *SEC* pp. 173–4.

6 This is an exact parallel to the religious art of the period – MS. illustrations range from the exquisite work of court painters to the simplest drawings, wall-painting from the artistry of St Stephen's Chapel to the efforts of what Tristram calls 'rustic daubers'.
7 *CB XV* No. 155.
8 See *EEC, SEC* Introduction, Robbins, 'M. E. Carols as Processional Hymns', *SP* lvi (1959), 559–82, John Stevens, *Medieval Carols* (Musica Britannica iv, London, 1952), Margit Sahlin, *Étude sur la Carole médiévale* (Uppsala, 1940).
9 *CB XIV* No. 88. Sahlin (p. 58) suggests rather a cradle-rocking ceremony (see below p. 112). There is no direct reference in the lyric to this, but it is not inconceivable that it might have been used in some such ceremony as that satirically described by Naogeorgus (*The Popish Kingdome*, ed. Hope, p. 45): after the three Masses on Christmas day:

This done, a wooden childe in clowtes is on the aulter set,
About the which both boyes and gyrles do daunce and trymly set,
And Carrols sing in prayse of Christ, and forto helpe them heare,
The Organs aunswere every verse, with sweete and solemne cheare.
The Priestes doe rore aloude, and round about the parentes stande,
To see the sport, and with their voyce to helpe them and their hande.
Thus woont the Coribants perhaps upon the mountains Ide,
The crying noyse of Jupiter new borne with song to hide,
To daunce about him round, and on their brasen pannes to beate,
Least that his father finding him should him destroy and eate.

10 See p. 81 and note 25. Cf. Lydgate, *A Kalendare* (EETS (ES) cvii, p. 363):

> Now pray for me, blessid Seynt Lucyan,
> That I myght be (l)adde forth unto youre daunce,
> There God reulith both angel and man,
> In right true love withouten variaunce.

11 See Sahlin, pp. 142–53, L. Gougaud, 'La Danse dans les églises', *Rev. d'Hist. ecclésiastique* xv (1914), 5–22, 229–45, J. Morris, *The Month* lxxvi (1892), 495–513.
12 *Remains of Gentilisme and Judaisme*, ed. J. Britten (London, 1881), p. 5.
13 Sahlin, p. 146.
14 A sect of 'dancers' appeared in the Low Countries in the fourteenth century (see *Dictionnaire de Théologie Catholique*, s.v. 'Danseurs', and references), and earlier examples of choreomania are attested (no doubt something like it lies behind the famous story of the 'Dancers of Colbek'): cf. J. F. K. Hecker, *Die Tanzwuth, eine Volkskrankheit im Mittelalter* (Berlin, 1882). Later examples of ecstatic 'dancing' in

Notes to pp. 63–70

the Christian tradition are perhaps the 'convulsionnaires' of seventeenth-century Paris, and modern Pentecostal 'Holy Rollers'. Frenzied dances are part of the South Italian phenomenon of tarantism, which can also be traced back to the Middle Ages. There is a fascinating account of this by E. de Martino, *La Terra del Rimorso* (Milan, 1961) (cf. *Times Literary Supplement*, 27 April 1967). Apparently neither of two possible spiders – *lycosa tarentula*, the popular favourite, a large and fast-moving wolf-spider, comparatively harmless, or *latrodectus tredecim guttatus*, a slower but much more venomous spider – are really responsible, although bites may have been the original stimulus. Tarantism is concentrated in particular families and certain villages (and is usually found in women), and is associated with the cult and feast-day (29 June) of St Paul.

15 Ed. L. F. Powell (Oxford, 1908), p. 8.
16 Auerbach, *Mimesis*, esp. ch. 2.
17 See J. Norton-Smith, *John Lydgate. Poems* (Oxford, 1966), pp. 192–5.
18 *CB XV*, No. 38.
19 W. J. Ong, 'Wit and Mystery: a Revaluation in Medieval Latin Hymnody', *Speculum* xxii (1947), 310–41.
20 *OBMLV*, No. 285.
21 Donne, *Holy Sonnets* 7, *The Divine Poems*, ed. H. Gardner (Oxford, 1952), p. 9.
22 *The Liturgical Poetry of Adam of St Victor*, ed. and tr. D. S. Wrangham (London, 1881), pp. 38 ff.
23 Intellect is by no means absent from affective devotional poetry; extended prose meditations (e.g. those of Anselm) often combine an intense personal emotion with an intellectual awareness and agility.
24 *CB XV*, No. 120.
25 *EEC* No. 318.
26 *EEC* No. 319.
27 EETS cxvii, p. 616.
28 Allen, *English Writings*, pp. 34 ff.
29 Images were usually painted and gilded. Cf. Evans, p. 106, *Rites of Durham*, Surtees Soc. cvii (1902), p. 33 – an altar triptych of the Passion of Christ was 'most richlye and curiously sett furth in most lyvelie coulors all lik the burninge gold'; above the 'story' of the Passion in stone on a wall is a border 'very artificially wrowght in stone with marvelous fyne coulers verie curiouslie and excellent fynly gilt with branches and flowres, the more that a man did looke on it the more desires he had and the greater was his affection to behold yt, the worke was so fynely and curiously wroughte in the said stone that it cold not be fynelyer wrowght in any kynde of other

Notes to pp. 70 –7

mettell.' An aesthetic judgment of a different sort is recorded by a mason in a *graffito* at Ashwell (Pritchard, p. 79), referring to bad work – 'I spit at it.'

30 Ed. J. F. Dimock (Lincoln, 1860), ll.882–3:
Inde columnellae, quae sic cinxere columnas,
Ut videantur ibi quamdam celebrare choream.

31 See Gervase Mathew, *Byzantine Aesthetics* (London, 1963), esp. pp. 30, 87, 89, 150. The description of Hagia Sophia (that church which drew from the envoys of the Grand Duke Vladimir the amazed comment 'when we were there we thought we were in Paradise, and we forgot everything that had gone before') by Paulus Silentiarius (sixth century) is especially noteworthy (text and Latin translation in *Corpus Scriptorum Historiae Byzantinae* vol. xl (1837)).

32 See W. W. Greg, *MP* vii (1909), 165–7. Other examples of lyrics apparently in the process of completion (*CB XIII* 26, *Index* 3926.5) or of re-working (e.g. in Ryman's collection) are interesting, but much less successful.

Chapter 5 Christ and the Virgin Mary

1 *Index* 114. MS. Bodley 26, f. 200r.
2 Proleptic treatments of the Fall are already found in catacomb paintings and early sarcophagi (see J. B. Trapp, 'The Iconography of the Fall of Man', 231). On Christ as the second Adam see *RDK*, s.v. 'Adam-Christus'.
3 *Index* 3357. On Mary as the second Eve, see E. Guldan, *Eva und Maria: eine Antithese als Bildmotiv* (Graz, Cologne, 1966), Trapp, 258 ff.
4 See A. O. Lovejoy, 'Milton and the Paradox of the Fortunate Fall', *ELH* iv (1937), E. M. Vetter, 'Necessarium Adae peccatum', *Ruperto-Carola*, xxxix (1966), 144–81.
5 *Index* 117. *CB XV*, No. 83.
6 Ed. 1859, I, ch. iii, p. 24. The first book of Durandus is translated by J. M. Neale and B. Webb, *The Symbolism of Churches and Church Ornaments* (1843).
7 *Index* *38. See Ross, *Speculum* xxxii (1957), 277–8. There is a very similar description in *Cursor Mundi* (EETS lxii, pp. 1078–81) ll. 18818 ff. Cf. Réau, pp. 36 ff., *RDK* s.v. 'Christustypus', *Lexikon der Christlichen Ikonographie*, ed. E. Kirschbaum, s.v. 'Christus, Christusbild', Mâle *XIII*, pp. 377 ff., W. Lowrie, *Art in the Early Church* (1947), p. 31.
8 Christ's beauty is timeless and eternal (see *The Wohunge of Ure Laverd*, EETS ccxli, and cf. the interesting discussion in Woolf, p. 61).

9 Ed. MacCracken, EETS (ES) cvii, p. 335. This image of course implies a happy conclusion to the quest of Orpheus; for the tradition, see Dronke, *Classica et Medievalia* xxiii, 198–215, Allen *MAE* xxxiv, 109 nt.
10 *EEC* No. 174.
11 *CB* xiv No. 112. Cf. *EEC* No. 48.
12 *EEC* No. 321; *Archiv* lxxxi, 83–5.
13 There is a full discussion of the treatment of the nightingale by F. J. E. Raby, 'Philomena Praevia Temporis Amoeni', *Mélanges Joseph de Ghellinck* (Gembloux, 1951), pp. 435–48. On the English poems see Woolf, pp. 232–3.
14 EETS (ES) lxxx, p. 5 (the rest of the poem is inferior). Cf. Lydgate's *A Seying of the Nightingale* (EETS (ES) lxxx, pp. 16 ff., cvii, pp. 221 ff.).
15 *OBMLV*, p. 414; the whole poem is in Dreves 1 (No. 398). The bird's cry 'oci' was apparently originally onomatopoeic, but was associated with the French *occir* 'to kill'. Pecham's poem is quoted by the Monk of Farne, ed. Farmer, p. 99.
16 *Index* 4196; *Archiv* clxi, 40.
17 *Index* 1133; *Reliquiae Antiquae* ii, 121.
18 *Index* 3727.5. MS. Lat. theol. d 1, f. 173v.
19 On the devotion to the Holy Name, see A. Cabassut, 'La Dévotion au nom de Jésus dans le nouveau testament', *La Vie Spirituelle* lxxxvi (1952), 46–69 (cf. also pp. 5–37); Woolf, pp. 172–9. Bernard's remarks (*In Cant.* xv) are in *Opera*, ed. J. Leclerq (Rome, 1957), I, p. 85; the famous hymn, *Jesu Dulcis Memoria*, which is sometimes echoed in poems on the Holy Name was sometimes attributed to Bernard, but seems not to be his – it may be the work of an English Cistercian (see A. Wilmart, *Le 'Jubilus' dit de S. Bernard* (Rome, 1944). R. W. Pfaff, *New Liturgical Feasts in Late Medieval England* (Oxford, 1970), ch. iv, discusses the Feast of the Name of Jesus. On magical rings, see J. Evans, *Magical Jewels of the Middle Ages and the Renaissance* (Oxford, 1922), pp. 130–2. On the sacred monogram in art, see *RDK* s.v. 'Christusmonogramm', C. Woodforde, *Stained Glass in Somerset* (Oxford, 1946), p. 195. The walls of English churches were often adorned with it – Dowsing, the iconoclast records finding and disposing of innumerable examples of 'IHS', 'Jesus–Maria', what he calls 'the Jesuit's badge'. A good surviving example is the church of Ewelme near Oxford. Among longer M.E. poems, the *Meditations on the Life and Passion of Christ* (ed. C. D'Evelyn, EETS clviii, ll. 1039 ff.) has a good passage on the Holy Name. For examples in later poetry, cf. Herbert's *Jesu* and *Love-Joy*, Crashaw's *To the Name above Every Name, the Name of Jesus*.
20 Allen, *English Writings*, p. xxii.

21 From *Index* 1692; ed. Horstman, *Yorkshire Writers* (London, 1895), i, p. 365.
22 John, the beloved disciple, was said by pious legend to have abandoned his wife to follow Christ; the union of their love is symbolized by his resting his head on Christ's breast at the Last Supper (cf. e.g. *EEC* Nos 102–5) – a scene which in the visual arts becomes a separate devotional image (see *RDK* s.v. 'Christus-Johannes-Gruppe', Pächt, *JWCI* xix, 78–9, H. Swarzenski, 'Quellen zum deutschen Andachtsbild', *Zeits. f. Kunstgeschichte* iv (1935) 141 ff.). The medieval treatment of the Redemption as the expression of Christ's love has been much discussed; see Woolf, esp. pp. 21 ff., Southern, *St. Anselm*, pp. 93 ff., J. Rivière, *Le Dogme de la Rédemption au debut du moyen âge* (Paris, 1934). Echoes of ancient ideas of the tricking of the devil are found; cf. in literature, the York *Harrowing of Hell*, ll. 248 ff., in art, the Mérode Altarpiece of the Master of Flémalle (Cloisters, N.Y.; reproduced in Whinney, pl. 6, Panofsky, *Early Netherlandish Painting*, II, pl. 91), where, on the side of the triptych, Joseph in his workshop has placed a mousetrap on his bench, which, it has been cogently argued, is the expression of the idea that 'God set a mousetrap for the Devil, and baited it with the human flesh of Christ'. (On this symbolic mousetrap, see Meyer Schapiro, 'Muscipula Diaboli; the Symbolism of the Mérode Altarpiece', *Art Bulletin* xxvii (1945), 182 ff.)
23 *Index* 2012; *CB XIV* No. 66.
24 *Index* 1311; *CB XIV* No. 129.
25 Cf. Hamman, *Early Christian Prayers*, No. 106, and the examples cited by István Kozáky, *Anfänge der Darstellungen des Vergänglichkeitsproblems* (Bibliotheca Humanitatis Historica, i (1936)), pp. 146 ff. (e.g. in the play *Mariä Himmelfahrt*, Mary and Christ dance with the angels in heaven, in Mechthild of Magdeburg Christ leads the soul to the dance). There may be an allusion to it in Wyclif (*Selected Works*, ed. Arnold, III, 360): 'And thus shuld the Churche drawe to acord bi Crist, that ledith the daunce of love.' In the apocryphal Acts of John, before the Crucifixion, Christ and his disciples take part in a mysterious dance (see M. R. James, *The Apocryphal New Testament* (Oxford, 1924), pp. 253–4; cf. Peter Dronke, *Poetic Individuality in the Middle Ages* (Oxford, 1970), pp. 194–5.
26 Fuller accounts of the development of Marian devotion are readily available in histories of spirituality and in various religious encyclopedias. There is a treasury of information in the *Lexikon der Marienkunde*, ed. K. Algermissen and others (Regensburg, 1957– (in progress)); cf. also *Katholische Marienkunde*, ed. P. Sträter (Paderborn, 1950–2), Yrjo Hirn, *The Sacred Shrine* (rev. English ed., London, 1958), A. Salzer, *Die Sinnbilder und Beiworte Mariens* (Linz, 1893).

Notes to pp. 82–5

27 See Raby, *Christian Latin Poetry* pp. 363–5. It expressed itself in new liturgical forms, notably the 'Little Office of the Blessed Virgin Mary' which formed a large part of the 'Prymer', widely used by the devout laity (see E. Bishop, 'On the Origin of the Primer', in *The Prymer*, ed. H. Littlehales, EETS cix), which is often echoed in devotional poetry.
28 Formerly attributed to St Albert the Great in his *Opera*, ed. Borgnet (1890), vol. xxxvi.
29 Formerly attributed to St Bonaventura. Two M.E. versions are found in the Vernon MS. (EETS xcviii, pp. 49–120). A nineteenth-century translation by the Rev. J. Cumming (1852) has a curious polemical preface: 'in order to let Protestants disposed to join Rome see what she is; and to make such who love evangelical and Protestant Christianity, thankful, and more disposed than ever to appeal to God's people in Rome, and yet not of her, saying, "Come out of her, my people..."'.
30 See Raby, p. 375, Mone II, No. 501.
31 Mone II, No. 483.
32 EETS (ES) cxx, p. 104, l. 197.
33 According to the *Speculum Beatae Mariae*, Mary heard 'Ave' three times, so that the three curses ('vae! vae! vae!') given by the eagle in the Apocalypse might be removed. Innocent's *De Contemptu Mundii* (*PL* ccxvii, 705) says that all children of men begin their lives by lamenting the sin of their ancestors – boys at birth cry 'A! A!' in memory of Adam, and girls 'E! E!' in memory of Eve.
34 See E. Harris, 'Mary in the Burning Bush', *JWCI* i (1937) 281–5; cf. *RDK* s.v. 'Busch (brennender Busch)', *LM* s.v. 'Dornbusch'.
35 *Index* 2107; *CB XIV* No. 32. For examples of other learned poetic lists of Marian figures, cf. *EEC* Nos 193, 194, 203, Dreves, Nos 120, 135, Adam of St Victor's Marian sequences, lxv, lxxiii, lxxiv. These have their counterpart in the depiction (at the end of the Middle Ages) of the Virgin (often in a garden) surrounded by her 'figures' (cf. the sixteenth-century tapestries at Rheims). There is much information on Marian figures in Raby pp. 365–75 (much of it drawn from the *Speculum Ecclesiae* of the mysterious Honorius 'of Autun' on whom see Southern, *St. Anselm*, pp. 209 ff.) and Hirn, *The Sacred Shrine*.
36 ll. 441–2. Cf. *EEC* No. 198, EETS xv pp. 291–2, ci p. 57, 1.50, Mone II, 510 (*imperatrix infernorum*), and an earlier example in the OE 'Christ', ed. Cook, ll. 284–6.
37 *EEC* No. 185 B. On the background to this sort of phrase, see *LM* s.v. 'Dreifaltigkeit'.
38 *CB XV* No. 69. This title is also used by Villon in the stanza quoted on p. 45. Cf. the adjective *dia/diva* used in Mone II, 508.
39 For other M.E. examples, see *EEC* Nos 182, 190, 192, 193, 203.

Notes to pp. 85–6

40 *EEC* No. 182. This figure is common in both art (cf. Mâle *XIII*, fig. 8, *Fin*, figs. 124, 125) and literature (cf. *EEC* Nos. 190, 192–4, Mone II, Nos 360, 346, 414, 480).
41 Cf. Mone II, 390, where the stone from Daniel's mountain is made into this missile.
42 Cf. *EEC* No. 190. The *De Laudibus BMV* (X, ch. 31, p. 523) works out the mystical resemblances in detail.
43 Another common figure; cf. *EEC* Nos 190–3, Chester Plays ed. Deimling (EETS (ES) lxii), p. 98, ll. 313 ff., Mone II, No. 326, Adam of St Victor, Seq. lxxix, 36–8.
44 Again, this is common: cf. *EEC* 192–3, Mone II, No. 372, etc. The *De Laudibus BMV*, typically, works through all the hills of the Old and New Testament.
45 For Sarah, cf. Mone II, No. 378; for Judith (a favourite story from the apocryphal book), cf. *EEC* Nos. 209–10, Mone II, 378, 507, 513; for Esther, cf. Mone II, Nos. 378, 507, *EEC* Nos 189, 199, 209, 210, 201 (with king Ahasuerus as Christ), 203 (in which the meekness of Esther finds favour with Ahasuerus (= God Almighty) after the wickedness of 'Vasty' (the previous queen, Vashti = the Synagogue)).
46 The Virgin is often compared to a town (cf. *De Laud.* IX, 1): no doubt the Vulgate's word *castellum* which is used of Emmaus (the A.V. has 'village') accounts for the feudal ring of *the riche castel* (it is called 'Emaus castel' in *Richard Coer de Lion* (l. 7124). A window in Great Malvern Priory church shows Christ and the disciples, dressed (as they often are) as pilgrims (the Vulgate has *peregrinus* in Luke xxiv, 18), meeting at Emmaus, with a castle tower in the background (G. M. Rushforth, *Medieval Christian Imagery* (Oxford, 1936), pp. 79–81). Emmaus is said to have been the last station of the crusaders on their way to Jerusalem in 1099; possibly the phrase 'thar resteth alle werye' may refer also to its use as a station by pilgrims.
47 Cf. Mone II, Nos 365, 507, etc.
48 *CB XIV* No. 132. It has been suggested that the Virgin's connection with the moon is an echo of earlier beliefs (cf. Hirn, p. 465) – like Artemis/Diana she cares for women in childbirth. In popular belief the Virgin is sometimes identified with the moon. Danilo Dolci (*To Feed the Hungry* (London, 1959), tr. from *Inchiesta a Palermo* by P. D. Cummins, pp. 256–7) records a Sicilian shepherd who thinks that the stars may be some 'queer sort of eyes', the sun is 'Our Saviour' and the moon is the Madonna (he prays to all of them).
49 *Index* 2645; *CB XIII* No. 17B.
50 See Odell Shephard, *The Lore of the Unicorn* (London, 1930), Mâle *XIII* pp. 148–52, Réau, pp. 191–2, *LM*, s.v. 'Einhorn'. There is a nice English illustration reproduced in the Bodleian booklet, *English Illumination of the Thirteenth and Fourteenth Centuries*, fig. 1 (b).

51 See *NED*. It may refer to sexual passion, as to animal 'wildness'. The Middle High German word *wild* in courtly poetry seems to have a similar intensity; one poet (Ulrich von Gutenberg) says that he was 'wild', however much he sang – his lady's fair eyes were the rods with which she overcame him.
52 See, for instance, the German dotted print reproduced in A. M. Hind, *An Introduction to a History of Woodcut* (London, 1935), I, fig. 76.
53 *Meditations on the Life and Passion of Christ*, EETS clviii, 26 ff.
54 At the end of the fifteenth century we find some interesting learned embellishments. A letter by Giles Robertson in the *Times Literary Supplement*, 24 April 1969 (p. 440) points out that the line *Ave virginei flos intemerate pudoris* behind the throne of Bellini's San Giobbe Madonna is an adaptation of a (spurious) line from *Metamorphoses* xiv, from Vertumnus's wooing of Pomona.
55 *Index* 3536; *EEC* No. 173. The first three Latin lines come from the *Laetabundus* sequence (*OBMLV* No. 113).
56 See the discussions by C. Joret, *La Rose dan l'antiquité et au moyen âge* (Paris, 1892), Peter Dronke, *Medieval Latin and the Rise of European Love-Lyric* (Oxford, 1965), I, pp. 184–8, D. C. Allen, *Image and Meaning* (Baltimore, 1968), ch. on Herbert's 'The Rose', Barbara Seward, *The Symbolic Rose* (N.Y., 1960), E. Wilkins, *The Rose-Garden Game*, pp. 108 ff., Woolf, pp. 287 ff. Cf. Hopkins's early poem, *Rosa Mystica*.
57 *EEC* No. 190 (cf. *Eccl.* xxiv, 18).
58 For the letters of the name, see Mone II, p. 272; for the Five Joys, cf. *EEC* No. 175 (on this theme which is especially important in English devotion, see Wilmart, *Auteurs spirituels*, pp. 317 ff., Woolf, esp. pp. 134–43).
59 From 'Caelum, gaude, terra, plaude' of Peter the Venerable (*OBMLV* No. 179).
60 See Ewald M. Vetter, *Maria im Rosenhag* (Düsseldorf, 1956).
61 *Partheneia Sacra* by H.A. (Henry Hawkins) (1633), p. 13; an interesting collection of Marian emblems and images, including Rose, Lily, Dew, Moon, Star, Nightingale, Pearl, Dove, Fountain, Sea, etc. Mary's womb is sometimes called a flowery meadow, or a *hortus deliciarum* (cf. Bernard, *PL* clxxxiv. 1011; Konrad von Haimburg's *Hortulus BVM*, Dreves iii No. 5). And she is associated with many flowers (see *LM* s.v. 'Blumen'), especially, because of her humility and modesty, with small flowers (cf. the innumerable Marian flower-names: Mary's flower, Mariet, herbmary, marigold, les yeux de Marie, rosemary (by popular etymology, for it originally comes from 'rosmarine', sea-dew), etc.).
62 On rose-windows (and their connection with cosmic wheels, wheels of fortune) see Helen J. Dow 'The Rose-Window' *JWCI* xx (1957)

248–97, Ellen J. Beer, *Die Rose der Kathedrale von Lausanne und der kosmologische Bilderkreis des Mittelalters* (Bern, 1952).
63 Mone II, No. 531.
64 Mone I, No. 39; cf. II, No. 346: Tota descendit deitas/In templum tui pectoris.
65 *CB XIV* No. 16; cf. Mone I, No. 47.
66 *EEC* No. 180.
67 There are some extraordinary examples in Latin (cf. Dreves xxxi, 125 et seq.); for more elaborate English examples see for instance 'Awey feynt love' (*Archiv* cxxxi, 52) or Lydgate's Ave Jesse Virgula (EETS (ES) cvii). There are some interesting references in *LM* s.v. 'Akrostichis'. See also Woolf, pp. 291–3, P. Vinc. van Wijk, *De Naam Maria* (Leiden, 1936).
68 Cf. *De Laud. BMV* II. 2, p. 87: et ista ubera (of Mary the mater misericodiae) tamquam pueruli petimus ad sugendum, quando dicimus ei:

>Virgo singularis
>Inter omnes mitis. . . .

or Dreves xxxi Nos 147, 148 (the second begins 'Mariae matris mammulae,/Nitentes velut faculae . . .). On the legends and illustrations of the 'Lactation of St Bernard' (in answer to his prayer 'monstra te esse matrem') see *LM* s.v. 'Bernhard' (pp. 716–19). Mary intercedes for man in heaven by making the classical gesture of maternal appeal, showing her breasts to Christ (Panofsky, in *Festschrift für Max J. Friedlander* (Leipzig, 1927), p. 302).
69 Cf. *Meditations*, EETS clviii, ll. 78 ff., *Archiv* cxxxi, pp. 60 ff. (based on the formal descriptions (from top to toe) of courtly ladies; but contrasted in the second half with the piteous aspect of Mary by the cross: there are some nice images – the brightness of her hair is compared to 'kiddes floke' descending from the 'mounte of Galaad' and her ears are the 'first gates of our salvation'), EETS xcviii, pp. 121–31.
70 *Index* 1836; *CB XIII* No. 27.
71 And turning away is a sign of disfavour; cf. *III Reg.* xxx. 9, *Is.* i, 15, *Ps.* cxxxi (Vg.), 10.
72 *Index* 420; *CB XIV* No. 130. Cf. the discussion by P. Dronke, *The Medieval Lyric*, pp. 69–70.
73 See pp. 133–4, and *NQ* ccviii (1963), 129–34.
74 See R. S. Loomis, *Arthurian Tradition and Chrétien de Troyes* (N.Y., 1949). Springs and fountains are regularly found in the other world, and are frequently the entrance to it (cf. H. R. Patch, *The Other World* (Cambridge, Mass., 1950), p. 54).
75 Other examples are mentioned in Patch, pp. 245 ff. Cf. *The Lays of Desiré, Graelent and Melion*, ed. E. M. Grimes (New York, 1928),

Notes to pp. 93–4

pp. 15, 20–3, T. P. Cross and C. H. Slover, *Ancient Irish Tales* (London, 1937), pp. 83 ff., 93–5.
76 Cf. for example, the ballad of *Thomas Rhymer* (Child, No. 37; cf. III, p. 504).
77 See R. C. Hope, *The Legendary Lore of the Holy Wells of England* (London, 1893), W. G. Wood-Martin, *Traces of the Elder Faiths of Ireland* (London, 1902), II, ch. 3, M. A. Courtney, *Cornish Feasts and Folklore* (Penzance, 1890), pp. 32–3, J. Rhys, *Celtic Folk-Lore: Welsh and Manx* (Oxford, 1901), I, pp. 332 ff.
78 Cf. Wood-Martin, II, p. 156.
79 Cf. *De Laud. BMV* pp. 33 ff., Mone II, No. 471. There is an early tradition that the Annunciation took place beside a well or fountain (cf. *Protevangelium, Liber de Infantia* (James, pp. 43, 74)), which is sometimes given visual form. Cf. also *LM* s.v. 'Brunnen' (almost all Marian pilgrimage sites have a healing well). A couple of stanzas in the carol 'Ther ys a blossum sprong of a thorn' (*EEC* No. 123A: 'ther sprong a well at Maris fote...') seem to allude to the miraculous springing of wells at the time of the Nativity.
80 Cf. *The Harley Lyrics*, ed. G. L. Brook (Manchester, 1948), Nos 5, l. 9, and 3, l. 21. The phrase is used in both secular and religious contexts (cf. the 'Love Rune' of Thomas de Hales, l. 125, *CB XIII* No. 5, l. 17, *CB XV* No. 78, l. 42).
81 *Index* 1337; Owst, *Literature and Pulpit*, p. 21. For another example of the phrase in a secular lyric, cf. Brook, No. 12, l. 36.
82 *Carmina Burana*, ed. A. Hilka and O. Schumann (Heidelberg, 1930), p. 54.
83 See R. Freyhan, 'The Evolution of the Caritas Figure in the Thirteenth and Fourteenth Centuries', *JWCI* xi (1948), 80 (pl. 15 f.).
84 *Index* 1467; Robbins, *MP* xxxvi, 348.
85 R. W. Southern, 'The English Origins of the "Miracles of the Virgin"', *Medieval and Renaissance Studies* iv (1958), shows that most *mariales* were based on English collections of the first half of the twelfth century. The miracles are known to most readers from the French stories in *The Tumbler of Our Lady and other Miracles*, tr. A. Kemp-Welch (London, 1907) (cf. Gautier de Coinci, *Les Miracles de Nostre Dame*, ed. V. F. Koenig; Rutebeuf, ed. E. Faral and J. Bastin); for English legends cf. Beverley Boyd, *The Middle English Miracles of the Virgin* (San Marino, 1964) (see the review by J. A. W. Bennett, *MÆ* xxxvi (1967), 93–5). The courtly atmosphere of the *Cantigas de Santa Maria* of Alfonso the Wise is nicely illustrated by Peter Dronke, *The Medieval Lyric*, pp. 71–2; in German legends too the Virgin is an 'edele vrouwe' (cf. *Marienlegenden aus dem Alten Passional*, ed. H. G. Richert (Tübingen, 1965)). Scenes from the stories are often found in the visual arts; Mâle *XIII*, pp. 259–67, gives some French examples.

Notes to pp. 94–8

86 The De Quincey Apocalypse Theophilus is reproduced in Brieger Pl. 60. For other English examples (e.g. in glass at Ely, on the reredos at Beverley), see M. D. Anderson, *Drama and Imagery in Medieval Churches* (Cambridge 1963), pp. 187–8, A. C. Fryer 'Theophilus the Penitent, as represented in Art', *The Archaeological Journal* xcii (1935), 287–333, Bennett, p. 95. The best known Theophilus play is that by Rutebeuf; there is a M.E. fragment (pr. J. Cooling, 'An unpublished Middle English Prologue', *RES* NS x (1959), 172–3; see Bennett, pp. 93–4).
87 Talbot, p. 75.

Chapter 6   Annunciation and Nativity

1 *Sermo in Nat.* iii, *PL* xxxviii, 1000.
2 *Sermo I in Adv., Opera* ed. Leclerq, IV, pp. 167–8.
3 See Henrik Cornell, *The Iconography of the Nativity of Christ* (Uppsala Universitets Årsskrift (1924)), ch. 1; cf. also the illustrations in *LM* s.v. 'Birgitta'. The idea that the child's body shone like a sun is found in popular belief (cf. R. Hofmann, *Das Leben Jesu nach den Apokryphen* (Leipzig, 1851), pp. 109 ff.); Clement A. Miles, *Christmas in Ritual and Tradition* (London, 1912), p. 66, quotes a charming Spanish song in which flame is said to issue from the porch at Bethlehem – it is a star from heaven which has fallen among the straw. More learned treatment of the imagery of light is found in the *Carmen Paschale* of Sedulius (II, 48 ff.; *PL* xix, 597):

> Quae nova lux mundo, quae toto gratia caelo!
> Quis fuit ille nitor, Mariae cum Christus ab alvo
> Processit splendore novo? . . .

See also the important article by Millard Meiss, 'Light as Form and Symbol in some 15th century paintings', *Art Bulletin* xxvii (1945), 175–81.
4 *OBMLV* No. 113 (*c.* 1100).
5 A.-F. Oxanam, *Les Poètes franciscains en Italie au 13e siècle* (Paris, 1852), p. 213.
6 *CB XIV* No. 88, *EEC* No. 12.
7 *EEC* No. 26.
8 *EEC* No. 35B. Cf. *EEC* Nos 34, 75; *CB XV* No. 80, etc.
9 *Index* 2733; *EEC* No. 30. For the music, see J. and C. Stainer, *Early Bodleian Music* II, pp. 122–3.
10 Cf. Cornell, ch. ii, 'Miracles of Christmas Eve', Réau, p. 218.
11 See David R. Cheney, *NQ* ccxiii (1968), 136–7, and the references given there.

Notes to pp. 98–100

12 *EEC* No. 7B. Cf. the Anglo-Norman Wassail song ('Si jo vus di trestoz; Wesseyl!/Dehaiz eit qui ne dira: Drincheyl!' ('And I say to you all "Wassail!" Cursed be he who will not say "drink-hail"')). Seventeenth-century attacks on Christmas festivities ('Christmas Day, The Old Heathens feasting Day, in honour to Saturn their Idol-God. The Papists Massing Day. The Prophane mans Ranting Day', etc.) have an interesting antecedent in Wyclif (see R. Kaiser, *Medieval English* (Berlin, 3rd ed., 1958), pp. 328–9).
13 *EEC* No. 3.
14 Ed. E. Mackay Mackenzie (London, 1932), p. 154.
15 On the iconography of the scene, see Réau, pp. 174–94, D. M. Robb, *Art Bulletin* xviii (1936), 480–526, M. B. Freeman, *Metropolitan Museum of Art Bulletin* (1967), 130–9. Mr John Sparrow (*Visible Words* (Cambridge, 1969), p. 57) points out an instance of a Madonna with the first three stanzas of Dante's invocation to Mary 'umile e alta' embroidered on the hem of her robe. Cf. also M. Meiss, 'The Madonna of Humility', *Art Bulletin* xviii (1936).
16 Luke says that Mary was 'troubled' by the words of the angel. There is a very dramatic representation of this in a *sinopia* of the Annunciation by Ambrogio Lorenzetti (active 1319–47) (see *Frescoes from Florence* (The Arts Council of Great Britain, 1969) pp. 62–3).
17 *CB XV* No. 70.
18 *Index* 1061; MS. Adv. 18. 7. 21, f. 23v (the bottom of the page has been cut off).
19 *CB XIII* No. 22; Dreves xxxi, No. 172.
20 On this see Hirn, pp. 211–13, and especially J. Vriend, *The Blessed Virgin Mary in the Medieval Drama of England* (Purmerend, 1928), pp. 150–60. It occurs in Zeno of Verona (*PL* xi, 352) and Bernard (*PL* clxxxiii, 327: missus est ... Gabriel ... ut verbum patris per aurem virginis in ventrem et mentem ipsius eructaret (he contrasts it with the poison in Eve's ear)); in Latin hymns Gabriel is spoken of as *seminiverbius* and Mary as *verbo foeta*. The image was not unchallenged. Agobard of Lyons (779–840), correcting the Lyons antiphonary (*PL* civ, 331), fastened on the phrase in a responsary 'introivit per aurem Virginis in regionum nostram', which he said 'could not be borne by Catholic ears' (it was changed in fact to *per virginem matrem*). It is quite common however in vernacular literature (among the examples quoted by Vriend comes one from the Old English Martyrology). See also Réau, pp. 190–1. It has been suggested that Rabelais may be parodying it in having his Gargantua born from his mother's ear. (Molière's Agnes in the *École des Femmes* also thinks that children are born through the ear.)

Notes to p. 101

21 The M.E. poem is in the Vernon MS. (EETS xcviii, p. 126, ll. 211 ff.). See Vriend, p. 152, Réau, p. 191. Yeats alludes to it at the beginning of 'A Nativity': 'What woman hugs her infant there?/ Another star has shot an ear', and of 'The Mother of God': 'The threefold terror of love; a fallen flare/Through the hollow of an ear'; his note in *The Winding Stair* says 'I had in my memory Byzantine mosaic pictures of the Annunciation, which show a line drawn from a star to the ear of the Virgin. She received the Word, through the ear, a star fell, and a star was born' (for this reference I am indebted to Mrs J. C. Gray).

22 Cf. E. S. Hartland, *Primitive Paternity* (London, 1909) I, ch. i, Stith Thompson, *Motif-Index of Folk-Literature* (Copenhagen, 1955), T.517. In Christian literature the image of conception through wind or breath is also found (cf. e.g. Dreves xxxii, No. 96, etc.). Hirn suggests an origin for this in the ancient belief that wind can bring about fertilization (so Hera conceived Hephaistos by inhaling wind; see also Hartland, *Perseus* I, 136, 180). Pigafetta, the author of a narrative account of Magellan's first circumnavigation (ed. and tr. by R. A. Skelton (New Haven–London, 1959), I, p. 142) was told by an old Malayan pilot the story of the island (perhaps Enggano) off the coast of Sumatra which was inhabited only by women, who were made pregnant by wind, and who killed off all male offspring and visitors. The similar popular idea of conception through a snowflake (cf. the German story of the *Schneekind* (see Holthausen, *Anglia Beiblatt* xxxv, 96)) is caustically used by one of the detractors of Mary in the Coventry *Trial of Joseph and Mary*:

> In feyth I suppose that this woman slepte
> Withowtyn all coverte whyll that it dede snowe
> And a flake therof into hyre mowthe crepte,
> And ther of the chylde in hyre wombe doth growe. . . .

and the second tells her to beware, for if the sun shines it will turn him to water.

23 *CB XIII* No. 4. Cf. *EEC* Nos 174, 208, *Ludus Coventriae*, ed. Block, p. 181, 97, Dreves xxxi, No. 143, Mone I, No. 47, II, No. 370, Hirn pp. 244–6, etc. There is a very interesting later example in Herrick's *Noble Numbers:*

> As Sun-beames pierce the glasse, and streaming in,
> No crack or Schisme leave i' th' subtill skin:
> So the Divine Hand work't, and brake no thred,
> But, in a *Mother*, kept a *maiden-head*.

24 See Meiss, *Art Bulletin* xxvii, especially pp. 177 ff. Mâle *Fin*, p. 215, mentions a window at La Ferté Bernard with the inscription

fenestra coeli; no doubt this figure was in the mind of the designer of the famous 'Notre Dame de la belle Verrière' window at Chartres. Cf. J. Dagens, 'La Métaphore de la Verrière de l'apocalypse à Rutebeuf et à l'école française', *Revue d'Ascétique et de mystique* xxv (1949), 524–32.

25 An example from St Augustine was used as a *lectio* for Matins on the third Sunday in Advent (*SEC*, p. 191).

26 *Enthusiasm* (Oxford, 1950), p. 125. He also mentions the view of the Paulicians that Christ's celestial body passed through Mary as 'water through a pipe' (in fact the *De Laud. BMV* IX, uses the word *aquaeductus* of the Virgin). An origin in non-orthodox sources for these images is possible, but in our poems from the later Middle Ages they do not seem to have caused trouble. Interestingly, when the light image is used in De Guilleville's *Pèlerinage Jhesucrist*, ed. J. J. Stürzinger, Roxburghe Club, 1897, ll. 1141–64, the orthodox theological point is made explicit (Christ will descend like light):

> Que de la substance de toi
> Il convertira tant en soi
> Qu'en sera non pas seulement
> Coulouré, mez realement
> En sera couvert et vestu,
> Tres parfait homme devenu.

27 *Index* 1367; often reprinted, and discussed (see especially Davies, pp. 14–18, S. Manning, *Wisdom and Number* (Lincoln, Nebr., 1962), pp. 158–67, Barbara C. Raw, *MLR* lv (1960), 411–14). It seems to be based, more or less remotely, on a thirteenth-century Annunciation lyric (*CB XIII* No. 31; see *MP* vii, 166). There are close verbal parallels in two of the stanzas. The later poet's changes (if changes they be) are invariably improvements – the almost separable nature-opening of the earlier poem has been worked into the central texture; Jesus's choosing of Mary has been significantly reversed.

28 Cf. *CB XIV*, No. 112, l. 3, *CB XV* No. 74, ll. 15, 78, l. 31; and images such as the 'taking' of the unicorn. In the Coventry Plays Mary says 'I conceyvyd God at my consentynge' (cf. the similar idea in the *Blickling Homilies*, ed. Morris, p. 9: Eala þu eadige Maria, eall þeos gehæftworld bideþ þinre geþafunga); Sedulius, in the 'A solis ortus cardine' even uses the word *creavit – intacta nesciens virum/verbo creavit filium* (see the discussion of this word in Walpole, *Early Latin Hymns*, p. 152).

29 The theme of 'coming' is of course important in the Advent liturgy (cf. p. 4).

30 'She was sitting in time, untimely ... a creature uncreaturely ...

Notes to pp. 103–5

she was liberated from creatures and set upon God alone . . . she was in the land of freedom', Johannes of Sterngassen, quoted by E. Wilkins, *The Rose-Garden Game*, p. 94.

31 *CB XIII* No. 19B, l. 13.
32 Cf. Manning, op. cit. The threefold repetition of 'he cam also stille' may be a feature taken from popular poetry, but it would also have appealed to the symbolic imagination, since Trinitarian imagery is not inappropriate to the Virgin who was called the 'couch of the Trinity' or the 'ark bearing the threefold blessing'. There were three Masses on Christmas morning, sometimes taken to symbolize three 'births' of Christ (see Miles, *Christmas*, p. 94).
33 *CB XIV* No. 31.
34 See below, pp. 131–2.
35 *CB XIV* No. 32, l. 23.
36 *Pélerinage Jhesucrist*, ed. Stürzinger, ll. 1017–29:

> En ce point le fil s'enclina
> Et vers terre jus regarda.
> 'Pere', dist-il, 'je voi ja bien
> Que Gabriel ne ment de rien.
> Je voi la douce pucelle
> Dont parle as, qui si belle
> Est du tout selonc mon plaisir
> Que nulle rien tant ne desir
> Com devers li tantost aler
> Pour moi dedens li hosteler
> A fin que le mariage
> De moi et humain lignage
> Soit fait en li et celebré. . . .'

See also *LM* s.v. 'Braut', 'Brautgemach'.

37 For parallels in word and phrase, cf. *CB XIII* No. 44, 49 ('maiden, moder makeles'), *CB XIV* No. 57, 79; Lydgate, *Life of Our Lady*, has 'mayden and moder was never non'.
38 Cf. *De Laud. BMV* xii, 5, pp. 707 ff.; Mone I, No. 29, II, Nos 364, 365, 379, 385, 496; and especially Dreves xxxi, No. 141:

> Cardine de supero
> Rore salutifero
>   Venter fecundatur,
> Peperit fecunditas,
> Et sacra virginitas
>   Integra servatur.
>
> Sicut ros in gramine
> Descendit in virgine
>   Verbum summi patris,

Patrem non deseruit
Et mortalem induit
Forman alvo matris.

Sicut terram pluvia,
Sic divina gratia
Virginem fecundat. . . .

Mechthild of Magdeburg expresses the idea more mystically: 'Der susse towe der unbeginlicher drivaltekeit hat sich gesprenget us dem brunnen der ewigen gotheit in den blumen der userwelten maget' (*Offenbarungen* ed. G. Morel, Regensburg, 1869, p. 11).

39 It is used to good effect in Dunbar's poem on the Nativity. The verse comes from the Old Testament (Isa. 45:8), where, as one would expect in Middle Eastern literature, the images of dew, rain, etc. as blessing and grace are very frequent (cf. Isa. 41:18–19; 55:10; Deut. 33:28; Ps. cxxxii (Vg.); 3, Hos. 14:5 quoted in the York plays (ed. Toulmin Smith, p. 96) though attributed to Joel ('a gentill Jewe'), while from Judges comes the figure of Gideon's fleece). The idea of spiritual activity is forcefully expressed in a little prayer (*Index* 963):

God send us the dew of hevene: *gratiam Spiritus Sancti*,
And reyn fro the cloudes of hevene *per doctrinam Divini Verbi*
And thirle our erthe and open our land *ad contricionem animi et confessionem peccati*,
And bryng forth a blome of sich feng and sich fuysoun
That be our bote and our savacioun; *i. Jesum filium Dei vivi*.

The most famous example from later times is probably Herbert's 'Grace', where the refrain 'drop from above' seems to be echoing the *rorate* verse.

40 *Opera*, ed. Leclerq IV, p. 173. Cf. the belief that the vines of Engaddi flowered at the Nativity (see, e.g., Mone II, No. 483). Cf. also Prudentius 'Quid est quod arctum circulum'.

41 Bartholomeus Anglicus states the traditional view that dew makes the earth plenteous – it brings forth and increases flowers, and corn, and fattens oysters. There was a German peasant belief in recent times in the magical powers possessed by bread baked at Christmas, especially when moistened by Christmas dew (Miles, *Christmas*, pp. 288–9; cf. Bächtold-Stäubli, *Handwörterbuch des deutschen Aberglaubens*, s.v. 'Tau', 'Weihnachtsgebäck', 'Weihnachtsbrot'. Something very similar is recorded in Britain by Gervase of Tilbury (*Otia Imperialia*, ed. F. Liebrecht (Hanover, 1856), p. 2) – on Christmas night oats or barley were put out, which, when moistened by heavenly dew at the hour of the Nativity and

made into bread, were efficacious against plague and fever. May-dew is also important in folk-belief.
42 See the discussion of 'The Foggy Foggy Dew' in James Reeves, *The Idiom of the People* (London, 1958), pp. 54–7.
43 Quoted by Hirn, p. 221.
44 Byrhtferth, *Manual*, ed. S. J. Crawford, EETS clxxvii (1929), pp. 152–3.
45 In the *Chronicle of Pierre de Langtoft*, ed. T. Wright (R.S. 47) II, pp. 426 ff.
46 Dreves xxxi, No. 18:

> Nox silentium tenuit
> Medium, dum sponsus venit
> A regalibus sedibus
> Donans pacem hominibus

(Cf. Mone I, Nos 29, 52; Introit for Sunday in Octave of Christmas, 'Dum medium silentium tenerant omnia. . . .') There are legends concerning the silence of the elements at the moment of the Nativity (Stith Thompson *Motif-Index* V, 211. 1. 5).

47 *Sermo* cxc (*PL* xxxviii, 1008): 'Quis est iste infans? Infans enim dicitur, quod non possit fari, id est loqui. Ergo et infans et verbum est.'
48 *EEC* No. 65.
49 *EEC* No. 56.
50 See Auerbach, *Mimesis*, especially pp. 151 ff.
51 *In Nat. Dom.* IV, 1.
52 *EEC* No. 50.
53 *CB XIII* No. 26.
54 *CB XIII* p. 192.
55 *Index*: MS. Adv. 18. 7, 12, f. 119r. Cf. EETS xv, p. 254:

> Ho art thou that comest so litel and so mithful?
> Ho art thou that comest so dredful and so rithful?
> Ho art thou that comest so yonge and so connynge?
> Ho art thou that comest so pore and al weldynge?. . . .

> Ich am a knyth for ou to fithten;
> Ich am a pledour ou to lede to rithte;
> Ich am a maister to teche the lawe;
> Ich am an emperour, a god felawe.

or Dreves xxxi. 23:

> Ave, Jesu parvule,
>   Regnum rex sublimis,
> Nobilis infantule
>   Deus magne nimis. . . .

Notes to pp. 108–10

Quam magnus, quam parvulus,
Quam tener, quam fortis,
Tu dominus, tu famulus,
Tu consors nostrae sortis.

56 Nicholas Love's paraphrase (*The Mirrour of the Blessed Lyf of Jesu Christ*), ed. L. F. Powell (Oxford, 1908), p. 46.
57 Ed. C. Dumont (Paris, 1961), p. 120.
58 See C. Woodforde, *The Norwich School of Glass-Painting in the Fifteenth Century* (London, 1950), Le Couteur, fig. 11.
59 See E. Panofsky, *Early Netherlandish Painting* (Cambridge, Mass., 1953), pp. 331 ff., M. Whinney, plates 47 ff., pp. 79 ff. The flowers in front of the picture are, Panofsky suggests, premonitions of the Passion – the scarlet lily suggests the shed blood, the iris the sword that pierces the heart of Mary. The coldness is often insisted on in popular verse – cf. the S. German song quoted by Miles, from K. Weinhold, *Weihnachtspiele und Lieder aus Süddeutschland und Schlesien* (Graz, 1870), p. 400:

Du herzliebste Muater, gib acht af dös Kind,
Es ist ja gar frostig, thuas einfatschen gschwind
Und du alter Voda, decks Kindlein schen zua,
Sonst hats von der Kölden und Winden kan Ruah.

('Dearest mother, take care of the child; it is freezing hard, wrap him up quickly. And you old father, tuck the little one up, or he will have no rest from the cold and the wind.')

60 No separate lyrics on the Nativity survive before those in Grimestone's book. Miss Woolf (p. 148) suggests that attention was stimulated by the mystery plays, in which the Nativity became detached from its liturgical season. But it is dangerous to argue from absence of manuscripts. One new 'find' in the thirteenth century might make the picture look entirely different.

61 *CB XV* No. 3. Some of Christ's words in the Old English 'Christ' (ll. 1420–6) are a premonition of this theme in medieval devotional literature:

... wearo ic ana geboren
Folcum to frofre. Mec mon folmum biwond,
Biþeahte mid þearfan wædum, ond mec þa on þeostre alegde
Biwundenne mid wonnum claþum – hwæt! ic þæt for worulde geþolade!
Lytel þuhte ic leoda bearnum; læg ic on heardum stane,
Cildgeong on crybbe, mid þy ic þe wolde cwealm afyrran,
Hat hellebealu....

62 *CB XIV* No. 75, Sisam, *XIV Century Verse and Prose*, pp. 167–8. See the discussion by Woolf, pp. 152 ff.

63 Cf. Millard Meiss, *Painting in Florence and Siena after the Black Death* (Princeton, 1951), pp. 145–56. On the Christ Child see *RDK* s.v. 'Christkind', and the elaborate account of the iconograph by Dorothy C. Shorr, *The Christ Child in Devotional Images in Italy during the XIV Century* (New York, 1954).
64 *EEC* No. 60. Note the homely word 'pappe' ('supposed' (*NED*) 'to have its origins in the sound made by an infant in opening and shutting the lips, as associated with the notion of food'). A nice visual parallel is an alabaster (Evans, pl. 53) where the child fondles Mary's breast and 'plays with her pap'.
65 Shorr, pp. 58–82, says that this is a very popular and ancient visual image, and finds a prototype for it in the Egyptian group of Isis nursing the infant Horus.
66 *Meditations on the Life and Passion of Christ*, ed. D'Evelyn, ll. 151 ff.
67 See Woolf, pp. 151 ff. There is also a Latin hymn with 'lully ... by by' refrains (*Processional of the Nuns of Chester*, ed. Legg (Henry Bradshaw Society), xviii, 18; see *New Oxford History of Music* III, p. 117), and an interesting post-medieval example in Verstegan's *Odes* (1691) – 'Upon my lap my soueraigne sits.'
68 *CB XV* No. 2.
69 *CB XIV* No. 56.
70 *EEC* No. 143.
71 *CB XV* No. 4
72 *EEC* No. 145.
73 See Miles, *Christmas*, pp. 109–11, T. G. Crippen, *Christmas and Christmas Lore* (London, 1923), pp. 81–2. There is an interesting example in Weinhold, *Weihnachtspiele* (p. 417), in which the singer says, as she contemplates the Christ child in the crib, 'even if myg little Hans were more beautiful than he is, he still would be nothing beside Him'. For other examples, see A. Tille, *Deutsche Weihnacht* (Leipzig, 1893), pp. 59 ff., *Oxford Book of Carols*, Nos 84, 87.
74 MS. Bodley 416, f. 12v. This passage is among those quoted in C. Kirchberger, *The Coasts of the Country* (London, 1952), pp. 73–4.
75 *CB XIV* No. 59, *EEC* No. 155.
76 *CB XIV* No. 65.
77 Though the crib was known before Francis. See Catholic Encyclopedia, s.v. 'crib'; cf. N. de Robeck, *The Christmas Crib* (London, 1930), R. Berliner, *Die Weihnachtskrippe* (Munich, 1955), Rouse, *Folklore* v (1894) 6–10.
78 The apocryphal Ps.–Matthew, xiv, applies a prophecy of Habakkuk (iii, 2 in the Old Itala version): 'in medio duorum animalium innotesceris' to the Nativity (see James, p. 74). The prophet Habakkuk is explicitly mentioned in *EEC* Nos 70, 72. In the ballad, *The*

Carnal and the Crane, 'wild beasts' come to worship Jesus on the flight into Egypt (from the *Historia de Nativitate Mariae*). On the ox and ass in art, see Réau, pp. 228–9.
79 *EEC* No. 45. They recognize the child's divinity. In popular tradition they sometimes express this by kneeling. In *Tess of the D'Urbervilles*, ch. xvii, the aged William Dewy saves himself from a bull by recalling this – 'he called to mind how he'd seen the cattle kneel o' Christmas Eves in the dead o' night' and burst into a Nativity hymn (cf. also Hardy's poem 'Christmas Eve, and twelve of the clock'). This belief is attested from other parts of England.
80 N. Hervé, *Les Noëls français* (1905), pp. 115 ff., P. Le Duc, *Les Noëls Bressans*, p. 145. Cf. Italian, German and Spanish parallels, Child I, pp. 241, 505, II, 501, IV, 451–2. Cf. Réau, 233n., Miles, 69, Tille, 311. H. J. L. Massé, *A Book of Old Carols* (London, 1910) has a Provençal 'Nouel des Ausèls' in which the birds come to Bethlehem and sing their songs. Simone dei Crocefissi (fourteenth century), in his 'Presepio' in the Uffizi, has the ass and the ox in the background of the Nativity scene, and the ass is uttering a loud bray (reproduced in L. Marcucci, *I Dipinti Toscani del secolo XIV* (*Cataloghi dei Musei e Gallerie d'Italia. Gallerie nazionali di Firenze*), Rome, 1965, pl. 123). T. G. Crippen, *Christmas*, pp. 83–4, describes an English broadside of 1701 showing a Nativity scene with angels, and birds and animals with Latin *tituli* for their noises – the cock has *Christus natus est*, the raven *quando*, the crow *hac nocte*, the ox *ubi*, and the sheep *Bethlehem* (cf. p. 22).
81 *Folklore* lxx (1959), 544.
82 See Réau, pp. 231–6. Of the numerous representations of the shepherds in English art, one of the best is the Adoration in the window at East Harling (Woodforde, *Norwich School of Glass-Painting*, pl. xi). The shepherds play an important part in popular art and devotion – they are prominent in the Neapolitan cribs, and in Provençal *santons*. At Les Baux in Provence, there is a famous ceremony on Christmas night, in which the shepherds offer a lamb.
83 See E. Winternitz, *Musical Instruments and their Symbolism in Western Art* (London, 1967), esp. pp. 80, 132 ff. (cf. fig. 58a, the scene from the Hours of Jean d'Évreux, where one shepherd has a bagpipe, another a pastoral shawm), who draws attention to the mingling of visual and musical symbolism – 'the characteristic union between the sound of reed pipes and the creche in the stable ... of pastoral music with its characteristic drone and Christmas, pervades more than five hundred years of music up to the *Christmas Oratorio* of Johann Sebastian Bach and to Handel's *Messiah* and still further.'
84 Ed. Hassall, p. 90.

85 H. Lemeignen, *Vieux Noëls* (Nantes, 1876), i, p. 29.
86 Ed. A. R. Waller (1902), p. 201 ('In the Holy Nativity of Our Lord God. A Hymn sung as by the Shepheards'); note the design which accompanies it.
87 *EEC* No. 79.
88 *EEC* No. 78. 'Mall' is apparently his favourite ewe, 'Will' the bell wether.
89 Poems and carols on the Magi and the Epiphany include *CB XIII*, No. 26, *CB XV* Nos 85–9, *EEC* 122–31; cf. *Index* *31, 2033.3, 3810.3, 4061. See also Réau, pp. 236–42, 255, G. Grigson, 'The Three Kings of Cologne', *History Today* iv (1954), 793–801.
90 *EEC* No. 123.
91 *Collected Poems*, p. 141. A more homely expression of their exotic nature is quoted by Réau (p. 244) from a German play:

> Ich bin's Melchior genannt
> Und bin von Saba her gerant
> Uf mynem dromedarie. . . .

92 *Itineraria*, ed. John H. Harvey (Oxford, 1969), p. 303.
93 These charms have a long history; cf. Scot's *The Discoverie of Witchcraft* (1584), pp. 231–2, MS. e mus. 243 (Bodleian, seventeenth century), f. 21v (the names appear also in a 'true experiment to fynde treasure y^t is hidde in ye grounde' (MS. e mus. 173, f. 64r)). A charm in the form of a prayer to the Magi was found on Jackson, a murderer and smuggler who was executed in 1749 (see *Gentleman's Magazine* (1749), p. 88); an accompanying note in French says that it is for accidents on journeys, headaches, falling sickness, fevers, witchcraft, 'toute sorte de malefice', and sudden death. Cf. Evans, *Magical Jewels*, pp. 125–7, Gray, *NQ* ccviii, 165.
94 *CB XIV* No. 58, Cf. *EEC* Nos. 258–60.
95 *Ludus Coventriae*, ed. Block, p. 110. The cult of St Joseph, which finally ended this sort of attitude, developed in the later Middle Ages, encouraged particularly by Bernardino of Siena and Gerson. Cf. Panofsky, *Early Netherlandish Painting*, pp. 164–5; Schapiro, *Art Bulletin* xxvii, 184–5.
96 F. J. Child, *The English and Scottish Popular Ballads*, No. 54 (see the notes). Cf. Vriend, ch. x. Here 'Joseph's trouble' has been combined with a miracle on the Flight to Egypt. The ballad was popular, and migrated to America, where it was discovered in the Appalachians in 1917 by Cecil Sharp.
97 *CB XV* No. 3.
98 *EEC* No. 112. Cf. *EEC* Nos 108–11, *Index* 414, and the four M.E. versions of the *Hostis Herodes impie*, *Index* 725, 1213, 3668, 4166.
99 Anthony Blunt, *Picasso's 'Guernica'* (London, 1969), pp. 44–7.
100 See *Norfolk Archaeology* xvii (1908), 113. The Christ child with a

crucifix is a common late medieval devotional image. Cf. also the symbolic sleep of the Christ child in some paintings (see Meiss, *Proc. Amer. Philos. Soc.* cx (1966), 348–52.
101 Mâle *XIII*, figs. 98–9. Cf. Réau, p. 219. Mâle quotes a version of the Gloss on Luke ii: *ponitur in presepio, id est corpus Christi super altare*. A different way of linking Annunciation with Crucifixion (legend had it that they both fell on the same day), and one which was popular in England, was the lily-crucifix (examples at Oxford (St Michael's), Long Melford, Abingdon, Westwood (Wiltshire), etc.; see Hildburgh, 'An Alabaster Table of the Annunciation with the Crucifixion', *Archaeologia* lxxiv (1924), 203–32, Woodforde, *Norwich School*, pp. 92–3, Tristram, *Fourteenth Century*, p. 24).
102 *MÆ* xxxiv, 16.
103 *CB XV*, No. 5.

Chapter 7   The Passion

1 In a devotional collection such as MS. Additional 37049, for example, the 'mind' of the Passion is dominant. Alongside the formal recalling of the Passion in the Holy Week and Easter liturgy existed a whole set of popular customs. Some idea of what these were like, at least in Germany, can be gained from the anti-Papist satire of Naogeorgus. He describes how on Passion Sunday boys go with a guy of death, how the guys of Winter and Summer were in conflict, the *Palmesel* – a wooden ass with an image of Christ (there is an example in the Victoria and Albert Museum) which on Palm Sunday was brought to the church and then taken round the streets (the people cast boughs on to it, which they later kept for protection against storms), the hurly-burly that breaks out after the candles are extinguished, the quenching of all fires on Easter Eve, the pageants, e.g. the Three Maries at the sepulchre, played by maskers on Easter Day, etc.
2 *CB XIV* No. 89.
3 'Luve is ase hard as helle,' says one poem attributed to Rolle (Sisam, *XIV Century Verse and Prose*, p. 39); cf. also *Index* 2678, a *chanson d'aventure* in which a bird sings as refrain 'fortis ut mors dileccio'.
4 *Index* 23; MS. Adv. 18. 7. 21, f. 40v.
5 See Esther C. Quinn, *The Quest of Seth for the Oil of Life* (Chicago, 1962), Betty Hill, 'The Fifteenth-century Prose Legend of the Cross before Christ', *MÆ* xxxiv (1965), 203–22.
6 See F. Wormald 'The Rood of Bromholm' *JWCI* i (1937–8), 31–45 (representations were sold to pilgrims; there are devotional verses which seem to be meant to be recited in front of the image), W. Sparrow Simpson, *J. Arch. Ass.* xxx (1874), 52–9.

Notes to pp. 123–7

7 *CB XIV* No. 40. The *Pange Lingua* is in *OBMLV* (No. 74). Cf. Paulinus of Nola, *PL* lxi, 550 (Hamman, No. 293).
8 *CB XIV* No. 62.
9 *CB XIII* No. 25, Child No. 23; see the discussion by Peter Dronke, *The Medieval Lyric*, pp. 67–9. On the legend of Judas, see Child's notes, and P. F. Baum, 'The Mediaeval Legend of Judas Iscariot', *PMLA* xxxi (1916), 481–632. Judas is shown being devoured by the devil in Southwark Cathedral; the Anglo-Norman *Passion of Judas* (MS. Laud Misc. 471) refers to Brendan's vision of him imprisoned on an island washed by icy waves.
10 Ed. Dumont, p. 104.
11 *CB XIII* No. 35B.
12 See Elisabeth Roth, *Der volkreiche Kalvarienberg* (Berlin, 1958).
13 On the development of this, see Réau, pp. 462–512, J. Reil, *Christus am Kreuz* (Leipzig, 1930); a brief popular account is C. E. Pocknee, *Cross and Crucifix* (London, 1962). There is much interesting material in V. Gurewich, 'Observations on the iconography of the wound in Christ's side', *JWCI* (1957), 358–62 (after the time of the Rabula gospels, the wound is regularly found on the right side (cf. *Dream of the Rood*, l. 20) – an interesting Irish exception is reproduced in Pocknee, pp. 29–30).
14 MS. Sloane 2499, f. 6r; cf. G. Warrack ed. pp. 15–16.
15 *Index* 156, 602; MS. Adv. 7. 21 f. 119r. On the same page there is another interesting quatrain:

> Cristes bodi maltth
> The soule it sualtth
> The blod was spiltth
> For mannis giltth.

16 Meditative lyrics are exhaustively discussed by Woolf, *passim*. Cf. Louis L. Martz, *The Poetry of Meditation. A Study in English Religious Literature of the Seventeenth Century* (New Haven, 1954); see also J. C. Hirsh, *NQ* ccxiii (1968), 7–9.
17 *Index* 1761; *CB XIV* No. 91. The second rubric may imply something like a rudimentary form of the *Via Crucis*. On the development of this form of public meditation (which has its origin apparently in the devout visits of pilgrims to the Holy Places), see *Catholic Encyclopaedia*, s.v. 'Way of the Cross', H. Thurston, *The Stations of the Cross* (London, 1906).
18 Cf. F. M. Comper, *Spiritual Songs* (London, 1936), p. 132 (from MS. Additional 37049); it is also found in the '*Quia amore langueo*' poem discussed on pp. 143–5.
19 *CB XIV* No. 90.
20 *CB XIV* No. 91.
21 *CB XIII* No. 63, ll. 21–2.

22 *CB XIII* Nos. 64 and 24.
23 *Index* 1761; *CB XIV* No. 91. The *Meditations* are in EETS clviii (ed. D'Evelyn). On John of Howden (who was chaplain to Eleanor, wife of Henry III, for whom a French translation of *Philomena* was made) and his poem, see F. J. E. Raby, *MLR* xxx (1935), 339–43, and D'Evelyn in *Essays and Studies in Honor of Carleton Brown* (ed. P. W. Long, New York, 1940), pp. 79–90.
24 *Index* 4088; *CB XIV* No. 1. See Woolf, pp. 28 ff.
25 See J. Leclerq and J.-P. Bonnes, *Un Maître de la vie spirituelle au xie siècle, Jean de Fécamp* (Paris, 1944).
26 *CB XIII* No. 33.
27 *Index* 1320; see B. D. Brown, 'Religious Lyrics in MS. Don. C 13', *Bodleian Qly. Record* vii (1932), 1–7.
28 *Index* 3743.3; cf. A. G. Little, *Franciscan Papers*, pp. 244 ff.
29 Ed. Curt F. Bühler, EETS cclxiv, p. 38. Cf. Little, *Franciscan Papers*, pp. 255–6.
30 On hornbooks, see A. W. Tuer, *History of the Hornbook* (London, 1896), which has profuse illustrations (see esp. I, chs 5 and 6 on the cruciform hornbook, which is presumably the type of which these poets are thinking). Cf. also Robbins, *MLR* xxxiv, 420 nt., B. Bischoff, 'Elementarunterricht . . . in der ersten Hälfte des Mittelalters' in *Medieval Studies in Honor of E. K. Rand*, ed. L. W. Jones (New York, 1938), who draws attention to the 'abecadarius' hung up in front of a class, and quotes a relevant passage from Odo of Cheriton: 'Sicut enim carta, in qua scribitur doctrina parvulorum, quatuor clavis affigitur in poste, sic caro Christi extensa est in cruce . . . cuius quinque vulnera quasi quinque vocales pro nobis ad Patrem per se sonant. Cetere circumstantes sunt consonantes et sicut abecadarium viam aperit in omnem facultatem.'
31 *Index* 1483. Cf. EETS xv, pp. 270–8, Woolf, 253n. *Index* 664 (*CB XV*, No. 101) alludes to the sign of the cross which was placed at the beginning of the alphabet (the formula 'Christs cross me spede' was said before repeating the alphabet (Tuer, I, pp. 80–1) (cf. the practice of making the sign of the cross on rising in the morning); the modern expression 'criss-cross' comes ultimately from 'Christ's cross').
32 For other examples of the image of Christ's body as parchment, cf. *Archiv* clxvi, 196–7 ('als touit als any tabour skynne our lord lay tyght on tente'), EETS cxvii, 647 (the 'testament' of Christ, with seals of steel and iron, the sealing wax from Christ's heart). Cf. also *Archiv* lxxix, 424–32, and J. G. Wright, *A Study of the Themes of the Resurrection in the Medieval French Drama* (Bryn Mawr, 1935), pp. 106 ff. Wright draws attention to the Passion of Isabel of Bavaria, where the vermilion colour used on the parchment is the blood of Christ, the blue his bruises. The Monk of Farne (ed. Farmer, p. 76) compares Christ's body on the cross to a book for the meditator's

Notes to pp. 130–3

perusal. The words are his actions, the letters his wounds (like Odo, he thinks of the Five Wounds as the five vowels).

33 *CB XIV* No. 16. On the Charters of Christ, see M. C. Spalding, *The Middle English Charters of Christ* (Bryn Mawr, 1914), Woolf, pp. 210 ff. The text of the version in MS. Additional 37049 is given by Spalding, p. 8.

34 See Woolf, pp. 44 ff., and 'The Theme of Christ the Lover-Knight in Medieval English Literature', *RES* n.s. xiii (1962) 1–16, W. Gaffney 'The Allegory of the Christ Knight in *Piers Plowman*', *PMLA* xlvi (1931), 155–68.

35 *CB XIV* No. 51.

36 *CB XIV* No. 79.

37 *CB XIV* No. 73.

38 See Woolf, pp. 234 ff.

39 See p. 51. Cf. Woolf, pp. 208 ff.; there are Latin examples also. On the relics, see H. M. Gillett, *The Story of the Relics of the Passion* (Oxford, 1935). For the theme in the visual arts, see R. Berliner, *Münchner Jahrbuch der bildenden Kunst* 3 Folge, vi (1955), 35 ff., Mâle, *Fin*, pp. 103–6 (figs. 52–3), C. Carter, 'The *Arma Christi* in Scotland', *Proc. of Soc. of Antiquaries of Scotland*, xc (1956–7), 116–29, Woodforde, *Somerset*, pp. 196–201, Evans, *Pattern*, pp. 148–9, M. D. Anderson, *The Imagery of British Churches* (London, 1955), pp. 196 ff. There are some interesting post-medieval examples in literature, cf. William Alabaster's *Sonnets or Ensignes of Christ's Crucifixion*, and Crashaw, ed. Waller, pp. 219 ff., 227 (note the pietà surrounded by the Instruments of the Passion which is the headpiece of 'Sancta Maria Dolorum'), and in visual form, e.g. in the painted gallery of Provost Skene's house in Aberdeen (?late sixteenth/early seventeenth century), and even later in popular churchyard sculpture (e.g. on a headstone of 1797 at Wolverton, Buckinghamshire (Burgess, *English Churchyard Memorials*, London, 1963, p. 188); cf. also L. Meynell, *Bedfordshire*, p. 342–3 (Leighton Buzzard)).

40 There are some good examples of this. See, for example, Brieger, pp. 137n, 209, plates 52b, 79a, etc.

41 *Index* 91; *Reliquiae Antiquae*, ii, p. 18. There is a beautiful illustration of this heraldic device in MS. Cotton Faustina B VI, Pt. ii (f. 123v) in the British Museum.

42 On the cult of the Precious Blood see *RDK* s.v. 'Blut', *NQ* ccviii, 130; cf. the summaries, with references, in the *New Catholic Encyclopaedia*, s.v. 'Precious Blood', III, *Dictionnaire de Théologie catholique*, s.v. 'Sang de Christ'.

43 Brieger, pl. 44b.

44 See Maj-Britt Wadell, *Fons Pietatis. Eine ikonographische Studie* (Göteborg, 1969), Mâle, *Fin*, pp. 110–15, Vloberg, pp. 164 ff., W. A.

Reybekiel, *Fons Vitae* (Bremen, 1934), Gray, *NQ* ccviii, 131–3. It was not common in England, as far as can be judged – there may have been one in St Mary Redcliffe, Bristol, and there is an example in a woodcut in Thomas Godfray's *The Fountayne or Well of Lyfe* (?1532; STC 11211, see Hodnett, *English Woodcuts* No. 2063). It reappears in emblem books in the seventeenth century (see, especially, Höltgen, 'Arbor, Scala und Fons vitae', 381–9). Other Protestant examples include Isaac Watts, *Hymns* I, 9, II, 90, III, 22, and *Hymns Ancient and Modern* No. 114:

> Come let us stand beneath the Cross;
> So may the blood from out His Side
> Fall gently on us, drop by drop....

Cf. also the traditional religious song, collected in the early twentieth century, 'There is a fountain of Christ's blood', *JFSS* iv (1910–13), 21–2 (Francis Douce collected a broadsheet version of this, from the end of the eighteenth century).

45 Cf. *Index* 1439, 3443; *EEC* p. 401, *CB XV* pp. 322–3.
46 On the Five Wounds see the study by L. Gougaud in *Dévotions et Pratiques ascétiques du Moyen Age* (Paris, 1925), Gray, 'The Five Wounds of Our Lord' *NQ* ccviii (1963), 50–1, 82–9, 127–34, 163–8 (there is also a book by Ignazio Bonetti, *Le Stimate della Passione: Dottrina e Storia della Devozione alle Cinque Piaghe* (Rovigo, 1952), which I have not been able to consult). The idea that they are the wounds of love is expressed in images discussed previously: in Lydgate's *A Seying of the Nightingale* the reader is asked to make of the Five Wounds a rose and to let it abide continually in his heart; in 'Christ's Testament' (EETS cxvii, p. 656) Christ takes to his Father a 'cotearmour' powdered with five red roses. On the Mass of the Five Wounds, see in addition to the studies mentioned, R. W. Pfaff, *New Liturgical Feasts*, pp. 84–91. There is an illustration of badges of the Five Wounds in the London Museum, *Medieval Catalogue*, pl. lxx, pp. 262–3. Some interesting examples (from the mid-sixteenth century?) appear in the vault of the painted gallery of Provost Skene's house in Aberdeen (see *Provost Skene's House*, pub. Art Gallery Committee of the Corporation of the City of Aberdeen, 1953).
47 See Gray, pp. 127–8. There is an early example (a liturgical fragment, recorded in the third century) in Hamman, No. 210.
48 *CB XV* No. 100.
49 On the Sacred Heart see Gougaud, op. cit.
50 *CB XIV* No. 71. Julian of Norwich has a vision of the wound in the side as 'a fair delectable place, and large enough for all mankind that shall be saved to rest in peace and love'; for other examples, see Gray, p. 129.

Notes to pp. 134–5

51 *Index* 644; it survives only in the facsimile of W. Bateman (Manchester, 1814). Crashaw's phrase is in the poem 'On our crucified Lord, naked and bloody', ed. Waller, p. 85.
52 It is sometimes the enthusiastic and perverse development of the idea of the imitation of Christ. See H. Thurston, *Physical Phenomena of Mysticism* (London, 1952), pp. 32–43 (who mentions, among other examples, one Christina of Spoleto, who perforated one foot with a nail in imitation of Christ's sufferings). The best-known expression of this is probably the processions of the Flagellants which caused great problems to ecclesiastical authorities on the Continent in the fourteenth century. The imitation of Christ is explicitly mentioned in their songs:

> Or, avant, entre nous tuit frère,
> Batons noz charoignes bien fort,
> En remembrant la grant misère
> De Dieu et sa piteuse mort,
> Qui fut pris de la gent amère,
> Et vendus et trahi à tort,
> Et battu sa char vierge et clère;
> Ou nom de ce, batons plus fort.

(Leroux de Lincy, *Recueil de Chants historiques français* (1841), I, p. 237). The Flagellants had no success in England, however. (Robert of Avesbury (R.S. xciii, 407–8) describes a procession in London in 1349 of Flagellants from 'Selond' and 'Houlond', who sang in their own language antiphonally 'in the manner of a litany'; Thomas Walsingham (R.S. xxviii, I, 275) has a brief note which ends significantly: 'qui sua corpora nuda usque ad effusionem sanguinis, nunc flendo, nunc canendo, acerrime flagellabant; tamen, ut dicebatur, nimis hoc faciebant inconsulte, quia sine licentia Sedis Apostolicae'.)
53 Dreves, xxxi, No. 61.
54 See *LM* s.v. 'Compassio BMV.'; there was an incipient liturgical feast of the Compassion of the Virgin (Pfaff, pp. 97–103).
55 Luke 2:34–5. The idea that the 'sword' which pierced her son's side also pierced Mary's is given direct iconographical expression in a fourteenth-century ivory, where the lance pierces simultaneously the right side of Christ and the left side of Mary (Gurewich, *JWCI* xx, pl. 27d, p. 360). More common is the rather gauche representation of the sorrows of the Virgin by a sword which pierces her, or indeed by a number of swords representing her Sorrows (seven is the favourite number: e.g. Simeon's Prophecy, the Flight into Egypt, the Search for the lost Child, the meeting with Jesus on the way to Golgotha, the death of Christ, the descent from the cross, the burial) (see Réau, pp. 108–10, Mâle, *Fin*, fig. 66).

Notes to pp. 135–9

56 *CB XIII*, No. 47 (a version of the hymn *Stabat Iuxta Christi crucem*). Ambrose, *De obitu Valentiani consolatio*, *PL* xvi, 1371.
57 See Hirn, pp. 274–9, Réau, p. 499. Cf. the beautiful crucifixion by Siferwas in the Sherborne Missal (M. Rickert, *Painting in Britain: the Middle Ages* (London, 1954), pl. 161); Evans, pl. 31 (Grandisson triptych), pl. 49 (Norwich Retable).
58 On Mary Magdalene, see F. Antal, 'The Maenad under the Cross', *JWCI* i (1937–8), 79–3. Her tears are of course a prominent theme in literature (cf. for instance the long late medieval poem 'The Lamentacyon of Mary Magdaleyne' (*Index* 2759), Verstegan's *Odes* (1601), and Crashaw).
59 *PL* clix, 271–90, clxxxii, 1133–42; see Woolf pp. 247 ff.
60 *Index* 4089; Lambeth Palace MS. 560, f. 118r.
61 *Index* 3211; *CB XIII*, No. 49. There is a recording of the music on Argo (Z)RG(5)433, 'Medieval English Lyrics', with notes by E. J. Dobson and Frank Ll. Harrison.
62 *CB XIV* No. 60.
63 On the Pietà, see Woolf, pp. 255, 392–4, Réau, pp. 103–8, Mâle, *Fin* 126–32, *LM* s.v. 'Beweinung Christi', W. Pinder, 'Die dichterische Wurzel der Pietà', *Repertorium für Kunstwissenschaft* xlii (1920) 145 ff. Some fifteenth-century poems of this sort refer to statues or images (see Woolf 257–8). On the *Planctus Mariae* see Woolf, 255 ff., Hirn, pp. 277 ff., H. Thien, *Über die englischen Marieklagen* (Kiel, 1906), G. C. Taylor, 'The English Planctus Mariae', *MP* iv (1907) 605–37, F. J. Tanquerey, *Plaintes de la Vierge en Anglo-français* (Paris, 1921), E. Wechssler, *Die romanischen Marienklagen* (Halle, 1893).
64 Skelton's *Phyllyp Sparowe* at one point (ll. 53–7) seems to have some fun at the expense of their style; Molanus, in his *De Picturis et Imaginibus* (1570 ed., ch. lxxvi, p. 140), says that some, following Bridget's revelations, show the Virgin swooning, but that most disapprove, because of the text in St John's gospel.
65 Woolf, p. 272.
66 *CB XV* No. 9.
67 *CB XV* No. 7. In devotional literature Mary sometimes at this grim moment remembers her son as a baby (the equivalent in the visual arts is the portrayal of the sorrowing woman, with her dead child, as a youthful mother (cf. Hirn, pp. 281–2); the most celebrated example is Michelangelo's Pietà in St Peter's).
68 *CB XV* No. 6.
69 *CB XIII*. No. 1. The quatrain is still found in the early sixteenth-century printed version, e.g. in the Treveris ed. (f. E iiii^v):

> Mervayle ye not though I be pale and broune. For I am dyscolored by heet of the sonne. Therefore an englysshe man moved with pyte made this:

Notes to pp. 139–40

> Now gooth the sonne under the woode
> Me reweth Mary thy fayre roode.
> Now gooth the sonne under the tre
> Me reweth Mary thy sone and the.

70 Dreves, iii, No. 42 (on Dionysius the Areopagite).
71 *Index* 158.3; Robbins, *Anglia* lxxxii, 5.
72 *Index* 1089; MS. Adv. 18.7.21, f. 119r. Cf. the similar complaint of the Christ-Knight on f. 122r:

> Behold thu man her myth thu se
> The armes that I bar for the;
> On my passioun be thi mynde
> That thin enemiye the idel ne fynde.

73 Cf. also an interesting story in MS. Additional 37049 (f. 45v):

It is sayd of Saynt Petyr of the Ordyr of Prechours that when he was emange gret persecucion and tribulacion, opon a nyght before a crucifyx he made gret lamentacyon, and ane other stode in a hyrne and herd his lamentacion, and Petyr sayd thus:

> Jesu Criste, Gods sone,
> That on the rode wald be done,
> What wo and wretchydnes hafe I wroght
> That in swylk perels I am broght?
> I frayst to fle all maner of syn,
> And yitt my angwys wil not blynne.

Than sayd the ymage thus to Petyr:

> Petyr, why wald I be slayne,
> That never deservyd to suffer payne?
> Was I owder prowde or covetowse,
> Envyos, slawe or lycherowse?
> This sorrow I suffered and wykkyd woo
> Thi saule to safe and other moo;
> Swylk payne sen I profed for thi prowe,
> For thi selfe sumwhat sal thowe.

And after this myrakil, Petyr toke swylk hardynes that he was al day afftyrward for Criste redy for to dye.

74 *CB XIV* No. 2A.
75 *CB XIV* No. 4.
76 *CB XIV* No. 46.
77 *CB XIV* No. 76.
78 *CB XIV* No. 47.
79 *Index* 494; MS. Adv. 18.7.21, f. 124v. On the theme '*homo, vide quid pro te patior*', see Woolf, pp. 37 ff.

Notes to pp. 141–4

80 *CB XIV* No. 74. See Woolf, pp. 42 ff. The *Lamentations* verse is later adapted by Herrick, 'His Saviours words, going to the Crosse'.
81 *CB XIV* No. 15. Cf. *CB XIV* No. 72, Woolf, pp. 40–2.
82 *CB XIV* No. 126.
83 *Index* 497; *CB XV* No. 103. See John Stevens, *Music and Poetry in the Early Tudor Court* (London, 1961), pp. 369–71.
84 See Panofsky 'Imago Pietatis', *Festschrift für Max J. Friedländer* (Leipzig, 1927), Woolf, pp. 184–7, 389–91, G. von der Osten, *Der Schmerzenmann* (Forschungen zur deutschen Kunstgeschichte, vii (1935)), C. Bertelli, 'The *Image of Pity* in Santa Croce in Gerusalemme', *Essays in the History of Art presented to Rudolf Wittkower* (London, 1967). It seems to have been immensely popular in England (Campbell Dodgson, 'English Devotional Woodcuts of the late Fifteenth Century', Walpole Soc. xvii (1928–9), says that it is the commonest of all subjects among English woodcuts of this period). Cf. also the 'Christ of St. Gregory' (Mâle, *Fin* figs. 49–51, pp. 102–3; J. A. Endres, *Zeitschrift f. Christliche Kunst* xxx (1917), 145–56), the vision of the *imago pietatis* which the saint is held to have seen as he celebrated Mass. The *imago pietatis* is sometimes found surrounded by tools; this is not a reference to Piers Plowman, as was once supposed, but a warning against reopening the wounds of Christ by working on Sunday (see Evans, Appendix, Caiger-Smith, pp. 55–59, R. Wildhaber, 'Der Feiertagschristus als ikonographischer Ausdruck der Sonntagsheiligung', *Z. f. Schweizerische Archäologie u. Kunstgeschichte* xvi (1956).
85 *CB XV* No. 109; see Woolf, pp. 196–7.
86 *Index* 1463; ed. Furnivall, EETS xv, pp. 180–9. See Woolf, pp. 187–91. The phrase *quia amore langueo* is from *Cant.* ii, 5, v, 8.
87 See G. van der Osten, *RDK* s.v. 'Christus im Elend', 'Job and Christ' *JWCI* xvi (1953) 153–8 (he argues that it originates in Germany in the late fourteenth century, and that its typological origin is in the common 'figure' of Christ, Job sitting *in sterquilinio*; cf. Réau, 469. There is a good example in the cathedral of Rouen; see also Mâle, *Fin*, figs. 44, 48.
88 Cf. the poem in MS. Additional 37049 (*Index* 269; pr. Ross, *Speculum* xxxii, 278–9, Bowers, *Univ. Florida Monographs: Humanities* xii, 32) in which Christ's bloody body hanging on the cross (to draw back man's sinful soul) is compared to the 'rede flesche' that the falconer uses as bait to attract his hawk.
89 On this image see Woolf, 189–90, A. Cabassut, 'Une Dévotion médiévale peu connue, la dévotion a Jésus notre mère', *Revue d'Ascétique et de mystique* xxv (1949), 234–5, 'God is our Mother', *The Life of the Spirit* ii, No. 15, (1945), 49–53. It is used most remarkably by Julian of Norwich (see Warrack ed., p. 150); cf. also the Monk of Farne, ed. Farmer, p. 64.

Chapter 8   Resurrection and Assumption

1 The note of triumph is of course dominant in the Easter liturgy (even more so, possibly, in the Eastern Church, where the words θανάτῳ θάνατον πατήσας, 'by his death he has trodden down death' are part of a troparion which is repeated many times on Easter day). Cf. also Hamman, No. 93 (a prayer from a papyrus).
2 *CB XIV* No. 37. For the full text of the *Aurora lucis rutilat* (*c*. sixth century), see *OBMLV* No. 38.
3 *Index* 1289; Coxe, *Cat. Merton MSS.*, p. 97.
4 MacCracken, EETS (ES) cvii, p. 250.
5 *CB XV* No. 111.
6 *Devotional Pieces in Verse and Prose*, ed. J. A. W. Bennett, STS, 3rd series, xxiii, p. 275.
7 Ed. W. Mackay MacKenzie, pp. 159–60.
8 On the Assumption and Coronation of the Virgin in the visual arts, see Réau, pp. 615–26, *LM* s.v. 'Aufnahme', Mâle XIII, pp. 248 ff., etc. Brief summaries of the doctrine and its development can be found in, e.g., *Dictionnaire de Théologie catholique*, s.v. 'Assomption de la sainte vierge', *New Catholic Encyclopaedia*, s.v. 'Assumption'.
9 *CB XIII* No. 3, ll. 25–30.
10 *CB XIV* No. 132.
11 *CB XV* No. 37.
12 E.g. *Index* Nos. 897, 1804, 1807.
13 Cf. *CB XV* Nos. 27–9, etc. This had powerful associations in the late Middle Ages (cf. H. Thurston, *The Month* cxxi (1913), 384–8), for it was associated by tradition (in the *Legenda Aurea*) with St Gregory and the ceasing of the great plague in Rome in 590. Gregory caused the picture of the Virgin painted by St Luke to be carried in procession, and when it came to the Ælian bridge, a troop of angels hovered over the picture, and were heard singing the words *Regina caeli laetare*.
14 Ed. Mackenzie, pp. 160–2.

Chapter 9   The Christian Life

1 *Index* 2342; *EEL* p. 177. Cf. Julian of Norwich's 'all manner of thing shall be well'.
2 *Index* 3359; ed. Patterson, *Loomis Studies*, 487–8.
3 See the studies by Rossell Hope Robbins, 'Popular Prayers in ME Verse', *MP* xxxvi (1939), 337–50; 'Private Prayers in ME Verse' *SP* xxxvi (1939), 466–75; Wilmart, *Auteurs spirituels*, ch. i.
4 And sometimes lapse into prose: cf. *Index* 1679 (Magdalene College, Cambridge, MS. 13, f. 28v):

Jesu Cryste I beseche the for the clennes of thyn Incarnacion,
And for the merites of thy woundes and of thy passion,
And of thi bittur dethe, and of thy glorios resureccion,
Strength me and defende me mercifully in all temptacion,
And bringe us to the blysse, where we maye have joye of thy glorious ascencion,
and graunt us of thi grace that to thonour and worship of thy holy name, and to the laude and praysing of thy blessid moder and virgen oure lady Seynt Mary, and to the profyte of oure moder holy cherche, we may do owre duty and homage ech with other and for other, Suete Jesus. Amen.

5 Cf. the *Cloud of Unknowing* (ch. 37), which says of mystical prayer, that if it is in words, which is seldom, then the fewer the better: 'ye, and yif it be bot a lityl worde of a silable, me think it betir then of to, and more accordyng to the werk of the spiryte....' – when a man or a woman is suddenly afraid, they call for help, not in many words, but with a single syllable, 'fire!' or 'out!'.
6 *Index* 1600; EETS cxxix, p. 12.
7 *Index* 1666; Lambeth Palace Library, MS. 541, f. lv.
8 Index 2988; ed. Zupitza, *Eng. Studien* xi, 41. Methley's *Epistle* is printed in E. M. Nugent, *The Thought and Culture of the English Renaissance* (Cambridge, 1956), pp. 388–93.
9 See *Index* 2099. These short prayers are often incorporated into longer ones; this couplet occurs in the third stanza of *CB XIV* No. 122.
10 See Gray, *NQ* ccxii (1967), 131–2.
11 *Index* 939; (cf. *Index* 942, 2796.5).
12 They sometimes form part of epitaphs: cf. William Goldwyre, d. 1514, Coggeshall, Essex (Ravenshaw, *Antiente Epitaphes*, p. 19):

> Mary Moder, mayden clere,
> Pray for me, William Goldwyre
> And for me Isabel his wyf;
> Ladye for thy joyes fyf,
> Hav mercy on Christian his second wyf
> Swete Jesu for thy wowndys fyf.

or, at Fairford (Murray's *Gloucestershire Guide*, p. 45):

> Jesus Lord that made us
> And with thy blood us bought
> Forgive us our trespasses.

Similar Latin prayers also occur as *tituli*: cf. *Norfolk Archaeology* xvi, 197 (St Peter Mancroft, Norwich), Pritchard, *Medieval Graffiti*, p. 129 (Cowlinge, Suffolk). J. C. Hirsh, *NQ* ccxv (1970), 44–5, prints an example of a short prayer of this type which is

accompanied in the MS. (Douce 54) by a short commentary (the thirty-three words represent the years of Christ's life; there is a pardon of 5,475 years in memorial of all Christ's wounds; five parts of the prayer are associated with five coloured beads of a rosary), suggesting a method of using it in private meditation.
13 *Index* 954; *Customary of St. Augustine's* (Henry Bradshaw Soc., 1902) p. 69.
14 *Index* 620; MS. Harley 2339, f. 122v.
15 Ed. Talbot, pp. 36–7.
16 *Index* 3844; *CB XV* No. 127. Very similar are the prayers to guardian angels; cf. *Index* Nos. 1051, 1341, 1560 (= *CB XV*, Nos. 133, 132, 134), 2174, 2385, Wilmart, *Auteurs spirituels*, pp. 537–58. There is a nice passage in which the Monk of Farne (ed. Farmer, pp. 127–37) thanks his guardian angel for looking after him – when he was eight, he remembers, he would have been crushed by a wall if he had not been caught up and carried fifteen feet away, and on another occasion he nearly fell from a plank crossing the Cherwell; if it had not been for his angel, he would often have fallen in a pond, down a well, or cut himself when he was cutting wood. A good example of a private prayer used as a pious charm is this, from Scot's *Discoverie of Witchcraft* (1584), p. 260 (N.B. the sign of the cross is used as a protecting *lorica*):

> In nomine patris, up and doune,
> Et filii et spiritus sancti, upon my crowne,
> Crux Christi upon my brest,
> Sweete Ladie, send me eternall rest.

Pious charms, like prayers, often use the device of recalling previous acts of grace, so that a charm to stop bleeding may well refer to the wounds of Christ, or to the shedding of the Precious Blood.
17 *Archiv* lxxxix, 283, 318–19.
18 *Eng. Studien*, xi, 249. Cf. Southern, *Anselm*, p. 36 and n.; the cult in the West was encouraged by the translation of St Nicholas to Bari in 1087 (Anselm has a prayer to him).
19 *Index* 1786.5; f. 107v. See the account of the book by M. R. James in *A Descriptive Catalogue of the Second Series of Fifty MSS. in the Collection of Henry Yates Thompson* (Cambridge, 1902), p. 225.
20 *Index* 1900; *EEC* No. 313. Cf. also *Index* 588 (an acrostic), 860.5 (a charm against despair; *EETS* xxxiii, p. 404), 508 (in a grace). St Catherine appears in charms in later tradition (she is especially associated with spinsters). Aubrey, *Remains* (ed. Britten, pp. 28–9) records an amusing story from his 'old cosen Ambrose Brown', concerning old Symon Brunsdon of Winterborne Basset in Wiltshire: 'When the Gad-flye had happened to sting his Oxen, or Cowes, and made them to run away in that Champagne-countrey,

he would run after them, crying out, Praying, Good St. Katharine of Winterborne stay my Oxen, &c.' (Aubrey also says that shepherds prayed to St Oswald to keep their sheep safe.)

21 *Index* 4229.5 (*SEC* No. 62), 2902.
22 *Index* 2903 (Robbins, *Sec. Lyr.* p. 61); cf. also *NQ* 6 ser. I, 54, Kittredge, *Witchcraft in Old and New England* (Cambridge, Mass., 1929), p. 220 (further examples).
23 *Index* 3903.3; see Bennett, *NQ* clxxvi, 387. On St Christopher in wall painting, see Tristram, *Fourteenth Century*, pp. 25-6 (he says that unlike the knightly St George, Christopher was especially associated with common people), Caiger Smith, *passim*, H. C. Whaite, *St. Christopher in Mediaeval English Wall Painting* (London, 1929), J. Salmon, 'St. Christopher', *J. Arch. Ass.* N.S. xli (1936), 76-115, Brindley, *Antiquaries Journal* iv (1924), 227-41 (a number of the paintings have traces of inscriptions). The huge size of St Christopher is traditional – one painting at Erfurt measures some twenty by thirty-five feet (cf. E. K. Stahl, *Die Legende vom heiligen Riesen Christophorus* (Munich, 1920)) – Stow records an allusion to it in a couplet by a 'merry poet' on the sumptuousness of the tomb of Sir Christopher Hatton (d. 1591) in St Paul's (compared with the resting places of Sidney and Sir Francis Walsingham):

> Philip and Francis have no tombe,
> For great Christopher takes all the roome.

On Christopher medals, see Evans, *Magical Jewels*, pp. 138-9. The protection that the saint's image was thought to give against a 'bad death' is made explicit in an inscription in Wood Eaton church (Oxfordshire): Ki cest image verra le jur de male mort ne murra. Erasmus, in the colloquy 'The Shipwreck', has much fun at the expense of popular 'devotion' to Christopher (and to other saints as well!). See also Browne, *Pseudodoxia Epidemica* V, ch. 16.

24 Ed. T. F. Simmons, EETS lxxi.
25 See *Minor Poems Vernon MS*, EETS xcviii, pp. 168 ff. Cf. *ME Sermons*, ed. W. O. Ross, EETS ccix, pp. 61 ff., 125 ff. There is a similar story told of St Wulfstan (see Brieger, p. 153) – the saint stands before the altar and holds up, not the Host, but a naked Christ child. Cf. L. MacGarry, *The Holy Eucharist in ME Homiletic and Devotional Verse* (Washington, 1936).
26 EETS clxxxiv, p. 67 (cf. EETS lxxi, pp. 131, 367-8, etc.). On the sacramental value of the sight of the Host, see H. Thurston, 'Seeing the Host', *The Tablet* (1907) 684-7.
27 *Displaying of the Popishe Masse* (cf. *Prayers and Other Pieces of Thomas Becon*, Parker Soc. 1844, p. 270).
28 See Robbins, 'Levation Prayers in ME Verse', *MP* xl (1942), 131-46; for similar Latin verses, cf. Dreves xv, Nos 40 et seq.

29 EETS lxxi, pp. 40–1 (cf. *Index* 3882–4).
30 *Index* 1729; Robbins, *MP* xl, 137–8.
31 Allen, *English Writings*, pp. 70, 15, 104.
32 *Index* 834. Cf. Grimestone's book, MS. Adv. 18.7.21, f. 125v (*Index* 7):

> A Jesu so fair an fre
> Suettest of all thinge,
> Thu ful art of pite,
> Of hevene and herde kingge.
> The love that is in the
> No man may rede ne singge
> Blithe may that herte be
> That hat of the meningge.

Crashaw's motto to *Steps to the Temple* sounds like a more polished version of the same type of prayer:

> Live Jesus, live, and let it bee
> My life, to dye for love of thee.

33 *Index* 1727 (cf. 1752): *CB XV* No. 64. See D. Harford, *Norfolk and Norwich Arch. Soc.* xvii, 221–4.
34 *Processional of the Nuns of Chester*, ed. J. Wickham Legg, Henry Bradshaw Soc. xviii (1899), pp. 26–7.
35 *Index* 4181; *CB XV* No. 119. It is echoed in a seventeenth century inscription; see Gray 'An Inscription at Hexham', *Archaeologia Aeliana* 4th s. xl, (1962), 185–8.
36 *EEC* No. 319.
37 Child, No. 1.
38 *Index* 2503; ed. MacCracken, *Archiv*, 41–3.
39 *Index* 2018; ed. Halliwell, *Early English Miscellany* (Warton Club), pp. 1–6.
40 *EEC* No. 323, *SEC* No. 68.
41 W. Sparrow-Simpson, *J. Arch. Ass.* xlviii, 46. The charm was quoted in a slightly different version in the Lancaster witch trial of 1612 (see Robbins, *Encyclopedia of Witchcraft and Demonology* (New York, 1959), p. 86; Potts, *The Wonderfull Discoverie of Witches in the Countie of Lancaster* (1613), ff. K1^v.–K2^r. Greene, *SEC* p. 232, mentions a seventeenth-century Norwegian folk-charm in which Christ 'walked to the church with a book in his hand' (see Robbins, *Encyclopedia*, pp. 363–4), and draws attention to the phrase 'While Christ was priest and I was clerk' in a version of *The Famous Flower of Serving-men* (Child, No. 106).
42 All the texts are printed in *EEC* No. 322, *SEC* No. 67.
43 See, for example, *JFSS* iv (1910–13), 53–66, E. C. Batho. 'The Life of Christ in the Ballads', *Essays and Studies*, ix (1924), 93–5; other references are given by Greene (see below).

44 R. L. Greene, 'The Meaning of the Corpus Christi Carol', *MÆ* xxix (1960), 10–21, and *MÆ* xxxiii, 53–60.
45 Cf., for example, the dove which takes Alberic to the other world (H. R. Patch, *The Other World*, p. 110).
46 Ed. A. Ewert (Oxford, 1947).
47 L. MacGarry, *The Holy Eucharist*, pp. 235 ff.
48 See D. Rock, *The Church of Our Fathers* (London, 1899), I, pp. 243 ff.; A. A. Barb, 'Mensa Sacra, the Round Table and the Holy Grail', *JWCI* xix (1956), 40–56. Cf. also H. Adolf, *PMLA* lxi, 307.
49 See *RDK* s.v. 'Christussymbolik', p. 731, Coomaraswamy, *Speculum* xiv (1939), 66 ff.
50 There is a vast literature on Wolfram's grail and on the mysterious name *lapsit exillis*. See M. F. Richey, *Studies of Wolfram von Eschenbach* (Edinburgh, London, 1957), ch. viii, and the references given by Barb. A forthcoming study by Mr A. D. Horgan in *Medieval Studies* will explore this further.
51 *Index* 3339; MS. Laud Misc. 213, f. 2v. Cf. the similar verses in MS. Laud Misc. 77: f. 46v 'In wedlocke/That knotte that is knytte scholde not be broken/Trw love in hertes togyder scholde be lokene'; f. 77v: 'Corrupciun of synne/That we han fallun inne/we schul now forsake/The sacrament of penaunce/Schal be owre delyveraunce/and so amendus make', etc. William Worcestre, the antiquary, records a similar couplet (Itineraries, ed. Harvey, p. 250): 'Wyrk wysely and sey but few/and ovyr thyn hede loke thou not hew.'
52 *Index* 4286; MS. Adv. 18.7.21, f. 40v.
53 See *CB XIV* Nos. 95–120.
54 *Index* 3408; *CB XIV* No. 42.
55 *Index* 230; Horstmann, *Yorkshire Writers*, II, pp. 70–1.
56 *Index* 1822; EETS xv, p. 222 (251). Cf. Brieger, p. 88, pl. 22a (De Brailes Psalter), or the example at the beginning of the *Carmina Burana* (cf. Hilka-Schumann ed., frontispiece).
57 *Index* 3504, 3437; *CB XV* No. 171. See Bühler, *MLN* lv, 567.
58 *Index* 3151; *CB XV* No. 191.
59 EETS xv, pp. 289–90; it is an example of the 'miseries of courtiers' theme (cf. Aeneas Silvius Piccolomini, *De Miseriis Curialium*).
60 *Index* 1218; H. A. Person, *Cambridge ME Lyrics* (Seattle, 1953), No. 60. The second couplet appears at the end of 'Take Tyme in Tyme' in the Maitland Folio MS. (Craigie, STS n.s. vii, 344) and elsewhere (cf. *Index* 512.8, 513, 3256.6, 4137; *Archiv* clix). Cf. Barclay's *Ship of Fools*, ed. Jamieson, I, p. 188; Tilley, *Proverbs*: C413 'hasty climbers have sudden falls', C414 'the highest climbers have the greatest falls', H 466 'praise a hill but keep on the plain'.
61 *Collected Poems of Sir Thomas Wyatt*, ed. K. Muir and P. Thomson (Liverpool, 1969), No. clxxvi, ll. 1–10.

62 *Archiv* cvii, 50.
63 *Index* 2008; EETS xv, p. 228 (257). This type of poem (often based on ps.–Cyprian, *de xii abusivis* (S. Hellmann, *Texte und Untersuchungen* xxxiv (1910), 32–60) is common. See e.g. Robbins, *Historical Poems of the Fourteenth and Fifteenth Centuries* (New York, 1959), Nos 54 et seq., and notes. An interesting example of a slightly different type occurs in a *graffito* at Ridgewell, Essex (Pritchard, *English Medieval Graffiti*, p. 75, fig. 103):

> A yong rewler wytles
> A pore man spendar haveles
> A ryche man thif nedeles
> A old man leche(r luve)les
> A woman rebolde sameles.

64 One example which has been missed is *Index* 2531, which reads, I think:

> q^d ye devill to ye frier
>
> O my good brother
> You ar no nother
> at you I have no spitt.
> Stonde still and praye
> All night and day
> Even like an yppecrite.

65 *CB XV* No. 179.
66 EETS (ES), lxxi, pp. 371 ff.; cf. M. D. Anderson, *Drama and Imagery*, pp. 173–7.
67 Cf. Pantin, *English Church in the XIV Century*, pp. 156, 189 ff. D. W. Robertson, 'The Cultural Tradition of Handlyng Synne', *Speculum* xxii (1947), 162–85.
68 *Index* 1965; Robbins, *MP* xxxvi, 346.
69 *CB XIV* No. 5.
70 *Index* 837; Ross, EETS ccix, p. 168.
71 Damned souls: cf., for example, *Index* Nos 994, 1218.15, 3901. Heart and Eye: *Index* 3699; cf. *MLN* xxx, 197–8, xxxvi, 161–5, Pfander, p. 51n. Deadly Sins; *Index* 4150; EETS clxxxii, pp. 58–71. Penitent usurer: *Index* 3600; PMLA xxxiii, 417. Udo: *CB XIII* No. 14 and notes (cf. also *Index* 3818.5, in the *Gesta Romanorum*; see J. A. Herbert, *Catalogue of Romances in the Dept. of MSS., British Museum*, III, p. 258).
72 *CB XIV* No. 113. A seventeenth-century ballad (Bodleian Library, Wood 401, f. 179v–180r) makes a similar penitential use of an earthquake at Hereford in 1661.

73 *CB XIV* No. 121. Cf. *Index* 3714, 773, 893.
74 *Index* 1454; EETS ci, p. 80, xxiv, pp. 91–4, A. G. Rigg, *A Glastonbury Miscellany of the Fifteenth Century* (Oxford, 1968), pp. 51–2.
75 *CB XIV* No. 10.
76 *CB XIII* No. 5.
77 See *Facsimile of B.M. MS. Harley 2253*, with introduction by N. R. Ker, EETS cclv, ff. 76v–77v.
78 *CB XIII* No. 51; on Maximian, see F. J. E. Raby, *A History of Secular Latin Poetry in the Middle Ages*, I (Oxford, 1934), pp. 124–5 (his elegies are printed in E. Baehrens, *Poetae Latini Minores* (Leipzig, 1910–), v).
79 *CB XV* No. 147; Honorius 'of Autun' in his *Gemma Ecclesiae* (PL clxxii, 633) compares the Ages of man's life to the canonical hours of the day.
80 *Index* 2282 (cf. *Index* 1259, 1587, 3858, 4277); cf. York, *MLN* lxxii, 484–5, Bowers, *Shakespeare Qly* iii, 109–12. Cf. also Browne, *Pseudodoxia* iv, xii, *Gentleman's Magazine*, May 1853, 494–502, *The Archaeologia* xxxv, 167 ff., *As You Like It*, Variorum ed. Furness, pp. 272 ff., Owst, *Literature and Pulpit*, pp. 534–5. The Seven Ages of Man form part of the paintings in Longthorpe Tower (cf. Caiger-Smith p. 162). For an example in which the ages are linked with the wheel of life, see Brieger, pl. 88b (cf. also Kozáky, *Anfänge der Darstellungen des Vergänglichkeitsproblems*, pp. 75 ff.; *Die Todesdidaktik der Vortotentanzzeit* Bibliotheca Humanitatis Historica, v, Budapest, 1944), pp. 165 ff. In St Swithin's Church, Swanbourne (Buckinghamshire), there are fragments of what must have been an interesting panoramic view of man's life, with the devil and death claiming the body, and scenes of souls in blessedness, purgatory and hell (see *Records of Buckinghamshire* iii (1870), 136 ff.). Near to it there was once a Judgment, a figure of a saint, and three evil spirits (with names, e.g. *timor mortis*). There was a Latin legend above and an inscription beneath all in English, seven to eight lines deep, which even in 1870 was too mutilated to read. Only '... Man lyvyth to dye', '... in wynde a dream at his fate' could be deciphered.

Chapter 10   Death and the Last Things

1 The ancient image of the 'iter ad mortem' is charmingly brought up to date in a couple of nineteenth-century railway epitaphs:

> ... my steam is now condens'd in death,
> Life's railway's o'er, each Stations past,
> In death I'm stopp'd and rest at last ...

The Line to heaven by Christ was made,
With heavenly truth the Rails were laid. . . .

(see Burgess, *English Churchyard Memorials*, pp. 237, 252).
2 Horace, *Carm.* I, iv, 13. Cf. *NQ* ccvi, 135; other examples can be found in the general books on the tradition of death-literature by Kozáky, Weber, etc.
3 Dreves, li, No. 259.
4 *OBMLV* No. 284.
5 Cf. 'What is man . . . but a stynkynge slyme, and after that a sake ful of donge, and at the laste mete to wormes', etc. (Owst, *Preaching*, p. 341.)
6 Cf. *Pardoner's Tale*, 347, Owst, *Lit. and Pulpit*, p. 532.
7 *CB XIV*, No. 27, ll. 57–60; cf. *Ayenbite of Inwit*, EETS xxiii, p. 264. So in the visual arts devils are sometimes depicted trying to catch the soul with hooks.
8 *CB XIV* No. 23 (from a French original).
9 *CB XIV* No. 100.
10 *CB XV* No. 156.
11 From 'Grace'.
12 Pritchard, *Graffiti*, p. 44 (cf. Coulton, *Proc. Camb. Ant. Soc.* xix, p. 58, pl. ix).
13 *Poems*, ed. Mackay Mackenzie, p. 99.
14 *CB XIV* No. 101.
15 *Index* 491; *Archiv* clxvii, 24 (for the legend in M.E. verse cf. *Index* 39, 41, 1794, 3918, 1585.5 (cf. 348, 3176)). Among recent books on the story, see D. M. Lang, *The Balavariani* (London, 1966), *The Wisdom of Balahvar* (London, 1957), *The Georgians* (London, 1966), pp. 159–65; it reproduces 'quite closely the ancient Buddhist doctrines of the impermanence of the world, the impurity of the human body, the worthlessness of human existence, the conquest of sin, and the life of the hereafter.' In the Georgian version a man is pursued by an elephant to a chasm and climbs up a tree. The two mice gnaw it, and beneath him he can see a dragon, etc. The unicorn takes the elephant's place in St John Damascene (*Barlaam and Josaphat*, ed. G. R. Woodward and H. Mattingley (Loeb, 1914), pp. 186–91), the *Gesta Romanorum* (ed. H. Oesterley, Berlin, 1872, p. 168), etc. On the scene in the visual arts, cf. S. Der Nersessian, *L'Illustration du Roman de Barlaam et Joasaph* (Paris, 1937), I, pp. 63–8, L. Pillion 'Un Tombeau français du 13e siècle et l'apologue de Barlaam sur la vie humaine', *Rev. de l'Art ancien et moderne*, xxxviii (1910), II, 321 ff., Saxl, *JWCI* v, 98.
16 See E. Panofsky, *Tomb Sculpture* (ed. H. W. Janson, London, 1964), pp. 63 ff. Another late example is the tomb of Robert Cecil, Earl of Salisbury (d. 1612) at Hatfield. E. H. Kantorowicz, *The King's Two*

Bodies (Princeton, 1957), pp. 431–7, suggests that the idea that the individual is subject to death and decay is contrasted with the idea that his 'dignity' as nobleman, prince of the church, etc. has a permanence not connected with the immortality of his soul but with his social or institutional status. This is not found in the treatment of this type of image in devotional literature.

17 English ed. (London, 1924), p. 124. Much material on *contemptus mundi* is collected together in D. R. Howard, *The Three Temptations* (Princeton, 1966). See the very thoughtful and cogent remarks of T. P. Dunning in *MÆ* xxxv, 134–6. Innocent, the author of the notorious treatise on the contempt of the world in fact promised a further treatise on the dignity of human nature (cf. also G. di Napoli, '"Contemptus Mundi" e "Dignitas Hominis" nel Renascimento', *Rivista di filosofia neoscolastica* xlviii (1956), 9–41).

18 G. Negri, *Julian the Apostate* (tr. the Duchess Litta-Visconti-Arese, London, 1905, I, 287); *Julian*, Loeb ed. (W. C. Wright), pp. 414–15. The Emperor is thinking primarily of the widespread and popular cult of martyrs.

19 Cf. Hamman, *Early Christian Prayers*, No. 131 (note the gentle tone of the dead man's speech). Early Christian art seems to regard death primarily as a deliverance (*vivas in domino, in pace* are frequent inscriptions; cf. R. Morey, *Early Christian Art*, p. 62). This is by no means unknown in later periods: cf. the fine figure of Conrad von Busang (d. 1464) by Nicholaus Gerhaert von Leyden in Strasbourg (Panofsky, *Tomb Sculpture*, pl. 231), in which the dead canon is shown side by side with the Madonna and Christ, and the Christ child reaches out to touch his praying hands.

20 There are many references in Elizabethan drama – in *Love's Labour's Lost* (V, 2), the countenance of Holofernes is compared to a death's head in a ring (for illustrations, see F. P. Weber, *Aspects of Death* (London, 1922) pp. 749 ff.). Cf. also, *inter alia*, Herrick's poem *His Winding Sheet*. Later funerary images are discussed in Burgess, *English Churchyard Memorials*, pp. 168–72.

21 Among recent books are P. Ziegler, *The Black Death* (London, 1969), G. Deaux, *The Black Death, 1347* (London, 1969), J. C. Russell, *British Medieval Population* (Albuquerque, 1958), and an especially interesting study by an author with medical expertise, J. F. D. Shrewsbury, *A History of Bubonic Plague in the British Isles* (Cambridge, 1970) (the bacterium *Pasteurella pestis*, an internal parasite of rodents, especially the rat, was carried by the flea, *Xenopsylla cheopis*, of the house-rat (*R. rattus*); Professor Shrewsbury thinks that bubonic plague probably alternated with typhus fever, which was also spread by *X. cheopis* and the body louse).

22 Knighton, *Chronicon* II, 61 ff., quoted by E. Rickert, *Chaucer's*

World (London, 1948), p. 355-6. There is a moving record of it in a Latin graffito at Ashwell, Hertfordshire (Pritchard, *English Medieval Graffiti*, pp. 181-2): 'wretched, fierce, violent; the dregs of the people survive as witness.'

23 See Mâle, *Fin*, pp. 200 ff., V. Sussmann, *Maria mit dem Schutzmantel* (Marburg, 1929), P. Perdrizet, *La Vierge de Miséricorde* (Paris, 1908).

24 See P. Heitz and W. L. Screiber, *Pestblätter* (Strasbourg, 1900).

25 Cf. the Mass *pro plaga pestilentiae cessenda in populo*, *The York Missal* (Surtees Soc., lx) ii, p. 233, F. E. Warren, *The Sarum Missal in English* (London, 1911), ii, pp. 122, 202, 208, 213, etc.

26 Cf. R. H. Bowers, *Southern Folklore Qly*. xx (1956) 118-29. The M.E. verse prayers (cf. *Index* Nos. 2444, 2459, 3477.6) mostly echo the anthem *Stella celi extirpavit* (Dreves xxxi, No. 207).

27 Cf., e.g. Egill Skallagrímsson's *Sonatorrek* or Jorge Manrique's *Coplas por la Muerte de su Padre* (see the study by P. N. Dunn *MÆ* xxxiii (1964), 169-83).

28 ll. 92 ff.

29 On *ubi sunt* passages in O.E., see J. E. Cross, Vetenskaps-Societeten i Lund, *Årsbok* (1956), 25 ff.

30 Ed. Longnon-Foulet, ll, 329 ff.

31 Cf. E. Gilson, 'De la Bible à François Villon', *Les Idées et les Lettres* (Paris, 1932) (see Wisd. 5:8-15; Isa. 33:18; 2 Kgs. 19:13, Baruch 3:16 ff.; I Cor. 1:19-20). The rhetorical formula does occur in classical literature but not usually in mortality contexts. C. H. Becker, 'Ubi sunt qui ante nos in mundo fuere', *Islamstudien* I, 501 ff., suggests that the *ubi sunt* may come from Greek rhetoric (he draws attention to some lines of the second century B.C. quoted by Plutarch (cf. A. Nauck, *Tragicorum Graecorum Fragmenta*, p. 909, No. 372)).

32 *Opera*, Corpus Christianum, Series Latina, ciii, ed. G. Morin (1953), *Sermones* I, p. 135, quoted by Cross, *JEGP* lvi, 434.

33 Gilson, pp. 20-1. Cf. the interesting illustration of Alexander (Brieger, p. 150, pl. 50) in a Cambridge manuscript which is accompanied by a Latin poem describing how he sank to the depths of hell. A curious ascetic Latin *ubi sunt* inscription is mentioned by G. Holles, *Lincolnshire Church Notes*, ed. R. E. G. Cole, Lincoln Record Soc., i (1911), 123.

34 Amadas and Idoine are celebrated in a thirteenth-century French romance, and are often mentioned in M.E., e.g. *Sir Degrevant* U.1493 ff., *Emare* 122 (where they appear in a tapestry with Tristan and Iseult, and Floris and Blancheflur).

35 *CB XIII*, No. 48. See J. E. Cross, 'The Sayings of St. Bernard and the Ubi Sount Qui Ante Nos fuerount', *RES* (1958), 1-7.

36 *PL* clxxxiv, 491.

Notes to pp. 189–94

37 Ed. MacCracken, EETS, cxcii, pp. 783–4.
38 Ed. Sir Egerton Brydges (1810).
39 Cf. Sparrow, *Visible Words*, p. 112, on the inscription said to be on the tomb of Alexander: *brevi hac in urna conduntur cineres magni Alexandri*.
40 Cf. the 'shroud' brasses, e.g. at Appleton (Berkshire), Oddington (Oxfordshire). In the latter (cf. L. Stone, *Sculpture in Britain. The Middle Ages* (London, 1955), p. 215), snakes emerge from the entrails, eyes and mouth of the priest, Ralph Hamsterley, and his image is accompanied by the *titulus:* Vermibus hic donor . . . (cf. the brass of John Andrew (1428), St Lawrence, Reading). Abbot Wakeman's tomb at Tewkesbury has worms, lizards, frogs, mice and snails on it. Panofsky, *Tomb Sculpture* (figs. 257, 258) has a very grim Swiss example from La Sarraz (north of Lausanne): Francis de la Sarra (d. 1362) with long worms on his decayed body, toads on his face, and toads' heads in place of his eyes.
41 Dreves xv, No. 235.
42 *Index* 1563; Brunner, *Archiv*, clxvii, 30–5.
43 Sermon xcv, *Works* (London, 1839), iv, pp. 231 ff.; quoted, with similar examples by R. M. Frye, 'Swift's Yahoo and the Christian Symbols for Sin', *J. of the History of Ideas* xv (1954), 201 ff. The less ascetic traditions of melancholy (cf. R. Klibansky, E. Panofsky and F. Saxl, *Saturn and Melancholy* (London, 1964)) continued alongside this, and find expression later in graveyard themes which afforded 'a sort of delight . . . alternately mixed with sorrow in the contemplation of death'.
44 The phrase is used very dramatically at the death of Hotspur (*I Hen. IV*, v, 4; note, incidentally, how the old image of the grave as narrow house comes easily to the Prince's lips). The joking 'diet of worms' is recorded in the eighteenth century in Grose's *Classical Dictionary of the Vulgar Tongue*; the phrase 'made worm's meat of me' is used as late as 1677 by Otway in his translation of the *Cheats of Scapin* (*NED* worm, *sb.*, 6c).
45 And life – the poet Beddoes, author of *Death's Jest Book* and amateur of Elizabethan drama, left pinned to his breast when he committed suicide in 1849 a note beginning 'I am food for what I am good for – worms. . .' (H. W. Donner, *Thomas Lovell Beddoes* (Oxford, 1935), p. 380).
46 L. F. Peck, *A Life of Matthew G. Lewis* (Cambridge, Mass., 1961), discusses (p. 126) the background of the ballad (primarily Bürger's 'Lenore') and its subsequent fame (p. 32) – it was made into a ballet, a melodrama, etc.
47 See Peter and Iona Opie, *The Lore and Language of Schoolchildren*, (Oxford, 1959), p. 33, and the discussion in the *Times Literary Supplement* (1921), pp. 43, 60, 126. Another version, reported to

Notes to pp. 194–7

me by Mr C. G. Barker, involves a 'homiletic' exchange between a woman and a vicar – 'Will I be like that when I'm dead?' 'Yes, you'll be like that when you're dead.'

48 The *Prognostics* of Hippocrates. See the note by J. H. Walter in the Arden ed. of *Henry V* (London, 1954), II, 3, and the discussion by Woolf, pp. 78ff., 330–2.

49 *CB XIII*, No. 71.

50 *Index* 853.8, 4040.6. Cf. *CB XIII* No. 29A, l. 30 (one of many examples), Woolf, pp. 82 ff., 94, Owst, *Literature and Pulpit*, p. 43, etc. The ironic image of the grave as house survives in a curious epitaph, of Rebecca Rogers (1688) at Folkestone (Burgess, p. 227):

> From chimney-money too this cell is free:
> To such a House as this who would not tenant be.

51 Cf. *Index* Nos. 1220, 3998, 4031, 4033, 4035, 4036.5, 4045–7. A similar poem, 'Memorare novissima tua' (*CB XIII* No. 13), which was popular for a long time (and is found as a *titulus* e.g. at Stratford, Saffron Walden, Faversham) is sometimes attached to it. Cf. the O.E. homiletic examples quoted by G. V. Smithers, *MÆ* xxvi, 142–3. Is it possible that the *Proprietates* lie behind the lines on the coming of death to every man in *The Seafarer* (91 ff.)? At the other end of our period there is a very eloquent use of the theme in More's *Four Last Things* (*English Works*, ed. W. E. Campbell and A. W. Reed (1931), I, p. 468): 'Thou seest ... thyself ... lying in thy bed, thy head shooting, thy back aching, thy veins beating, thine heart panting, thy throat rattling, thy flesh trembling, thy mouth gaping, thy nose sharping, thy legs cooling, thy fingers fumbling, thy breath shortening, all thy strength fainting, thy life vanishing, and thy death drawing on.' Innocent also uses it in his *De Contemptu Mundi* (*PL* ccxvii, 706).

52 Cf. Jeremy Taylor, *Holy Dying*, ch. 1, section 1.

53 *Ulysses* (Bodley Head ed., 1960), p. 149.

54 *The Big Sleep*, ch. 2. The theme does appear in the New World in a more traditional context (whether from authority or experience): cf. Oscar Lewis, *Life in a Mexican Village: Tepoztlán Restudied* (Urbana, 1963), p. 415 – when a person is about to die 'his eyes go up and become whitish, his nose sharpens, his hands get cold and still, and his body becomes loose'.

55 *CB XIII* No. 30.

56 *Index* 3939; *CB XIII* No. 73. The various versions are edited by H. M. R. Murray, EETS cxli..

57 Cf. R. B. Wheler, *History and Antiquities of Stratford-upon-Avon* (Stratford, n.d.), pp. 98–9, Thomas Fisher, *Ancient Allegorical, Historical and Legendary Paintings on the Walls of the Chapel of the Trinity ... at Stratford-on-Avon* (described by J. G. Nichols,

London, 1838), W. P. Reeves, *MLN* ix (1894), 201–6. The paintings are again 'coloured over'.
58 John Weever, *Ancient Funerall Monuments* (London, 1631), p. 534.
59 See Murray, pp. xxxvi ff., Burgess, pp. 227–8, Bridges, *The History and Antiquities of Northamptonshire* (compiled by P. Whalley, London/Oxford/Northampton, 1791), I, pp. 403–4, G. Lipscomb, *The History and Antiquities of the County of Buckingham* (London, 1847), I, p. 93, Ravenshaw, *Antiente Epitaphes*, pp. 12, 13, 35.
60 Cf. Gray, 'Two Songs of Death', *NM* lxiv (1963), 71, 74, EETS clxxiii, pp. 206–8. There is a curious use in Herbert's *The Church Porch*, where the reader is advised to look to his mouth:

> Look on meat, think it dirt, then eat a bit;
> And say withal, Earth to earth I commit.

(Cf. also *The Priesthood*: 'I do not greatly wonder at the sight,/If earth in earth delight.')
61 *Themes and Variations in Shakespeare's Sonnets* (London, 1963 ed.), pp. 61–2.
62 John Skelton, *Poems*, ed. R. S. Kinsman (Oxford, 1969), pp. 8–10.
63 *Opera*, ed. G. Morin, *Sermones* I, p. 135. See J. E. Cross, *JEGP* lvi, 434–9.
64 It is common both in Latin and the vernaculars (for a French example, cf. the epitaph on the Black Prince, for an example in Georgia, U.S.A. cf. *Southern Folklore Qly* xx, 100). See, for instance, Lipscomb, *Bucks*. I, 112, 347, 431, II, 133, 358, Bridges, *Northants.*, I, 98–9, Holles, *Church Notes*, 167, etc.; the examples in Burgess, pp. 220 ff., 249, include a rather tetchy reversal of the homiletic theme (West Down, Devon, 1797):

> Reader pass on, nor waste your precious time
> On bad biography and murdered rhyme.
> What I was before's well known to my neighbours
> What I am now is no concern of yours.

Cf. *Index* 237, 3701.
65 In a brass; the English verses are arranged around the slab so that the opening 'Such as ye be' is above the heads of the two figures. Cf. Evans, p. 173. A nice *orate* is recorded at Fairford (John Tane and Alice, d. 1471):

> For thus, love, pray for me
> I may not pray more, pray ye
> With a pater noster and an ave
> That my paynys relessyd be.

Notes to pp. 201–2

66 Formerly in St Michael at Basinghall, London (destroyed in the Great Fire); from Stow, (ed. Kingsford), I, p. 289. John Barton died in 1460.
67 *Index* 1119.5; Evans, 175, Pettigrew, p. 44, etc.
68 Evans, p. 213. Cf. Holles, *Linc. Church Notes*, p. 143 (Tattershall):

> Have mercy on the Soule (good Lord) we thee pray
> Of Edward Hevyn layd here in Sepulture
> Which to thine honour this Chappell did array
> With ceiling, deske, perclose and pourtrayture,
> And paviment of Marble longe to endure,
> Servant of late to the excellent Princesse,
> Mother to King Henry, of Richmund Countesse.

69 *Index* 2736.5; Ravenshaw, p. 5 (Snodland, Kent).
70 *Index* 4028.3; F. Blomefield, *An Essay towards a Topographical History of the County of Norfolk* (London, 1806), V, p. 3, Pettigrew, p. 49. Cf. the very similar epitaph of the goldsmith Robert Trappis (d. 1526), formerly at St Leonard's, Foster Lane (Ravenshaw, p. 20). A much earlier example in a MS. seems to be the couplet (*Index* 1276.5):

> hic am Michel of Airas
> Wl sone ic am viryeten alas.

Ingenuity is rare, but not totally absent. Cf. the acrostic (*Mors solvit omnia*) in *CB XV* No. 152 (see Cutler, *MLN* lxx, 87–9), or this patterned palindrome (*Index* 3097.3; Pettigrew, p. 63, Davies Gilbert, *The Parochial History of Cornwall* (London, 1835), II, p. 128 (with a different arrangement)), formerly at Gunwalloe, Cornwall:

> Shall we all die
> We shall die all
> All die shall we
> Die all we shall

(Cf. Sparrow, *Visible Words*, p. 112; Tesauro's *Il Cannochiale Aristotelico* (1654), pp. 294–7, gives seventy-seven witty ways of re-phrasing Alexander's epitaph (see note 39).)
71 *Index* 334.5 (St Martin's Vintry (1469)); Weever, p. 406. Cf. Ravenshaw, pp. 18–19, the epitaph of Robert Fabian (d. 1511), at St Michael Cornhill:

> Lyke as the daye hys course doth consume
> And the new morowe springyth agayne as faste
> So man and wuman by natures custome
> Thys lyff to passe, at last in erth are caste,
> In joy and sorowe, which heer theyr tym doe waste

Never in on state, but in course transitorie
Soe ful of chawnge is this worlde the glorie.

72 *Index* 2050.5.
73 Evans, p. 155n. points out the similarity with an exemplum in the *Disciplina Clericalis* of Petrus Alphonsus. A philosopher sees the inscription in a cemetery, and is moved by it to become a hermit. See A. Hilka and W. Söderhjelm (Heidelberg, 1911), p. 48 (Latin text only), *Acta Societatis Scientiarum Fennicae*, xxxviii (Latin and French).
74 Pp. 8–9.
75 Cf. the three essays on Epitaphs printed in *The Prose Works*, ed. A. B. Grosart, (London, 1876).
76 Ed. Arber, pp. 70–1. Burgess, p. 249, lists a number of late sixteenth- and seventeenth-century painted boards.
77 See Robbins, *NM* lvi (1955), 241–9.
78 *CB XV* No. 159.
79 Cf. *CB XV*, No. 149, l.8, Audelay, ed. Whiting, EETS, No. 2, ll. 280–1, *EEC* No. 371, *Speculum Misericordiae*, ed. Robbins, *PMLA* liv (1939) 935–66, ll. 71 ff. See also *Troilus and Criseyde* v, l. 1840.
80 *NED* quotes Lydgate: 'Galle in his breste and sugre in his face'.
81 Cf. *NED*, s.v. 'dance' *sb*., especially 5, 6.
82 The word is sadly appropriate, for Edward was for a short time exiled from his kingdom (1470–1); he returned triumphantly to a successful reign.
83 Cf. Tilley, H 8–10 for proverbial uses.
84 Though it must be said that this was a mark of distinction for a medieval and Renaissance ruler.
85 Cf. Dreves, xxxiii, No. 244:

>Totum evanuit
>Ut ros, ut nebula,
>Ut breve theatrum
>Ut brevis fabula,

Index 3610 (EETS xv, 265):
This is a wondir merie play, and longe ssal laste;
Bot for thi sete is perilous, war the ate laste.

More, *The Four Last Things* (*English Works*, p. 479): 'If thou shouldst perceive that one were earnestly proud of the wearing of the gay golden gown, while the lorel playeth the lord in a stage play, wouldst thou not laugh at his folly, considering that thou art very sure that when the play is done he shall go walk a knave in his old coat? Now thou thinkest thyself wise enough while thou art proud in thy players garment, and forgettest that when thy play is done,

Notes to pp. 205–11

thou shalt go forth as poor as he. Nor thou remembrest not that thy pageant may happen to be done as soon as his.' Cf. also *NQ* ccviii (1963), 99–101, and the references given there.

86 *CB XV* No. 149; cf. Gray, 'A ME Epitaph', *NQ* ccvi (1961), 132–5.
87 EETS clxxiii, p. 208. Cf. *Oxford Dictionary of Proverbs*, p. 131, Tilley, D. 59.
88 ff. 86v–87r. *Index* 789.
89 *Index* 143.8; R. Gough, *Sepulchral Monuments of Great Britain*, II, p. 187 (with illustrations). Cf. Gough, II, p. 274 for a Latin dialogue between Archdeacon Ruding (d. 1481) and death. Of the poems which do not appear as *tituli*, Henryson's *Ressoning betwix Man and Deid* is the best.
90 Another dramatic example is *Dethe and the Goer by the Waye* (see *Hudson Review*, vii, 414–18).
91 E. P. Hammond, *English Verse between Chaucer and Surrey* (Durham, N.C., 1927), p. 134.
92 See K. Künstle, *Die Legende der Drei Lebenden und der Drei Toten* (Freiburg, 1908), S. Glixelli, *Les cinq Poèmes des trois morts et des trois vifs* (Paris, 1914), W. Rotzler, *Die Begegnung der 3 Lebenden und der 3 Toten* (Winterthur, 1961), Réau, pp. 642–5.
93 Cf. Evans, pp. 94 ff., Brieger, pp. 225 ff., Pollard, *Bibliographica* iii (1897), for examples in Horae. Wall paintings are listed in Caiger-Smith, and E. C. Williams, 'Mural Paintings of the Three Living and the Three Dead', *J. Arch. Ass.* 3rd ser., vii (1942), 31–43. There is a good example at Raunds, Northamptonshire – a big painting high on the wall, with another beside it of a huge figure of death with a dart attacking a lady.
94 MS. Arundel 83, f. 128 (reproduced, e.g. in W. F. Oakeshott, *The Sequence of English Medieval Art* (London, 1950).
95 See Tristram, *Fourteenth Century*, p. 262. A number of the paintings, e.g. at Ampney Crucis, Gloucestershire, Ditchingham, Norfolk, Bovey Tracy, Devon, once apparently had inscriptions. One at Battle, Sussex, had the proverb *Mors sceptra ligonibus equat* (Walther, *Lateinische Sprichwörter . . . des Mittelalters*, 15198); cf. Shirley's lines, 'Sceptre and crown must tumble down. . . .' (and see Weber, *Aspects of Death*, pp. 261 ff.; *The Heroicall Devises of M. Claudius Paradin*, tr. P.S., London, 1591, p. 373, etc.).
96 Whiting, EETS clxxxiv, No. 54.
97 See W. F. Storck, *Zeitschrift f. deutsche Philologie* xlii (1910), 422–8.
98 *CB XV* No. 158.
99 The debate of the soul and the body is an ancient, widespread and interesting type. There is a good extended example in ME, *The*

Desputisoun bitwen the bodi and the soule, ed. W. Linow (Erlangen, 1899), as well as traces in the lyrics. See Woolf, especially pp. 89–102.
100 *CB XIV* No. 28.
101 *OE Homilies*, EETS liii, p. 181, Owst, *Literature and Pulpit*, p. 37. Cf. Innocent, *PL* ccxvii, 705, *Speculum Misericordiae*, ll. 73–4:

> With woo and wepyngge born was I
> My ferste voys was a sorwefull song;

EETS xv, p. 263:

> Allas! in gret sinne, alle beyete we were
> Stronge pines tholeden the moderis that us bere
> Here we live bisiliche wit stronge serwe and care
> Deye we ssulin sikerliche; but God wot wanne and were.

William Worcestre, *Itineraries*, p. 180, has a similar tag:

> Ve michi nascente; ve nato; ve morienti;
> Ve michi; quod sine ve non vivit filius Eve.

102 *CB XIV* No. 106.
103 EETS viii, p. 85.
104 See G. Sitwell, 'A Fourteenth-Century English poem on *Ecclesiastes*', *Dominican Studies* iii (1950), 284–90.
105 *Poems*, ed. Mackay Mackenzie, p. 146.
106 Ibid., p. 150.
107 Ibid., p. 151.
108 Ibid., pp. 20–1.
109 Ibid., pp. 26–7. See the fine discussion in the *Times Literary Supplement*, 18 April 1958, p. 208.
110 *CB XV* No. 163 (see the note), p. 342.
111 *Index* 233; University College, Oxford, MS. 181, f. 42r.
112 *Archiv* lxxxix, 267–8.
113 *CB XV*, No. 164. See Greene, *MLN* lxix, 307. In the first word I have restored the (N) of Walton's MSS. The man who copied this stanza was using the early printed version, which has Howe.
114 *De Senectute*, ch. xix.
115 *Convivio*, IV, ch. 28 (tr. Wicksteed).

Conclusion

1 There is an example in the MS. copy of the poem '*Hoc factum est a Domino*', mentioned above, p. 162, where a stanza containing a reference to transubstantiation has been crossed out.

2 See *SEC*, pp. 20 ff., *ELH* vii (1940), 223–38. Carols seem to have found their way into sixteenth-century printed versions more often than meditative lyrics; *Christmas carolles newely Imprinted* (c. 1550), for example, preserves the unique copy of a remarkable complaint of Christ, 'Blow the winde styl and blow nat so shyl/My blode man I shed for the all at wyl. . . .'
3 Cf., for example, A. L. Lloyd, *Folk Song in England* (London, 1967). Traditional songs on the subject of the Joys of Mary, and even of the symbolic Pelican, are recorded.
4 *Remains*, ed. Britten, pp. 31–2.
5 Scott quotes from a British Museum MS. an interesting account of Cleveland, Yorkshire, in the reign of Elizabeth:

> When any dieth, certaine women sing a song to the dead bodie, reciting the journey that the partye deceased must goe; and they are of beliefe (such is their fondnesse) that once in their lives it is good to give a pair of new shoes to a poor man, forasmuch as after this life they are to pass barefoot through a great launde full of thornes and furzen, except, by the meryte of the almes aforesaid, they have redeemed the forfayte; for at the edge of the launde an oulde man shall meet them with the same shoes that were given by the partie when he was lyving; and after he hath shodde them, dismisseth them to go through thick and thin without scratch or scalle. (This is the 'shoe of the dead', the *Totenschuh*, attested elsewhere in folk-belief.)

6 Lloyd, pp. 140–1.
7 Cf. Patch, *The Other World*, passim (*The Lyke-wake Dirge* is discussed on p. 123), Ettlinger, *JWCI* xix, 155–6. There is an English visual parallel in a wall-painting at Chaldon, Surrey (see Caiger-Smith, pp. 36–7, pl. xii, J. C. Wall, *Medieval Wall Painting*, pp. 218 ff.).
8 Cf. Gray, 'Two Songs of Death', *NM* lxiv (1963), 52–74.
9 There is an example in one of Francis Douce's collections in the Bodleian Library (Douce Addit. 137), a volume which also contains broadsheet versions of *Dives and Lazarus, The Holy Well, The Seven Joys of Our Lady*, and *Joseph was an Old Man*.
10 See A. L. Maycock, *Nicholas Ferrar of Little Gidding* (London, 1963), pp. 220–2; cf. *Conversations at Little Gidding*, ed. A. M. Williams (Cambridge, 1970).
11 *The Shape of the Liturgy*, (London, 1945) pp. 605 ff.
12 A. Hanham, *Churchwardens' Accounts of Ashburton, 1479–1580* (Devon and Cornwall Record Society), p. 140 (1558–59).

Index

'A barge to beren fro depe groundes', 123
'A God and yet a man', 68-9
'A, Jesu so fair an fre', 280
'A lyoun raunpaund wit his powe', 39
'A man of ple and motyng', 129
'A Prisoner's Prayer', 172-3
'A roose hath borne a lilly white', 77
'A scheld of red, a crosse of grene', 133
'A sory beverich it is', 124
'A virgyn pure', 113
'A yong rewler wytles', 282
'Abyde, gud men, and hald yhour pays', 140
Ad Herennium, 40
'Adam, alas and waylaway', 75
'Adam lay ibowndyn', 61, 76
Adam of St Victor, 65, 67-8, 84
Ailred, St, 108, 124
'Al mi blod for the is sched', 125
'Al stant on change like a mydsomer rose', 189
'Al this world was forlore', 86
Alabaster, William, 270
'Alasse, Deth, alasse', 207
Alcuin, 10
Aldhelm, St, 58
Alfred, King, 10
'All hyt is fantome that we withe fare', 212
'Allas, alas, si haut, si bas', 38
'Allas! in gret sinne', 293

'Allas, Jesu, thi love is lorn', 125
'Also Adam wyt lust and likynge', 75
Ambrose, St, 12, 135, 273
'An ernemorwe the daylight spryngeth', 146-7
Ancrene Riwle, Ancrene Wisse, 26, 131
'And by a chapell as y came', 163-4
Anselm, St, 19-20, 27, 33, 125, 232
'Antiochenus', 206-7
Arma Christi, 51, 52, 132-3
'As flowers in feeld', 202
'As I me lend to a lend', 170
'As I up ros in a mornyng', 112
'As I walked me this endurs day', 111
'As I went one my playing', 174
'As reson rywlyde my rechyles mynde', 138
'As walnot barke his hare is yalowe', 76-7
Asser, 10
'At a sprynge-wel under a thorn', 92-4
'At his burth thow hurdist angell syng', 38
'At this court this lawe is set', 38
'Atte wrastlinge mi lemman I ches', 37
Aubrey, John, 222, 278-9
Audelay, John, 21, 209
Augustine, St, 9, 12, 95, 106, 171, 232
Aurora lucis rutilat, 146

Index

Ave Maris Stella, 83, 86
'Ayenis my fadris wille I ches', 112–13

Bacon, Francis, 239
Barlaam and Josaphat, 179
Becon, Thomas, 158–9
'Behold man, wat is my wo', 140–1
'Behold thu man her myth thu se', 274
Bernard, St, 19, 20–1, 79, 82, 95, 105, 107, 225
Bernardino of Siena, St, 25, 79, 233
Biblia Pauperum, 49–50
Billyng, William, 134, 197
Black Death, 181–2
'Blod wetyng', 39
'Boar's Head Carol', 222
Bonaventura, St, 22
Bridget, St, 95–6, 135, 273
'Brother, abyde', 143
'By a forest syde walkyng', 172
Byron, 190

Caesarius of Arles, 185–6, 199
carols, 62–3
charms, 34–6, 118, 164, 237, 243, 266, 278
'Charter of Christ', 30, 270
Chaucer, Geoffrey, 5, 25, 30, 57, 61, 84, 102, 182, 215, 220
Chester plays, 115
'Child, it is a weping dale', 113
'Christ', 4, 263
Christina of Markyate, 25, 26, 94, 156
Cicero, 40, 220
Convercyon of Swerers, 54
'Corpus Christi Carol', 164–7, 222
Coventry plays, 84, 103, 118, 119, 258
Cranach, Lucas, 28
Crashaw, Richard, 68, 115, 134, 249, 270, 272, 280
'Crist criyede', 125
'Crist makith to man a fair present', 126
'Crist that breed brak', 155
'Cristes bodi maltth', 268

Cur Mundus Militat, 177, 189–90

Dance of Death, 50–1, 55, 62, 198, 208, 224, 242
Dante, 5, 64, 82, 87, 90, 220, 244, 257
David, Gherard, 28
Davies, John, 225
De Laudibus Beatae Mariae Virginis, 82–3, 86, 87, 104
Death and the Lady, 224
'Death, the Port of Peace', 219–20
Devil and the Maid, The, 161–2
Dies Irae, 66
Digby plays, 130
'Disputacioun betwyx the body and wormes', 191–2
Disputation between Mary and the Cross, 69
Dives and Pauper, 44–5
'Done is a batell on the dragon blak', 148
Donne, John, 66, 68, 91
Dowsing, William, 42
Dream of the Rood, The, 48, 268
Dunbar, William, 61, 65, 99, 148, 150, 178, 216–18
Duns Scotus, 28

'Earth upon Earth', 196–8
'*Ecce, ancilla Domini*', 99–100
'*Ecce, quod natura*', 106
'Edi beo thu, hevene quene', 56–7
Edmund of Abingdon, St, Archbishop of Canterbury, 21, 31
Edward IV, Lament of the Soul of, 203–5
'Ellas, mornyngh y syngh', 139
Emare, 34
emblem poems, 52–4, 293–4
Ephraem Syrus, 82, 105
epitaphs, 200 ff., 283–4
'Erly on morwe', 51
Everyman, 208

'Farewele, Advent', 98
'Farewell, this world', 205–6
Farne, monk-solitary of, 26, 278
'For my love he ys nou asslawe', 38

Index

Francesco da Holanda, 27
Francis, St, 21–3, 37, 55, 108, 113, 218, 225, 232, 233
'Friday spell', 164
Froment, Nicholas, 84

Gerson, Jean, 36
'Glade us maiden, moder milde', 100
'God and Seynt Martyn', 155
'God send us the dew of hevene', 261
Godric of Finchale, St, 26, 155
'Goe, lytyll byll', 56
Grimestone, John, 38, 93, 100, 123–4, 125–6, 132, 134, 136–7, 139, 140, 167, 171
Gude and Godly Ballatis, 169

'Haile be thu, Mari maiden bright', 104
'Hale, sterne superne', 150
Hawes, Stephen, 54, 206
'He that was al hevene', 107
'He yaf himself as good felawe', 78
'Heil, Marie, and wel thu be', 100
'Helpe, crosse, fayrest of tymbris three', 35
Henryson, Robert, 61, 182
Herbert, George, 15, 25, 63, 68, 91, 127, 141, 178, 249, 253, 289
Herebert, William, 12–17, 24, 83, 130, 141, 147, 230
'Herkneth to mi ron', 173
Herrick, Robert, 36, 170, 258
'Hiegh towers by stronge wyndes full lowe be cast', 169–70
Hill, Richard, 61, 165, 172
Hilton, Walter, 32, 44, 240
'Ho art thou that comest so litel', 262
Hoccleve, Thomas, 61
Holcot, Robert, 29
'Hold yowre tung and sey the best', 48
Holkham Bible picture book, 50, 114
'Honnd by honnd we schulle ous take', 62, 96

Honorius of Autun, 87, 283
Horace, 176
'How suld I now, thu fayre may', 109

'I come vram the wedlok', 147
'I hafe set my hert so hye', 80
'I have laborede sore', 147
'I herd an harpyng on a hille', 129
'I ne wat quat is love', 93
'I slepe and my hert wakes', 160
'I syng of a mayden', 61, 101–6
'I wolde ben clad in Cristes skyn', 134
'I wolde witen of sum wys wiht', 212–16
'Ich delede the see vor the', 141
illustrated poems, 50–5, 174, 206–7
'In a noon tijd of a somers day', 172
'In a tabernacle of a toure', 149
'In all this worlde ys none so tru', 94
'In everi place men mai see', 130
'In my bed liyng', 62
'*In nomine patris*, up and doune', 278
'In the vaile of restles mynd', 143–5
'In this tyme of Chrystmas', 110
'Into thi handes, lorde', 154
'Into this world this day', 107

Jessup, 42
'Jesu be thou my joy', 160
'Jesu Cristes milde moder', 135
'Jesu Cryste I beseche the', 277
'Jesu, lorde, that madest me', 160
'Jesu, lythe my sowle with thi grace', 155
'Jesu, my joy and my lovynge', 79
'Jesu, swete is the love of thee', 122–3
'Jesu, swete sone dere', 110
'Jesu that hast me dere ibought', 126–8
'Jesu, whom ye serve dayly', 156–7
'Jesus doth him bymene', 142
'Jesus woundes so wide', 134

Index

'John Barton lyeth under here', 201
John of Howden, 127
Judas, 124, 268
Julian of Norwich, 26, 78, 125, 126, 239, 271

Kempe, Margery, 26, 28
'Kinge I sitte', 168

'Lament for the Makaris', 216–17
Lancaster, Henry, Duke of, 32–3
Langland, William, 9, 131
Ledrede, Richard de, Bishop of Ossory, 58
'Let fal downe thyn ne', 47
'Levedie, ic thonke the', 91–2
'Levedy for thi joyyes fyve', 155
Lewis, M. G., 193–4, 288
Livre de Seyntz Medicines, Le, 32–3, 70, 236
'Loke, man to Jesu Crist', 140
'Lollai, lollai, litil child', 211–12
'Loued be thou, keyng', 160
'Louerd, thu clepedest me', 171–2
Love, Nicholas, 63
'Love is out of lond iwent', 171
'Love me brouthte', 80
'Love Rune', 57, 58, 186–7, 245
'Lovely lordynges ladys lyke', 162
'Lullay, myn lykyng', 111
Lydgate, John, 15, 32, 46–7, 50, 51, 61, 65, 77, 147, 189, 235, 291
'Lyke as the daye hys course doth consume', 290–1
Lykewake Dirge, the, 222–4

'Make the poure to pray well', 50
'Man and wymman, loket to me', 140
'Man, com and se how schal alle dede be', 202
'Man, hef in mynd', 178
'Man, in what state that ever thou be', 46
Mannyng, Robert, 31
Martini, Simone, 99, 100–1
'Marye, mayde mylde and fre', 84–6, 101

'Mary moder, mayden clere', 277
Maximianus, 173
Meditations on the Life and Passion of Christ, 87, 110–11, 127
Meditations on the Life of Christ (Meditationes Vitae Christi), 22, 63, 108–9, 113, 126–7
'Meditatioun in Wyntir', 217–18
'Men rent me on rode', 131
'Merowre ys deth', 39
Merure de seinte Eglise, 21, 31, 139
'Mi love is falle upon a may', 132
Michael of Kildare, 24
Michelangelo, 27, 28, 30, 273
Milton, John, 83
'*Mirabile misterium*/In forme of bred', 69, 161
'*Mirabile misterium*/The Son of God', 106
More, Sir Thomas, 10, 291
'My trewest tresowre sa trayterly was taken', 132

'Nakyd into this warlde', 174
'Nou goth sonne under wod', 139
'Nou skrynketh rose and lylie flour', 55, 172
'Now is wele and all thing aright', 153

'O dredeful deth, come make an ende', 219
'O Jesu, lorde, wellcum thu be', 159
'O man thow marrest in thy mynd', 162
'O man unkynde', 53–4
'O my good brother', 282
'O sisters too', 119
'Of M.A.R.I.', 91
'Of one stable was his halle', 107
'Off alle women that ever were borne', 137–8
On God Ureisun of Ure Lefdi, 148–9
'Owt of your slepe aryse and wake', 96–8

'Palmers all our faders were', 201

Index

patterned poems, 54, 244
Pearl, 56, 84–5, 103, 182
Pecham, John, Archbishop of Canterbury, 78
Pecok, Bishop, 44, 161
Peter Damian, St, 15
Peter of the Order of Preachers, St (St Peter Martyr), 274
Pettinagno, Pier, 21
Pierce the Ploughman's Crede, 22–3
Piers Plowman, 131
Pilgrimage of Perfection, The, 41, 60
Pilgrimage of the Soul, The, 218
'Pleasure it is', 60–1
Pricke of Conscience, The, 50
Proprietates Mortis, 194–5
Psalterium Beatae Mariae Virginis, 83, 251

'Quanne ic se on rode', 124
Quarles, Francis, 224–5
'Qwan the Belle ys solemplye rownge', 201

'Reuthe made God on mayden to lithte', 39
Richard de Caistre, 160
Ridevall, John, 40
Rolle, Richard, 19, 26, 69–70, 79, 159–60
'*Rorate celi desuper*', 99
Ryman, James, 24, 36, 219

'Sainte Marie virgine', 155
Sawles Warde, 64
'Sayings of St Bernard', 188
Seneca, 169, 170
'Seynt Jorge, our lady knyghth', 157
Shakespeare, William, 98, 119, 174, 180, 190, 192–3, 195, 198, 203, 211, 285, 290
Sheppey, Bishop, 38
Skelton, John, 61, 142, 198–9, 203
'Sodenly afraide', 137
'Somer is comen and winter gon', 55
Splendor Patris et Figura, 67–8, 84

Stabat Mater Dolorosa, 66–8, 96, 135
'Steddefast crosse', 123
'Stond wel, moder, under rode', 136
'Such as ye be such wer we', 200
'*Surge mea sponsa*, so swete in syghte', 149

Talbot, Sir John, 156–7
'That thi brother in heven', 78
'The fende oure foo', 167
'The gladsom byrd, the deys mesanger', 154
'The levedi fortune', 168
'The minde of thi passiun, suete Jesu', 41
'The rede stremes renning', 40
'The sheperd upon a hill he sat', 115–17
'The worlde so wide, th'aire so remuable', 169
'The yates of Parais', 75
'Thenke mon thi liffe', 48
'Ther is no rose of swych vertu', 88–91
'Think on Yesterday', 178–9
'This brede geveth eternall lyfe', 69
'This endres nyght about mydnyght', 111–12
'This have I done for my true love', 81
'This is a wondir merie play', 291
Thomas de Hales, 24, 57
Thomas of Celano, 55
'Thou wommon boute vere', 90
Three Living and Three Dead, 208–9
'Thu thad madist alle thinc', 129
'Thynk, man, qwareoff thou art wrought', 218
'Thys mayden hyghth Mary', 120
Tiptoft, John, Earl of Worcester, 33
tituli, 45 ff., 200 ff., 240–2
Towneley plays, 109, 115, 131, 171, 199
'Trewlove trew on you I truste', 58

Index

Tutivillus, 171
'Tyrle, tyrlo', 115

'Under a tre, in sportyng me', 56
'Under the Leaves of Life', 222
'Upon my right syde y me leye', 156
'Uppon a deedmans hed', 198–9

Vado Mori, 209–10
Van der Goes, Hugo, 109, 120
Van Eyck, Jan, 28
Villon, François, 45, 183, 184–5, 186, 195, 286

Walton, John, 220
'Wan ic myself stond', 127
Wanderer, The, 183–4, 185, 187
'Wanne mine eyhnen misten', 194
'Welcome, lord, in fourme of brede', 159
'Wen the turuf is thi tuur', 195
'What art thou that art so yynge?', 158

'What manere of ivell thou be', 35
'What ys he, thys lordling', 12–17
'When Chryst was born of Mary fre', 222
William of Ockham, 28–9, 214
'With notis cleer, and vois entuned clene', 78
'Witte hath wondir', 161
'Wofully araide', 142
Wolfram von Eschenbach, 167
Worcestre, William, 118, 293
'Wy have ye no reuthe on my child?', 136–7
Wyatt, Sir Thomas, 169, 170
Wyclif, John, 44
'Wynter wakeneth al my care', 55
'Wyth was hys nakede brest', 128

'Ye ben my fadrer eternally', 120
'Ye that pasen be the wyye', 141
Yeats, W. B., 101, 118, 158
'Yit is God a curteis lord', 172
York plays, 109
'Yungthe ne can nouth', 167

For Product Safety Concerns and Information please contact our EU representative GPSR@taylorandfrancis.com
Taylor & Francis Verlag GmbH, Kaufingerstraße 24, 80331 München, Germany

www.ingramcontent.com/pod-product-compliance
Lightning Source LLC
Chambersburg PA
CBHW070723020526
44116CB00031B/1174